TYNE & WEAR

Edited by Jenny Edwards

First published in Great Britain in 1998 by
POETRY NOW YOUNG WRITERS
1-2 Wainman Road, Woodston,
Peterborough, PE2 7BU
Telephone (01733) 230748

HB ISBN 0 75430 085 4
SB ISBN 0 75430 086 2

FOREWORD

With over 63,000 entries for this year's Cosmic competition, it has proved to be our most demanding editing year to date.

We were, however, helped immensely by the fantastic standard of entries we received, and, on behalf of the Young Writers team, thank you.

The Cosmic series is a tremendous reflection on the writing abilities of 8-11 year old children, and the teachers who have encouraged them must take a great deal of credit.

We hope that you enjoy reading *Cosmic Tyne & Wear,* and that you are impressed with the variety of poems and style with which they are written, giving an insight into the minds of young children and what they think about the world today.

CONTENTS

Fulwell Junior School

Rachel Hennessey	42
Lauren Taylor	42
Andrew Birkenshaw	42
Mark Simpson	42
Rebecca Lowdon	43
Jake Bonallie	43
Daniel Rodley	43
Angela Scott	44
Maddie Harrison	44
Hannah New	44
Philip Chisholm	44
Nicola Wyness	45
David Bent	45
Paul Lowe	45
Michael Downey	45
Sara Hamod	46
Abigail McCardle	46
Annie Dorner	47
Christopher Bell	47
Helen Boyd	48
Adrienne McDonough	48
Katherine Dorans	49
Rachel Price	49
Catherine Blakelock	49
Rosanna Upright	49
Richard Fowler	50
Ross Atkinson	50
David Beckinsale	50
Lauren Hart	50
Lauren Barnes	51
Stacey Derivan	51
Kate O'Reilly	51
Lauren Barker	51
Kate Jackson	52
Rachael Clifton	52
Holly Waites	52
Alex Birkenshaw	52

Lucy McBeath		69
Katie Sanderson		70
Allix Nichols		70
Jordan Burdis		71
Rebecca Nelson		71
Tanya Charlton		71
Liam Downing		72

Hadrian JMI School

Stevie McAskell		72
Layla Hakim		73
Lia Rachael Sefton		73
Craig Gray		74
Faye Ironside		74
Deena Welsh		75
Lindsey Smurthwaite		76
James Cowie		76
Andrew Dorrian		77
Laura Swan		78

Harraton Primary School

Laura Rump		78
Laura Armstrong		79
Claire Clasper		79
Hannah Greenhow		80
Sarah Crossling		80
Claire Morris		81
Laura Magee		81
Michael Temple		82
Darrin Richardson		82
Rachel Kendall		82
Craig Scott		83
Daniel Ferry		83
Stacey Merrigan		84
Nathan Keogh		84
Victoria Bowden		85
Curtis Connor		85
Danielle Crossling		85

Shauna Allan	86
Anthony Goundry	86
Ken Cavanagh	86
Jason Wilson	87
Ashleigh Stewart	87
James Douglas	87
Scott Parry	88
Mark Nugent	88
Rhianne Greenwell	88

Hetton Primary School

Christopher Stammers	88
Claire Harrison	89
Melissa White	90
Christopher Sutherland	90
Stacy McBeth	91
Rebecca Cardy	91
Jayne Soppitt	92
Carly Lambton	92
Marc Loscombe	93

Hill View Junior School

Rebecca Walton	93
James Ferguson	94
Daniel Vasey	94
Charlotte Carlin	95
Tahmina Rokib	95
Jonathan Loach	96
Lian Kirton	97
Mark Watson	98
Natasha Meldrum	98
Rachael Thornton	99
Michael Wilkinson	99
Rosemary Ferries	100
Michael Telford	100
Philip Lorenson	101
Louise Brown	101
Emma Knott	102

Catherine Jones	102
Stacey Ferguson	103
Kirsty Lebihan	104
Philip Hall	104
Laura Howey	105
Gary Playle	105
Kayleigh Brannigan	106
Maddi Chismon	106
Ashley Moody	107
Stephen Mitchell	108
Stephen Porter	108
Lindsay Dagg	109
Helia Kasiri	110
Anthony Tennant	110
Ashley Laws	111
Kirsty Bramley	111
Rebecca Miller	112
Samantha Dawson	112
Gemma Haynes	113
Dominic Hogg	114
Rachel Hall	114
Phillippa Sellars	114
David Edgeworth	115
Laura Rutter	115
Martin Metcalfe	116
James Dent	116
Alex Keith	117
Samantha Nicholson	117
Richard Smith	118

Hylton Red House Primary School

Amy Jayne Cook	119
Joanne Prior	120
Sean Wilson	120
Tiffany Powell	121
Kristina Hodgson	121

Newlands School

	Greg Eckhardt	137
	Guy Silver	138
	Guy Halbert	138
	William Howie	139
	James Robson	139
	William Johnson	140
	Matthew Johnston	140
	James Mitchell	141
	Ben O'Brien	141
	Alasdair Upton	142
	Aidan Waters	142
	Andrew Bolam	143
	James Keyes	143
	Philip Davison	144
	Simon Brown-Adams	144
	Christopher Robinson	145
	Hugo Clerey	146
	Richard Pearson	147
	James Horn	147
	Simon Walker	148

New York Primary School

	Kimberley Lyon	148
	Karl Sharp	149
	Carly Nicholson	149
	Mark Walker	150
	Craig Evans	150
	Richard Thompson	150
	Nicola Lindsay	151
	Darren McDermott	151

North Fawdon Primary School

	Sarah Rice	152
	Julie Armstrong	153
	Alison Langley	154
	Joanne Shields	155
	Scott Henry	156

Samantha Jennings	175
Jay Bent	176
Katie McDermott	176
William Straker	177
Andrew Clissold	177
Amy Louise Longstaff	178
Hayleigh Spry	178

St Anne's RC Primary School

Paul Burn	178
Christopher Bagnall	179
Joanne Smith	180
Kayleigh Scott	180
Alexander Hamilton	181
Hanna Fenton	182
Adam Parker	182
Stephen Carr	183
Rose Brear	183
Victoria Spalding	184
Michael Mollett	184
Jack Doran	185

St Anthony's CE Primary School

Carly Blackburn	186
Caroline Briganti	186
Louise Thompson	187
David Lee Hamilton	187
Mark Anderson	188
Natalie Lockhart	188
Jenna Anne Allen	189
Gemma Collinson	190
Alan Halliday	191

St Cuthbert's RC Primary School

Rachael Wales	192
Kieran Burn	192
Andrew Brown	193
Emma Douglas	193

THE POEMS

THE WORLD IS FULL OF ANIMALS

The world is full of animals
Animals are fantastic creatures
Creatures like giraffes with long, strong necks
Necks to eat leaves at the top of trees
Trees have panthers in, with babies
Babies of lions running around
Around the corner a cheetah is having her dinner
Dinner time for a jaguar, a delicious gazelle
Gazelle running away from the crocodile pond
Pond reeds with a stork eating fish
Fish swimming away from danger
Danger! Shark in the sea
Sea, seaweed floating on the water
Water gets you very wet
Wet star fish in the rock pool
Rock pool is crabs' paradise
Paradise is where I want to be. So come with me!

Kimberley Wrigley (10)
Atkinson Road Primary School

THIS TREE

This tree has once been hollow and hard
He lives with his father and his mother
His leaves are torn and dropped from his twigs
This tree has grown apples and plums for years
This tree has no leaves at all

Karl Wails (9)
Atkinson Road Primary School

WHERE AM I

I am in a house
I sit on an old, broken chair
In the corner there is a man wearing a suit
I hear the sound of water
Outside the window I notice animals
It is foggy and windy.

I can smell flowers. I pick a flower up
It feels smooth and it looks like a yellow sun
I can hear people talking and I do not understand them
The words are coming from the sky
I feel scared and lonely.

Tammy Hindmarsh (10)
Atkinson Road Primary School

POLLUTION

Pollution
People must care about rubbish
Or the trees will die
Look at the dirty water
Look at the rubbish floating
Up in the sky there is grey smoke
Try to keep the land and water clean
In the car exhaust there is pollution
Our trees are dying
Now the world is a mess.

Nichola Hopkinson (9)
Atkinson Road Primary School

AT THE BOTTOM OF THE SEA

The first thing I see is a swordfish
I sit on a lumpy octopus
There's a shark in the room
I hear bubble, bubble in the corner
Outside the cave is a giant squid
Plump, wriggly, spotty, humungous
I smell rotten fish in the water
I scoop up a stingray
It feels rubbery, smooth, massive
It's grey
I hear screeching.
It's saying, 'Come here now.'
I feel so very, very shaky. My bones are rattling.

Leanne Jackson (11)
Atkinson Road Primary School

WHERE AM I?

I notice shiny trophies as I enter the smoke-filled room
I sit down on a leather chair with four small wheels
I see my Dad buy his friend a drink of wine
I hear glasses of beer being placed on a wooden table
I stare at a green football pitch from high up in the stadium
There is a fresh smell of grass in the air
There is a cold coin on the ground and I pick it up
I hear a man say, 'Howay the Lads!'
The match is just about to begin
I feel wildly excited!

Joseph Charlton (10)
Atkinson Road Primary School

SPACE TRAIN

                    Train
                    running
                            through
                                    space
                                        p
                                        a
                                        s
                                        t
                                    the
                    stars
            and
through
            the
                    planets
                            swirling
                                    around
                            and
                then
comes
            the
                    last
                        planet
                                    P
                                    l
                                    u
                                    t
                                    o
                            with
                    holes
                            We're
                                    gone!

Christina Watson (10)
Atkinson Road Primary School

UPS AND DOWNS

```
                                    up
                                  back
Riding                            way
   down                           the
     the                          all
      hill                        go
     very                         to
      fast                        having
    on                          of
       my                       thought
       bike                  The
              But Oh!
```

Tracie Wright (10)
Atkinson Road Primary School

SWIMMING LESSONS

I'm trying to learn how to swim
I'm just about to jump in . .
I've leapt in now and my arms are . . .
Over here, over there, in my face and in my hair
I'm in the middle of the pool
When everyone else is on their way back (to school)
I'm kicking here, I'm kicking there
I'm sick of my life, I wish I was somewhere (else)
Oh my God! I can see the end
I'm going to make it, but . . .
My head is getting sore. Now it's gone dead
I've reached the end. '*Yeah!*' I said.

Kerry Johnston (10)
Atkinson Road Primary School

THE PIRATE SHIP

This pirate ship was built by a workman
It took him nine years

This pirate ship has been everywhere where you haven't
I wish I knew where

This pirate ship has no one to look after it
And it's sick of the parrot!

This pirate ship is full of junk
And the parrot has earache from the captain
Yelling and screaming, 'Scrub the deck.'

This pirate ship is staring and glaring at me
Oh no, it's wrecked!

Christina Robson (10)
Atkinson Road Primary School

UTOPIA

P eace in harmony every day
A nger never occurs in paradise
R oses pop up and never die
A s things grow, more life comes
D ying does not exist
I   nside of this is love and hope
S ilky cloth, if it were a material
E ndlessly, life smells just as good.

Kaleigh Redhead (9)
Atkinson Road Primary School

THIS BOOK

This book has been torn and scarred
This book has been bounced in a bag, and thrown
across the room
This book has been handled by boys and teachers,
many times
The cover bruised, and blue
The torn plastic, rough and crumbly
Yet this book will be passed on next year
and will be used again
This book hopes the boy's next book will be happy
and have a book of a time.

Sean Gowing (10)
Atkinson Road Primary School

POLLUTION

Pollution
People pollute the country
Or throw rubbish on the floor
Like so many, they don't care
Look at how the country is
Unpleasant for the animals
Try not to pollute the countryside
It is disgusting on the ground
Our people are trying to care.

Jeffrey Mason (8)
Atkinson Road Primary School

PARADISE

Paradise smells like burnt-out candles

It feels like highly polished wood

It looks like a tremendous pasture with dewdrop
Diamonds sitting in the middle of the clover

It tastes like thick strawberry milkshake

It sounds like the smooth notes of the pan pipes.

Stacey Burke (9)
Atkinson Road Primary School

THIS FOOTBALL

This football has been pumped up and put in a cardboard box
This football has been left in the window of a shop with many others
This football has seen millions of people walking by
This football has been bought by a man
This football has been given to a child and kicked about
This football has been muddy and wet
This football has seen boys cheering and silver cups
This football has been popped by a dog and chewed.

Michael Saleeb (10)
Atkinson Road Primary School

PARADISE

Paradise is a fantastic place
It is a summery, fine day
I can see that paradise is full of dreams
Princess Diana is in paradise.
She is always smiling
I can sing to the animals and the birds
I am not telling how I got here.
It is a secret
I can hear people shouting, 'It's a fantastic place.'
We are not going back.

Sarah Holmes (9)
Atkinson Road Primary School

PARADISE

Paradise is an imaginary place
It never rains
And I am allowed to play football every day
                                    of the week
I watch the rockets blast off into space
I dream every night a perfect dream
And the animals are singing a beautiful song to everyone.

David Walker (10)
Atkinson Road Primary School

A JOURNEY THROUGH THE PAST

An old haunted house
House covered with dust
Dust on the cups
Cups cracked and broken
Broken lights on the ceiling
Ceiling covered with cobwebs
Cobwebs on furniture and all over
Over in the corner there are noises
Noises coming from ghosts
Ghosts up and downstairs
Stairs scratched and creaky
Creaky banisters on the landing
Landing covered in paint
Paint on the stairs and on the walls
Walls scraped and scratched
Scratched tables with broken legs
Legs are shaking, on me and everywhere
Where is the television?
Television with its screen smashed
Smashed glass everywhere
Where am I?
I need to get out
Out I go. Fast!

Marc Robson (10)
Atkinson Road Primary School

THE BEAUTY OF AUTUMN

The grass is covered in dew,
The leaves have started to fall,
Not long until there will be
No leaves on the trees so tall.

As I sit in my garden
I see red, yellow and brown,
I admire the autumn leaves
As they flutter to the ground.

Nature is so beautiful,
No words can describe
The wonderful things
I picture in my mind.

Soon animals will be hiding
For their winter sleep,
Now it's getting dark
And the sky begins to weep.

Autumn has arrived
And my mind is all a flutter,
Autumn has arrived
And its beauty is discovered.

Hester Lloyd (10)
Bede Burn JMI School

WAR

The grey fumes
All in the air
Covering the wrecked buildings.
Lies and betrayal
Soldiers surrounding
Innocent people
Bang!
Cities wiped out
By one bomb
Ash, bloodshed, rubble.

Sam Frank (11)
Bede Burn JMI School

WAR AND PEACE

Grey soldiers marching up the street,
Fear of walking out your door,
Air raids,
Missiles fired,
Misery.

The white dove remembered,
Joy of skipping up the road,
Fun, laughter,
Children making friends,
Happiness.

Stacey Morland (10)
Bede Burn JMI School

Food

I like cheese, that's very funny,
I like marmalade but I don't like honey,
Apple's sweet and grapefruit's sour,
Carrots get crunchier by the hour.

Mushy peas, yuck what a taste,
Yorkshire pudding and potatoes,
                    they're not waste,
All this food, Oh what a treat,
When it comes to cheese
Chicken can't beat.

Spaghetti hoops, Lots of jelly,
Yummy food
In my belly.

Ice-cream creamy
Bacon's fat
Sticky toffee pudding,
I like that.

Mandy Henderson (10)
Bede Burn JMI School

Evacuee

Alone,
In the station.
His face worried, anxious,
Rejected, with no relation.
Lonesome.

Rhiannon Logan (10)
Bede Burn JMI School

WHAT THE GIANT HAD FOR DINNER

First
He ate a
Group of trees.

Then
He had a
Hive of bees.

Next
He had a
Whopping key.

Last of all
He drank
Some tea.

Then he turned and looked
At me . . . Oh no!

Laura Tennet (9)
Bede Burn JMI School

OUTSIDER

On the outside looking in,
She looks empty drained of happiness.
Standing abandoned
Feeling alone,
Drifting away into the distance
Friendless forever.

Stephanie Forster (11)
Bede Burn JMI School

MEMORIES

One. Standing in a cardboard box, moving house oh what a shock.
Two. New-born baby brother for me, I gave him a blue teddy.
Three. Riding on my yellow bike, this is what I really like.
Four. A new era has begun, I've started school and it is fun.
Five. Michael's three, I am five, our baby rabbits do arrive.
Six. I can't believe I'm not dismayed, Palmer won on Sport's Day.
Seven. We all go to the Isle of Wight, see the Victory in all its might.
Eight. We went to Cornwall with our tent, hired bikes and cycling went.
Nine. Big Thunder Mountain at Disneyland, Mam was dragged on by
the hand.
Ten. We went to Holland with our bikes, saw lots of windmills and
loads of dykes.
Eleven. My junior school I must leave, for friends and teachers I will
grieve.

Samantha Forster (10)
Bede Burn JMI School

THE DOG BY THE RIVER BANK

The water looks quite inviting
Should I chance a swim?
Or wait until the sun is hot,
Before I tumble in?

The water may be warm enough,
But one thought does occur,
Do I really want to hang about
In a coat of soaking fur?

Corrinne Towsey (11)
Bede Burn JMI School

THE MOON

At night,
Every night,
The stars have a football match.
The moon is their ball,
A black hole is their goal
And a Milky Way is the ref.
Last night 2-nil.
Tonight, who knows?
The starting whistle blows.

Jessica Bathgate (10)
Bede Burn JMI School

THE MOON

The moon is round and cheesy,
Its glittering face sparkles in the dark,
The ghostly moon is soft,
It feels like a marshmallow.
The moon is alone
In the middle of nowhere.

Lucy Hardman (10)
Bede Burn JMI School

MY HISTORY

When you look in my hands
You see ghost-writing.

When you look in my feet
You see footballers on the field.

When you look in my heart
You see rivers running by.

When you look in my head
You see bright red blood.

When you look in my soul
You see memories forgotten.

Hayley Kane (11)
Bede Community Primary School

MY HISTORY

When you look inside my hand
You see a basketball
Falling to the ground

When you look inside my feet
You see people crying
And running for their mams

When you look inside my heart
You see long lost friends
Fading away

When you look inside my head
You see a picture of me
And my friends

When you look inside my soul
You see a big picture
Of me and my family.

Rebecca Whitfield (11)
Bede Community Primary School

MY HISTORY

When you look inside my hand,
you see my Great Grandad
and a book full of writing.

When you look inside my feet,
you see travellers running
home to the families.

When you look inside my heart,
you see memories of friends,
fading away.

When you look inside my head,
you see my Great Aunty who
died.

When you look inside my soul,
you see a book full of blank
pages.

Jasmine Burns (11)
Bede Community Primary School

MY HISTORY

When you look inside my hand,
You see missing parts of your life,
Like missing parts of an orange.

When you look inside my feet,
You see a football with no one to kick it,
Like a boy with nobody to play with.

When you look inside my heart,
You see two dogs sitting on their own,
Like a girl with no one to help her.

When you look inside my head,
You see people talking to a big man,
Like a boy talking to a teacher.

When you look inside my soul,
You see Frank walking about the globe.

Tony Walker (11)
Bede Community Primary School

MY HISTORY

When you look into my hand,
You see a ball bouncing,
Like a pebble bouncing,
On a river.

When you look into my feet,
You see people playing,
In the street,
As calm as the sea.

When you look into my heart,
You see Kevin Keegan,
And my dad like,
Happy feelings.

When you look into my head,
You see tangles,
Like people thinking.

When you look into my soul,
You see people trying to get,
Away from me.

Stephen Faetz (10)
Bede Community Primary School

MY HISTORY

When you look inside
My hand,
You see water dripping off
My fingertips
Like a waterfall.

When you look inside
My feet,
You see the big green fields
I have walked across
Like the soft sand.

When you look inside
My heart,
You see a picture of poor
People crying for help.

When you look inside
My head,
You see a picture
Of the forgotten friends.

When you look inside
My soul,
You see a big picture of
My family.

Kelly Hopkins (11)
Bede Community Primary School

My Deep Sleep

I dreamt I went up in space
Without any hands feet or face.
When I passed the stars so bright
I saw myself and got a fright.
I said, 'What could have happened to me?'
I wondered will I ever be free.

When I awoke from my deep sleep
Really loud I started to weep.
My mam and dad opened the door
Then again I started to snore.
Hoping to dream about very nice things
Like little angels with tiny wings.

Raymond Davey (11)
Bexhill Primary School

My Trip To Space

One day I went to space
I had a funny look on my face,
I packed some clothes in a case
And tried to go at a fast pace.

The next day I went up to the moon
I hoped to get there very soon,
I bounced through space on a red balloon
While listening to a funny tune.

I decided to go home the very next day
I had a snack on the way,
I can't wait until I get my pay
To go up there for another stay.

Kate Brown (11)
Bexhill Primary School

I WAS ABDUCTED BY ALIENS!

One day through a telescope I was looking up at space,
When a big ray of light came and beamed me up to base,
Aliens *Ahh!* So big and so ugly,
So big and so fat they look like Pugsly,
Can I escape, which way and where?
Oh no the aliens have started to stare.

Sharp teeth and claws and rainbow hair,
Their eyes are floating in total mid-air,
The aliens stepped back I got ready to run,
I stopped when the aliens shouted 'Fun fun fun.'

Suddenly I fell down and was lying on the ground,
I ran home and there Mum and Dad I found,
'Mum Mum, up there' to the sky I pointed,
'Calm down boy with you I'm disappointed,'
'Aliens!' I shouted 'I was abducted.'

Kim Elstob (11)
Bexhill Primary School

WHEN JACK AND JILL WENT TO SPACE

Jack and Jill went up to space,
In a supersonic case.
The suitcase landed much too soon,
It landed heavily on the moon.

Alien passed and fastened his lace,
And then he saw the old suitcase.
Soon Jack's face went bright red,
Alien had found his new bed.

Keelie Langley (10)
Bexhill Primary School

SPACE IS A WONDERFUL PLACE

Space, space is a wonderful place,
So why don't you go and pack your case.
Icy rings and shooting stars so why don't you
visit Mars?

Go with spaceships or a spoon,
I don't care if you land on the moon.
I jumped in a red rocket,
with something in my pocket.
The rocket went *zoom!*
I landed with a *boom!*
Saturn is such a wonderful place,
So why don't you pack your case!

Kayleigh McCully (11)
Bexhill Primary School

I WANT

I want to be an astronaut.
So I can fly in space.
I want to see the stars
And the human race.
I want to see Neptune,
Jupiter and Mars
And I really want to
ride on the shooting stars.
I hope one day it will
come true.
So I can see
space too.

Rachel Dagg (11)
Bexhill Primary School

SPACE IS A GOOD PLACE

Humpty Dumpty went to space
Saw two aliens in a race
One said 'Hi' and one 'Bye'
And one fell down from the sky.

Humpty Dumpty went to space
Saw an astronaut fastening his lace
He saw his face while on a race
And ended up in some place.

Kayleigh Briggs (11)
Bexhill Primary School

MY TRIP TO THE MOON

I went to the moon one day,
It is very very far away,
I flew up there in a rocket,
Sitting eating the sweets in my pocket,
When I got up there,
I sat and ate a pear,
I ran about investigating the moon,
And then I came across a big balloon,
I got a hold of the string,
When I got back on Earth I fell down with a ping,
I wish I'd seen an alien up there,
Anyway I don't really care.

Kayleigh Brown (11)
Bexhill Primary School

It's Time For Lift Off!

10 Fasten seat belts ready to go,
9   Counting down it seems so slow,
8   I can't believe I'm lying here,
7   My stomach feels kind of queer,
6   I'm on my way to the moon,
5   I should get there very soon,
4   Hear the rumble hear the roar,
3   Up in the sky we will soar,
2   Off we go at a fast pace,
1   To that unknown world called
                              Space!

Anthony Huntrod (11)
Bexhill Primary School

Up In Space

Up in space where no one goes
Way up there no one knows
Is there life on Mars and Venus?
Who will know? No one's seen it
Why does the Earth spin round the sun?
Finding out is so much fun.

Lynsey Maclaughlan (10)
Bexhill Primary School

SANTA MARIA

She softly silently slides among the
swirling shining shimmering sea.
Scattering spray upon the ship.
Mysteriously magically moving to
another new land.
They come across glittering glistening gold.
Gladly singing glory to God forever.

Samantha Findlay (10)
Bexhill Primary School

MY TRIP TO SPACE

I want to go to the moon
On a big blue balloon
Fly high and high in the sky
When people below are waving goodbye
Then I'll fly through the stars
On my way to bright red Mars
I'll see an alien with huge paws
Growling madly with big black claws
Later I'll go straight back home
And that's the end of my space poem.

Joanne Hutchinson (10)
Bexhill Primary School

OCTOPOEM STAR

Sapphire star shining in space,
Sometimes looks like a light floating
in the sky.
Winter wind blows around in space
Bits of stars fooling in the sky
Like snow floating down from the clouds.
Pluto has come from Disneyland to planet Pluto.
Bits of sparkling stars shout like winter ice
A long sparkling dress, the stars like to wear
A settee to sit on in space
A cake with smooth silver
Icing on it.
Luminous flowers
floating . . .

Nicola Ferrell (9)
Brighton Avenue Primary School

STARS

The stars are like silver plates
shining in the sky,
The stars are like autumn leaves falling
from the sky,
The stars are like a treasure chest full of diamonds
The stars are like jars of sunshine,
The stars are like a Chinese silk yellow dress,
The stars are like a bright orange chair,
The stars are like a piece of white Milky Way chocolate,
The stars are like marigolds.

Beth Baldwin (9)
Brighton Avenue Primary School

OCTOPOEM

The moon is a creamy colour.
The moon is a wintry place.
The moon is Antarctica.
The moon is a snowstorm.
The moon is a wedding dress.
The moon is a white leather chair.
The moon is a white potato.
The moon is a white rose.

Kristofer Bendelow (9)
Brighton Avenue Primary School

HUMPTY DUMPTY AT THE MOON

Humpty Dumpty went to the moon
On a rocket shaped like a spoon
He went to land and fell off his stand
And didn't wake up until noon.

Stacey Lowdon (7)
Brighton Avenue Primary School

HAMSTER

Hamster
at
midnight
sings in
the
empty
room.

Lewis Ennew (7)
Broadway Junior School

WINTER

Lots of icy trees
The children's frosty faces
Howling in the wind.

Laura Simpson (9)
Broadway Junior School

A SUNNY DAY

The sun is shining.
It is very hot outside.
We go to the beach.

Laura Farley (9)
Broadway Junior School

ABOUT MY GAMEBOY

Gameboys are compact
My Gameboy is exciting
I've got ten great games.

Michael Simpson (9)
Broadway Junior School

WINDS

Winds are powerful,
Violent winds can destroy trees,
They are mighty too.

Neil Smith (9)
Broadway Junior School

THE TWISTING TORNADO

The tornado twists,
The tornado twirls through town,
Tornado swirling.

Emma Shelley & Jamie Kennedy (8)
Broadway Junior School

BRIGHT SNOW

Light snow swirling round,
Cold snowflakes fall on huge trees,
White soggy bushes.

Samantha Byers & Martin Metcalf (9)
Broadway Junior School

WINTER

Cold nippy air,
Sparkling rainy days,
Icy brittle branches.

Mark Head (8)
Broadway Junior School

STORMS

Storms are breathing out,
Skies turning grey, trees breaking,
Ground is getting wet.

Terri Marsh & Kyle Milley (8)
Broadway Junior School

DEEP FOREST

In the dark forest,
Heavy snow falls as blizzards,
Freezing animals.

Luke Trueman (8) & Andrew Ingram (9)
Broadway Junior School

CHILLY MORNING

Dark chilly morning,
Frosty and icy windows,
Cold hands feet and face.

Harvey Robson, Stewart Hill (8) & Neil Smith (9)
Broadway Junior School

WAR

Terrified people,
Brave soldiers dying and lost,
Despicable war.

Stewart Robins (9)
Broadway Junior School

TORNADOES

Twirling in the air,
Frightening and powerful,
Sucking everything.

Gary James (8)
Broadway Junior School

RAINBOW

Colourful rainbow,
Bright and cheerful feelings,
Spreading through the sky.

Rachael Myers & Melissa Hay (9)
Broadway Junior School

RAINBOW

Rainbow in the sky,
It is beautiful and high,
It is wet and dry.

Stacey Richards (9) Terri Muncaster & Gail Herron (8)
Broadway Junior School

SPRINGTIME

Winter trees soon die,
Springtime leaves start to grow now,
Animals are born.

Robert Laing (8) Stefan Fisher & Jamie Bell (9)
Broadway Junior School

WHEN THE SNOW SETTLES

Harsh snow covers grass,
Find bird tracks in the cold snow,
Settles on the ground.

Mitchell Clark (9) & Rebecca Riley (8)
Broadway Junior School

SUMMER'S DAY

Scorching hot weather,
Warm sweat on all our foreheads,
Lazy from mild heat.

Colin Hudson (8) & Christopher Wilkinson (9)
Broadway Junior School

SNOW

Soft snow starts to fall,
Flakes are dancing in the air,
Turning grass to white.

James Shelley & Graham Reed (8)
Broadway Junior School

SUN

Rising in the air,
Fiery, blazing, burning sun,
Sweat runs down my face.

Hayley Barry & Courtney Hutchinson (9)
Broadway Junior School

WIND

Roaring wind blowing,
Strong punches hitting my face,
Making me shiver.

Bill Hedley (8)
Broadway Junior School

FOG

Whirling misty air
Depressing damp foggy day
Sadness all around.

Mark Dugga, Louie Groody & Nicholas Cooney (8)
Broadway Junior School

RAIN

Heavy wet cold day,
Balls of water splashing down,
Making puddles big.

Beau Cook (8) & Luke Trotter (9)
Broadway Junior School

RAINBOW

Rainbow shining through,
My curtains in the morning,
Happily I wake.

Dionne Pickersgill (9)
Broadway Junior School

TORNADOES

Dangerous terror,
Twirling around buildings tall,
Disaster is near.

Luke Moralee (8) & Martyn Coddington (9)
Broadway Junior School

LIGHTNING

Silver blood punches
Slicing through the gloomy sky
Flashing deadly too.

Michael Thompson (9) & Neil Hewison (8)
Broadway Junior School

HALLOWE'EN

Hallowe'en is spooky
Hallowe'en has spirits
Hallowe'en is dark
Hallowe'en is the time you can go trick or treating.

Richard Barker (8)
Broadway Junior School

HOT

Baking hot houses,
Sizzling warm garden path,
Limp, drooping flowers.

Clare Scott & Jane Minniss (8)
Broadway Junior School

A LONG LONG WINTER

It is cold outside.
Snow is falling on the ground.
Winter days are long.

Danielle Boyle (9)
Broadway Junior School

KEVIN

Where are you going Kevin taking deep sniffs?
I'm going to the fish shop to buy some fish and chips!

Where are you going Kevin rushing out from school?
I'm going to buy a new fan to keep me cool!

Where are you going Kevin licking your lips?
I'm going to the fruit shop to buy some grapes
without pips!

Where are you going Kevin looking so sad?
I'm going shopping with my mum but I'd rather go mad!

Siân Donkin (8)
Broadway Junior School

MY MAM MAKES ME . . .

My mam makes me happy
My mam makes me sad
My mam makes me bored
My mam makes me proud
My mam makes me my breakfast
My mam makes me pictures
My mam makes me paper aeroplanes
My mam makes me tidy my room
My mam makes me eat my food
My mam makes me go places and
My mam makes me lock the door.

Tony Barrs (7)
Broadway Junior School

WINTERTIME

Wintertime is fun
The animals are asleep
They will wake up soon.

Vicky Cowans (9)
Broadway Junior School

WINTER

W   inter is good.
I   cicles hanging from the window it is
N   ice for me.
T   errible snow is falling from the sky.
E   veryone is having a
R   ainy snowy day.

Jonathan Glenwright (8)
Broadway Junior School

PERFECT DAY

S   unny day
P   erfect day.
R   eading a poem about spring.
I   ce nowhere
N   ot a spot of rain.
G   olden day.

Anthony Mackay (8)
Broadway Junior School

WINTER IS . . .

W inter is
I cy
N ice and cold hanging from
T rees and snow is falling
E verywhere and it feels like
R ain.

Daniel Dodsworth (8)
Broadway Junior School

WINTER

W indy
I   cicles hanging
N ear my window
T   rees are white
E verywhere is
R eally cold
        Brrrrrr!

Scott Donkin (8)
Broadway Junior School

WINTER

W inter flows
I   n the air
N earer and nearer
T   wists and turns
E verywhere
R   ustling the trees.

Stephanie Stubbs (7)
Broadway Junior School

ROCK CAN BE . . .

Rock can be rough.
Rock can be white.
Rock can be bumpy.
Rock can be big.
Rock can be little.
Rock can be sandy-coloured.
Rock can be greyish.
Rock can be smooth.
Rock can be flat.
Rock can be fat.
Rock can be thin.
Rock can be slippery.
Rock can be round.

Liam Mole (8)
Broadway Junior School

THROUGH MY WINDOW

Through my window
Who can I see?
Oh it's Chewy my dog and
My mummy.
My mum's getting the washing in,
And look at me all snug
Or should I have helped her
I should have because the
clothes are all curly.

Xanthe Robinson (9)
Cragside Primary School

ANIMALS

Cats are cuddly
Dogs are cute
Mice are tiny
Insects are minute

Giraffes are tall
Lions are grumpy
Pigs are fat
Camels' backs are lumpy

Tigers have stripes
Elephants eat lots
Bears like to roar
Leopards have spots

Ostriches run fast
Owls sleep through the day
Ducks like to swim
Parrots repeat what you say
Parrots repeat what you say.

Charlotte Cawthra (8)
Cragside Primary School

MY BABY BROTHER

My baby brother
Eats when he is lying down.
My baby brother . . .
When he is in a mood
You'd better not come close
He is a little rascal!
. . . But he does
Love me the most.

Katherine Logan (8)
Cragside Primary School

THE SEA

The swishing, swashing sea
There's the bright
Gleamy sun in the sky
The palm trees are
Swaying all around from
Side to side
There's
The white fluffy
Clouds in
The sky too,
And the smooth
Pale blue sea dying down
There's the seagulls
Passing by,
Then the colourful sunset
Rises all around.

Melanie-Jane Williams (9)
Cragside Primary School

SUMMER AND WINTER

Summer is hot
There's no clouds in the sky
The birds will sing
And the sun will shine

Winter is cold
The grey clouds in the sky
The raindrops will fall
And the birds will not sing.

Tanya Shand (9)
Cragside Primary School

STARS IN THE NIGHT

Stars sparkling, black night.
Stars fly in the sky, darkness.
Stars shine in moonlight.

Rachel Hennessey (9)
Fulwell Junior School

STARS AT NIGHT

Stars bright in the night
Silver, gold sparkling, gleaming
Inky jet-black night.

Lauren Taylor (9)
Fulwell Junior School

STARS

Stars fly in the night
Sky black, deep, endless, lonely
New stars say goodnight.

Andrew Birkenshaw (9)
Fulwell Junior School

VELVET

Stars fly on the night
Sky is black, darkest velvet
New stars say goodnight.

Mark Simpson (9)
Fulwell Junior School

THE TERRIBLE TWITS

The wicked Twits are a nasty bunch
They have bird-pie for their lunch
I hate the Twits very much
They should live in a little hutch

These gruesome people who live next door
Have little insects under the floor
Spiders, bugs, they like to eat
They pick out all the juicy meat.

Rebecca Lowdon (9)
Fulwell Junior School

THE HORRIBLE TWITS

Mr Twit was a horrible man
He slapped his wife with a frying pan
She did the same to him one day
And that's how she made him pay

Mr Twit was mighty mad
He made his wife very sad
If they would go away
Everyone would dance and play.

Jake Bonallie (9)
Fulwell Junior School

LIGHT RAIN

Showering lightly
Dripping all the time to earth
Drizzling on and on.

Daniel Rodley (9)
Fulwell Junior School

A CAT

Loving playful cat
Cuddling up snugly so sweet
Sleep my cat. Night's here.

Angela Scott (8)
Fulwell Junior School

DAISY

Broken-stemmed daisy
all alone after the storm
swaying in the field.

Maddie Harrison (9)
Fulwell Junior School

LIGHT RAIN

Showers but soaking
light but extremely soggy
I'm soaked to the skin.

Hannah New (9)
Fulwell Junior School

SUNSET

Sunset reds blues pinks
enjoyable to my eyes
as day turns to night.

Philip Chisholm (9)
Fulwell Junior School

SNOW

Arctic conditions,
A carpet of crystals lie.
Milky ghosts' eyes stare.

Nicola Wyness (11)
Fulwell Junior School

SNOW

Cloudy, silky sky,
Spiky sharp lashing blizzards;
It feels like daggers.

David Bent (11)
Fulwell Junior School

SNOW

Soft sinking carpet,
Settling on dewy grass.
A silent cat stalks.

Paul Lowe (10)
Fulwell Junior School

SNOW

A blizzard rages,
Flakes of arctic crystal,
Plummeting downwards.

Michael Downey (11)
Fulwell Junior School

FRIENDS/BULLIES/GANGS

A friend is someone who cares for you,
Who shares and plays in all they do,
Who's kind and happy and never quite unhappy.
A friend is someone who cares for you.

A bully is someone who hurts your feelings,
Who leads you into trouble,
Who makes you feel left out and
Has a bad reputation.

A gang is a group who's good or bad,
Who meets at a certain place,
A gang is a group that may have a promise
And may not include bullies.

Sara Hamod (9)
Fulwell Junior School

THE AWFUL TWITS

The Twits are an awful pair
They put worms in my hair
They stole then hid my front door key
I wish they would jump in the sea.

They hit the animals with big sticks
They play nasty little tricks
Mrs Twit has a glass eye
It looks like a big fat pie.

Abigail McCardle (9)
Fulwell Junior School

FRIENDS/BULLIES/GANGS

A friend is someone who cares for you
Thinks of you
Is nice to you
A friend is someone who shares with you
That's what a friend is.

A bully is someone who's nasty to you
Doesn't like you
Hates you
A bully is someone who bullies you
That's what a bully is.

A gang is a group of people
Who leave you out
Make you shout
A gang is a group of people
Who make you scream and kick.

Annie Dorner (10)
Fulwell Junior School

THE TWITS

The Twits are a brutish pair.
They never ever wash their hair.
They put glue on a tree.
If a bird lands it'll never get free.

I wish the Twits would go away.
So I can have a normal day.
They put a frog in my hair
Next to the toad already there.

Christopher Bell (9)
Fulwell Junior School

EARTH EARTH EARTH

Earth is a place where we live,
Earth is a place that spins round and round.
Earth is a place we must respect,
Earth is a place of many sights and sounds.

Earth is a place where it's mostly blue,
Earth is a place where the land is green.
Earth is a place where we are,
Earth is a place we must keep clean.

Earth is a place like a great big bubble,
Earth is a place deep out in space.
Earth is a place where we should do our part,
Earth is a lovely place.

Helen Boyd (10)
Fulwell Junior School

PLANET EARTH

Deep in dark outer space
There is a blue and lovely place
It is the home of the human race
We call it Earth
Around the Earth live the stars
And lots of planets like Saturn and Mars
The moon and sun are out there to
They shine in our sky for us to view
They bring to us night and day
On our amazing planet in the Milky Way.

Adrienne McDonough (10)
Fulwell Junior School

RAIN

Spitting, drizzling rain,
making me cold, damp, then wet,
frozen to the bone.

Katherine Dorans (9)
Fulwell Junior School

SNOW

Soft feather carpets,
Fall in circular spirals,
Floating down to earth.

Rachel Price (10)
Fulwell Junior School

SNOW

Gliding down to earth,
Like children pillow-fighting,
Settles, peacefully.

Catherine Blakelock
Fulwell Junior School

SNOW HAIKU

Snow quietly floats
Snowflakes glittering shining
Icicles sparkle.

Rosanna Upright (11)
Fulwell Junior School

SPRING

Leaves growing on trees
spring is here the lambs are born
flowers all around.

Richard Fowler (8)
Fulwell Junior School

SUNDERLAND

Super stadium
Is full of Sunderland light
Red and white fly high.

Ross Atkinson (9)
Fulwell Junior School

RAIN

Pounding the windows,
Water bouncing off the ground,
Splish splash fell the rain.

David Beckinsale (8)
Fulwell Junior School

EARTH

An active planet.
Slowly spinning peacefully,
Giving life to all.

Lauren Hart (10)
Fulwell Junior School

CAT

My cat Tiger is a
Scary vicious fighting cat
Spiky fur hunched back.

Lauren Barnes (8)
Fulwell Junior School

WINTER

Sleek ghostly figure
Shimmering in moonlit hills
Smiles delightfully.

Stacey Derivan (10)
Fulwell Junior School

WINTER

Freezing icy weeks,
Slushy snowy frosty winters,
Bleak chilly winter days.

Kate O'Reilly (11)
Fulwell Junior School

WINTER

Sliding sledges slip,
Freezing sparkling snowflakes,
Gleaming swirling snow.

Lauren Barker (10)
Fulwell Junior School

DAFFODIL

Velvety petals,
Waving in the wind softly,
Crackly underneath.

Kate Jackson (8)
Fulwell Junior School

DAFFODIL

Golden daffodils,
Waving happily in fields,
Silently swaying.

Rachael Clifton (8)
Fulwell Junior School

FEET

Feet are like five snails,
With big toe as leader
Slithering along.

Holly Waites (8)
Fulwell Junior School

DAFFODIL

Such fragile petals,
Growing from a tall green stem,
Gold trumpets sway.

Alex Birkenshaw (8)
Fulwell Junior School

WHY?

Why is falling snow so cold?
See me tomorrow and you'll be told.
Why is Sunderland Football Club so red and white?
So they are seen on a dark night.
Why isn't it Christmas every day?
We would get bored straightaway.
Why is it not always a summer day?
Because we'd miss out on snow, okay!
Why do cats daintily say miaow?
Well go and find out - now.
Why are rich people so wealthy?
Is it because they're fit and healthy?
Why do people forget our names?
They think they're playing little games.
Why do things get lost?
Especially things with a very high cost!

Lesley Mearns (11)
Fulwell Junior School

FRIENDS/BULLIES/GANGS

A friend is someone
who stays with you
no matter what

Bullies are people who
play rough and think
they're tough

Gangs are people who
stick together and are
friends forever.

Lucy Tindle (9)
Fulwell Junior School

WITHOUT ADULTS

Without adults I would . . .
Get a tattoo of a swallow on my shoulder
Change my name to Lara Vicki Tuner
And eat loads of sherbet and junk food
But I would miss . . .
My dad pretending to be a chef in a restaurant
every time he makes something
Dad fighting me and sitting on me in his stupid way
And taking me out on trips to Blackpool and going on
all the rides.

Without adults I would . . .
Play music full blast which would break all the windows
Get my ears pierced and wear dangly earrings
And climb loads of trees and swing from the tops
But I would miss . . .
My nanna fussing over me and giving me sweets
My mam and dad serving my food
And Mam mopping up my burst lip
when I smacked into the wall.

Nicola Turner (9)
Fulwell Junior School

THERE ARE GHOSTS IN MY SCHOOL

I've heard there are ghosts in the school
They're even down the loo
They float around the playground
And in the bell tower too
At playtime we laugh and play
We hope the ghosts don't bother us
Or we'll have to run away.

Michael Armstrong (9)
Fulwell Junior School

SNOWFLAKES

Shining crystals gleam,
Coming from high up above,
Landing on rooftops.

Gavin Stoker (11)
Fulwell Junior School

SNOW

Freezing cold fingers
Shivering in the cold wind
A horrible day.

Ashley Padgett (11)
Fulwell Junior School

SNOW

Silky shiny snow
Soft playful snowflakes shimmer
Sparkling icicles glow.

Emma Galer (10)
Fulwell Junior School

SNOW

Showery snowflakes
Sailing quietly downwards
Landing on rooftops.

Jill Scott (11)
Fulwell Junior School

WHY?

Why does my ink pen blot?
My teacher must think I'm a clot.
Why do I have a hard and painful brother?
Life is so cruel, couldn't I have another?
Why are teachers so nice?
I suppose it's better than a bowl of rice!
Why do people grow and grow?
When you can stay like Teletubby Po.
Why are Ross's glasses on a slant?
Is it because he jumped over a plank?
Why is Rebecca so kind?
Is it because of her mind?
Why is Greg so keen on cricket?
Is it because he takes the wicket?
Why is Mark so clever in maths?
Why couldn't he be clever in crafts?

Tanya Grant (11)
Fulwell Junior School

FRIENDS AND BULLIES

A friend is someone who cares for you
Plays and looks after you the whole day through
But there's something special about a friend
She's the only one on whom you can depend
A bully is someone who bullies you
And does not share their sweets and food
But there's something strange about a bully
Do they know they're doing it?

Gemma Scott (9)
Fulwell Junior School

WHY?

Why is it never sunny on a Sunday?
The sun might be having a rest in the bay.
Why do we day-dream while in a lesson of French?
Or do we fall asleep on the bench.
Why are my school books always so messy?
Maybe I'm thinking about catching Nessie.
Why do cats and dogs have claws?
They might be fighters with weapons on their paws.
Why doesn't everyone look the same?
Well I suppose if we did it would be a shame.
Why is fire so burning hot?
If I touched it I would be a clot.
Why do parents always know the answer?
They say you'll get bad feet if you're a dancer.
Why do babies pull long hair?
I could frighten them off and give them a scare.
Why is my cousin always so silly?
I'll put him in my budgie's cage (he's called Billy).
Why are Goosebumps books always so short?
I've read all the ones my mam bought.
Why are writing skills so hard to remember?
I think I'll be trying to remember them until next December.

Laura Scott (11)
Fulwell Junior School

SLY BOOKS

Books are really sly,
You can never let them go,
They really grasp you.

Rachael Goodchild (10)
Fulwell Junior School

WHY?

Why are crocodiles' teeth so sharp and pointy?
Is it because they like animals crunchy?
Why is an orange the same as the colour?
Has it got some sort of strange brother?
Why have foxes got big, bushy tails?
Is it to wipe away its small footprint trails?
Why are firemen so strong and tough?
Is it because they can't get enough?
Why do young drivers drive so fast?
Is it because they want to look back at their past?
Why do clouds fly in the sky?
Is it because they're not afraid to go high?
Why do churches have a bell?
Is it just to keep people well?
Why is the Earth so big and round?
Are two giants kicking it around?
Why are there so many people on the Earth?
Is it just part of mankind's birth?
Why did dinosaurs die out for?
Did God want people just a little bit more?
Why are magpies so silly and thick?
They can't even build a little wall out of brick.
Why does water pressure crush your ears?
Is it to scare people with water fears?

Adam Lock (11)
Fulwell Junior School

THE TWITS

The Twits are a mean old pair,
They never never wash their hair,
They stand on spiders, worms and flies
This is what they have in their pies.

I wish they didn't live near me,
They are as dirty as they can be,
They couldn't be nice even for a day,
They always have to get their way.

Lindsay Coates (9)
Fulwell Junior School

SOUNDS OF THE PLAYGROUND

The playground is peaceful
There's silence all over.
Then the bell goes.
From the silence breaks a rumble of thunder.
Then it sounds like a herd of elephants -
Everybody goes crashing down the stairs.
Then they tumble out of the school.
I come hurtling down with them.
It's very loud, you can't hear yourself.
Girls skipping, boys kicking a ball.
'Goal! I've scored a goal! Yippee!'
'Ow! I'm telling!'
'Miss, he hurt me!'
'Come here'
Peep - the whistle blows.
'Bye-bye, see you tomorrow.'
'Okay.'
The school was quiet until now.
Back to class.
Pencils ready, back to work.

Paul Allinson (8)
Fulwell Junior School

LATE FOR SCHOOL

I woke up one morning and I gazed outside,
Kids were in the playground I very nearly died!
I went to see my mum and dad and shouted in Dad's ear,
'Wake up, wake up it's time to go,
School time is drawing near,'
Dearest Dad jumped out of bed
And on a bedpost bumped his head,
I had my breakfast very fast,
Wondering how long this nightmare would last,
I grab my bag and slam the gate,
'Hurry up Clare, we're going to be late!'
Oh no there must be some mistake
It's only half-past eight.

Kathryn McCandless (9)
Fulwell Junior School

GOOD FRIENDS BAD BULLIES LOUD GANGS

A friend is someone who cares for you
A friend is someone who shares with you
A friend is someone who plays with you
A friend is someone who waits for you

A bully is someone who's horrible to you
A bully is someone who doesn't play with you
A bully is someone who makes you cry

A gang is happy
A gang is sad
A gang is quiet
A gang is *loud!*

Rachel Grieves (9)
Fulwell Junior School

ART

We come into class and shout '*Yippee,*'
Art lesson's just begun,
Anne's already got glue on her knee,
The tap is starting to run.

Cover the tables with newspaper,
Get out the glue and the paint,
Michael, don't get out the stapler,
The teacher is starting to faint.

We've done our art lesson now,
The classroom is a tip,
We'll go home to the warm TV,
The cleaners can clear up,
You'll see.

Helen Ritchie (10)
Fulwell Junior School

I'M NOT GENEROUS

I'm not generous,
My real name is Greedy,
I wouldn't give a penny to the poor and needy,
Cars, credit cards, a slot machine,
I guess you could say I'm really quite mean,
As the world goes round I'm getting richer,
While the poor and homeless all get sicker,
Yes you could say I'm mean and greedy,
I wouldn't give a penny to the poor and needy.

Emma Graham (11)
Fulwell Junior School

I Ain't Greedy

I'm not the kind
The kind to mind,
When people are greedy,
I ain't greedy.

I like to care,
I like to share,
To make it fair,
Oh yeah.

I ain't mean,
It ain't my scene,
If I've got two,
There's one for you.

I like to care,
I like to share,
To make it fair,
Oh yeah oh yeah.

There's too much wanting,
Ain't that daunting,
See what I got,
You can have the lot.

I like to care,
I like to share,
To make it fair,
Ain't square, so there!

Jennifer Greaves (10)
Fulwell Junior School

WHY?

Why can't we go for a holiday to the moon?
I hope we can go soon.
Why is the Earth so large and round?
It travels quickly without a sound.
Why are horror books so very scary?
If I read another one I'll have to be wary!
Why does a helium balloon float into the air?
Nobody knows, nobody cares.
Why are brothers really mean?
They are naughty and so unclean.
Why are clever people always neat?
Even when they're walking in the street!
Why is football such a popular game?
Rugby and cricket are just the same!

Robert Coates (11)
Fulwell Junior School

SOUNDS OF THE PLAYGROUND

Bell goes, teacher sighs and off we go,
Screaming, giggling, shouting down the stairs.
Doors shoot open,
Torpedo into the playground.
Boys shouting, *'Goal!'*
Girls shouting, *'Tig!'*
Cartwheel for luck.
A boy swears - gets wrong.
Whistle goes,
Back to class,
Ready for work.

Katie White (8)
Fulwell Junior School

WHY?

Why are people so good at art?
I suppose you don't have to be very smart!
Why do people always talk?
It's much healthier to walk.
Why do mean people always complain?
They get on my nerves again and again.
Why do people never play in the rain?
They're probably doing their homework and using their brain.
Why do plants sadly shrivel up and die?
A keen gardener would start to cry.
Why is the sun so fiery and hot?
Is it because it's angry, maybe not!
Why are gorillas really scary?
Is it because they're big and hairy?
Why is jelly wibbly and wobbly?
Jelly eating is my hobby, probably!

Lucy Cuthbertson (10)
Fulwell Junior School

A FRIEND

A friend is for you
A friend is for me
A friend is for everybody
A friend cares for you
A friends stays with you
A friend sticks up for you
And plays nice games with you.

Lydia Cresswell (9)
Fulwell Junior School

TIME TICKS

Time is ticking by,
Daytime, night-time, every time,
Tick tock, ticking tock.

Carolyn Mearns (10)
Fulwell Junior School

CROCASAURAS DILLEY

The Crocasauras Dilley
Has big black eyes,
And two sticky up ears,
With a squidgy brown nose,
He might be found in the Mediterranean
Or in the River Thames
I'm not quite sure
Because I've never seen him
But I know he's there!

He has scaly skin
And he can swim
He has two big fins
And is very big,
He eats anything
Because he has sharp teeth
I'm not quite sure
Because I've never seen him
But I know he's there!

I don't think you'll ever see him though,
Because he's make-believe
But I know he's there!

Amanda Thompson (10)
Goathland Primary School

I LOVE MY BROTHER!

I've got one brother
I don't want another!
And that's the way
I want it to be.

He is nice
And likes lots of spice.
He's lovely and sweet.
Makes me things to eat.

It would just not be right
If I did not have a fight
For days without him!

I love my brother!

Laura Brett (10)
Goathland Primary School

I MISS MY DAD

I miss my dad
Because he left us alone
With no one to laugh with,
He used to take me on his motorbike,
Down a hill,
Taking turns with my brothers
And now that he's gone,
There is no way back.
I miss my dad
I miss my dad.

Sophie Stobart-Kilgallon (10)
Goathland Primary School

LONELINESS

Lonely,
The girl,
Standing on her own.

Watching,
The others,
Playing chasing games.

Everyone ignores her,
No one sits by her at lunch,
Her mother told her not to worry
She said it was just a phase,
There is no way, it seems,
To ease those lonely days.

No one seems to realise,
Until they're on their own,
That loneliness isn't when there's only one,
But when nobody knows.

Kathryn Cox (10)
Goathland Primary School

CHRISTMAS PARTY!

Christmas party underneath the sea,
Little fishies happy as can be,
Hear the cheers, loud applause,
Merry, merry Christmas *Santa Jaws!*

Laughing and screaming,
Shouting and smiling,
And! Fancy clothing,
Merry, merry Christmas, *Santa Jaws!*

Danielle Bellwood (9)
Goathland Primary School

MY DOG!

My dog!
My dog's name is Angus,
with cute brown eyes
and is very excitable.
He has a soft coat like velvet.
He runs like the wind
and eats everything
like a vacuum cleaner
but I love my dog!

Rebekah Wilkinson (9)
Goathland Primary School

PIRATE PETE

There was an old pirate called Pete,
Who very much liked a treat,
He got in a tizzy,
And then he was dizzy,
Poor old Pirate Pete.

Alison Janes (10)
Goathland Primary School

EPITAPH

Here lies the body
of little Snow White
who went out in the night
and died in a fight.

Katie Field (7)
Grange Park Primary School

I LOVE FOOD

Juicy apples after lunch
Sizzling bacon in a pan
Crackling Rice Crispies for my breakfast

Beefy beefburgers for my tea
And hard lime drops for afters
Pancakes and salt for my supper

I can hear the popping of the toaster
I can hear popcorn crackling

Popping toasters, crunching candy,
Icy ice-creams, sizzling sausages.

Deborah Thompson (10)
Grange Park Primary School

BUTTERFLY

Butterfly, butterfly,
I love it when you flutter by,
I see you land on petals and nettles,
Then I see you happily settle.

Butterfly, butterfly,
I love it when you flutter by,
I see you weave through the trees,
Then you flutter in the breeze.

Lucy McBeath (10)
Grange Park Primary School

BOUNCE

What goes bounce?
I just can't think.
Does a car go bounce?
No that's stupid
I know, a ball goes bounce.

What goes bounce, bounce?
I just can't think.
Does a Hoover go bounce, bounce?
No that's crazy
I know a trampoline goes bounce bounce.

Bounce, bounce, bounce,
No more things I can think of
Go bounce

Bounce!

Katie Sanderson (11)
Grange Park Primary School

EPITAPH

Here lies the body
of Mickey Mouse
killed by a brick
that fell out of a house.

Allix Nichols (7)
Grange Park Primary School

EPITAPH

Here lies the body
of Ba Ba Black
Killed by a cow
that gave it a whack.

Jordan Burdis (7)
Grange Park Primary School

EPITAPH

Here lies the body
of Mickey Mouse
he went on a diet
and died in the house.

Rebecca Nelson (7)
Grange Park Primary School

EPITAPH

Here lies the body
of a silly little cat
who died this morning
because he was fat.

Tanya Charlton (7)
Grange Park Primary School

EPITAPH

Here lies the body
of a poor pussy cat
squashed by an iron
and ended up really flat.

Liam Downing (7)
Grange Park Primary School

MY BEST FRIEND LIVES BEYOND THE EARTH

My best friend is funny,
She lives very far away,
She's never heard of money.
She always says 'OK'
We never see each other,
Only when I'm sleeping,
She really hates my brother.

One night she was weeping
So I asked her what was wrong
She was really upset.
She'd burned her head with the tongs.
So we rushed upstairs to the bathroom,
And she got soaking wet.
I dried her up with the towel.
She gave a great big howl.
That was a bit of a quiz
Can you guess what she is?
She's an alien
She's called Zorlien.

Stevie McAskell (9)
Hadrian JMI School

MARILYN MEND

Once I had a friend
Her name was Marilyn Mend
She always whizzes around the house
Trying to wake the baby up
Every time she knocks
She always rattles at the locks.
My mam keeps saying 'Keep that Marilyn
Mend out of my house she's nothing but trouble.'
This is what my mam has to say
Every time I look at her.
I go all red inside with the anger
I just can't keep in
But there's nothing I can do
She's my best friend
She's Marilyn Mend.

Layla Hakim (10)
Hadrian JMI School

BEYOND THE EARTH

Space is beyond the earth.
There're aliens there.
Big green slimy monsters everywhere.
Martians fly through the air.
Howling aliens with long raggy hair.
Ugly creatures with spiky backs.
And a statue holding an axe.
Space is an unusual place.
But they don't care!

Lia Rachael Sefton (9)
Hadrian JMI School

THE UNIVERSE

Space is very dark and glittery
The stars shine and twinkle,
You can even see the sun glowing down on the earth.
The stars were glowing and twinkling
Next to the sun you could see nine planets
They are all lovely, but I came from earth
When you looked deep into Mars you could see some aliens
Well of course, we didn't want to bother them.
So we went on all the way around space.
We had a look at the glittering stars and the flaming sun.
But I live not in space but on earth.
So we went home to land the spaceship.

Craig Gray (9)
Hadrian JMI School

APPLES

Apples are nice
Especially when they're ripe
I love apples.
I like food
When I'm in a mood
But always apples
They're my favourite fruit.
Apples are fresh
Straight from the tree
I have apples every single day.

Faye Ironside (9)
Hadrian JMI School

THE DAY I WENT INTO SPACE

I went into space one day
And saw to my surprise,
Planets all around me
Blazing before my eyes.
First I went to Jupiter
Then I went to Mars and Pluto,
But the last planet I went to,
Wasn't a planet at all.
It was the moon,
I landed on the moon,
I had a look around.
I saw lots and lots of craters,
All around me.
I looked in one
And it was deep,
I looked in another
And I fell right down
I shouted 'Help.'
But no one was on the moon
So I had a go at climbing out
And finally I did.
I started to run out of oxygen
So I went into my rocket,
And on the way home,
I saw planets all around me
Blazing before my eyes.

Deena Welsh (10)
Hadrian JMI School

MY IMAGINARY FRIEND

My imaginary friend is Pippy,
She is annoying and a pain.
She is not allowed to my house,
She can come with her mum.
She has red hair and weird eyes,
She has a face like a goblin.
She has a normal nose as well.
She is so tall.
She reaches to the ceiling.
We play together all the time.
When she is asleep she turns small
When she gets up she changes to tall.
She is really weird. we play *passies* but she
                          can't catch the ball.
When she goes to school she can't read all
                          that well.
She enjoys school a lot.
Wherever I go all I hear is
'Can I come with you?'

Lindsey Smurthwaite (9)
Hadrian JMI School

MY DOG, MULDER

My dog, Mulder, is my friend
Humans and him don't really blend
When I take him out to play
If I left him he would be there day after day.
I love him and he loves me
I will tell you and you will tell me.

Mulder gulps his water down
When he's naughty we have to frown
When I cuddle him I don't hold him tight
If I do he will get a fright.
Because I love him and he loves me
I will tell you and you will tell me.

James Cowie
Hadrian JMI School

WHEN YOU GO INTO SPACE

When you go into space
It's great. Bouncing around
like on a bouncy castle.

When you go into space
It's scary. You might
meet an alien. Like
meeting a ghost.

When you go into space
It's dark. Like night-time
all the time. So you've
got to go to bed.

When you go into space
there's no school to go to,
So you laze around
like the six weeks holiday.

Space is great!

Andrew Dorrian (9)
Hadrian JMI School

ALL ABOUT SPACE

S is for the stars that twinkle in the sky so high
P is for the planets that are very colourful.
A is for the aliens with six eyes, four heads, eight arms, green and
slimy,
C is for the comets that shoot across the sky.
E is for earth amongst the other planets.

Laura Swan (10)
Hadrian JMI School

WHEN I WAS A BABY

When I was a baby I cried and cried
And I always stayed inside
I slept and slept
Sometimes I wept
And I made my nappy wet.
When I was two
I was sick on my mam's shoe
I could not walk
I could not talk
And I could not crawl.
When I was three
I never drank tea
All I drank was juice
I ate chocolate mousse
But then I liked any other food.
There was a hard knock at the door
It was my Auntie Marie
Her cat was up a tree
We could not help her.

Laura Rump (8)
Harraton Primary School

My Hamster

My hamster, Fudge
he is a kind hamster of course
he bit my mam once
but she did not care.
We called him Fudge
because he was fudge-coloured
with white on him.
He is very, very, cute indeed.
Fudge is a smelly hamster.
Cleaning him is hard
always asleep
wakes up at 8.00 at night.

Laura Armstrong (8)
Harraton Primary School

Sparky And Lucky

Sparky and Lucky are two little hamsters!
Who eat their cages
And fill their cheeks with food
They bury their food as well.
Sparky and Lucky
They are such little rascals
They bite my hands
But they sleep all day.
Sparky and Lucky
Are a girl and a boy
Sparky is a boy and Lucky is a girl.
Sparky and Lucky
Have sharp teeth
But that's just hamsters!

Claire Clasper (8)
Harraton Primary School

IN THE BATH

In the bath I scrub my toes.
In the bath I nearly drowned.
In the bath there are lots of bubbles.
It is like a jungle.
It scares me,
Even though I'm eight.
I like the bath when it is hot.
The towels are very soft.
The bathroom is light.
With lots of air.
I like it a lot.
It is lovely there.

Hannah Greenhow (8)
Harraton Primary School

MY BUDGIE

My budgie is cute
When we play Trivial Pursuit
He runs after the dice.
He stands up straight
After he ate
And he is really nice.

He flies around
Then falls to the ground
He stands on my head before bed
He plays with his toys
And makes a lot of noise
I will really cry when he is dead.

Sarah Crossling (8)
Harraton Primary School

AT THE BEACH

When the sea is thrashing,
And the children splashing,
There are seagulls screaming
And the surf is gleaming,
You might hear people talking,
And the sound of walking,
Because when you're by the sea,
It may be cold, clean or dirty,
Or the sea might be trickling,
But it could be rippling.
There are children playing,
And sometimes they're saying,
'When the sea is thrashing against the sand,
You know you're at the beach
When you're at the sandy land.'

Claire Morris (9)
Harraton Primary School

MY CAT

My cat Ellie has a furry belly
She eats all day and watches telly.
She likes to roam outside at night
Her tail gets bushy when she gets a fright.
When I stroke her head it makes her purr
She keeps herself clean by licking her fur.
When she goes to sleep she snores
She covers her face with her front paws.
Ellie is a very special pet
Best cat you could wish to get.

Laura Magee (8)
Harraton Primary School

MY RABBIT

My rabbit is white,
But it never bites.
We gave it some food
And a carrot to chew.
It goes to sleep at night
It has very good eyesight.
Its eyes are bright
In the light.

Michael Temple (8)
Harraton Primary School

MY SCHOOL

School! School!
Boring school!
Hard work
Getting shouted at!
Kids shouting
Rather loud!

Darrin Richardson (8)
Harraton Primary School

STREAM

Flowing stream
Fast flowing stream
Gentle fast flowing stream
Flowing gently under the bridge.
Stream.

Rachel Kendall (9)
Harraton Primary School

THE SEA WALL

I'm standing by the sea wall
watching all the boats,
All the waves smashing, crashing,
then the waves fall.
Ships moving on the water.
Small waves, large waves
big whales, little whales
Even lovely dolphins
Tiny little fishermen's boats
other boats too, some big, some small.
I can hear the roaring of the water
and the crashing of the sea.
The flow sometimes smooth, sometimes rough.
I can hear the wind and rain.
I'm standing by the sea wall.

Craig Scott (9)
Harraton Primary School

ME

I was playing football
A bunny came onto the pitch.
The bunny was lovely and furry.
He had big pointy ears
And big black eyes
I was scared because of the big
                    black eyes he had
He did a very funny dance
It was good fun.
The bunny went back into its hole
And we scored.

Daniel Ferry (8)
Harraton Primary School

RIVERS

Whirling,
  Curling,
    Crashing rivers
      Fly down by the trees

Round the bend,
  Round the rocks
    Crash into
      the sea

Birds chirping
  Fish gurgling
    Children swimming
      past the pier.

Stacey Merrigan (10)
Harraton Primary School

MYSELF

Nathan is my name.
At school I like to play a game
At home I like to play with my toys,
Just like the other boys.
I have a dog called Ben
And he is over ten
I take him for a walk
If I see my friends I have a talk
I have a friend called Mark
My mam takes us to the park
We love to play all day.

Nathan Keogh (7)
Harraton Primary School

MY BROTHER

My brother is fat
He can't get through the door!
When I went to the park,
He got stuck in the swing!
We had to get the saw and cut it
Then he went down the slide
He broke it!
He went on the see-saw
He broke that!
I was glad when we went home.

Victoria Bowden (7)
Harraton Primary School

PICKLED FEET

In the bath the bubbles
make my feet tickle.
Sometimes after football
My feet smell like pickles
But I wouldn't like to eat them
Because I would be 'sickles'.

Curtis Connor (7)
Harraton Primary School

FRIENDS

Friends are kind and always happy,
Friends are always helpful,
Friends are special in a way.
Friends can make you smile all day.

Danielle Crossling (10)
Harraton Primary School

SPLASHING

I am sitting by the water's edge,
Wondering what to do,
I see the rippling of the river,
Circling round and round.
There are children nearby,
Splashing and sploshing,
Just like children do,
The water's clean and fresh,
See the little fishes there.

Shauna Allan (9)
Harraton Primary School

RAIN

Rain, raining all day long.
Rain, still raining when the clock goes *dong!*
Rain, raining all the time
Rain, I hate the rain,
I wish the sun was mine.

Anthony Goundry (9)
Harraton Primary School

RIVER

Cold river
 fast, cold river
  deep, fast, cold river
   going to the sea.
    River.

Ken Cavanagh (10)
Harraton Primary School

RIVER WATER

Fast river water,
Flowing and crashing against the rocks.
Fish in the water.
Swimming and playing with each other.
Slow river water.
Dripping and trickling through the trees
Rock in the water crashing and sloshing
                          against the side.

Jason Wilson (10)
Harraton Primary School

WATERFALL

Sparkling waterfall
Crashing, sparkling waterfall
Cold, crashing, sparkling waterfall,
Splashing on the bank.
                    Waterfall.

Ashleigh Stewart (9)
Harraton Primary School

OCEAN

Rough ocean
Roaring rough ocean
Crashing roaring rough ocean
Battling it out with the ship
Ocean.

James Douglas (10)
Harraton Primary School

LAMBORGHINI

Fast sporty yellow Lamborghini
Moving very fast
Electric windows, alloy wheels
Black windows.

Scott Parry (9)
Harraton Primary School

RIVER

Cold river
Sparkling cold river
Shallow sparkling cold river
Sparkling to the sea.

Mark Nugent
Harraton Primary School

RIVER

River,
Smelly river
Dirty, smelly river.
Swishing, flowing through
Night and day.

Rhianne Greenwell (9)
Harraton Primary School

ALIENS ARE MAD

Aliens are mad!
They are mean which is quite sad,
On *Independence Day* they were quite bad,
Killing people with the lasers they had.

To be an alien it would be sad,
To have sixteen arms I would be glad,
'Do they exist?' I asked my dad,
'All we know is that they are green my lad.'

Christopher Stammers (11)
Hetton Primary School

SPACE

Space is such a strange sight,
You can see the earth turn day and night,
You see the planets turn around,
And hear a noisy, gurgling sound.

Mercury's like a ball of fire,
But it's not quite as hot as the sun,
Venus is the planet I desire,
I think it would be a lot of fun,
Earth is the planet we know the best,
We know it better than all the rest,
Mars can get extremely cold,
Sometimes it's the colour of gold,
Jupiter has a big red spot,
It suffers from storms an awful lot,
Saturn has got some lovely rings,
Made up of rocks and other things,
Uranus is mostly green,
But it is not often seen,
Neptune is way out in space,
A very dark and eerie place,
Pluto is the furthest away,
From the sun and light of day.

Claire Harrison (10)
Hetton Primary School

MY ALIEN LOVES FOOD

As I woke one night from my bed
I looked out of my window, saw an alien,
And this is what he was eating.

Frogs' bellies with yellow jelly
I was very shocked indeed,
Rotten fish, horses' eyes,
Spiders, handbags and pork pies.
I wasn't feeling quite well at the time
But wait till you hear the rest,
I know you might not like the food
But this is what he likes best:
He likes noses with beans
Money with honey
Cars with Mars bars
And brains with drains.
Well now I think to myself,
Oh well he's my alien
Now I'll go and get him some shells!

Melissa White (10)
Hetton Primary School

UNLUCKY DAY

I was on my way to Mars one day
When I saw flashing lights, hooray!
But it wasn't my lucky day
It was a laser blaster, grade A.
A thousand volts went through my head,
In one second I was dead,
I was lying on the floor,
My heart was beating no more.

Christopher Sutherland (10)
Hetton Primary School

I HAVE BEEN TO MERCURY

Mercury is the hottest of them all.
Even though it is very small
If I was tall I could see
A funny little alien staring down at me.

Mercury is in space,
In a very large place,
With planets around both big and small,
If you went there you would easily fall.

As I pray to God
I give a little nod.
Look at the stairs
and look at the vase.

Look at Mars
And think of stars.
Up with the stars
And away with the cars.

Stacy McBeth (10)
Hetton Primary School

VENUS

This is what it's like on Venus.
It is brighter than you know
It has blue colours round it, but not anymore.

The sun is bright
The sun is hot
The sun is always there
I look out of my window
And the sun is always there.

Rebecca Cardy (10)
Hetton Primary School

MY ALIEN

Aliens live on Mars,
Aliens have no cars,
      But
My alien has three eyes,
My alien does not cry,
My alien is very fat,
He does not have a pet cat,
But he wears a blue hat,
My alien has three feet,
My alien likes to eat people's
      brains and their teeth,
My alien has some hair,
My alien walks around bare.
      That's my alien

Jayne Soppitt (10)
Hetton Primary School

SPACE

I look at the moon
And I think of a big lagoon,
Deep and dark.

I look at the sun
And I think of a nun
Kind and warm.

I look at space
And I think of a place
Dark and thick.

Carly Lambton (11)
Hetton Primary School

MARS

Mars is a big ball of rock,
Trapped in the sun's gravitational lock.

Mars, as cold as ice,
Living there would not be nice.

Balls of light, known as stars,
Are constantly shining down on Mars.

Mars from Earth looks like a star,
It gives its name to the chocolate bar.

Marc Loscombe (10)
Hetton Primary School

COSMIC

If you travel to space
you think it's ace.
Travel in time
you'll be home by nine.
In the sun
it's really fun.
Aliens ahead
are green, blue and red.
Stars so bright
twinkle in the night.
Planets come our way
every single day.
Shooting stars
passing Mars.
We all go home in a rocket ship
and have strawberry whip.

Rebecca Walton (10)
Hill View Junior School

SPACE

Earth and Mars,
Planets, stars.
Supernova!
Move over.
White dwarf, pulsar,
The universe so far.
Nebulas, gas and dust,
Constellations, earth's crust.
UFO
Time holes throw!
Solar flare
Bursts in air!
Telescope,
Gives us hope.
Visits to moon . . .
Coming soon!
Unknown race,
Lost in space.

James Ferguson (9)
Hill View Junior School

COSMIC POEM

The star is bright
Travels far
Light up the night
The shining star
The planets are far away
Far away in space
Never show in the day
They all look like a face.

Daniel Vasey (9)
Hill View Junior School

COSMIC

Get to space,
It's a race,
There's some stars,
They're very far,
Star Trek,
Is it a wreck?
On Saturn,
They speak Latin!
Black hole,
Space like coal,
Spaceships,
Do aliens eat chips?

Charlotte Carlin (9)
Hill View Junior School

COSMIC

The twinkling stars give the light,
To make the whole space so bright,
I look in the dark gloomy sky,
Astronauts passing by,
Different planets big and small,
I wonder why they never fall?
The moon is travelling round the earth,
Who in the world gave it birth?
The sun I always wish to see,
How big do you think it will be?
I look at the planets and dream,
How it will look? How it will seem?
To be in a planet unknown,
Will it feel as good as home?

Tahmina Rokib (9)
Hill View Junior School

COSMIC

Vile Venus
I wouldn't go there
No one's ever been
Why would I dare.

Sizzling stars
Light up the sky
They shine so brightly
I wonder why?

Magnificent Mars
The planet that's red
Pity if I went there
I'd soon be dead.

Unidentified Uranus
The planet that's strange
Like all of the planets
It's not going to change.

Emphatic earth
Is where I live
It's so exciting
It's got loads to give.

All the planets
Different by loads
Some have green creatures
(Not toads!)

Jonathan Loach (10)
Hill View Junior School

COSMIC

A Milky Way
starts to sway.
Shining lights,
I don't like heights.
Shining star,
don't go far.
Astronaut
an alien's been caught.
Black hole,
covered in coal.
Aliens met,
on a planet.
There's a UFO,
or you said so.
Open space,
in your face.
Here's your mission,
well why don't you listen?
Gravity,
stars on me.
Spaceship,
do a flip.
Moon life,
with strife.
Never ending,
the spaceship needs mending.
Very vast,
but very fast.

Lian Kirton (10)
Hill View Junior School

COSMIC

Don't mess with the sun
Because he weighs 10,000 tonnes,
The sun's light
has all the might,
The sun.

Just in case
You go to space,
I'm warning you now
Don't go right now,
Space.

Stars give light
With all their might
Shining with the moon
Which goes down at noon,
Stars.

Mark Watson (10)
Hill View Junior School

ALIENS

Do aliens fly around all day
in a very strange way?
Do they walk or do they crawl?
Do they jump and never fall?
Have they heard of homes and shops?
Have they heard of lollipops?
Have they heard of wasps and bees?
Do they have knobbly knees?
But the question that I need to know is . . .
Do they exist at all?

Natasha Meldrum (10)
Hill View Junior School

A COSMIC POEM

Super shining stars.
I wonder why?
Is there a black hole
up in the sky?
Man has gone
from earth to space,
landed on
an extraordinary place.
In a spaceship
to the moon.
No life did they find.
I hope the day will come
quite soon.
When I can go up
to the moon,
and see the stars,
and go to Mars.

Rachael Thornton (9)
Hill View Junior School

MARS

Mars is not one of those chocolate bars,
It's something that is in space or next to the stars.
Might it crash into something close by?
Nobody knows, do they?
Each day rockets must come crashing by making
lots of noise,
But none has hit Mars yet.
There must be lots of things in space all different
shapes and sizes.

Michael Wilkinson (9)
Hill View Junior School

COSMIC UNIVERSE

Way out in space,
There is a place,
That is called the universe.
It shines and sparkles
When we cannot see,
I wonder why I cannot
Spy the place I want to be.
I looked around every day,
But still no sign of it!
Early next morning at the start of day,
This is what my mam did say,
The earth is in the universe the same as all the rest.
But then she said just one more thing
'Now will you stop being a pest?'

Rosemary Ferries (9)
Hill View Junior School

COSMIC

Mobile, mistaking Mercury
Vital vast Venus
Evaporating, evergreen Earth
Magnifying, magnificent Moon
Moaning, mocking Mars
Jumping, jolly Jupiter
Sitting season Saturn
Upsetting, understanding Uranus
Nipping, nerve-racking Neptune
Polluting, political Pluto
Super, satisfying Sun.

Michael Telford (10)
Hill View Junior School

COSMIC POEM

Of all the planets,
In all of space,
Do they really,
Have little green men?

In the skies,
At night,
Can you really,
See UFOs?

Or are they,
Just stars?

Philip Lorenson (9)
Hill View Junior School

COSMIC

The universe is spinning,
In a unique kind of way,
Spinning with,
Sun,
Moon,
Earth and stars,
Spinning all the way,
Spinning with the universe,
In and out through space
Spinning,
In and out,
In a unique kind of way.

Louise Brown (10)
Hill View Junior School

COSMIC

Racing rockets
Through my pockets
Everlasting
Aliens passing
UFOs
Who knows?
Empty space
Travelling pace
Mass of black
Like a sack
Shooting stars
Men on Mars
Black hole
Bless my soul!
Moon craters
Plastic plates
Meteors flying past
Whizzing very fast
Moon, Earth
My own home, Perth.

Emma Knott (9)
Hill View Junior School

COSMIC

The sky so high
The moon shining on us
Planets up above us
Twinkling stars so bright.

Watch the rockets fly
Way up in the sky
Shooting stars above us
Why! Oh why! Oh why!

Astronauts upon the moon
They should be coming home quite soon!
Aliens from outer space
Satellites and Milky Ways!

At night the moon
Is very bright
Planets up above us
Twinkling stars so bright.

Catherine Jones (10)
Hill View Junior School

SPACE

Bright stars,
shine on Mars.
You can trace,
the space race.
Dark night,
need some light.
A world,
is curled.
Chocolate bar,
that is far.
The moon
comes soon.
UFO
on Pluto.
Earth and space,
have a race.
The sun,
makes fun.

Stacey Ferguson (9)
Hill View Junior School

COSMIC

Bright stars
Shine on Mars
Dark night
Need some light
UFO
Lands on Pluto
Up in space
It looks ace
Look at Saturn
Making a pattern.

Kirsty Lebihan (10)
Hill View Junior School

MOON

Some things up there,
are a little light,
Some things up there,
are a little bright,
Ahhh! I scream in my dream,
there is a beam!
Sometimes I think what's up there?
Sometimes I ask my parents but
they say 'What's up where?'
At night there is a light,
it gives me such a fright.
It had better go soon,
It is only the moon!

Philip Hall (9)
Hill View Junior School

MARS

I'm flying in a spaceship
to the planet Mars,
And no I'm not of course,
I'm not taking any cars.

I zoom past Mercury and Venus
They look quite like a genius,
Then I land on Mars.
I notice Mars is red.
Like my mother and father said.

So I decide to walk across Mars
And in case I get hungry I take two
chocolate bars,
It's quite soft and sandy.
My chocolate bars come in handy.

I walk round Mars,
Eating my chocolate bars,
Then I go back to the spaceship,
And fly back to earth.

Laura Howey (10)
Hill View Junior School

COSMIC

Space is ace
All the rockets zoom up into space
Making lights all over the place
Mars and Jupiter so near to see
Aliens jumping all over the sea
So clearly.

Gary Playle (9)
Hill View Junior School

ONE NIGHT AS I WAS LYING IN BED

One night as I was lying in bed,
I looked outside and saw ahead,
It was green, purple and red,
I was quite sleepy . . .
But I went to have a look instead.
When I went to have a look
An alien said 'Let's go up.'
When we went up we went to space,
And he said 'We are going to a place.'
Right ahead I saw the world,
It was green, purple and gold.

We landed on the alien world
and it was freezing cold, brr,
There were craters everywhere with
Feelers sticking out of there,
The alien suddenly said 'It's OK he's my friend.'
They then popped out from anywhere,
We danced, danced, danced all night,
And ten times I got a fright,
Then it was time to go
I said goodbye and flew back home.

Kayleigh Brannigan (10)
Hill View Junior School

WHEN I WENT TO BED ONE NIGHT

It was purple, red, yellow and green.
When I got to see the whole thing, I screamed!
He told me that I shall go up to space
But I said 'Wait a minute
I have to fasten my lace.'

At last in the spaceship now
I looked around and shouted *'Wow!'*
I saw the moon and the stars
And when I looked very carefully,
I saw some flying cars.
The aliens were gold, silver and black.
I missed my mum, I said 'Take me back.'

Maddi Chismon (9)
Hill View Junior School

COSMIC

In the dark, deep galaxy,
Spacemen on the moon
Jupiter, Venus, Saturn, Mars
What's it like up there?

In the dark, deep galaxy
I'll never want for home
Way out in the universe
Green aliens passing by.

In the dark, deep galaxy
In my rocket all alone
Travelling round the universe
Discovering all the planets.

In the dark, deep galaxy
Crashed on the moon
Help us somebody
I don't know what to do
I think I'm travelling home now
My cosmic adventure just had to end.

Ashley Moody (10)
Hill View Junior School

COSMIC

As I think of the universe
I think of the Roman gods.

Uranus is a planet of gas
It orbits on its side
It is my favourite colour green
Although it's full of ice.

Next there is the red one, Mars
It's nearest to Earth
The days are not much longer
But the years are off this earth.

Mercury the messenger
Obscured by cloud
Boiling hot in the daytime
Freezing cold at night.

Now the home planet, planet Earth
Perfect for the human race.

Stephen Mitchell (9)
Hill View Junior School

SPACE

Rockets zooming out to space
Making lights all over the place
Mars and Jupiter so clear to see
My family can sit and watch with me.

My mother said 'Look at the view'
But Dad said 'It looks like a zoo'
My sister said 'I'm going to get a closer look'
And my brother said, 'I need to read a book.'

Shooting star zooming round moon and Mars
Making other planets shiver
Rockets zooming out to space
Making lights all over the place.

Stephen Porter (10)
Hill View Junior School

COSMIC

Cosmic
Way out in space
Cosmic
A fantastic place

Cosmic
The dreams we use
Cosmic
Search for clues

Cosmic
Life on Mars
Cosmic
Where we see the stars

Cosmic
We look to the sky
Cosmic
And wonder why

Cosmic
Way out in space
Cosmic
A fantastic place.

Lindsay Dagg (10)
Hill View Junior School

A JOURNEY TO MARS!

I was lying in bed at midnight,
I looked out and got such a fright,
There was something bright,
I just thought I might jump
into the light.

I heard a scream,
Then I saw something that looked like
ice-cream,
It was like a red beam.

I was just about to scream,
When I fell in a room,
And the spaceship started to zoom.

I landed on Mars,
When I saw lots of flying cars,
There were also lots of chocolate bars,
That's why I stayed on *Mars!*

Helia Kasiri (10)
Hill View Junior School

THE LAND OF EARTHLINGS

I come from Mars
I come from space
I wish I wish I was in place
Earth and Mars, earthlings' cars
I wish I wish I was in their place
Earthlings' cars all gold and silver
So bright, what a sight!

Anthony Tennant (10)
Hill View Junior School

COSMIC

Is it dark?
Is it light?
Do the stars only come
out at night?

What is the sun?
What are the stars?
What is Jupiter?
What is Mars?

Is it hot?
Is it cold?
It is hard so I've been told.

What is the sun?
What are the stars?
What is Jupiter?
What is Mars?

Ashley Laws (9)
Hill View Junior School

COSMIC

The universe is spinning.
Round and round and round.
The universe has no shape.
It has a little sound.
Though it has a lot of creatures.
It is very peaceful.
For not many aliens are out in space.

Kirsty Bramley (10)
Hill View Junior School

COSMIC

Mercury, shining bright and sparkling,
Leader of the lot.
Venus, second to the front,
Jealous of the first,
Twirling, twirling lost in a black land
Earth, the most alive of all the eight,
And of course it's green.
Mars, it's not a chocolate bar,
But a planet like all the rest.
Twirling, twirling lost in a black land.
Saturn, with a ring around it,
Like a model globe.
Jupiter, you can spot it easily,
Although it's high above.
Twirling, twirling lost in a black land.
Neptune, like a bouncing ball,
That never touches the ground.
Pluto, the baby of them all,
Has little contact with the rest.
Twirling, twirling, lost in a black land,
They are all packed up into a big black sack,
And they act as a roof for heaven.
Cosmic.

Rebecca Miller (10)
Hill View Junior School

ONE DAY I WAS ON A PLANET!

One day I was on a planet!
No I think it was a star!
A space rocket landed
I think it was from Mars!

A funny green man with only four fingers
stepped out of the rocket!
And said he'd come to greet us.

Samantha Dawson (9)
Hill View Junior School

MY NIGHT FRIGHT

I was in bed, it was late at night,
I looked out of my window and saw my kite.
I was appalled at this awful sight,
I looked who was holding it,
It was something bright.

I ran across the kitchen floor,
And opened the utility door,
Suddenly I heard a splutter,
Then I heard an alien mutter.

I saw something gazing at me,
I couldn't believe what I had seen,
I stared and stared at this awful thing,
Then I heard a big loud ping.

No sooner than a second I was in Mars,
Looking at all of the planets and stars,
And on my way home, I saw a flying comb!
Then I saw the Milky Way,
But, I didn't want to stay.

I was one hundred feet off the ground,
Then I heard a thundering sound,
I let out a very loud scream!
Then I woke I'd just had a dream.

Gemma Haynes (10)
Hill View Junior School

THE LAND OF ALIEN TEACHERS

A spaceship appeared so I interfered
It was big and bright and what a sight.
There were two little creatures that looked
like teachers and acted like them.
They took me away and we had a little play
And after that, we flew straight back!

Dominic Hogg (10)
Hill View Junior School

COSMIC

There is a place,
Way out in space,
Where I would like to be,
The stars would twinkle as
well as winkle,
And shine where I would be,
And I would think about my family.

Rachel Hall (9)
Hill View Junior School

COSMIC POEM

The stars are sparkling
The moon is like a banana.
Where are the UFOs?
Who knows
Where they are!
Who cares!

Phillippa Sellars (10)
Hill View Junior School

THE BLOB

He's got really big eyes he lives on the planet Mongo.
He is very sweet but doesn't eat.

He is very fat and wears a hat.
His eyes are black and his teeth are green
His tongue is green.
He stinks!
He is very small, looks like a ball,
He has lumps on his face
And runs at a pace.
He's got a space machine.
He's plotting a scheme to get in his
machine and fly.

David Edgeworth (10)
Hill View Junior School

COSMIC

Space is the place,
Outer space, outer space,
Where aliens live,
Outer space, outer space,
Satellites circle round and round,
Outer space, outer space,
Stars like lights twinkle in the sky,
Outer space, outer space
Sun brightens up our world,
Outer space, outer space.

Laura Rutter (10)
Hill View Junior School

COSMIC

The dark sky,
People fly
They pass by,
The stars in the sky
The dark planets,
The Martians make a racket
The twinkling stars,
Come out again.
To rise another day.

Martin Metcalfe (10)
Hill View Junior School

COSMIC

In a big, black hole,
The moon and stars gather round Mars,
People float around,
People wear big suits,
And gigantic boots,
They whiz around in buggies all day,
Astronauts put flags on the moon,
Aliens in spaceships,
People in rockets,
All floating around in pitch black,
And that's why it's called
Crazy Cosmic.

James Dent (10)
Hill View Junior School

COSMIC

Riding through the unusual universe, universe, universe
Riding through the universe and jumping on the moon.
Riding through the unusual universe, universe, universe.
Riding through the universe and floating away in space.
Riding through the untidy universe, universe, universe,
Riding through the universe and sweating on the sun
Going away from the unbelievable universe, universe, universe,
Going away from the universe and sliding into an egg.

Alex Keith (10)
Hill View Junior School

WHEN I WOKE UP ONE NIGHT

One night I woke up,
I saw the planets around,
What a fright!
I woke up one night!
Everybody, everywhere, planets floating in the air.
When I woke up one night,
I started dancing around the room,
My father was a spoon,
My mother was a cat.
My friend's brother was my mother,
Then that was the end of that.

Samantha Nicholson (10)
Hill View Junior School

COSMIC

My brother is an astronaut,
My dad he stares at the galaxy,
My mum's in the laboratory.
My sister designs the rockets that shoot the stars.
I asked my brother 'What's out there?'
He said, 'The moon and stars.'
I asked my dad what he can see, he said
'Venus and Mars.'
I asked my mam 'What's in the lab'
She said 'Rocks from Venus, chocolate
from Mars.'
I asked my sister to help me design a rocket
to travel so far.
I'm just a simple little boy that reads the
classic books.
I play on my PC and sometimes watch TV.
But space just isn't my thing
I like cars and budgerigars,
But space really isn't my thing
It's millions of miles up in the sky.
Where the little green aliens live.
Now that's the brilliant universe.

Richard Smith (9)
Hill View Junior School

COSMIC

Upside down round and round
Bumps and shouts all about
The man in the moon pops
Down to say, 'Afternoon'
This is very crazy so I
Don't have time to be lazy
I cannot believe what I have
Just seen - a shooting star?
Nah!
Shooting stars are coming
Tonight
Watch out people it's very
Bright
Enough about stars
What about Mars?
Space is full of treats
Mars bars Milky Ways and all
Good sweets
But now, from way up high I,
Say bye bye from the sky.

Amy Jayne Cook (10)
Hylton Red House Primary School

SPACE

I think space is dark and gloomy,
But when I see Neptune it's scary and spooky.
When I go to Pluto I have a race,
But I have to stop to fasten my lace.

Next on my list is Mars,
But on the way, I stop and look at the stars.
They twinkle so bright,
In the moonlight,
And sparkle and gloom,
When I am on the moon.
Then I go to Saturn,
I buy a Chinese pattern
I take it back to my rocket
and find my keys in my pocket.

Joanne Prior (10)
Hylton Red House Primary School

THE PLANETS

First comes the sun mightiest of all,
Then comes Mercury closest of all,
Then comes Venus big and blue,
Then comes Earth and Mars too.
Then comes Jupiter biggest of all
Shining like a yellow ball,
Next comes Saturn with its ice rings round,
Then comes Uranus swirling around and around.
Then comes Neptune cold and blue,
Then comes Pluto and its moons too.

Sean Wilson (9)
Hylton Red House Primary School

UP IN SPACE

Up in space so far away,
Little green aliens come to play.

Look up there it's the Milky Way,
Let's go up there right away.

It's very blue but mostly white,
And it's a very silvery sight.

But right now it's time to see the moon,
But as for you I'll see you soon.

Tiffany Powell (10)
Hylton Red House Primary School

COSMIC

Cosmic's coming from night till day,
He's coming round and saw the Milky Way.
Shooting stars are light and bright,
In the space's moonlight.
Space has got lots of treats,
Especially with a lot of sweets.
Space is so faraway,
Even aliens still come to play.
Enough about the shooting stars,
How about the planet Mars.
Come on let's play on Mars,
We'll maybe get some Mars bars.
But now from way up high,
I'll have to say bye-bye.

Kristina Hodgson (10)
Hylton Red House Primary School

SEASONS

Jack Frost comes out at night
And leaves ice what a nice sight
Children play in the snow
With their faces aglow
Snowball fights
Children's delight
Spring comes, lambs are born,
Daffodils are blooming
Trees are budding
Summer will soon be coming
Summer's here
Sun is shining with glee
As we run into the sea
Waves are rushing towards us
That's summer
Last comes autumn
Leaves fall to the ground off trees
Leaves scattered on the ground
They're my seasons.

Sara Blacklock (9)
Ivy Road Primary School

THE MYSTERY CAT

Gus is a mystery cat, he's called the Secret Paw,
He's a crafty criminal cat who always breaks the law.
He can't be found say Scotland Yard with all hope and despair
For every time the police arrive,
The Secret Paw isn't there.

Gus is a sneaky animal, sneakier than a snake,
The investigators are losing hope, they just want a break.
Gus is the king of criminals no one can deny,
Strikes at 6pm carries on till morning is nigh.

Breaks through banks, breaks through shops,
Gus is just unstoppable,
No one on this earth can stop him,
It's just impossible.

Lukas Cowey (10)
Ivy Road Primary School

THE APPENDIX

There's a funny little thing that sits inside of you,
Quite what it looks like I'm not really sure.
Is it large or is it small?
I sometimes wonder if it is there at all.

It grumbles and rumbles when I'm in bed
And then I know it's really there.

I know a man who had a cheeky one,
After a meal it began to play.
It jumped about, it kicked a ball,
It made the poor man have a fall.

Then one day it really hurt, it was like a motorbike revving its engine.
It was doing skids and wheelies and dangerous things,
The man yelled out 'Oh help me oh do.'

The hospital men came in a rush,
They took out the appendix without any fuss.
Now the man has no more pain,
His grumbling appendix has gone down the drain.

Karim Chenouf (9)
Ivy Road Primary School

SUMMER

The summer sun is blazing hot
    cold it is not
You can go to the beach with a bucket
    and spade
But the sun gets hot so stay in the shade.

Bees buzz merrily in the flowers and
    trees
Leaves sway softly in the breeze.

Sam Hine (10)
Ivy Road Primary School

FOOTBALL FOREVER

Football forever
Football is a game.
They wear black and white,
But what is their name?
They've always been the same,
Forever they score goals,
But what is their name?
I've known them forever,
Football forever is their game.
They are black and white,
But what is their name?
So if it's football forever
And football is their game,
And black and white are the colours,
Newcastle must be their name.

Richard Sainsbury (10)
Ivy Road Primary School

STORMS

Like a wild thing through the night
Shining light and bright,
The big ships are tossing and burning
With the big tempest.
Many people are frightened and cold
But the wind goes on
Strong and bold
Now it's beginning to go down
All the houses mashed and crushed
People are hurt and bruised
But many live on for another time
Many dead under bricks and wood
The ships are sunk
Animals are hurt
Planes are lost in the hills.

Ben Bradley (10)
Ivy Road Primary School

WHAT IS BLUE?

Blue is the sky
The lakes nearby
Blue is the sea
It's the colour for me
Blue is for boys
Or so they say
It's my favourite colour
And it's here to stay.

Lisa Dibden (10)
Ivy Road Primary School

HANDS

Hands, hands in bands,
    hands in sands,
Hairy hands, beary hands, scary hands,
    hands are pink
        and stink.
Hands, long, short, pointy, sweaty,
    hands.
Hands, scruffy, mucky in the
    muck.
Magical hands doing tricks
    and picking up
        very heavy bricks.
We need them, we love them
    hands.

Rachel Nicholson (10)
Ivy Road Primary School

AUTUMN

Nuts are ripening
Birds flock around holly bushes
Berries red above my head.

Autumn leaves go red and brown
As they tumble to the ground
Dogs and children laughing, run
Through the crunchy carpet, having fun.

The harvest is in
The nights grow cold
Stories of witches and ghouls are told
As Hallowe'en pumpkins are lit at the window.

Matthew T Riall (10)
Ivy Road Primary School

ORANGE

Orange is the sun,
Playing with an orange ball is fun,
Running in the sunlight,
In the orange sun flying a kite.

Orange juice,
Let loose.

Oranges are orange,
Orange leaves in autumn,
Red and yellow too.

Golden orange sunlight
In the navy blue sky,
And clouds are floating by,
Then at night the sun
Will say goodbye.

Sarah Eastland (10)
Ivy Road Primary School

WHAT IS BLUE?

My eyes are blue,
And the sky is too.
So is my fish tank water,
Well, only a quarter.
The books are blue,
And the sea is too.
Parrots' feathers are blue,
And don't forget the elephants too!

Daniel Scott (10)
Ivy Road Primary School

RED

Red is a leaf that falls from the trees,
Red is my jumper,
Red is my nose,
Red is the sun,
Red is a carpet,
As red as the sun.

Charlotte Longstaff (11)
Ivy Road Primary School

BIRTHDAYS

Birthdays are fun
If you haven't got a gun
Birthdays are great
If you're not late
Do you like birthdays,
The parties and the presents?

Nicola Walker (9)
Ivy Road Primary School

EGYPT

Egypt is a land of sand
Where pyramids stand so tall
Kings and queens from long ago
Entombed within their walls.

Egypt is a land of sand
Where there's nowhere to catch a Metro
A camel is the thing to ride
To get where you want to go.

David Daglish (11)
Ivy Road Primary School

HANDS

Hands, hands can pick
Hands can click
Hands can twist and twist
Hands can dip
Hands can grip
Hands can hit, hit and hit.

Christopher Duggan (10)
Ivy Road Primary School

AUTUMN

Autumn is a windy season
Leaves fall off trees
And conkers ripen
Birds fly south
Blackberries grow
Windy October.

Danny Clark (11)
Ivy Road Primary School

AUTUMN

All the leaves fall off the trees,
To make a great big pile.
It makes the leaves soggy and wet,
The leaves are all sorts of colours,
Like red, gold, yellow and orange.
All are beautiful bright colours.
Bright colours, dark colours,
In the autumn it's really cold,
Most people wrap up with very warm clothes,
Sometimes it's freezing,
The paths are frosty and slippy and the sky is foggy.

Your ears go cold and all red,
And your nose glows like Rudolph's.

Autumn is a great season
To have fun with all the different coloured leaves.
When they're dry they crackle and pop,
Then you rake them up,
And put them into a compost pot,
To put on your garden.

Michael Embleton (10)
Ivy Road Primary School

KESTREL

It swoops off the fence
And hovers for a moment
Then swoops for a field mouse
In the long green grass.
It must have been successful
Because it flies away so happy.

Richard Law (10)
Ivy Road Primary School

TREASURED MEMORIES OF MY MUM

This person reminds me of a high bridge looking over
a bed of pink lily pads floating in the sea.
She is kind and loving,
She is a soft cuddly teddy.
She is a peaceful herd of cows standing eating
some green grass.
She reminds me of the letter D.
If she were an animal she would be a mermaid.
If she were an object she would be an expensive mirror.
If she was a lesson at school she would have to be geography.
She has Italian style.
If she were a day of the week she would be Friday
'going out' night.
If she were a programme on TV she would be the Clothes Show.

Adam Stephenson (8)
Monkhouse Primary School

A MUDDY LITTLE WESTIE

This person is a muddy little Westie.
She is sugar on a doughnut
This person is a stormy December
She is a box of allsorts
She reminds me of a sandy rockpool
She is an old walking stick.

Anneliese Wiseman (7)
Monkhouse Primary School

YELLOW AND GOLD

It feels like sand running
out of my hands.

It looks like corn waving
in the wind.

It tastes like cornflakes
in a bowl.

It sounds like dead grass
getting cut in summer.

Gold is my face when
I'm good.

Ross Marino (8)
New Brancepeth Primary School

CRIMSON

Crimson is like a ruby red apple
hanging on a tree.

Crimson is my face when I
get shouted at.

Crimson is jelly wobbling
off a spoon.

Crimson are my cheeks when I am
playing out in the cold.

Crimson is the colour of my jumper.

Christopher Barton (9)
New Brancepeth Primary School

BEACH BALL

B lue is the colour of the clear summer sky.
E ach and every child has a smooth cold ice-cream.
A nimals swimming in the sea and flying in the sky.
C hildren running around in their swimming costumes.
H iding in the background the shows swirl round.
B umper cars crash into each and every car
A nd you can hear the horror house creaking.
L ittle babies howl with laughter playing with a beach ball.
L ike me, I just love the beach.

Cassie Burnett (11)
New Brancepeth Primary School

ANGER

Anger is a volcano waiting to erupt inside me.
Fire waiting to burst out of my mouth and
burn anyone in sight.
A tornado swirling round in my head waiting to
burst out of my ears and suck up everyone around me.
A burning sun setting my face on fire.
A bull is charging around in my head.

Vicki Taylorson (11)
New Brancepeth Primary School

A TIGER HAIKU

The tiger is *huge*
Orange, black, fierce
Tiger in the wood
Killing instantly.

Andrew Gregory (11)
New Brancepeth Primary School

HARVEST

It's harvest time again
Time to cut the corn and collect it in.
The apples are ripe and ready to eat
It's harvest time again.

Time to celebrate
The vegetables are ready
To be dug out and eaten
Time to celebrate.

We're all enjoying ourselves
Celebrating and singing
The church bells are ringing
While we are enjoying ourselves.

Harvest's nearly over
We've all had our fun
Now it's time for winter to come.

Lauren Mickle (10)
New Brancepeth Primary School

BROWN

Brown is like mud in a hole.
It feels like a tree trunk.
Brown makes me cold.
Brown is like a raw plum.
It has brown crunchy leaves.
Brown is my face when I
come from my summer holidays.
Brown is my window frame
when I look out.

Natalie Ann Towning (8)
New Brancepeth Primary School

ANGER

When I'm angry I feel like
punching a wall down,
Anger is like a velociraptor
ripping out from inside.
It is dynamite set to blow you to bits,
When I'm angry I feel like
I'm crackling up with hate,
Anger is like a devil putting
a curse on you,
Anger is a horrible emotion
to deal with in life.

Craig Hindmarch (9)
New Brancepeth Primary School

WINTER

Winter feels like an iceberg,
Just about to fall on top of the world,
Winter looks like a white sheet,
On the bottom of my bed,
Winter tastes like an ice cube,
Melting in your mouth,
Winter is so crisp and clear,
Winter is the fun time of year,
When snowmen appear in your garden,
Winter is the clearest, coldest
        White.

Kelly Rank (10)
New Brancepeth Primary School

DREAM WORLD

I lie on the hot sandy shores
Watching the deep green waves crashing against the rocks,
The seagulls flying by pinching people's chips.
I look up into the blue and white sky.
I think this is the best feeling.
The clouds look like marshmallows.
The sun looks like a big yellow juicy lollipop,
How I wish I was a mermaid jumping in and out of the wave,
And playing with the fishes and dolphins.
Jumping over rocks.

Faye Alderson (11)
New Brancepeth Primary School

FIDGET AND FUDGE

I have two guinea-pigs, Fidget and Fudge.
When you put your hand over them
They give a little nudge.
Fudge just sits there while Fidget runs about.
When Fidget runs under the table
I can hardly get her out,
I give them a nurse at the end of the day.
Fudge sits on my lap and sleeps away.

Phillip Hughes (9)
New Brancepeth Primary School

GOLD

Gold feels like hard armour in the museum
Golf looks like a golden fish.
Gold tastes like golden cornflakes in a bowl.
Gold looks like a piggy bank full of money.

Emma Burton (10)
New Brancepeth Primary School

BALLOONS

I went to a party
It was great fun
We saw loads of balloons
and we ate lots of buns
It was Jonny Waitt's
We went to Metroland
It was very big
and it had lots of sand,
It was two hours long.
We played with balloons.
After the party
We watched cartoons.
We love playing balloons
So we played with them
I had a red one
and so did Ben.
We had to go now
I said 'Thank you,'
Thanks for the presents
See you again soon.

Greg Eckhardt (9)
Newlands School

THE BALLOONS

When it was my birthday
I had lots of balloons.
But four got popped
That happened quite soon.
We had something to eat
The balloons all over the place
Floating around like they were in space,
I nearly ate one.
When I heard a bang. *Pop!*
We all got one each,
Some let them go
And one balloon looked like Po.
Then we said goodbye to the balloons
And each other as well.
The end had come so soon.

Guy Silver (8)
Newlands School

THE BALLOON

I went to town
To buy a balloon
It was crescent-shaped
Like a long, yellow moon
It blew out of my hand
High, high into the sky
I could not reach it
No matter how I tried.
I ran and ran to try and catch it.
But soon I knew
It wouldn't survive.

Guy Halbert (8)
Newlands School

BALLOON

I went to the park
with my balloon.
I hit my balloon
with a stick.
I nearly fell on the grit
If I did my balloon
would have gone *bang!*
I took it home
And drew a face on it
a smiley face
on my balloon.
I went into the garden
and popped it with a pin.
It made a big *bang!*
So I threw it in the bin.

William Howie (8)
Newlands School

ON A BRIGHT MORNING

I see in the woods, trees touching each other
dark green, light green and yellow ones
I see birds singing to each other
Rabbits kissing each other
I see a carpet of blue from the bluebells
and a sprinkle from the daffodils
I smell garlic and mushrooms
that is if you are out early.

James Robson (11)
Newlands School

THE BALLOON

I went to the park
And bought a balloon
It sailed through the sky
Like a large orange moon
It bumped and fluttered
In front of my eyes
My mum came up
And held my balloon high
I let go of the string
My balloon soared to the sky
I started to cry
And said goodbye.

William Johnson (8)
Newlands School

WISHES

If the moon was a balloon
I'd fly it in the sky
If the moon was green cheese
I'd spread it on a cracker
If the moon was a watch
I'd never be short of time
If the moon was a football
I'd kick it over the clouds
If the moon was a banana
I'd eat it
If the moon was a boat
I'd sail it through the sky

But the moon is the moon
And it's where it is.

Matthew Johnston (8)
Newlands School

THE BAILDONS

One day I had a party
It was great fun
We had lots to eat
like ham in a bun.
I got some great presents
A pen which writes
and some lovely sweets
which were really nice.
We had some balloons,
there were four great colours,
red and blue, green, sunny yellow.
I blew them up, every one
then when the doorbell rang
I ran to the door.
It was Greg with a present
as big as the door.
As soon as we'd eaten,
we grabbed a balloon.
We kept them in our sight
until my dad gave us a fright
I jumped so high
I let go of mine
It went into the sky.

James Mitchell (8)
Newlands School

HUNGRY ELEPHANT

There once was an elephant who lived far away.
Who liked to eat an apple and an orange every day.
One day the fruit box did not have anything in.
So the elephant went hungry and became very thin.

Ben O'Brien (8)
Newlands School

WISHES

If the moon was a balloon
I'd fly it in the sky.
If the moon were green cheese
I'd throw it in the bin.
If the moon was a watch
I'd put it on my wrist.
If the moon was a face
I'd smile at it every day.
If the moon was a boat
I'd sail it through the sky.
If the moon was a dart board
I'd throw rockets at it.
But the moon is the moon
And it's better where it is.

Alasdair Upton (8)
Newlands School

WISHES

If the moon was a balloon
I'd fly it in the sky
If the moon was green cheese
I'd eat it if I please
If the moon was a watch
I would stay up at night
If the moon was a ball
I would kick it over the wall
If the moon was a grin
I'd smile back at it
But the moon is the moon
And it's better where it is.

Aidan Waters (8)
Newlands School

I AM

I am an old train
Once I roared down the track
Carrying five hundred people,
Burning up coal as I went
My shiny gold bell
Polished every day
My silver-coloured wheels
Reflecting the sun's light.
But now I am a wreck,
My bell is rusty,
My wheels torn off,
My engine broken,
Soon I will be cut up
and lie on the
top of the pit
A train no more.

Andrew Bolam (10)
Newlands School

THE SPARKLING GOLDFISH

The goldfish in the pond are like
a highlighter in a pack of black pens
like a sun shining brightly
a golden sovereign on the bottom of the pond
like a burning arrow in the water
they have eyes as round as marbles
at the end of the day they fade away to the bottom of the pond.

James Keyes (10)
Newlands School

I AM

I am
an old country house.
Once new and perfect.
Great bricks
perfect thatched roof
all beautifully decorated inside.
Everybody wanted me
Once I was loved
and used for a summer house

But now -
I'm old.
My roof is full of holes.
My bricks are cracked.
My garden is full of nettles.

Soon -
I'll be smashed into debris.
Then dumped on to the scrap heap
and used to make a bomb shelter.

Philip Davison (11)
Newlands School

SAUSAGE

I am a lonely sausage
sizzling in a pan
waiting to be eaten
by a fat and hungry man.

Through his mouth and down his throat
large intestine past
chewed by his stomach acid
chewed up really fast.

Once I was a happy pig
roaming in the muck
Led out to the slaughterhouse
we pigs don't have much luck.

Simon Brown-Adams (10)
Newlands School

IN THE HOUSE

'Get in the bath'
'But you always tell me if I jump
in the bath the water will jump out.'
'What have I said about being cheeky?'
'Not much, why?'
'You're addicted to that computer.'
'What else can I do? I've got no money.'
'Go and play football.'
'Where? Because there's no room in the
                              back garden.'
'Wash the dishes'
'The water will jump out'.
'Get the paper from the shop'
'You never let me go when I want sweets.'
'Put the tele on.'
'You tell me I'll get square eyes.'
'Fetch my slippers.'
'I'm not a dog!'

Christopher Robinson (11)
Newlands School

WHO DO YOU THINK YOU ARE?

'I thought I told you to clean your teeth.'
'Don't want to.'
'I thought I told you to wash the car about half an hour ago.'
'That's your job.'
'You are grounded so get inside.'
'Make me.'
'I thought I told you to do all these things.'
'You do it.'
'Who do you think you are, saying that?'
'I'm Hugo Clerey.'
'Turn off the tele now.'
'There's nothing else to do.'
'You can go down to the shops and get some bread.'
'That's boring.'
'Go to your room or else.'
'Or else what? You will lock me up in a dungeon
For ten years and throw away the key?'
'Now what have you got to say for yourself?'
'Sorry Mum!'

Hugo Clerey (10)
Newlands School

I AM AN OLD LADY

I am an old lady
Once I danced away at the Plaza
Hypnotising all men
Making other women jealous
Who couldn't dance like me,
Who couldn't entice other men.
Wearing my lovely flowery dresses
I was smothered in perfume
And massaged until relaxed completely
Such a lovely scent drifting off me.
But now I can't dance or hypnotise men
No perfume
My bones are always creaking
And I walk with a stick
Soon I'll be dreaming about how I could dance
And for a moment be young again.

Richard Pearson (10)
Newlands School

THE GOLDFISH

Little arrows in the pond.
They swim as fast as lightning.
Like a glinting submarine floating away,
A gold sovereign sitting at the bottom.
Like the sun on the pond.
Swimming along happily in the pond.

James Horn (11)
Newlands School

I AM

I am an old man
once a great hero
saving lives
helping people in danger.
I was very strong and fast
No one could beat me in the games
I was one of the best
I was a magnet to women
and everyone was jealous.
But now I am too old to go on
I am fat, slow, weak and stiff.
I get beaten in the games
soon I will be gone
but my name will be remembered forever more.

Simon Walker (11)
Newlands School

OUT IN SPACE

Flying in space
All the different planets
Red and green
All good colours
As I float free
I go to visit Mars
My favourite is Saturn.

Kimberley Lyon (7)
New York Primary School

OUT IN SPACE

I wish I was zooming in space
Like a meteor.
Crashing into the moon, boom
I wish I was flying through the stars.
Visiting Earth and Mars
But it is time to go.
I'm just joking - a day to go
So my favourite planet is Mars
Bye space.

Karl Sharp (7)
New York Primary School

OUT IN SPACE

Floating around in space
Lots of planets to visit
Mercury so hot
Pluto so cold
Earth just right
Saturn with rings
Venus so beautiful
Do you think Venus is beautiful?

Carly Nicholson (7)
New York Primary School

OUT IN SPACE

Flying in space
Lots to see
Me and Mars
Jupiter and sea
More planets to see
Some are red some are cream.

Mark Walker (7)
New York Primary School

OUT IN SPACE

I'm out in space floating free.
Lots to see
Zooming through the galaxy
I'd visit all the planets in the solar system
And the moon as twinkly as a gold penny
I like space don't you?
It's fun don't you think too?

Craig Evans (8)
New York Primary School

OUT IN SPACE

I'd like to be a spaceman
I'd go zooming through the galaxy
I'd visit every single planet in our solar system
I'd look for some form of life
I'd float around in my space suit
Jumping wild on Mars
I like space don't you?
It's fun, have a go at it.

Richard Thompson (8)
New York Primary School

OUT IN SPACE

Out in space
No one around
Just me around
It's just silence
I'm floating around
Stars in the sky
Twinkling with glee
The moon as well and he is as gay
I'm still floating I can't get down
I'm stuck up here - can you help?
I like planets they're such fun
I like it don't you?

Nicola Lindsay (8)
New York Primary School

OUT IN SPACE

Out in space all to see
        A big shiny moon
Some beautiful big stars
        All around me
There's a big big sky
        All full with excitement
And all you do is float around all day.

Darren McDermott (8)
New York Primary School

MY DOG WALK

I have a disobedient dog,
In many ways he's like a hog.

Once in a while he gets a walk,
He shoots out like a popping cork.

We're never home in time for tea,
'Why?' you ask me.

As soon as we get out,
He really makes me shout.

'Cause he starts to make his heart to heart,
With Mr Rogers' Crufts winner Bart!

I tap him on the nose.
He responds by stamping on my toes.

I tried to put him on the lead,
But, he ran away with mighty speed.

When I've got him tied up neat,
He pulls me up and down the street!

When we're finally on the field,
I have to use a tree as a shield.

'Cause he's charging at me like a ram,
'No, no!' I cry 'Don't do it Sam.'

He stands to pause,
So he can chew up Mrs Finkle's hose.

I finally get him home,
By bribing him with a juicy bone!

Sarah Rice (10)
North Fawdon Primary School

BROTHERS

It all started with the dreaded speech
'Tim dear you're going to have a sister'
'What, I'd rather soak in bleach,
Or have a big red blister!'

A few months later . . .
Came baby in incubator,
The scrawny thing was not well
What it was I could not tell.

A few days went by,
And Mum was home with tears in the eye
For in her arms she held as if a toy
A darling little baby boy

'What's his name?' I cried
'James' she replied.

Late that night,
I woke in a fright,
What was that I heard
It sounded like a screeching bird,

A *waaa a wooo a boo-hoo*
It sounded like a cat with flu,
That was it I couldn't take it anymore
So I went downstairs and slept on the floor.

Ten years later James and I are best of friends
So this is where the poem ends.

Julie Armstrong (10)
North Fawdon Primary School

IN THE JUNGLE

There is a jungle over the hills
You can often hear the birds' harsh shrills

There is a lion with a mane
Whatever he is, it isn't tame

There is a parrot with feathers bright
What a completely wonderful sight

There is a monkey with a long tail
He likes to drink a lot of ale

There is an elephant with a grand trunk
If he stays with the monkey he's sure to get drunk

There is a crocodile with a crooked smile
If you see him run a mile

There is a creature called a hog
He likes to play with his lucky Pog

I'm afraid I'm running out of time
So this is where I end my rhyme.

Alison Langley (11)
North Fawdon Primary School

WHEN I SAW DRACULA!

I had just put my foot on the stair,
When I looked up and saw Dracula standing there.
I ran to my mother shouting 'Ma, Ma
I've just seen Dracula.'
She looked up at me and she calmly said
'Don't be silly dear Dracula's dead'
I took her into the hall,
But would she believe me?
Not at all!
I looked everywhere
Even on the stair,
But I could see Dracula just was not there.
I remember the day I saw Dracula
I told some people but they just went 'Ha!'
But I know that it's not very funny
It gives me a sick feeling in my tummy.
Despite everything my mother said
I don't think Dracula's really dead!

Joanne Shields (10)
North Fawdon Primary School

SCAREDY CAT

John is such a scaredy cat,
he's even scared of his front doormat.
When he goes out he quivers with fright,
especially if he's alone at night.
His mum comes round every day,
but he'll run to his bedroom and there he'll stay.
His mum called up Doctor Smith,
he said it's a rare case called *'scaredycatarith'!*
Doctor Smith went round that night,
and gave John a terrible fright.
The neighbours heard a horrific scream,
and then they saw a bright green beam.
Ten hours later the doc came out,
but John did not yell or shout.
John was never scared again,
and only screams when he's in pain.

Scott Henry (10)
North Fawdon Primary School

SPRING IS HERE

The buds come out,
The lambs are born.
The daffodils spring,
Hedgehogs yawn.

Snowdrops spring out of the ground,
Blossom in the trees is all around.
The kids play out late at night,
Because it's not dark it's going to be light.

Spring is brill, spring is here,
Spring is everyone's time of the year.

Richard Brown (11)
North Fawdon Primary School

ORBIT

Really far away in distant space,
All of the planets were having a race.
Ready steady go!
Mercury was fast but Pluto was slow!
Around the sun, Mercury zoomed!
Like a million jets,
The earth assumed!
Venus' exhaust fumed!
Then it crashed!
It was doomed!
Then we were entering the asteroid belt,
All the hard rocks were really felt,
Saturn raced into a star!
Earth's moon stopped at the bar,
It put earth behind,
So it had to catch up,
It found some boosters
And put them to the top,
Earth was in front and ready for fame,
But the year was over,
So they had to start again!

Andy Atherton (11)
St Aloysius' RC Junior School

THE CAT AND THE HAT

I have a fat cat called Nat
Who loves to wear a hat
In the middle of the mat
When the mice come along
He takes off his hat
And squashes them flat!

Ashleigh Lockford (10)
St Aloysius' RC Junior School

THE WEATHER

I feel the sunshine
Sinead don't you
Sinead don't you?
There it is, there it is
I am hot all through
I am hot all through
And so are you.

I hear thunder
Sinead don't you
Sinead don't you?
Flash, flash, flash
I am scared.
Are you?

I feel the wind
Sinead don't you
Sinead don't you?
In my hair
And I am cold all through
Are you?

Laura Nicol (10)
St Aloysius' RC Junior School

MY SISTER JANE

My sister Jane is a pain
She messes my room up
Again and again
But I get the blame
So don't have a sister
Called Jane!

Shelley McCaffery (10)
St Aloysius' RC Junior School

MY HOUSE

I live in a house
That is 20ft tall
It has a big bathroom
It has a big hall

I have a big house
I think it's so nice
But the only problem is
That there are mice

I tried to chase them out
But they would not go
I asked if I could keep them
But my mother said *no!*

Lyndsey Lackford (10)
St Aloysius' RC Junior School

DREAMS

Dreams are the things that help me
Through the night,
They last until morning light.
Dreams can make you happy,
Dreams can make you sad
Dreams can make you feel good
And they can make you feel bad.
Some dreams are scary
Some dreams are nice,
Some dreams are carefree
Some dreams you think about twice.
You can have dreams in the night
Dreams in the day,
You can have dreams anywhere any day.

Faye McClurry (9)
St Aloysius' RC Junior School

FOOTBALL CAPERS

Maradona, West and Pele didn't stall
But who is the greatest of them all?
I would say Pele, others would say
West, others would say Maradona
is the best!

New players have come from nowhere
you see.
Shearer and Giggsy are top class to
me.
There's goalkeepers like Seaman, Schmeichel
and Bettee,
Oh I've forgot the Brazilian Betti.
On the pitch there's no mute, Ronaldo has come on he
is so bute.
Milan, Juventus and Inter
Arc all Italia teams
I'm telling you football is in all of my dreams.

David Waldock (11)
St Aloysius' RC Junior School

SISTERS

Sisters make you laugh
but sometimes make you cry.
All my sister wants to do
is buy, buy, buy.
My sister buys sweets
all day long.
Then she eats, eats, until
they're gone.

Amanda Doyle (9)
St Aloysius' RC Junior School

WHAT A DAY!

One day I woke up small I found a shoe upon
the wall.
A bunch of bananas were on the apple tree
oh boy this really frightened me.

Then I walked along the street I saw a man with no
head or feet.
That was really really scary, I saw a baby big and hairy.
I found a boot
with a wing and bunch of worms started to sing.
On the way back to the
house a black cat got chased by a mouse.

When I got back I changed back to a size that was a big
surprise
what a day!

Liam McCauley (10)
St Aloysius' RC Junior School

THE COMPETITION

I took my time to write this rhyme
to win a bottle of wine if I win it'll be
my mum's not mine.

Words words flow out of my head
even when I'm still in bed.
Rattle rattle they won't go away,
rattle rattle they're there to stay.
If I win I might get pay.

Martin Laffey (10)
St Aloysius' RC Junior School

THE BIG LESSON

I was shooting into space,
In my supersonic rocket,
I had a button to fire the thrusters,
In my outer jacket packet,
I went to the red planet Mars,
Then I had to dodge some shooting stars,
When it was safe I had to check,
My cosmic walking suitcase,
After,
I visited the moon
There I found an alien 'racoon'
I took the racoon,
And fed it with a spoon,
It did not like that,
But watch it,
Splat!
I've just been hit with some baked beans,
So for a punishment I fed it greens,
It bit off my hand,
So that told me, a lesson,
Not to be messin'
With an alien racoon.

Jonathan James-Gunn (11)
St Aloysius' RC Junior School

MY LIFE

I had a little hamburger
I had a plate of chips
And some chicken dips.

I went to McDonald's
I went to Burger King
And heard the burgers sing.

I went to the baths
I went to the fair
But somebody thumped me
And I gasped for air.

I went on a stall
I went on the roller-coaster
And I won a toaster.

Amy McCaffery (10)
St Aloysius' RC Junior School

MY MAM

She ties me up right to the neck,
honestly I look like a real wreck,
I have buckled up shoes
The girls take the mick,
They always have a good little pick,
I wear orange blue dungarees
They are wearing mini skirts and shoes up to their knees,
They say I'm not in the fashion
And give me a bashing
They give me a stare like an angry bear,
My mam makes me pull my socks up to the knees in case I get
cold,
She'll still think I'm her baby when I'm old,
My skirts are past my knees and no shorter it goes
everyone knows,
She gives me a kiss and a hug to say bye
I walk in the school beginning to cry,
I wish I could die and start a new life,
I don't know how my dad can cope with having her as his wife,
But deep down inside I love her a lot,
After all she's the only mam I've got.

Charlotte Jones (10)
St Aloysius' RC Junior School

SCHOOL

When I went to school today,
All we did was sing and pray.
Get out your grammar,
Sometimes I could hit her with a hammer.
In the hall we sit and eat,
Thinking what a lovely treat.
Then what do I see on the peas,
It's a whole load of fleas.
Then back to class we all go,
Get out your maths!
I can't cope with it anymore,
Sometimes I could walk out of the door.
Ring! Ring! Ring!
The bell has rung
Alleluia we all sung
Well that's life,
You have to cope with it!

Ashleigh Draper (10)
St Aloysius' RC Junior School

CATHERINE PARR

His sixth and last wife
Catherine Parr
Was a star.
She was the one that
Outlived him by far.
He died of old age
He was not a sage
And that was the end
Of Henry the Eighth.

Luke Shepherd (9)
St Aloysius' RC Junior School

HOMELESS

As I walk among the dusty streets
People come and go
They don't care what happens
No one wants to know

I sleep in shop doorways
In the grime and dust
I beg for my food
I hate it but I must

No charities come to help me
The government doesn't care
People just ignore me
Others stand and stare

I fend for myself
Because I have no friends
No one shares
No one lends

Anonymous at the soup kitchen
No one knows my name
Inconspicuous in the line
Every day's the same

When the winter winds are freezing
There aren't enough warm clothes
'Move along here!' the officer shouts
Where to does he suppose?

There is no one that will listen
What else can I say?
Through the streets I'll wander
Then I'll just drift away.

Christopher Smith (11)
St Aloysius' RC Junior School

SHOPPING

One Saturday I went shopping with my mum
and she gabbled 'Go round the shop and get all these:
Pickles
Onions
Bananas and
A cabbage
Chips
Fish and
A bottle of pop.'
So I went round the shop as fast as I could.
Then I took them to the trolley
Where I found my mum looking at a fresh pig's bum
Then we took them to the checkout
And the lady scanned them through.
The price came to £20.73
As we paid for them I said 'Can we go home now?'
My mum replied 'Yes darling we will go home now.'

Ian Crookston (11)
St Aloysius' RC Junior School

I ONCE SAW THE MILKMAN

I once saw the milkman
Without his hat or coat
I once saw the milkman
Driving his daily float.

No matter if it's fog
No matter if it's rain
No matter if it's snow
He's always at my door.

Jonathan Olley (10)
St Aloysius' RC Junior School

DANCING

There is a nice thing
it is dancing
I like to dance all day
I have a dancing show in May
I could dance for hours
all around the beautiful flowers
I like it lots and lots
because I get to wear skirts with
polka dots.
My mam likes to take me
just before I have my tea
I like to dress up in fancy clothes
and I can even dance on my tiptoes.
When I get old I would like
to win a lot of gold.

Nichola Farrell (10)
St Aloysius' RC Junior School

THE BOY NEXT DOOR!

The boy next door is very easy to ignore but his mother isn't.
With her constant singing and the doorbell always ringing
is very hard to miss.

The boy next door is easy to ignore but his father isn't.
With his constant drilling and his ugly grinning is a vulgar
sight to see.

The boy next door is easy to ignore but his brother isn't.
With his music blasting and the windows cracking is a real
sound to hear.

Susan Brown (11)
St Aloysius' RC Junior School

THE RAINY DAY

The rain pours down
on everybody
but I don't know why it does.

It splashes on cars and trains

The rain pours down
on everybody
but I don't know why it does.

Everybody gets wet in this horrible rain
on this rainy day.

The rain pours down
on everybody
but I don't know why it does.

When the rain goes away
everybody is happy.

Laura Tatum (9)
St Aloysius' RC Junior School

WHAT?

What is the matter with kangaroo?
It looks like she has lost her shoes!
She's looked over here she's looked over there,
She's even looked on the stairs!

What's the matter with Freddie the frog?
It looks like he has fell off a log!
He's broken his ankle and broken his wrist
And boy! He's driven me round the twist.

Ashley Hunter (9)
St Aloysius' RC Junior School

THE ONE WHO FORGOT

Someone forgot
to make their bed!

Someone forgot
to clean the pancakes
off the kitchen wall!

It was you you *you!*

You were the one who
forgot to flush the toilet!

You were the one who
forgot to make their bed!

You were the one who forgot
to clean the kitchen!

You were the one who
forgot to clean the
bathroom!
But Mam it was not me!

Stephanie Tolson (11)
St Aloysius' RC Junior School

FRIENDS

F riends are
R eally cool
I   n the garden we play
E ach and every one of us
N eed friends
D o we like them?
S ure we do.

Kaylee Rogan (9)
St Aloysius' RC Junior School

SHE MADE ME WEAR

When I was young she made me wear . . .
A fluffy little hat so pink and flared,
A fat red coat all stitched and sewed,
Some pretty purple shoes all coloured and
bowed,

She made me wear . . .
Some stripy blue tights,
And pigtails with bobbles that look like kites,
She made me wear all those ridiculous clothes,
She probably didn't mean it I suppose.

Kelly Stewart (11)
St Aloysius' RC Junior School

WHY OH WHY?

Why do birds fly in the sky
Why do fish swim in the sea
Why do birds live in trees
Why do bears live in forests
Why do you have a brain?

Why oh why?

Why do astronauts float in space
Why do planets have an orbit
Why do things happen?

Why oh why?

Christopher Spargo (10)
St Aloysius' RC Junior School

I KNOW THIS MAN

I know this man that lives in a house
And acts like a mouse.
He eats like a pig
And smells like a rat.
He likes bees
And eats lots of fleas.
He's not very nice
And likes his dice.
He hates cats
And he's not keen on bats.
He likes going to the beach
But hates the colour peach.
He hates his mat and
Dreads his hat.
His favourite colour is blue
And he'd like to live in an igloo.

Jamie Hamilton (9)
St Aloysius' RC Junior School

DENTISTS

Everyone is afraid of the dentist
With his drill and tools
When you need a filling
You would jump through the ceiling

When you have a check-up
You don't know what to expect
You may need this or you may need that
But when you are finished
You are glad it is over.

Garret Power (10)
St Aloysius' RC Junior School

MARTIE'S PARTY

Martie's party
Eddy came seemed very rude
To Jude
Eddie's Coke so fresh and fizzy
Showered Lizzy
Eddy fired a lemon seed
At Steve
Bubble gubble double trouble
Very messy very sticky
Where's Martie, don't know
He just gave the
        Party!

Craig Connolly (10)
St Aloysius' RC Junior School

THE SWIMMING POOL!

I listen to the water
I gaze away into the pool
It's oh so quiet until people start
        Diving
        Shouting
        Screaming
        Singing
        Talking
        Crying
And then suddenly the pool is empty
I stop gazing
I come back to earth to find it was raining
And my mind was dull once more.

Kayleigh Scott (10)
St Aloysius' RC Junior School

FOOTBALL MAD

Turn the telly on
Look at them draws, no look at them wins
Shearer scores for 1-0 win at Newcastle.
Villa have a draw a draw put them
Down on the door.
Southampton won at the Dell
Get them out of the cell.
Man U won look at that terrible pun
Sunderland lost, they're compost.
Well that's another bad day for football.

Jamie Matthews (11)
St Aloysius' RC Junior School

COLOURS OF THE DAY

I watch the sky change each day,
from dusk to dawn each day,
from blue to grey each night and day.
I once thought why have night when
most creatures can survive in the day?
Then I thought as I watched one day,
how the sky represents a painter's water jar
with the paint curling and swirling while
the colours change like dark to light.
My eyes are paralysed to this wonderful
sky by the colours, clouds and anything
that flies by and cries,
for attention.

James Clarke (11)
St Aloysius' RC Junior School

SHOPPING

I do think it's funny
the way she spends money
although she's my mummy
she can't stop spending money

from cake and jam
to bread and ham
in no time at all
the bill is tall
the till is ringing
and my mummy is singing
because she is happy the week's
shopping is done.

Jamie Baxter (10)
St Aloysius' RC Junior School

THE BIRTHDAY PARTY

There was cake on the wall,
There was custard on the floor,
There was paper on the chair,
There was egg in my hair,
The TV was washed in Coke,
It was letting out smoke,
There was jelly on the wall,
There was no quiet at all,
So I went home and left the mess to them.

Faye Welsh (11)
St Aloysius' RC Junior School

RAINBOW

Rainbow rainbow come with me,
Rainbow rainbow let me see.
Rainbow rainbow come with me,
Rainbow rainbow let me see.

Red is the colour of roses,
Yellow is the colour of the sun.

Rainbow rainbow come with me,
Rainbow rainbow let me see.

Pink is the colour of dresses,
Green is the colour of grass.

Rainbow rainbow come with me,
Rainbow rainbow let me see.

Orange is the colour of clementines,
Purple is the colour of violets.

Rainbow rainbow come with me,
All the rainbow rainbow let me see
And all the colours around me.

David Woods (9)
St Aloysius' RC Junior School

RAINBOW

Rainbow is blue
Rainbow is pink
Rainbow is red and purple
Rainbow is white and yellow and green
This is my rainbow shining on you.
This is a rainbow nice and bright.

Samantha Jennings (8)
St Aloysius' RC Junior School

BREEZE

I feel the breeze from the air
It softly blows through my hair.
I feel the wind like the breeze
Blowing hard on my cheeks, they go
Red upon my face.
I wonder how or why or who makes
The wind.
How it goes through me like a ghost.
Wind, wind why are you so cold
Who makes you?

Jay Bent (8)
St Aloysius' RC Junior School

MY NAUGHTY LITTLE PARENTS

My naughty little parents
Glasses, papers, chocolate,
They leave everything everywhere.
They say to me 'Don't buy chocolate!'
And they do!
'Don't leave papers!'
And they do!
They say 'Don't leave glasses.'
But they do!
My naughty little parents.

Katie McDermott (9)
St Aloysius' RC Junior School

TOYS

Toys, toys, toys,
Toy aeroplanes, toy boats, toy people
Everywhere you look there are toys.
Toys, toys, toys you go in a shop
There are toys. Don't you get sick
Of toys that make a noise?
Toys, toys, toys you look at a toy
You think 'Oh what a great toy'
Because it's new
And then what?
It breaks all over you!
Toys, toys, toys your littler brothers
Play with your toys
They break them
Oh boy!
They make a noise
Toys, toys, toys.

William Straker (8)
St Aloysius' RC Junior School

ABOUT MY MAM

Your eyes are like roses
Your heart is as light as a cloud
Your hand is as straight as a star
And your hair is like the sun.
I dream about you all day,
You are so smooth like thin ice,
You are so beautiful like the morning sun.

Andrew Clissold (9)
St Aloysius' RC Junior School

SNOW

Sledging and snowballs
Angel prints in the snow
Snow is good fun.

Making a snowman
Dressing him up
Snow is good fun.

Skids and skiing
Snow is good fun.

Amy Louise Longstaff (9)
St Aloysius' RC Junior School

SNOWFLAKES

Snowflakes sparkle like glitter and gold
Snowflakes come when it is winter
I love building snowmen with snow
Sometimes I build little ones
With my sister on the wall
I love snowflakes very much.

Hayleigh Spry (9)
St Aloysius' RC Junior School

THE GHOST

I went into my room last night,
And I saw a scary ghost,
It told me what its name was,
It was Beans on Toast.

It told me not to be scared,
It said it wasn't bad,
But when I saw its face,
I shouted for my dad.

I went a little nearer,
He came closer too,
I moved my hand towards him,
But it went straight through.

My dad came a-running,
He got to the top stair,
But when he reached my bedroom,
I'd woken from my nightmare.

Paul Burn (10)
St Anne's RC Primary School

MORNING

Don't want to get up,
  Outside it is cold,
    I'm as snug as a bug in my bed.

Too lazy to rise,
  But can't sleep no more,
    The birds' twittering enters my
    Head.

Crawl out of bed,
  Scratch my head,
    Yawn and stretch as I walk across
    The floor.

Put the kettle on,
  Shovel breakfast down,
    Splash of soap and water then out
    The door.

Christopher Bagnall (9)
St Anne's RC Primary School

THE OLD HOUSE

I think the old house is haunted,
It just stands there on the hill,
It's dark and gloomy on the brightest day,
Just seeing it gives me a chill.

I went up there last Hallowe'en,
It was a moonless night,
I heard a really spooky laugh,
That made me jump with fright.

The house is over 100 years old,
And very big it is too,
Once I crept into the bathroom,
And a monster jumped out of the loo!

There's a witch lives in the kitchen,
She's always casting spells,
When people visit the old house,
Her cauldron makes nasty smells.

I'm really scared of the old house,
I'm sure you would be too,
Because whenever you're in it,
A ghost is chasing you!

Joanne Smith (10)
St Anne's RC Primary School

THE OLD CAT

There's an old black cat comes down
our street,
I see it most every day.
He's lost an eye and half an ear,
He's a hundred, so they say.

Mum says she saw it when she was a
girl,
I think it's a witch's cat.
I've never seen its owner,
To be honest, I'm glad about that!

Kayleigh Scott (10)
St Anne's RC Primary School

IN THE FASHION!

The Great Wizard Ho-Ho
Always used to fly
On his magic carpet
Way up in the sky.

'But now that is old-fashioned,'
Said the great Ho-Ho.
'These magical carpets
Are really too slow!'

And so he quickly ordered
His three servants to bring
A little blue saucer,
What a peculiar thing!

But see the Wizard Ho-Ho,
A clever man is he,
He made the little saucer
As large as can be.

So swiftly through the heavens
His saucer now will go.
Neither UFO nor Superman
But the Great Wizard Ho-Ho.

Alexander Hamilton (8)
St Anne's RC Primary School

HOLLY

Piercing yellow eyes stare
Through tufty black fur.
Ever alert for mice and birds,
She purrs loudly for hours on end.
Scratching all the furniture
Stretched on the sofa,
Pleading eyes crying for food.
Moving silently like a shadow,
But leaving a trail of hair everywhere.
Creeping into my bed
She cuddles up for warmth.
A furry hot water bottle,
That is my cat Holly!

Hanna Fenton (9)
St Anne's RC Primary School

THE RACE

I turn the key,
The engine roars,
I put my seat belt on.

The race begins,
I set off fast,
Position number one.

I reach the corner,
Far too quick,
I speed right off the track.

My wheel falls off,
I'm in a mood,
As the tow truck takes me back.

Adam Parker (8)
St Anne's RC Primary School

THE TORNADO

The tornado passes furiously
       through the street,
Demolishing everything in its path.
Roaring winds mask babies'
       screams,
The once blue sky now black as
       tar,
Houses tremble,
Floorboards creak,
The trees moan angrily.
Objects fly through the air,
Like the birds that fled before.
Cars deserted
As people scurry to their houses,
When this visitor came to town.
No one would answer their door.

Stephen Carr (10)
St Anne's RC Primary School

THE GHOSTS

When I go to bed at night,
My mum says, 'Turn off the light.'
That is when the ghosts come out,
And begin to fly about.
Straight away I start to scream,
Because of the way their eyes gleam.

      'Coko Coko, what was that?'
      'I don't know but it's not a bat.'

Yes it was just a dream.
. . . . . Or was it really just a dream?

Rose Brear (8)
St Anne's RC Primary School

THE STORM

I feel my heart pounding,
The wind roars like a thousand
Werewolves howling,
Umbrellas whizzing as they flee the
Loosened grips
Of icicle fingers.

Thunder beats time
Like a heavenly drummer,
Bright silver moonbeams peak
Through rushing clouds.

Cats running wild
As electricity cables fall,
The most horrid day of my life.

Thumping head,
Terrified,
Horrified infants yelling,
What a *nightmare!*

Victoria Spalding (8)
St Anne's RC Primary School

MY FAMILY

My mam's on a diet,
My dad's on the booze,
My gran's out playing bingo,
She was born to lose.

My brother's out with his friends,
Drinking a bottle of wine,
But me, I'm just sitting here,
Writing you this rhyme.

My mam's now lost half a stone,
My dad's come in mortal,
Gran, at last has hit it rich,
With money from the Bigball.

My brother's stayed out all night,
If my mam finds out she'll kill him,
Gran has run off to Portugal,
To spend her bingo winnings.

Michael Mollett (9)
St Anne's RC Primary School

HOMELESS

My house is a torn and ragged box,
The only shelter from wind, rain
And snow.
Terrified of the night ahead,
Yet little comfort brought by dawn.
I started with a little, but now I've got
Less,
Just a box and dog to call my own.
No clothes but those I have now,
They're warm but three sizes too
Small.
My hands numb with the cold.
I look to strangers for help.
All I want is a warm place to stay,
A pillow for my head,
And some food to see me through the
Day.

Jack Doran (9)
St Anne's RC Primary School

MY POEM ABOUT A MONKEY

I have a little monkey,
His name is Minnie Moo.
He went into the sun house,
To see what he could do.
He saw another monkey and
Jumped up to the moon,
The other monkey's name was Mr Moo.
He always liked to go to the zoo,
And play fights with you too.
He clawed a lion and the lion ate him too.
He went down the basin and into
The laces of a little shoe.
He went to Spain and had a pain
He went to France to have a dance.

Carly Blackburn (11)
St Anthony's CE Primary School

POETRY IS FUN

Poetry, poetry is such fun,
If you don't like it,
I'll smack your bum.
It's cool!
It's good!
It's better than a test,
Poetry, poetry is the best.

Caroline Briganti (10)
St Anthony's CE Primary School

FRUIT BUNS

Fruit buns are fruity,
Fruit buns are tooty,
Fruit buns are cutie.

So keep off my fruity, tooty,
Cutie, fruit buns.

It's fun to eat fruit buns,
I don't want a hot cross bun,
I don't want a salad bun,
I don't want anything except,
My fruity, tooty, cutie fruit buns.

I like hot cross buns,
I like salad buns,
What I like best are
My ooo fruity, tooty, cutie
Fruit buns
So please give me a fruit bun.

Louise Thompson (11)
St Anthony's CE Primary School

A RAINBOW

There is a rainbow in the sky,
It is so very high,
No one can reach it.
It has lots of different colours in,
There's red, yellow, green and blue,
Not to forget violet too.
Can you see a rainbow?

David Lee Hamilton (11)
St Anthony's CE Primary School

GHOSTS

Ghosts can come in twos
Ghosts can make scary boos
Ghosts can come through walls
Ghosts don't go to balls
Ghosts aren't scared
Ghosts are really dead
Ghosts aren't bored
Ghosts are sometimes frauds
Ghosts don't care
Ghosts aren't fair
Ghosts are scary
Ghosts are weary
Ghosts are bad
Ghosts are mad
Ghosts aren't fed
Ghosts don't go to bed
Ghosts are daring
Ghosts aren't caring
Ghosts are bare
Ghosts aren't there!

Mark Anderson (10)
St Anthony's CE Primary School

YUMMY SCRUMMY BISCUITS

Yummy scrummy biscuits,
Taste so good
You can have orange and chocolate,
Even have some fudge.

Yummy scrummy biscuits
Are a delight
You can dip them in your cup of tea,
Every single night.

Natalie Lockhart (10)
St Anthony's CE Primary School

MY FAMILY

My room is a mess,
I am a pest,
Oh no, my blister!
Oh no, my sister!
Why is she so sad?
She is never so bad.

Then there's my mother,
Who shouts at my brother.
He is always to blame,
He is a right little pain!

Now then there's my dad,
Who is never very sad,
Except when I'm bad,
Then he's a mad little dad.

Now then there's my dog,
Who doesn't like frogs,
That sit on logs,
So that's my dog.

Then there's my grandad,
Who goes to the bar,
He has a few drinks,
Then sleeps in his car!

Jenna Anne Allen (10)
St Anthony's CE Primary School

ALL ALONE

All alone,
Nobody to talk to
I stop and stare at the boy across the street.

His clothes,
They are just rags.
His hair is very dirty,
His home is a box.

The poor boy's name?
He hasn't got one.
When it rains,
He gets wet.
He can't go inside,
Because he has no home.
I often wonder how he feels.

If it was up to me,
He could live with me,
But it's not up to me,
My mum is in charge.
He begs for money,
I usually give him some.
One day he is gone,
All that is left is a box.
I often wonder where he is,
I hope he is somewhere warm.

Gemma Collinson (11)
St Anthony's CE Primary School

MY LIFE STORY . . .
SO FAR

When I was one,
I had a gun.
When I was two,
I lost my shoe.
When I was three,
I climbed a tree.
When I was four,
I flew through the door.
When I was five,
I went for a dive.
When I was six,
I did lots of tricks.
When I was seven,
I learnt about heaven.
When I was eight,
I sat on the gate.
When I was nine,
I went down the Tyne.
When I was eleven,
I visited heaven,
(And came back home again of course)
And that's the end of me for now.
By a boy aged eleven.

Alan Halliday (11)
St Anthony's CE Primary School

EASTER

Easter is a time for a new start,
At this time of year, love is in
everyone's heart.
The new born animals that come,
The new chicks as yellow as the
sun.
The lambs they jump around gaily,
they thank their mothers daily,
for she has made them happy
but oh she's made them chatty.
Easter eggs are being sold,
The best are Cadbury's we are
being told.
The children are excited
for Easter Sunday.
Has Easter Bunny been?
Or has he stayed away?

Rachael Wales (10)
St Cuthbert's RC Primary School

PHILLIP

Phil thinks there's a ghost in the pool,
He is the daftest in the school,
He likes to get his very own way,
He never ever likes to pay.

He never wins competitions,
Quickly! He needs an optician.
He picks on all the girls in the yard,
Phillip thinks sums are hard.

Kieran Burn (9)
St Cuthbert's RC Primary School

THE RIVER

Dribble dribble goes the rain
On the hills the river starts.
Gurgle bubble
down the hills
Goes the stream.
The other rivers come together
The river gets faster and faster
Then whoosh
Down the
Waterfall
Scratching and snatching
Lash and splash
Goes the river
Down the city
Into the sea.

Andrew Brown (8)
St Cuthbert's RC Primary School

THE SUN

The sun will shine all day so bright
The sun goes down in the dark night
He sinks behind a distant hill
Will he stay there? We hope he will.

Behind the mill behind the hill
In the distance we see him still
Here come the birds eating the bread crust
The bikes are getting covered with rust.

Emma Douglas (9)
St Cuthbert's RC Primary School

FOOTBALL CRAZY

England are my favourite team
Their strips are as flash as a
lightning beam.
Shearer up front
Beckham on the wing
All the fans shout and sing.
Ince in midfield
With Gazza too
All the fans shout
'God bless you.'
Adams rises in the air
All the attackers look round
and stare
The England defenders are
incredibly hard
Whilst their attackers slip away
from defenders like lard
When I watch their home games
I try to recognise all the players
and chant their names.

Paul Bunyan (10)
St Cuthbert's RC Primary School

THE SUN

The sun will shine all day so bright
The sun has gone to take a flight.
He sinks behind a distant hill
The sun goes down with a big crown.

The sun is round and light
It is the sun that gleams so bright.
The sun grins at me it is so bright
He is bright he gleams at me in the night.

Faye Robertson (8)
St Cuthbert's RC Primary School

CAPTURED

I want to capture the sound of dogs barking
I want to capture the feel of my mam
hugging me because then I know that my mam
is with me.
I want to capture the smell of the Christmas
dinner because you only get it once a year.
I want to capture the sight of flowers
and butterflies because the colours look beautiful
and bright.
I want to capture the taste of my mam's lovely
dinner because it tastes gorgeous.
I want to capture the moment when I
made two friends on holiday called Jade and
Natasha.
I want to capture the memory of when
I first came to this school.
I want to capture the silence when I am
on my own because I think of my
friends.
I want to capture the feeling of when I
think of my friends and what happened.

Naomi Lilley (8)
St Cuthbert's RC Primary School

CAPTURE

I want to capture the sound of the music
that my mam has on her CD player.
I want to capture the feel of my mam
kissing me goodnight.
I want to capture the smell of my mam's
perfume as it reminds me of my mam.
I want to capture the sight of my dad's
car to remind me of my dad.
I want to capture the taste of my mam's
dinners that she makes me every day.
I want to capture the moment when I
look at a photo and think of my nana.
I want to capture the memory of when
it was my first day at school.
I want to capture the silence of the
dark dark night.
I want to capture the feeling of
my friends touching me.

Janine Matfin (8)
St Cuthbert's RC Primary School

ON YOUR BIKE

On your bike,
little Miss Messy,
girls,
stop fighting,
be quiet Megson,
I am home now,
your bedroom's like a bomb shell,
but you're lovely still.

Christine Amy Murray (10)
St John The Baptist RC Primary School

DISCO DANCING

Dramatic movements fill the room
Screaming, shouting, banging
Drums banging boom! Boom! Boom!
Arms and legs moving around
People stamping up and down
Dance
Tired legs, hurting toes
Pop on sale, bleeding nose
Stretch them legs, move them arms
Lights flashing, bright colours
Tap tap tap tap!
People dancing to the rap.
Then it's all quiet
Crisp wrappers on the floor
Won't come here anymore!

Hayley Brown (10)
St John The Baptist RC Primary School

TORTOISE

T ortoise crawls slowly,
O ver the ground,
R ocking back and forwards on its
T ough shell,
O r sleeping nice and warm,
I t's all different shades of colours,
S leeping all day,
E xcept for lunch.

Carlo Franchi (10)
St John The Baptist RC Primary School

CRICKET

The teams are ready to come out,
All you hear is laughter,
Booms of shouts and cries of joy,
The match is ready to start.
Whiz, spin,
The ball goes in,
The batsman hits it hard,
The ball is away, the crowds stand up,
Oh! The fielder drops the ball.
What a shame!
The next ball is bowled in,
Fielders scatter around,
Looks like he's going to catch it . . .
How's that! Brilliant, super, terrific,
What a catch,
It's back to the dressing room for him!
Oh well that's the way the game goes!

Simon Wood (10)
St John The Baptist RC Primary School

MY MAM

My mam is bright pink with happiness
She is a warm spring evening
On a hot beach
She is a clear sky
She is a skirt and jumper
And a warm fire and a comfortable couch
She is a comedy programme
She is a hot cup of coffee and a digestive biscuit.

Kerrie Pankhurst (11)
St John The Baptist RC Primary School

COSMIC POEM

Cosmic, a quick race into outer space,
Planets floating, slowly rotating,
I don't know how planets stay up there
without any air,
but gravity is up there keeping things afloat,
the sun is definitely no fun,
it can burn and scorch,
like a red-hot torch.
Part of the moon is like daylight,
but the other half is dark as night,
the ring of Saturn is full of gas,
but it doesn't let anything past.
The stars don't go anywhere,
they don't go anywhere!
They just stay there,
high in the sky,
until they eventually die,
but space has no start and no finish.

Christopher Smallman (9)
St John The Baptist RC Primary School

FIREWORKS

When a firework goes off
Lots of beautiful colours explode.
Red, purple, yellow, silver and gold
all at the same time.
Catherine wheels, rockets and all kinds of fireworks
have beautiful colours
They could be white, green
all at the same time.

Michael Farrow (9)
St John The Baptist RC Primary School

DOLPHINS

The dolphins
are swaying
through the water
soft and gentle
as ever
lifting their tails
in the air
in among the fish
they swim
full of grace
they are
when danger comes
they know
the way to escape
still full of grace
their jump is like
a cycle.

Laura Stafford (8)
St John The Baptist RC Primary School

PARROTS

They talk
and they squawk
and they flap
their beautiful
wings
and they live
in a cage
and they talk
too much!

Laura Lannighan (8)
St John The Baptist RC Primary School

FALCONS

Falcons
swiftly
flow
to
the
ground
for
food,
falcons
are
streamlined
fly
so fast
they seem
to
vanish
swooping
to
their
prey
down
they
go.

John Bee (8)
St John The Baptist RC Primary School

RABBITS

Rabbits hop
high and low
in a bush
over a hill
over a road.
They don't care
they hop
everywhere.
Side to side
up and down
everywhere.

They get hunted
every night
jackals and
foxes
everywhere
sometimes hawks
maybe not.

Jonathon Horn (7)
St John The Baptist RC Primary School

SOMETHING'S OUT THERE

I'm walking home,
On a pitch-black night,
There's something down the road
That's filling me with fright.

Its illuminating brightness,
Is lighting up the street,
It's floating, motionless,
As white as a sheet.

I'm close to home,
Should I run?
It comes towards me
What *have* I done?

I enter my garden,
I open my door,
I turn around . . .
Aaagghh!

John Whale (11)
St John The Baptist RC Primary School

COSMIC

The planets are far away,
and they are there to stay,
For every night and day,
They are watching over us,
The moon is shining
from the sun's rays
because it does not have any light of its own.
Every night the moon is bright but not
always the same shape,
But when a new moon comes you
cannot see any moon,
But there will be a time when the
sun will shine upon our faces,
Then we will know that the sun will
not go and leave us.
The sun will be up there for many, many years,
and be smiling with happiness
with other planets in deep space.

Nikki Boyle (10)
St John The Baptist RC Primary School

MONKEYS

Monkeys jump
jump about
tree to
tree with
their hands
they are
cuddly
and sweet
and they
like to
hang about.

Emily McGinley (7)
St John The Baptist RC Primary School

WARS

Wars, wars
People fighting
with guns and swords
Being stabbed and shot
It is not a nice sight.
Cannon balls going
over to enemies
and blowing up.
Houses getting burnt.
Blood coming out of dead bodies
Men shouting
'Keep shooting, we can win.
Do it for your country.'

James Kiney (9)
St John The Baptist RC Primary School

AUTUMN

In the autumn the leaves are crispy
The leaves are falling down, down, down
The air is cold,
Swishing and swooshing,
Winter is coming,
The leaves are dancing and prancing,
Walking down the street the air is
Getting colder,
Colder and colder making me shiver and
Chatter,
Walking down the street.

Rebecca Spooner (8)
St John The Baptist RC Primary School

SPRING

In spring flowers grow,
They grow very tall.
Lambs are born,
As white as snow.
Bulbs have been planted there,
Growing, growing, growing.
People can see colours,
Colours, colours, everywhere.
Spring is here,
Spring is here.
Hurrah, spring is finally here!

Danielle Rowley (8)
St John The Baptist RC Primary School

RACING ROUND THE BEND

Racing, racing, racing,
round the bend the crowd's
going wild.
I need a new mind.
It comes to the end
of the day
coming up to the month
of May.
I come home to my
mam sitting down,
eat jam.
Raring to get started
off on the track,
I never have time
to look back.

Matthew Campbell (8)
St John The Baptist RC Primary School

SUMMER

Summer is light
Summer is bright
The wind has stopped
The acorns don't drop.

Spring is gone,
Summer is here.
Hot and sweaty
We all feel.

Summer is fading,
Autumn is coming.
There is the end of a
Nice hot season.

Simon Lyons (9)
St John The Baptist RC Primary School

MARCH WINDS

March is the month when you wonder,
Is it winter or summer?
March makes you blink,
March makes you stare,
When you blink March is not there,
March, March, March away,
March to Christmas day,
For today is the day we come to
March,
And spring is here time to play,
A blue day,
A blue jay,
And a good beginning.
One crow. Melting snow. Spring's winning.
It's the first mild day of March,
Each minute sweeter than the first.

The wind is hidden in the night,
He jumps on the roof you hardly
Notice him ruffling through your hair
He quietens down,
And in the end,
Notice him go,
Whistling down the road,
To find another place to blow.

David Saville (9)
St John The Baptist RC Primary School

NEVER YOU MIND

That's your lot!
I never said yes!
Dream on!
Turn your music down!
You're arrested!
Do you ever stop talking?
My little princess!
What do you want for tea?
Never you mind!
You're lovely!
What are you after?
Get in the bath!
But Mam!

Catherine Neil (11)
St John The Baptist RC Primary School

SPACE

There is space up there,
Where?
There,
Where we stare,
It is an amazing place,
Thousands of little twinkling things,
Nobody knows how many there are,
Up there,
Where we stare, stare, stare.

Michael Costelloe (9)
St John The Baptist RC Primary School

WATERLOO

Canons going off,
Cavalry galloping into battle,
Infantry marching into battle,
The French walk into battle
With their muskets over their shoulders.
With the flag and eagle high in the air.
Advance, retreat,
What should we do?
Volley, present, *fire!*
Onward we'll advance.
We have won lads,
Victory is ours!

Christopher Harland (9)
St John The Baptist RC Primary School

AUTUMN

Twisting, twirling
drifting down.
I fly up, you go down.
I'm flying, floating through the air.
I fall everywhere.
You go up I go down,
You're so high, I can't fly.
Autumn is light, sometimes dark
Leaves fly all over in the park.

Lindsay Taylor (9)
St John The Baptist RC Primary School

TEETH

I wish I had looked
after my teeth,
I should not have eaten
all those sweets.
I should have listened to
my mum.
Now my teeth are all yellow,
What should I do?
What,
oh what,
should I do?

Arron Pattison (9)
St John The Baptist RC Primary School

COSMIC

Here we are bobbing up in the air.
I can't go beyond our earth.
I don't think that is very fair.
I would like to fly off in a spaceship
and see all the stars.
I would have to hold on tight and keep my grip
I would visit the moon.
Then I would get back into my spaceship
and I'm off again with a *boom!*
But I know that won't happen so I'll just
have to sit here in gloom.

Elizabeth McGinley (10)
St John The Baptist RC Primary School

DAY AND NIGHT

The sun is shining through the day
Children coming out to play
Hopping, skipping, running, jogging
along the big clear road.
The moon is bright through the night
Sleeping, snoring in your bed
Snuggle up and sleep instead
Watch you don't bash your head.

Dominic Hornsby (9)
St John The Baptist RC Primary School

OH WHAT A FRIGHT

Ghosts and bats, *ooh, ooh*
Skeletons and rats, *ooh, ooh*
Watch where you go,
Crackle, crackle,
Creeping up the stairs,
Skeletons rattle.
All alone in the dark of night.
Oh what a fright.
Getting closer and closer.
Terrified, terrified.
Bang!

Kerry Boyd (11)
St John The Baptist RC Primary School

STARS

When I go to bed,
I look up to the stars,
Imagining there's a man waving at me
With his rocket and other people,
I make up my own aliens on paper,
Green ones, pink ones, yellow ones and more,
I wish there *were* people like that up there.

Rachael Goodacre (9)
St John The Baptist RC Primary School

RABBITS

Fluffy, furry, brown, black, white
Rabbits are all around,
Hopping here, hopping there,
Fluffy rabbits everywhere
In their burrows
Out of their burrows
Hopping all around everywhere.

Giulio Franchi (9)
St John The Baptist RC Primary School

NIGHT FRIGHT

Closing door, creaking stair,
Trying to ignore it, trying not to care.
But turning around, nothing to see,
it's just dreaded fear taking over me.

With trembling fingers I creep into bed,
Scary visions alive in my head.
Too scared to sleep, for fearful dreams,
but it's nothing, no matter how scary it seems.

I'm biting my lip, I'm shaking away,
Why is my bedroom so scary today?
I did let the cat out and locked the back door,
but I'm not going downstairs, that's for sure.

I jump out of bed, I switch on the light,
and no longer do I feel any fright.
I'm trying to think, what is this lark?
It's simple really, I'm afraid of the dark!

Helen Saville (10)
St John The Baptist RC Primary School

MY BEST FRIEND

My best friend is yellow,
She is like a cool breeze in summer,
On a warm field.
She is a warm cup of hot chocolate.
And sweet like an apple.
She's got a shoulder for me to cry on.
And is like a warm bed in winter.

Jacklyn Connelly (10)
St John The Baptist RC Primary School

CRABS

Crabs move slow
they crawl sideways.
They go clip clip clip
they hurt when they nip.
Crabs.

Anthony Johnson (7)
St John The Baptist RC Primary School

MIKE TYSON

Mike Tyson is purple
He is sharp like the frost
On a cold winter's day.
He is a boxing ring
He is like the wind
He is like a pine table
He is like *Men Behaving Badly*
He is like boiled sweets.

Michael Wilden (11)
St John The Baptist RC Primary School

I'M BEING BULLIED

There's a ring of children older than me,
I'm in the middle being teased by three,
Scared stiff as usual.
Trapped in confusion that must be me,
Kicked and punched, crying alone.
No one to go to, I'm left alone.
Bell goes, I'm lonely again,
I'm hurt and in pain.
'Help,' I called but no one came.
I'm left alone, crying in pain.

Sarah Jary (10)
St John The Baptist RC Primary School

YOU'RE GIVING ME A HEADACHE

You're giving me a headache.
Don't answer back!
Up the stairs and tidy your room!
That room is in a right state.
Do you ever listen to a word I say?
Am I talking to a wall?
Pack the cheek in.
Turn the music down!

Danielle White (10)
St John The Baptist RC Primary School

MY BEST FRIEND

My best friend is pink,
She is a blossom in summer,
She is a field of flowers,
She is a summer's day,
She is my colourful shorts,
She is my sofa,
She is *Eastenders*,
She is my fish fingers and Smiles.

Naomi Bloomer (10)
St John The Baptist RC Primary School

ANIMALS AND BIRDS

Think about a golden eagle
Soaring through the sky.
Think about a graceful antelope
Leaping through the plains.
Think about a tiger,
Silently watching its prey.
Think about a beautiful peacock
Impressing its mate.
Think about a tree frog,
Leaping through the air.
Think about a lion,
Roaring into the night.
Think about a flamingo,
Sleeping, perfectly balanced, on one leg.
Think about a crocodile,
Waiting in the river.
Think about a field mouse,
Looking for little snacks.
Think about all the animals,
And the fact that God,
Created this beautiful world.

Emily Baldwin (10)
St Lawrence's RC Primary School

NIGHT SKY

The silent, soundless, shadowy night
Awakes from a restful sleep.
The twinkling stars come zooming from Mars,
On horses of silver moonbeams.

Then those elegant stars
Jump off their horses
And land on Venus,
Without jumping too far.

'The ballroom on Venus
Is enough to please us,'
Said one of the beautiful,
Glittering diamonds of the night.

The stars began dancing,
The moonbeams were prancing,
Until the stroke of midnight struck.

Then those handsome horsemen
Rode off with their majestic beasts
Back to Mars
For a long, lazy sleep.

Eleanor Beckford (10)
St Lawrence's RC Primary School

A WINTER WHITE BLANKET

The trees are like tall, white angels,
Floating back and forwards in the storm.
So they are waving their arms,
It looks like they were calling for
The nine, nine, nine, helicopter.

The house looks like a big, white Roman wall.
The satellite dish looks like a snowdrift.
The roof looks and sounds like a horse,
Charging across the roof.

I think that the roof is going to collapse,
The windows look like they are little snowflakes,
The path looks like a white cloudy sky.
The garden is covered in snow-white frost,
Glittering on the ground.
The cars are like a giant's snowball,
Firing along the road.

William Jarvis Smith (8)
St Lawrence's RC Primary School

NIGHT-TIME BLITZ

A veil of fear drapes over me,
As I dread the moment when hope
Disappears into flames.
Smoke billows from the fire.
The flames that arise when an explosion calls them.
I start to panic when hope becomes too scarce,
Too scarce to restore,
The fear overwhelms me,
Taking over me, trying to drive away,
The calmness and courage that still remains.

Rachael Bailes (10)
St Lawrence's RC Primary School

NIGHT-TIME TERROR

The night silence is shattered by an ear-piercing wail,
Darkness is banished by the bomb's sly flames,
Smoky smells enter my confused brain.
Night-time terror.
The army takes over marching steadily along,
Ready to kill and cause massive destruction,
Night-time terror.
All evil forces join into one whole body,
Laughing, jeering, mocking me,
Fear overtakes, I'm losing control.
Night-time terror
Night-time terror!

Alice Hickman (11)
St Lawrence's RC Primary School

ANOTHER FACE OF EVIL

Another face of evil heading this way,
Reminds me of an eagle watching its prey.
Bombs dropping.
Fire like an eagle's golden tail,
Swooping down to earth,
Screeching
A high-pitched wail.
Curiosity is conquered by fear.
Smoke fills the air,
The golden eagle spreads over the town.
Life's
Not
Fair!

Gemma Robinson (10)
St Lawrence's RC Primary School

SILVER AND SILENT

Silver and silent,
The moon shines down,
At my window,
In her shimmering crown.

The moon is bumpy and lumpy,
Slow to turn,
With a heart so bright,
It is ready to burn.

It is high in the sky,
With company of stars,
And night creatures,
All high up in Mars.

Her crown has jewels,
Which were found in pools,
They were big, they were bright,
And fitted so tight,
They could not fall out
And be broken.

Rebecca Maguire (8)
St Lawrence's RC Primary School

SILVER PAINT

One cold, misty night,
Something lit up the sky.
It was the bright, beautiful moon,
In a beaming, silver shoon.
It was a full moon.
Cold as it was,
The moon was my friend.
It lit up the world,
More and more.
I stared at the moon,
And, there, to my surprise,
Appeared a face, winking at me,
Then it disappeared.
This happened again,
Perhaps it was my imagination.
Then the moon said to me
'Goodnight,'
And it painted my room silver.

Lydia Malcolm (8)
St Lawrence's RC Primary School

THE MOON

The moon is big,
It sits on a tree,
And the moon always shines
Down on me.

The moon is really high,
In the sky,
It looks like a ball,
As it floats by.

The moon looks like a sphere,
But it's always here.
When it's big and full,
The rest of the sky looks dull.
The moon is always there,
And it floats
Everywhere.

Jayde Hill (8)
St Lawrence's RC Primary School

CABOOM!

Caboom!
Glittering sparks flew up in a blaze,
Painful cries pierced through the skies,
Caboom!
As the planes soared through the indigo night,
Bright colours arose from buildings and stores,
Thumping feet marched through the streets.
Cries of a child made me sigh,
And think what the world should be.
Sirens warning, shouts and screams,
As the doodle-bugs fly overhead.
The droning and moaning *stops!*
Caboom! Caboom!

Rachel Farrier (10)
St Lawrence's RC Primary School

BOMBING

In my shelter underground
I lie in my bed thinking
What will happen next?
The bangs sound like giants' feet.
Then fire like dragons' breath.
The sign on the planes
Looks like a dart board,
A gun shoots on the blue, scores,
But just fifteen.
I lost the game.
Germany out
And we're in!

Nicola McLanders (10)
St Lawrence's RC Primary School

ONE WHITE WINTER'S DAY

A snow-white blanket covered the earth,
Trees swayed back and forward,
Trying to get the snow off their shoulders.
An icy blast hits the roof
And snow comes fluffing off.
Cars are blue with cold,
Start up! Start up! Start up!
There, it has started.

A white world,
Snow everywhere.
Up here, and down there.

Jak Milor (9)
St Lawrence's RC Primary School

MY BEST FRIEND (MY MUM)

When I'm down
And need a friend
She's always around
Ready to give me a friendly hug.
Her gentle smile, tender and mild,
Makes me glad I am who I am
And not another child.

Even though sometimes we argue
And have our little disagreements,
I'm glad I have my mum
To love and share my secrets with.

When I was little
She put me to bed
And took me to school.
Even though I'm now growing
And I don't need her as much
I've still never found a better friend than
Her, my dear mum!

Ashton Hewson (10)
St Oswald's RC JMI School

TRIP TO SPACE

When I was about 25,
I went up in space to see what's alive.
It took me about a couple of days
To get out in space in any ways.
I was going to Venus for a few hours,
It was so steamy like boiling hot showers.
As last we were there, I got out of the shuttle,
It was so hot there wasn't a puddle.
I crept around in a hurry,
It was so hot like a prawn madras curry.
I saw in the distance a funny looking guy,
When I first saw him I thought I was going to die.
I stopped for a second and thought he'll turn me into pies,
But he was too busy eating flies.
I sniffed, I looked, I said 'Uh oh.'
Instead of that I flew to Pluto.
Now that I'm back on Earth,
I bet that alien has given birth,
And I can't cope with that
Aahhh!

Scott Hunt (9)
St Oswald's RC JMI School

WINTER

There was once a man
He saw a girl
He said 'Hello little girl
It's a cold day isn't it?'
She said
'It's freezing,
It's cold,
It's snowing,
It's blowing,
It's frosty,
It's slippy,
It's slosh
I'm going home.'

Craig Kennedy (9)
St Teresa's Primary School

WINTER

Shining bright
Crisp and white
Like peaks
Of icing on a
Xmas cake.
The snow is
Such a
Delightful
Sight, it
Really is a
Christmas card
Bright.

Luke Taylor (9)
St Teresa's Primary School

IT WAS SNOWING LAST NIGHT

The car won't start,
It is too cold.
It was snowing last night.

My brothers and I are in the back,
- Freezing cold.
It was snowing last night.

The car starts with a rumble,
Off we go on the gritted surface.
It was snowing last night.

We arrive at school.
'We're late!' We shout.
We're running down the bank!
Slipping and sliding everywhere.

Why did it snow last night?

Kieran Corcoran (9)
St Teresa's Primary School

WINTER

I walked through the back door.
The icy leaves under my feet.
The frost bites against my cheeks.
Everything is white, mysterious and bright.
The crispy sound of someone walking,
The sound of the wind wisping by.
I sighed and went back inside.
The fire burning bright, how cosy at night.

Stuart Watson (10)
St Teresa's Primary School

WINTER'S WONDER

The sun has gone
From his spot in the sky
And the black clouds
Scuttle across the air
And little drops of water
Bounce off the ground
While the sky gets darker
And the ground gets wetter.
Our little minds are set
On the atmosphere.

The little black drops
Get louder and louder still
Till, silence.
We all rush to see
The sun has come back out
And now it's time to play.

Melanie O'Brien (10)
St Teresa's Primary School

WINTER

Winter is cold
Winter is bold
Winter is not very nice.

There's lots of snow
And the wind does blow
And the ground is covered in ice.

Snowball fights
Darkened nights
And noses that turn all red.

I'm cold and wet
So I'll go and get
My covers and curl up in bed.

Jonathan Keelan (9)
St Teresa's Primary School

CAN YOU IMAGINE WHAT IT'S LIKE?

Can you imagine what it's like
Living on the streets on a winter's night?
Looking around for somewhere to go.
All alone.

Can you imagine what it's like
Nesting down on the frosty ground?
Trying to sleep on the lonely street.
All alone.

Can you imagine what it's like
Scavenging for food and looking about?
Out of date scraps from someone's meal.
All alone.

I can imagine what it's like
Sitting around on a cold winter's night.
Looking about for somewhere to go.
All alone.

Jack Wilkinson (9)
St Teresa's Primary School

SPACE

5, 4, 3, 2, 1, a flash of light then I was gone.
Rocket flying to the moon,
Through the darkness, rocket zoom.
Past the stars that shine at night,
Fading in the pale moonlight.
Past the planets Jupiter and Mars,
All around us shooting stars.
We're nearly at our destination,
We'll soon be docking at the space station.
Rocket ship to earth below,
Systems here are all go.
The earth looks like a ping-pong ball,
Down there all so very small.
There's satellites and lights out there,
The sun is just a distant glare.
As we're orbiting the moon,
We know we're coming home soon.
Our journey's over, down we go,
Dropping through the clouds below.
At last we've landed safe and sound,
It's good to be back with our feet on the ground.

Christopher Troughton (8)
St Teresa's Primary School

WINTER

No leaves.
Robins hopping, searching.
Silence.

My toes crackling,
My hands freezing.
Turkey crackling.

Rich foods,
Hot chocolate,
In the warming pan.

Mince pies,
Home-made marzipan,
Dissolving on my tongue.

Naomi McDonnell (10)
St Teresa's Primary School

WINTER

Dancing stars of pearl-white snow,
Slowly falling to the ground,
Landing softly with such ease,
Floating slowly as it falls.

Soaring stars of pearl-white snow,
Slowly falling to the ground,
Landing where I do not know,
Happily swirling round and round.

Gliding stars of pearl-white snow,
Slowly falling to the ground,
Twirling, twirling as they go,
Taking off for graceful flight.

Flying stars of pearl-white snow,
Slowly falling to the ground,
Twisting, turning, down and down,
Safely spinning with such grace.

Matthew Davidson (9)
St Teresa's Primary School

WINTER

Pink nose, cold toes, red rosy cheeks.
Winter has come all-right.
Days are getting shorter,
Though they seem longer.
Smoking chimneys, bright fires;
Snuggle up warm.

Sun, set fire to the sky,
Wrap up warm, hat, gloves and all.
Slip and slide on ice,
Throw snowballs, make snowmen.

Silver moon high in the sky,
Stars shine bright in the night.
Ground covered in a white blanket,
At the end of the day snuggle up tight.

Aisling Wootten (9)
St Teresa's Primary School

WINTER

Winter to me is lots of fun,
It makes some people rather glum.
Jack Frost bites my toes and nose,
My cheeks glow like a red rose.
Frozen ponds and frozen rivers,
It's enough to give the shivers.
Icicles shimmer in winter light,
Oh how beautiful! Oh how bright!
Robin red-breast comes to say,
'It's the end of another real short day.'

Nataliya Mulhall (9)
St Teresa's Primary School

WINTER

I wish it would snow
Soft white flakes,
Just like clouds,
Falling, falling,
Softly and quietly
Covering the ground.

I wish it would snow
Big white flakes,
Just like cotton wool,
Soft and fluffy,
Changing the shape of everything.

I wish it would snow
Cool white flakes,
Just like small marshmallows,
Springy and squeaky,
With every footstep.

I wish it would snow
Soft, big, cool white flakes,
Just like cotton wool,
Marshmallow clouds,
Or a big, soft fluffy
Feather pillow.

Spring is nice with its early flowers,
Summer is great with its hot sun and long days,
Autumn is good with its damp smells, leaves
And mists.
But winter is brill because:
Walking, running, jumping, sliding, falling
I love *snow*!

Robin Knox (10)
St Teresa's Primary School

THOSE POOR WOMEN!

Henry VIII was very greedy,
A son for him was very needy.
Catherine of Aragon was his first wife,
Did not get to see Mary in all of her life!
With Anne Boleyn, Henry got in a tiz,
Because all she gave him was baby Liz!
Jane Seymore had a son (at last),
But her life after him was very fast,
Anne of Cleves didn't last very long,
Henry's feelings for her were not very strong.
Kathy Howard married at 20,
Death for her was all at the plenty!
Catherine Parr lasted longest
Next to all of the wives
She was the strongest.

Fiona Conway (10)
St Teresa's Primary School

WINTER THOUGHTS

The echoing red and green of Christmas.
Snuggling into a big fire-coloured armchair.
The icy, freezing, blue snow.
Cuddling up to frizzy, furry friends.
Listening to classical FM, sipping a cup of hot chocolate.
The whistling whimper of the wind.
Toasting my feet on the sizzling radiator.
Lights in the dark of night, glowing.
Foggy days with hailstones pattering off my head.
My images of winter, all around.

Helen Cunningham (10)
St Teresa's Primary School

HENRY VIII

Henry was a Tudor King, throughout his life he bought six rings.
He excelled at war and ate lots of wild boar
at his many feasts where he ate like a beast.
He was very good at singing and even better at dancing.
He hated the French unless it was a pretty wench,
many wives went to the substitute bench.
At the end of his life he was left with only one wife
but it was his son Ed who was at his death bed.
Ed has a sister called Mary who at times was quite contrary.
Then there was Liz who was a whiz
who always knew the biz.
Now you know the history of King Henry
the man with the very fat belly.

Nathan Cunningham (9)
St Teresa's Primary School

HENRY VIII

Henry the VIII was fat and florid,
To his wives he was really horrid.
Never to be missed or even missed out,
He was that because he was so fat and stout.
Liked for the wrong reasons,
Unliked for the right,
In my eyes he's a terrible sight.
He lacked in kindness and soul,
That's why he put people's heads on a pole.
It's not surprising his wives married for money,
For he had no looks, charms and he wasn't very funny.

Helen Sales (10)
St Teresa's Primary School

WINTER

The snow drifts slowly down
To the cracked concrete ground.
Inside the houses children glow
To wait for their presents tomorrow.

The Christmas tree lights
Shine out to you.
Some presents are toys,
Some are shoes.

The children go down to bed.
Sleeping quietly, they can't wait
For their presents tomorrow.

Tomas Garvey (9)
St Teresa's Primary School

WINTER

Snow is white, snow is bright
Glittering over the ground.

On a cold, dark morning you
Will see snow falling all around.

So look out the window
And you will see white, bright snow.

Snow is cold on a dark winter's day
Falling on rooftops that's what

It has been like today

Maybe winter has had its day.

Laura Dodds (10)
St Teresa's Primary School

WINTER

Winter is that time of year
When everybody starts to cheer.
Rugby grounds and football pitches,
Full of mud and water ditches.

Christmas trees and fairy lights,
Children's toys and chocolate delights.
Whistling wind rushing by,
Snowflakes falling from the sky.

Winter is damp and cold
And so difficult for the old.
Soon it will be spring
And the birds will come out to sing.

Michael Astley (9)
St Teresa's Primary School

SNOW

As the snow is falling from the sky,
forming a blanket on the ground,
the birds are scavenging food,
but there is nothing left to eat.
As us humans sit in front of our fires,
warming up our feet,
I look out of the window and it's
dropping from the sky,
dancing and doing cartwheels in the air.

Faye Boustead (9)
St Teresa's Primary School

UP IN SPACE

The dark and gloominess,
Affecting all around,
It all seems quiet,
In fact silence is the only sound.

Silver glittering stars shining in every little spot,
Like a baby with measles in its cot.

The patterns that they make are incredible to see,
We wouldn't believe them, you and me.
You see other planets some big and some small,
Coming towards you like a floating football.
Planet Earth is a tiny speck of dust,
As you look down from above you can only see it just.
Space is a miracle, perhaps a dream,
Has it all been imagined by the supersonic team?

Josephine Cunningham (8)
St Teresa's Primary School

WINTER TIMES

When it's winter, people like me
Are sitting on the settee
Drinking hot cocoa watching TV.
Lightning flashes and thunder with rain
A few more months of this and
Spring will be here.
Flowers blossom, ivy grows,
Chicks hatching, lambs being born,
Soon it will be nice and warm.

Lucy Willis (10)
St Teresa's Primary School

WINTER

W ind whistling through the trees
I ntergalactic snow storms falling down on earth.
N orth breezes whooshing down the open chimneys
T he wind is rising, the air is swirling
E veryone huddled in winter clothes
R ed hot coals steaming in the chilling air.

Jonathan Prinn (10)
St Teresa's Primary School

PLANETS

P luto is blue and icy cold,
L oads of miles from here,
A nd it is next to
N eptune, which still isn't very near,
E ven now we're getting closer,
T o the planet of my birth,
S o goodbye other planets, hello good old earth.

Caroline Henzell (9)
St Teresa's Primary School

GOING TO THE MOON

I'm going to space in a rocket,
I pass some stars and a comet.
I reach the moon,
And I'll be back soon,
I wish I'd brought Wallace and Gromit.

Emily Gray (8)
St Teresa's Primary School

LIFT-OFF

My friends and I (and Mrs Pope)
Are going to have a race.
We're going to see who can be first
To step out into space.
The rocket took off very fast so I think,
That very soon my friends and I (and Mrs Pope)
Will shortly reach the moon.
We're going to take some pictures
When we are having fun,
Dancing in the darkness beside the stars and sun.
But I might meet an alien
He might bite off my head, so let's just
Turn the rocket round
And go back home to bed.

Jennifer Armstrong (8)
St Teresa's Primary School

MERCURY AND MARS

I wish that I could go to Mars,
I could go and see the stars.
But I couldn't see because of the gas,
And whereabouts would I go to Mass?

But if I went to Mercury,
I would go all purpley.
But there would be steam, absolute scream
And I'd think it was only a dream!

Joseph Ingoe (9)
St Teresa's Primary School

THE BIG PLACE

Space . . .
The moon's white face.
I take one pace
From the human race.

Space . . .
I radio base.
I love the place
I think it's ace!

Space . . .
I lost a lace,
And there's no trace
Of my suitcase.

John Downs (8)
St Teresa's Primary School

LUCK

One day I went down to the fair,
But in my trouser leg I find,
Nothing but a tear.
With my mam I go to shop,
Down my shirt I spill my pop.
I was thinking about my luck,
With a step I'm in the muck.
The wind outside starts to blow,
I fall over and hurt my toe.
Up I get on my way,
Hope nothing else spoils the day.
How come my life's gone wrong?
Days and days seem so long.

Amanda Harrison (8)
Springwell Village Primary School

PLANETS

Saturn has a big ring
like an empty road.
Mars is red
like a glowing fire.
Earth is a busy world
with lots of cars for hire.
The sun is a burning fire ball,
high in the sky it's very tall.
The moon is a reflected light,
it's very high in our sight.
Pluto is the smallest planet,
there is an alien I have met.
All around is darkness
nothing to be seen in sight.

Laura Wilkinson (9)
Springwell Village Primary School

MY HEDGEY

Hedgey was a hedgehog,
Hedgey was *my* hedgehog.
He lived in the hedge.
But he came to live with me.
We gave him slugs,
We gave him worms
And sometimes dog food.
He had a wife and four children as well,
We gave them names, Hatty, Henry, Holly and Harry.
But Hedgey is not here now
He died.
But his family didn't.

Amy Birdsall (10)
Springwell Village Primary School

MY DREAMLAND

My dreamland is Disneyland,
Mickey Mouse, Minnie Mouse,
Donald Duck, Daisy Duck.
Treasure island would be fun.
Going to the dolphin show.
The Epcot centre all lit up,
On a night.
Glowing up the whole world,
Roller-coasters flying fast,
Waltzers spinning fast,
Mickey Mouse's car,
Minnie Mouse's bow,
The teacups are spinning fast,
I love the parade in the street,
Disneyland is fun!

Kelly Johnson (8)
Springwell Village Primary School

TREES

Trees, trees.
The trees are everywhere.
Now it's autumn,
No leaves upon the trees.
Trees are everywhere.
I like trees.
They're big and strong,
They hold themselves up,
And hold the leaves tight.
But in the autumn they drop them from their height.
So remember they work hard for the day and hard for the night.

Christie Patterson (7)
Springwell Village Primary School

IN THE WILD

Don't kill the wild for food,
Or chop down trees to make our floor.
Don't go hunting wild boar.
It's all part of nature, so do not kill,
Let animals rest through the night,
If you trap them they will bite.
Don't take bees' honey from their hive.
Let birds roam free,
Instead of having their eggs for tea.
This isn't the way it's meant to be.
Leave owls alone;
Don't destroy their homes.
Leave wild bears.
Don't go hunting hares.
Leave animals' homes,
Let animals live their lives.
Leave alone snakes.
Don't eat ducks that come from lakes.
Let animals live their lives!

Joanne Garnett (9)
Springwell Village Primary School

THE EARTH

Seas, paths, roads and parks
People, animals and even sharks.
A round sphere,
Noises, noises which I can hear.

People, cars, wagons and fumes,
Buses, lorries and empty tombs.
A round sphere,
Fumes, fumes, fumes are near.

Noises, buzzes, cities and towns,
The circus in the countryside.
With clowns that juggle all around,
And mice that don't make a sound.

England, Spain, Italy and France,
Lots of people like to dance.
A round sphere,
Cities, towns and countries here.

Danielle Patterson (9)
Springwell Village Primary School

SATURN

Saturn is big and round,
It's got a couple of hundred rings around,
I don't know if there's any sound.

I want to ride on the big round slide,
I want to slide down the side,
On the big and round planet.

I would be an astronaut and fly away,
And won't come back the next day,
And I would come back in May.

I would slide down the Milky Way,
And make myself stay another day,
In space, far away.

I would make a hut of wood and clay,
And meet an alien friend called Fay,
Then go back to earth and play,
And remember the Milky Way.

Mandy Anderson (9)
Springwell Village Primary School

LOOKING AROUND YOU

Look,
Look at the earth.
Look,
Look around you.
Look,
Look at the filthy ground.
Look,
Look at the long, green grass.
Look,
Look at the smelly old bins.
Look,
Look at the plants - dead.
Look,
Look at the people squashed.
Look,
Look at the trees - dead.
Look,
Look at all the babies crying.
Look,
Look at all the people ill.
Look!

Kelly Swinburn (8)
Springwell Village Primary School

PLANETS

Spacemen in their spacesuits,
All have their very special boots.
Planets always spinning round,
There is no sound, all around.
Why is there no gravity at all?
I wonder what happens if you bounce a ball?

Katherine Oliver (9)
Springwell Village Primary School

SPARKLING STARS

Stars are mini planets,
Spinning around.
Lots of things up there,
Never to be found.
Stars have a secret that
We will never know.
Stars are spinning round,
So fast, millions more
Than we will ever know.
I wish I could go
Up there to see the stars,
Spinning round so fast.
They glitter when it is night,
And sparkle when it is light.

Amy Postlethwaite (9)
Springwell Village Primary School

MY OAK TREE

I like oak trees they are very nice
But they make a lot of noise,
Cracking, cracking, cracking.
Winter, winter, winter on the trees,
Glowing, glowing, glowing on the leaves.
Autumn is when the leaves go
Rustle, rustle, rustle.
And when it is summer the leaves need
Water, water, water
In the spring the trees
Blossoming, blossoming, blossoming.

Justine Redhead (7)
Springwell Village Primary School

MY FAVOURITE TREE

Rubber tree, rubber tree,
How do you get your rubber?
Can it walk?
Can it slither?
When I am older
I'm sure I will find out.
Rubber tree, rubber tree,
Thank you for your rubber.
Peach tree, peach tree,
Thank you for your peaches.
Peach tree, peach tree,
How are your peaches so juicy?
Apple tree, apple tree,
Thank you for your apples,
Are your apples juicy?
I want a juicy apple.
I like red apples,
Because they are ripe.

Jordan Kendal (7)
Springwell Village Primary School

THE SILVER ROCKET

Like a huge metal bird,
About to soar through the sky.
It's going to travel through space,
Which is so very, very high.

So powerful the engine,
It travels much faster than fast.
So many miles it travels,
But will soon reach its place at last.

You lose count of the miles it journeys,
The planet Neptune is in sight.
It's getting there gradually,
It's at such a tremendous height.

Its journey's almost ended,
It's very nearly there.
It will soon go on another journey,
But no one knows where.

Michael Hills (10)
Springwell Village Primary School

DARKNESS

Darkness is nasty,
Dismal and black.
Darkness is danger,
Darkness is a bat flying through the night.
Darkness is a vampire giving you a fright.
Darkness is a roller-coaster giving you a shock.
Darkness is a poltergeist stealing your sock.
Darkness is looking at the stars,
Waiting for an alien coming from Mars.
Then the laughter coming from a child,
Like a panther coming from the wild.

As the light comes, the vampire fades.
The bat turns back and heads for a tree.
The roller-coaster stops.
And the poltergeist comes to return your sock.
Now the alien floats back to the stars
On its long journey back to Mars.

David Liddle (11)
Springwell Village Primary School

SPACE

Planets spinning,
Round and round.
Millions more,
Than we've found.
Saturn, Mars,
Earth and stars.
Solar systems,
Universes,
Galaxies, the lot.
I don't know what's out there.
Maybe I forgot.
Maybe there are aliens,
Maybe there is water,
We might have to live out there
Space . . .

Zoë Birdsall (10)
Springwell Village Primary School

LEAVES

Since I was born
my grandad had a tree,
and in the winter,
when I went,
I used to stamp on
the leaves.
I used to love
the crackling
of the tree leaves
falling on the ground.

Alex Fife (7)
Springwell Village Primary School

MY UNUSUAL DOG

My unusual dog
He has massive eyes,
And he eats pies.
He can talk
Just like you.
He is never ill,
And he can work a till.
He is funny
When he does jokes.
He is 1,
I am 8.
My dog is called Ben.
He is a Cavalier King Charles spaniel.
He is the best.

Rebecca Palmer (8)
Springwell Village Primary School

DRAGONFLY

I am a dragonfly
I hear you say 'Why oh why?'
I hover over ponds and lakes
Then I find some more drakes.
I like to eat insects,
They look like tiny specks.
I like to live in jungles hot,
In this cosy and lovely spot.
As I fly across the road,
I'm the opposite of a great big load.
In the winter I slowly fly
Then I simply start to die.

Matthew Thomas (9)
Springwell Village Primary School

SPORTS DAY

Here comes Martin for the big jump,
Someone's sorting out the cricket stump.
Chris is on the run,
The others are waiting for the starting gun.
The thrown Frisbee weighs a ton.
There's one of the sportsmen's sons.
Here comes out the shiny sun,
All the racing is fun.
All the races want to be won,
All the races are nearly done.
Chris is disqualified from the race,
While everyone else is on the pace.
Someone's come on holiday with their suitcase,
Just to watch the final race.
Martin is the champ,
The children have all gone back to the camp.

Craig Boyles (9)
Springwell Village Primary School

IN MY CHRISTMAS BOX

From my aunty I got a Christmas pud made out of mud.
A bike with no wheels, a pair of pink high heels.
A Christmas tree, a little dead flea.
A size 28 bra and my old grandpa.
I picked out a bit of chewed chewing-gum and there I found
my mum.
Some toy cars which the wheels don't go round and a big
bloodhound.
I just wonder what I'll get next year!

Joe Wardle (11)
Springwell Village Primary School

MY LITTLE OAK TREE

I had a little oak tree since I was three.
Every morning I see my tree
With its green leaves fluttering.
When I go and touch it,
I hear leaves crackling under my feet.
At night time when I feel lonely
I hear owls hooting.
In the morning
I hear birds singing.
Soon as I am dressed, I go straight down
To see my tree grow.
I like picking acorns off the tree
In late summer.
My little oak tree.

Ryan Miller (7)
Springwell Village Primary School

A TREE

An apple tree is from a seed,
That sprouts from the ground,
And grows and grows
Until it's huge.
Leaves and branches
Rise on the tree
And it looks lovely
For the rest of its life.

Katie Mulholland (8)
Springwell Village Primary School

TREES

Trees are brown,
Trees have twigs,
Trees have roots,
So they can drink.
Trees' leaves
Falling from the sky,
Crackling on the ground.

Lianne Robinson (7)
Springwell Village Primary School

LEAVES

Walking on the leaves,
In the autumn breeze.
High in the sky,
In the clouds,
Flying with the birds.
Leaves, leaves are the best.

Katie Carr (7)
Springwell Village Primary School

AT SCHOOL AGAIN

One, two, three, four,
Lost my temper,
Slammed the door.
Five, six, seven, eight,
Wiped the chips from my plate.
Nine, ten,
At school again.

Sara Oliver (7)
Springwell Village Primary School

WINTER THINGS

When the farmer defends the sheep, the fox goes away,
It goes away to find easy prey.
Night-time is coming, the farmer rounds the sheep up.
Tomorrow is going to be a freezing cold day.
Earth is frozen, snow across the land,
Robin redbreast in the bony trees.
Farmers scattering corn for the birds,
The birds coming down in a flock starving and hungry.
The rats are looking for some seeds.
The barn crinkles with ice.
The barn owl sleeps throughout the day.
The fox scavenges everywhere.
Ponds are frozen over.
The frogs are struggling for air.
Doves are cooing, cooing, on the roofs.
Twinkling, strong icicles.

Gregg McGuire (11)
Springwell Village Primary School

MY TREE

My tree is brown all the time
And it has leaves on it some of the time,
Then the leaves begin to change.
Then in the autumn,
They fall off
And it starts again.

Caroline Hills (7)
Springwell Village Primary School

In My Christmas Stocking

Today is Christmas day and in my stocking I found . . .

A pair of smelly socks,
A book about how to get chickenpox.

A bottle of whiskey,
And a teletubbie, it was Dipsy.

A ticket to see Santa next year,
How could this occur.

I also got a reindeer suit,
And a horn, toot, toot.

Before I got to the bottom,
Two more things came.

A half-eaten Christmas cake,
Half-eaten, half-baked.

Last, but not least,
There was the wonderful misspelt wrapper
That said 'Chr Baocolate!'

This is not what I expected in my stocking.

Lucy Johnson (10)
Springwell Village Primary School

DARKNESS IS . . .

Darkness is spooky.
Darkness is witches at night,
Making a spell to give you a fright.
Darkness is about the devil,
Darkness is cold and wet and gloomy.
Darkness is all about ghosts
Flying through the night.
Darkness is blind.
Darkness is mysterious.
Darkness is death.
Darkness is the full moon and the werewolf
Howling at midnight.
Darkness is the mummy walking
Like a zombie.
Darkness is what people fear,
They always have, they always will!

Ben Lowery (11)
Springwell Village Primary School

TREES AND LEAVES

In autumn, leaves go crunch,
While we eat apples for our lunch!
In the winter trees are bare,
No leaves are there.
All the leaves
Come from trees!
But trees come from seeds.

Alan Foley (7)
Springwell Village Primary School

WINTER

Grey sky turning black,
Darkness falls on the village.
Stars and the moon come out,
In the icy sky.
Winter has begun,
For some people this is not fun.
Trees are standing there,
Without a leaf for a friend.
Gleaming snow, thick and deep.
Animals in hibernation for a long deep sleep.
The whole village covered in white.
Children play with delight.
People watch snowflakes falling from the sky
Out of the frosty window.
Night has come, not much fun.
Not a noise in the village
Except the carol singers singing softly.

Laura Waltham (10)
Springwell Village Primary School

MY TREE

Apple tree, apple tree,
Are you juicy?
Are you red?
And are you fruity?
Apple tree, apple tree,
You make me feel hungry.

Stuart Anderson (8)
Springwell Village Primary School

THE SECOND MILLENNIUM

The second millennium, oh no,
If we have a war, where will people go?
A war in the second millennium,
If we have one we will beat them,
The second millennium.

But think of the good it might bring,
One day, we might have a king,
He will help us to live,
And food and drink he will give,
The second millennium.

What about crime?
Oh turn back the time,
Please don't rob us of our money,
If you do, it's not very funny.
The second millennium.

Let us go to school,
And don't be cruel,
If you don't we will not learn,
And when children grow up, money they won't earn.
The second millennium.

Let people work and have jobs,
Only do things if people nod,
Leave people alone,
On their own.
The second millennium.

How will it be?
How will it be for you and for me?
Don't leave it horrible for the third world,
And put everything straight and not curled.
The second millennium.

Laura Ward (10)
Springwell Village Primary School

THE WORLD IN 1998

Wars stop people's lives,
And children should not carry knives.
It's not the people's fault if they are poor,
It's not their fault if they have no roof or floor.
So stop it now and make it better.

Children working,
Where animals are lurking,
Is cruel.
And people who have no cars, have to be pulled by mule.

Charities help people in all situations,
And they are in all nations.
Every child should go to school,
And learn to obey the rule.

We chop down trees to make our floor,
We don't care if we kill wild boar.
What will happen if our Queen dies?
Will our world be full of lies?

If you kill killer whales,
All they'll be in is stories and tales.
If we start another war,
Will we sink in to the earth's core?

Long ago when the world was clean,
That's the way it should have been.
So make the world that way.

Rebecca Lee (9)
Springwell Village Primary School

MAGIC HORSE

'Magic horse, magic horse,
Where are you going?
Will you take me to the land that you go to every night?'

He said 'I am going to the land
Where horses rule
The magical land I call home.

I will take you young Jonathan
As long as you don't tell
Where the magic land is hidden.'

'How will you take me, magic horse?
Will we run with the wind together?
How magic horse, how?'

'We will fly to the land
The magical land
Where all horses are kings and queens.'

'When magic horse, when magic horse?
Will you take me next week?
Or maybe on the Sabbath day?
Oh please could we go now?'

'Yes young Jonathan I will take
You right now.
Jump onto my strong back
And we will fly together
To the magical land I call home.'

'Magical horse what is it like
The land I am going to?
Is it near or is it far?
I will see all of it in minutes.'

Carly Foster (9)
Springwell Village Primary School

I'VE SEEN A . . .

I've seen a penguin's waiter suit.
I've seen a panda's frilly frock.

I've seen a crocodile's dinner suit.
I've seen a cheetah's tracksuit.

But between you and me
I've never seen an
Elephant in yellow spotted underwear.

I've seen a parrot's fancy hat.
I've seen an octopus' shoes.

I've seen a frog's parachute.
I've seen a crab's walking stick.

But between you and me
I've never seen an
Elephant in yellow spotted underwear.

I've seen pigs flying.
I've seen hippos jump.

I've seen a monkey at a park.
I've seen a beaver build a house.

But between you and me
I've still never seen an
Elephant in yellow spotted underwear.
Oh well, never mind
I've still seen a penguin's . . .

Catherine Ellwood (11)
Springwell Village Primary School

WIZARDS

Wizards and wizardry,
Things like that,
Fighting the goblins,
Wearing a pointy hat.

Merlin or Gandalf
Are they the same?
Are the people who believe
Really insane?

Gandalf, was it good
To be in 'The Hobbit'?
Is it good being in a book,
Or is it a habit?

Merlin, oh, Merlin
You are so famous.
Do people say,
'Please will you entertain us?'

I like wizards,
And things like that,
Especially the ones
That wear a pointy hat!

Garry Mowbray (10)
Springwell Village Primary School

TREE

Trees have leaves in the summer,
Trees have trunks that twist and turn.
All the leaves fall off in autumn,
But then they grow back in spring.

Max Downs (8)
Springwell Village Primary School

LOST

People die at war,
Families cry with sorrow.
Children scared but still laughing.
Families pray.
Husbands die, wives cry.
Why did it happen to them?
They lost their family.

People lost their loved ones
But still they have them in their heart.
People lost their lives
But they will rise again.
People lost their family,
Still they will be strong.

So people of this world, listen to what
War has done to us.

War should be lost
Like all those people.
We still remember the people
Who died for us.

War destroys everything
Everything in its path.
War is like a lost world
War kills innocent people.

So wear a red poppy to remember
The people who died for us.

Gemma Swinburn (11)
Springwell Village Primary School

DARKNESS IS . . .

Darkness is scary
Darkness is spooky
Darkness is ghosts
Darkness is danger
Darkness is witches flying through
the night sky
Darkness is owls screeching in the night
Darkness is black cats running through
the night
Darkness is death walking down your
street
Darkness is spiders giving you a fright
Darkness is bats flying down your neck
Darkness is vampires trying to bite your neck.

Christopher Rowlands (11)
Springwell Village Primary School

REMEMBER THE WORD

Love dies in the back of your heart,
Like soldiers in the war.
They fought for our lives,
All the people in the trenches.
Helping to save our lives,
Then the poppies are spread around.
Then war stops,
But just for two minutes,
The world is abandoned,
All to the mind then . . .
Soldiers remember the word, kind.

Kate Robinson (10)
Springwell Village Primary School

EASTER SUNDAY

On Easter Sunday I go to church,
my budgie Joey, sits on his perch.
I open up my Easter eggs,
washing hanging out on pegs.
Easter Sunday is great,
I play out and come in late.
On Easter Sunday I always play,
and I eat Easter eggs all day.
I love Easter Sunday and opening stuff,
opening eggs, *puff, puff, puff.*
Easter Sunday is fun,
at night I have a hot cross bun.
Easter Sunday is class,
I love playing in the grass.
I always eat all my eggs,
little goose bumps grow on my legs.
My brother is very greedy,
he always speaks to Mr Weedy.
I love Easter Sunday,
it's great on that day.
It is totally excellent,
I give up sweets for Lent.
Easter Sunday I go the pub for lunch,
I love the drink, punch.
It's great on Easter Sunday,
what a lot of money
my mam has to pay.
That is all that happens on Easter Sunday!

Lauren Nikrandt (10)
Springwell Village Primary School

MOTHER AND FATHER

You helped me through the worst times,
You never gave up hope.
You cuddled me and loved me,
When I couldn't cope.
When the darkness came,
You showed me the light,
You kept me warm and cosy,
Through the cold, dark night.
You looked after me,
There is no other
As loving as you,
My dear mother.
But then there's Father,
If it wasn't for you,
I wouldn't be here,
Your voice is so soothing,
Your eyes are so dear.
You stand up tall and proud,
Looking down at me,
You helped me to understand,
You taught me how to see.
You helped me through the times
When I was so sad.
I will always need you,
My loving caring dad.

Love

Sarah

xxx

Sarah Devanney (10)
Springwell Village Primary School

THE SHADOW MAN

When I'm in my bed at night,
I look around my room,
Every corner, every crack,
The shadow man will be here soon.
I look around at the wall,
See the clothes on the floor,
What's that over there,
A crash of a door?
He's here, look there,
I pretend to be asleep,
As he's turning things into beasts,
When I take a peep,
A witch on my cupboard door,
A beast on my floor,
The moon on my curtains,
Standing on my bed, the hammer of war,
The stars on my bookshelf,
A shadow dog and shadow bone,
Running on my ceiling,
A rhino with a horn!
The shadow man smiles with glee,
Looking at the shadow hound,
'The best I've done in years' he whispered
Then leaves . . . without a sound.

Sarah Cook (10)
Springwell Village Primary School

WHEN I GROW UP

When I grow up
I want to be,
An author or an astronaut
or an explorer of the sea.

If I was an author
for children I would write.
To teach them what is bad
and what is good and right.

If I was an astronaut
I would go into space.
To go and look for aliens
to tell them of our race.

If I explored the sea
I would go and look at fish.
And every other sea creature
that I could ever wish.

There's lots of things
I want to do.
Which one to choose
I haven't a clue.

Kelly Fenwick McFarlane (10)
Stanhope JMI School

SURPRISE

Just before Christmas I had a surprise
three little kids came into our lives.
Two little boys and one little girl
named after me.

24 little fingers and 6 little thumbs
all so fragile
as everybody knows.

They are still wicked
all of the time.
So much I love them
forever more.

Shaun Bell (11)
Stanhope JMI School

COME INTO MY ROOM

Come into my room
What do you think?
It looks like a tip, a tip that's what I think,
Come into my room
What can you see?
I see books, clothes, games and a mess.
Come into my room
Why do you think it's such a tip?
It might be a tip
But I know where everything is.

Nadia Jones (11)
Stanhope JMI School

TELL ME . . .

Tell me a poem that I've never heard,
of witches and giants and of a song bird.
Tell me of monkeys, tell me of sun,
tell me of angels, tell me of fun.

Tell me a story that I've heard before,
it's called Sleeping Beauty and I could
listen to it forever more.
Tell me why she falls asleep and before
you read it can I have a peep?

There are some things in life
that you just can't get.
But try and try
they will come to you I bet.

Katharine Parker (11)
Stanhope JMI School

WHY

Why do we have to die?
It is so sad to see someone *die.*
Why do we have to hate?
It brings anger in your heart.
Why do we have bad feelings?
They are so sad.
Why can't it be love?

   Why?

Darren Tooley (10)
Stanhope JMI School

SEASONS

Spring is full of colour and birth.
Summer is hot all over the earth.
Autumn is full of blowing leaves,
Winter is cold it is not just a breeze.
For all of these reasons
I love the seasons.

Lorin Briggs (10)
Stanhope JMI School

WHEN MY NANNA DIED

One day when I was at school
my nanna died.
It was after school when I heard the news,
My mam said to me, 'Your nanna has died.'
When I got home, I ran to my room and cried.
I went to her house and had a look round.
Then my mam said she died in her sleep.
There's nothing I can do to get her back
I miss her every day.

Mark Smith (10)
Stanhope JMI School

LOVE IS

Love is Jesus all around the world.
Love is your mum and dad.
Love is the friendship between a child and his pet.

Terry Kennedy (9)
Stocksfield Avenue Primary School

St Lucia Is . . .

St Lucia is hot and sunny
St Lucia is blue sparkling sea
St Lucia is classy clubs and entertainment
St Lucia is relaxing, soothing and cool
St Lucia is romantic honeymoons
St Lucia is luscious, tropical drinks
St Lucia is full of luxury and lots and lots of fun!

Jill Allen (10)
Stocksfield Avenue Primary School

If Only . . .

If only I was a footballer,
I could win trophies and sign autographs!

If only I was rich and famous,
I could buy whatever I wanted and appear on TV!

If only I had a PlayStation,
I could play on amazing games and listen to
great music!

If only I was Prime Minister,
I could make new laws and feel powerful too!

If only I was an astronaut,
I could swim and jump in mid-air!

If only, if only, if only,
I could be grateful for what I have.

Christopher Mullan (10)
Stocksfield Avenue Primary School

NIGHT IS

Night is dark, dull and dim.
Night is silent, quiet and still.
Night is black, grey or white
Night is anything but light.
Night is frightful, scary and dark,
Night is a time when the moon comes out.
Night is cloudy, stormy and misty.
Night is full of twinkling stars.
Night is night, mysterious and mystical.

Jodie Kirkley (9)
Stocksfield Avenue Primary School

ST LUCIA IS . .

St Lucia is love!
St Lucia is romantic!
St Lucia is changing!
St Lucia is tropical!
St Lucia is sparkling!
St Lucia is family!
St Lucia is volcanic!
St Lucia is an early bird!
St Lucia is beautiful!
St Lucia is the best!
St Lucia is the romantic place!
St Lucia is the place to be!
St Lucia is sparkling in my heart!
St Lucia is my friends!
St Lucia is love!

Rosie Copping (9)
Stocksfield Avenue Primary School

If Only . . .

If only I was rich and famous
I could travel around the world.

If only I was a fast runner
I could win medals and more.

If only I had a dog
I could play games with him.

If only I could meet the Spice Girls
I could sing with them.

If only I was a teacher
I could tell the kids what to do.

If only I could trust my friends
I could tell them big secrets.

If only I could join the army
I could save the world.

If only I was a rugby star
I could play for England.

. . . in my dreams of course!

Stephen Mowbray (10)
Stocksfield Avenue Primary School

WILD WISHES

I wish I was a dog so I could be taken for a walk.
I wish I was a lion so I could be powerful and proud.
I wish I was a leopard so I could be the fastest runner in the world.
I wish I was a panther so I could blend into the shadows of the night.
I wish I was an ape so I could laze about all day and swing from tree
                                                          to tree.
I wish I was an elephant so that I could carry a king on my back.
I wish I was a giraffe so I could nearly touch the sky.
I wish I was an ant so I could squeeze into a crack and hide from
                                                          the world.
I wish I was a butterfly so I could be beautiful and delicate.
But most of all I wish I could be thankful for just being me.

Nathaniel Frame (10)
Stocksfield Avenue Primary School

ST LUCIA

St Lucia is full of grapefruit greens,
Yelling yellows, ringing reds, original
oranges and beautiful blues.
St Lucia is full with fruits of nature,
fruits of fun.
St Lucia is covered by fantastic sun.
Relaxing and romantic evenings
followed by sand and sea.
Then I fall into a deep sleep
and imagine the sun setting above me.

Emma Tominey (10)
Stocksfield Avenue Primary School

St Lucia Is . . .

St Lucia is a soft drink sipped from a long straw,
St Lucia is the sea glistening in the night,
St Lucia is the wind against my cheeks,
St Lucia is the rain from the sky,
St Lucia is the place to go,
St Lucia is a small soft pillow on the sea,
St Lucia is changing,
If only I was there.

Carl Griffin (9)
Stocksfield Avenue Primary School

Fruits

Some things are true
but only in our class.
We did fruit today,
in science.
We learned that a tomato,
is a fruit.
We learned that a strawberry,
is not a fruit.
A cucumber is a fruit,
but rhubarb isn't.
I copied down the diagrams
and I made some notes,
because I knew
I had to pretend it was true.

Victoria Crow (9)
West Rainton Primary School

THE PIT DISASTER

When I was working on a late night shift
I heard a noise it was only the lift.
Something was shaking on top of the ground
And then I realised it was only a sound.
Then the ground started to shake
Then there was an enormous lake.
I picked up my pickaxe, I started to dig
Then I looked up and the ground started a jig.
Then there was a mighty rumble
And all the ground started to crumble.

Stephen Allen (9)
West Rainton Primary School

DOWN THE MINE

I am a young boy working down the mine,
Opening and shutting the door every
single time.
Sitting in the dark, feeling all alone
Listening to the miners as they walk past
and moan.
A very young boy leading his own way
Opening and shutting doors every single
day.
How I wish I wasn't a miner
Staying home would be kinder.
But I have to earn my pay
So I come here every day.

Joanne Pallister (10)
West Rainton Primary School

SPRINGTIME BEGINS

In the soil see the buds.
Snowdrops growing in the woods,
Lambs are jumping high and low.
Find new fields so off they go.
On the trees, blossom of pink and white.
This is spring's familiar sight.
See the cows getting milked by the maid.
See the farmer using his brand-new spade.

Terry Fisher (10)
West Rainton Primary School

THE WAY THE MINE WORKS

As the workers get their pay
They are dying day by day
As you are working, you get no air
But the owner doesn't care.
As the canary tests the air,
Why the birds? It's not fair.
Rockfall, explosion no good air
Why do we work? It's just not fair.
There are all kinds of people
Rich and poor
Who is that person at the door?
My husband is dead
I don't believe you
What have you found?
A bit of his sleeve.
How did he die?
In a rockfall they say.
So when you get older, keep away.

Patrick Mongan (11)
West Rainton Primary School

THE BLAST

Working at the face,
Taking out the black gold.
Stop,
Listen,
Thundering sound.
Cave-in!
Try to run,
Dust surrounds me,
Cough and splutter,
Try to breathe.
Props collapsing.
Fall to the ground.
Legs heavy.
Silence.
Then the groaning
Crying for help
The pain. The fear!
Someone help.
The end of my life has come at last
I was a victim of the blast.

Emily Burns (11)
West Rainton Primary School

AN ANGEL FOR US

A blue dancer
A golden healer
A beautiful singer
A soft cuddler
A touch giver
A silver hugger
A star gazer
A people carer
An old people sharer
A nightmare stopper
A God watcher
A gold guider
A baby blesser
A moon dancer
A golden healer
A purple saver
A happy helper
A flower grower
A present giver
A children watcher
A white flyer
A golden angel for everybody.

Christopher Salem, Kristopher Edwards,
Kimberley Scott, Jason McKay, Anna-Marie
Loraine, Hayley Robinson, Daniel Donaldson &
Steven Wildsmith (7-8)
Windmill Hills Primary School

POT OF GOLD

Rainbows bright, like the sun
When it rains the sunshine will come

Like an arc, swooping across the sky
Colour sparkling in the sun
And at the end -
A golden dream.
Perhaps never to be seen.

A golden tree
Some golden coins
Sparkling at the rainbow's end
Or perhaps there lies,
Beneath the rainbow
A dream house
Full of golden memories,
That are for everyone
In the world.

Samantha Wildsmith
Windmill Hills Primary School

THE BEAT ON THE STREET

Running down the street,
Running with the beat,
Scared from the cat -
Or something like that.

Getting to my home.
Do I live all alone?
My mam's through the door -
I'm not lonely anymore!

Natalie Edwards (9)
Windmill Hills Primary School

THEY CALL ME LEE

They call me Lee,
Because I'm so cool,
With my bike,
Because I've got a race tonight.
With the fire on the back of my bike,
I'm 6 years old and it's a mighty jungle
out there.
I'm halfway through the race and I'm
third.
All the people are shouting for me -

Lee! Lee!
That's me!
I'm first and I've won my first race.
You should see the look on my face!
Lee! Lee!
That's me
That's me!

Lee Hand (9)
Windmill Hills Primary School

ALONE

A n angel with a golden halo,
   like a ring sparkling bright above her head.
N obody knows the world she's come from or
   where she is going.
G lowing so high in the sky until she reaches
   her destiny.
E verybody wondering the secret she brings.
L onely people gaze at her and hope that her
   secret is for them - alone.

Victoria Morrison (10)
Windmill Hills Primary School

MUM! MUM!

Mum, Mum, the garden is
full of witches.
Come quick and see the witches.
The full moon is out,
and they are flying about.
Mum, please come and see the witches.

One is green,
and one is red.
One is eating mouldy bread.
Mum, come quick and see the witches.

One is black,
and one is brown.
One has got a broken crown.
Mum, come quick and see the witches.

Raymond Shek (9)
Windmill Hills Primary School

FIZZY COLA COLA

Fizzy, busy,
Whizzy, fizzy,
Bubbles in Cola Cola.

Squirting, hurting,
Burping, squirting,
Bubbles in Cola Cola.

Bubbling, huggling,
Guggling, bubbling,
Bubble in Cola Cola.

Now I've drank it all!

Gary Styles (9)
Windmill Hills Primary School

ADVICE TO STAN

I was brave, I was in goal,
You should have seen me kick that ball.
I kicked it so hard it disappeared
Like a pound of lard melting in a warm
atmosphere.
Sizzling save!
Then it nearly hit striker Stan,
'Go on man.' I shouted,
'Do your best.
Take it on around all the rest'
Perfect positioning.
'But first take it down upon your chest
'If you score, we will do the rest.'
Here we go!
Here we go!
'Then when we win the Premier League
We might even play for
Kevin Keegan!'

Tommy McCartney (11)
Windmill Hills Primary School

THE BEST MATCH OF THE YEAR

Did you see it?
Did you see it?
John's brilliant goal from the outside box
Top hand corner of the net -
The defence had no chance!
Did you see it?
Did you see it?
James's super save,
Tommy deflected it
Did you see it?
Did you see it?
They tried to score
But we made a run for it
Antonio crossed it in,
and Rikki headed it in the net.
Did you see it?
Did you see it?
Lee's shot hit the bar,
Then Dean scored!

John Gaughan (9)
Windmill Hills Primary School

DREAMS

Dreams can be scary, dreams can be nice.
We all have dreams throughout the night.
Most are good ones, some are bad.
Most dreams are happy, some are sad.
Angry dreams
Silent dreams.
Noisy dreams
Hideous dreams
Dreams that can terrify.

We have dreams about rainbows.
Dreams about the sun.
Dreams that are in colour.
Dreams are for everyone.

Amanda Richardson & Gemma Cusick (11)
Windmill Hills Primary School

FRAGRANT FLOWERS

F lowers are fragrant, soft and bright.
L ove, care and look after the flowers.
O ver the hills, across the banks
    flowers are there.
W herever there's a flower there's
    usually a scent.
E very flower has something
    special - just like people.
R oses, tulips, daffodils and bells - all
    beautiful flowers for the world to
S hare.

Emma Keepin (11)
Windmill Hills Primary School

RAINBOW MAN

A rainbow man in his bedroom,
paints pictures with his rainbow paint.
Red, orange, yellow, green, blue, indigo
and violet.
Red is for a red, red apple.
Orange for a big juicy orange.
Yellow for the big round sun.
Green is for the spring grass.
Blue is for the summer sky.
Indigo is for a lush plum.
Violet is for a velvet flower.

Toni Guest (9)
Windmill Hills Primary School

THEY CALL ME WILL SMITH

They call me Will Smith.
I'm a Harley Davison fan.
I'm just a kid,
riding a motorbike with speed.
I'm seven years old,
but oh, I'm so bold.
I like stunts and leather seats.
I'm so cool.
I comb my hair
with boiling oil.

Andrew Noble (9)
Windmill Hills Primary School

A RECIPE FOR A GOOD NEIGHBOUR

Ingredients:

six - smiles
good manners
16 - nice hearts
three - good souls
a big bowl of happiness
four - honesties
four - freedoms

How to do it:

Get your bowl and put in some good manners
and three smiles.
Stir for three minutes.
Add 15 nice hearts, three good souls and put in
the other smiles and one heart.
Add the good manners and four honesties and mix.
Add the four freedoms and mix.
Wrap it all up in a prayer for an hour and . . . make
friends with your neighbour.

John Lewis (8)
Windmill Hills Primary School

presenting for professionals

presenting for professionals
phil baguley and janet bateman

The **teach yourself** series does exactly what it says, and it works. For over 60 years, more than 40 million people have learnt over 750 subjects the **teach yourself** way, with impressive results.

be where you want to be
with **teach yourself**

For UK orders: please contact Bookpoint Ltd., 130 Milton Park, Abingdon, Oxon OX14 4SB. Telephone: (44) 01235 827720. Fax: (44) 01235 400454. Lines are open from 09.00–18.00, Monday to Saturday, with a 24-hour message answering service. You can also order through our website www.madaboutbooks.co.uk.

For U.S.A. order enquiries: please contact McGraw-Hill Customer Services, P.O. Box 545, Blacklick, OH 43004-0545, U.S.A. Telephone: 1-800-722-4726. Fax: 1-614-755-5645.

For Canada order enquiries: please contact McGraw-Hill Ryerson Ltd., 300 Water St, Whitby, Ontario L1N 9B6, Canada. Telephone: 905 430 5000. Fax: 905 430 5020.

Long renowned as the authoritative source for self-guided learning – with more than 30 million copies sold worldwide – the *Teach Yourself* series includes over 300 titles in the fields of languages, crafts, hobbies, business and education.

British Library Cataloguing in Publication Data
A catalogue record for this title is available from The British Library

Library of Congress Catalog Card Number: On file

First published in UK 2003 by Hodder Headline Plc., 338 Euston Road, London, NW1 3BH.

First published in US 2003 by Contemporary Books, A Division of The McGraw-Hill Companies, 1 Prudential Plaza, 130 East Randolph Street, Chicago, Illinois 60601 U.S.A.

This edition published 2003

The 'Teach Yourself' name and logo are registered trade marks of Hodder & Stoughton Ltd.

Typeset by SX Composing DTP, Rayleigh, Essex, UK

Printed in Great Britain for Hodder & Stoughton Educational, a division of Hodder Headline Ltd., 338 Euston Road, London NW1 3BH by Cox & Wyman Ltd., Reading, Berkshire.

Impression number   10 9 8 7 6 5 4 3 2 1

Year   2009 2008 2007 2006 2005 2004 2003

In the twenty-first century world of work the presentation has become the default mode of group communication. It's an ever-present, ever-ready event. As a result there must be few – if any – of you who *don't* do presentations. These, as you know, can be about almost anything – the new or the old, the bold or the cautious, the quick or the slow, the hesitant or the sure. Their aims and objectives are just as diverse – to persuade or to inform or to influence. These are all important – to both you and your employer. For they hold within them the potential to change your world of work. But doing that, getting to the point where that potential becomes actual, can only be achieved when your presentations have the four Ps. Presentations like this are:

- powerful
- passionate
- persuasive and, above all,
- professional.

Teach Yourself Presenting for Professionals aims to enable you to create and perform 'four P' presentations. The result will be presentations that are different; they will be interesting, enjoyable, seductive and compelling. But it isn't a beginner's guide to presenting. It assumes that you have the basic skills of that process. Its objective is to help you to build on these skills, to lift them – and your presentations – to a professional level; to create presentations that *really* reach people. To do that it covers the how, why, what and when of presenting in greater depth than has been done before. It's rich in practical and useful presentation tips, jam-packed with insider advice and information and big on multi-media know-how. In short, it's a book that you'll find yourself reaching for every time you prepare for a presentation.

how?

Mastering the skills of professional presenting isn't an instant process. It'll take time, effort and commitment. You're going to have to shift up a gear, move on to doing things differently. To do that you're going to need two things:

- the right sort of information, and
- quick and easy access to that information.

In short, you're going to need to:

- find your way around this book quickly and easily, and then
- use what you find there.

We've done quite a lot about both of these. The result is a book that's different. You'll be able to access its contents easily and read, understand and absorb any one of its sections within ten minutes. But these sections are very different to the sort of thing that you find in 'ordinary' books on presentation skills. Printed in alphabetic order, each of them focuses on a single aspect of professional presenting. They are listed in a Contents section that doubles up as an index and follows shortly. Once you get into them you'll find that you can read this book whichever or whatever way you want to. You can be logical, linear and alphabetic or intuitive and impulsive; you can dip in and dip out or be a systematic page-turner. It's really up to you. Why not start off by looking at the 'route-map' guide on page ix?

navigation marks

Once you're into this book you'll find its pages contain a couple of icons. These are used to highlight specific parts of the text – to bring them more sharply to your attention. Here they are:

 When you find this icon on a page it means that the text adjacent to it contains a key point – an issue or piece of information that's vitally important to upgrading your presentation skills.

 When this icon appears it's a 'heads-up' warning sign. It's there to warn you about a potential mistake – one that could cost you time, money and embarrassment.

why?

By now you should have a pretty good idea of what this book is about. But in case you haven't, let's check it out. It's a book that will enable you to enhance your abilities – or to put it another way – move up a gear, in one of *the* core skills of management – that of presenting. There'll be very few – if any – of the management roles that you either aspire to or are already in that don't demand this skill. So being able to present and do that at a professional standard will be good for you, for your career and, last but not least, for your employer.

So how will this book help you?

The answer is that from this book you'll get:

- a clear understanding of how you can plan, prepare and deliver a presentation that's professional
- a wide range of ideas and appropriate methods/tools that you can use to enhance that presentation
- a firm foundation from which you can start and continue, with confidence and enthusiasm, to upgrade and develop your professional presenting skills.

But, despite all this, it isn't a book to be read through at one sitting. It's more a book to be dipped into, referred to and browsed over as your presenting skill grows – as it surely will! We've even provided a section at the back in which you can note down your own ideas and know-how and given you a list of further resources – such as books and websites – that will provide more relevant in-depth material.

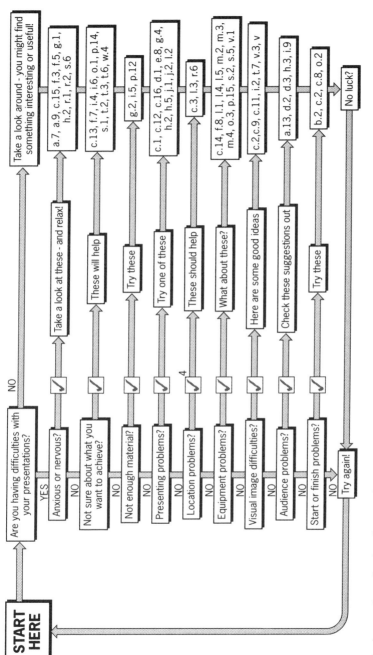

Route-map to professional presenting

contents

a.1 a, b and c

The a, b and c of professional presenting aren't immediately obvious. If you tried to find them on your own you'd have to work hard, tunnelling into the mountains of words that have been written about presenting. But, as this book is about enabling you to become a professional presenter, here's a short cut. For the a, b and c of professional presenting tell you that:

- a is about access (*see* **a.4 access**)
- b is about believability (*see* **b.3 believability**), and
- c is about courage (*see* **c.15 courage**).

But as you get further into professional presenting – and into this book – you'll realize that there's a lot more to it than that. For you'll find that there's a whole alphabet full of 'bits' that will help you to convert your presenting from the merely adequate to the outstandingly professional. You'll discover and use the fact that – amongst other things – p is for passion, c is for climax and t is for thank-yous – all of which will help you on your way to becoming a professional presenter.

a.2 accents and dialects

We all have an accent of one sort or another. It's to do with the way we pronounce words when we talk. We learn this accent at the same time as we learn to talk, by listening to the adults around us. It may get changed or modified when we go to school or university, move to a different part of the country or world or become involved with a different social or work group. Some accents are obvious or 'strong' while others are softer, more socially acceptable, even fashionable. We also all have what's known as a 'dialect'. Dialects are more complex than accents. They are to do with the range and type of words we use – our vocabulary – and the ways in which we use them, the grammar of our speech. If you think about these you'll soon realize that the differences between northern and southern English or New York and Alabama English are to do with accents. You'll also realize that the differences between the British 'I have got' and the American 'I have gotten' are to do with dialects.

If you have a strong or 'different' accent you'll be aware that there can be pressures for you to change or modify that accent. These pressures come about for a number of reasons, including social class, popularity and fashion. The same applies to dialects. People with 'strong' dialects can often find that they are encouraged to speak in a way that's 'standard' and have their speech 'corrected' until they do. When it comes to professional presenting and your accent or dialect the key questions are:

- does the way you pronounce your words get in the way of your audience understanding you?
- do the words that you use and the way that you use them inhibit or limit that understanding?

If your presenting – or even social – experiences give you a 'yes' on either of these then you need to do something about it. After all, you are trying to communicate – aren't you? But what you do needn't be radical. Here are some suggestions:

- Check out your audience – find out if there's a local word or local pronunciation that will help and then slip it (*after* practising it) into your presentation.
- Don't apologise for your accent or for your dialect – they are individual, what makes you, you.
- If you feel there's a problem, slow down slightly and make sure that you're articulating your words clearly (*see* **u.3 using your voice**).
- If there's still a problem, stop and ask the audience whether they are with you. If they are – great, but remember not to speed up. If they aren't, ask where you lost them, then backtrack, checking as you go that they're still with you.
- Remember that having an accent needn't necessarily be bad. It may even, in the audience's eyes, give you more credibility or authority.

a.3 accentuate the positive

Being positive is a key element in professional presenting. But this positivity isn't the unconditional, unqualified, 'gung-ho' sort. It's based on the firm foundations of hard work and experience. It reflects the way that you've prepared your presentation (*see* **p.12 preparing your material**), the time you've spent rehearsing (*see* **r.1 rehearsal**) and the willingness that you've shown to learn, to stretch yourself and to achieve even better presentations. All of this – and more – will give you firm grounds for being positive. This positivity will show itself in both your relationship with your presentation and the content of that presentation.

For you and your presentation will have reached the point where your relationship is one of mutual respect. You'll show this in the easy and assured way that you speak. The pace, pitch, pauses and tone of your speech (*see* **p.4 pauses, u.3 using your voice**) will assure your audience that you've a right to be where you are – presenting to them. Your head-up, shoulders-back posture (*see* **p.9 posture**) and the gestures (*see* **g.4 gestures**) that you make will tell that audience that you are confident about what you're saying. What you tell them will use an 'active voice' (*see* **s.3 simplify**) – rather than a passive one. You'll use sentences like:

'Quality has improved.'

rather than:

'An improvement in quality has been made.'

Your sentences will be short, have direct links between subject and verb, use familiar words and won't use vague, diffuse, unclear expressions such as:

'failure to adhere to proscribed procedures'.

You'll feel good, alive and happy about being up there presenting – as you ought to. After all, you are a professional presenter, aren't you?

a.4 access

Access to your audience or – more precisely – access to their minds and imaginations, is a 'must-do' for professional presenters. This involves communicating with them (*see* **c.12 communication**). The keys to the success of your communication with your audience lie in their ability to see and hear. Most of them (*see* **d.3 disability awareness**) will see you and what you show them and will hear what you say to them. Of these two senses, sight and hearing, it's their ability to see that is the more significant (*see* **n.2 non-verbal communication**). For they see:

- the movements of your hands, arms, head, feet and legs
- your gestures, posture, eye movements and facial expressions
- the way you dress, the jewellery that you wear
- the images that you project upon the screen (*see* **i.2 images, v.4 visual aids**).

Their seeing all of these is a commonplace, normal, almost unconscious activity. It's one that most of us take for granted. But what results, when your audience sees what you present and the way that you present it, *can* be – if you get it right – unusual, amazing and extraordinary. But this will only happen if you touch, tap into their curiosity and their imagination.

For when you touch these, your audience will literally 'lean forward in their seats'. You will fully engage their minds and this will give you access to their enthusiasm and their creativity.

a.5   ad-libs

The verb 'to ad-lib' was first used in the USA. It's an abbreviated form of the Latin *ad libitum*, meaning 'to the full extent of one's wishes'. As such, ad-libbing is usually used to describe what you do when you improvise – say something without premeditation or preparation. Ad-libs are often humorous (*see* **h.5 humour, j.2 jokes, l.2 laughter**) but can also be sarcastic or cutting. They almost always represent a response – on the part of a presenter – to an unplanned event, such as a heckler, a projector breaking down or a total power failure. Sounds great, doesn't it? To be able to ad-lib well, to respond with one of those great, off-the-cuff, quotable witticisms at the drop of a hat, spontaneously, is an art. It certainly sounds like the sort of thing that you'd expect a professional presenter to be able to do.

But real ad-libs are very rare events in professional presenting. The reason for this is the risk involved in using them (*see* **r.5 risk**). For the off-the-cuff 'flip' remark that seems funny to you may actually be deeply offensive to someone in your audience; the impromptu witty response that springs to your lips in answer to a question from that audience may well be seen to be dismissive, even arrogant, by the questioner. Ad-libs also have the potential to lead both you and your audience astray. They can take you off-course, draw 'red herrings' across the carefully planned course of your presentation and consume – to no real effect – the time span you've been allocated.

What then, given that they *seem* to ad-lib, do professional presenters do? The answer is almost always that what appears to be an off-the-cuff 'ad-lib' is actually a well-used response that has been carefully rehearsed and practised. It's also one from a catalogue of responses that cover a wide range of circumstances and events. Building up such a catalogue takes time and effort. But it's worthwhile – as you'll find the next time your projector fails.

a.6   aims

See o.1 objectives and targets, w.4 why

a.7   alcohol

Let's be very clear about this – alcohol and professional presenting *do not* go together. You may feel that a drink will give you the 'dutch courage' that you need to get-up-and-go. You may even feel that having a drink with your audience before the presentation helps the way they feel about you and you about them. But alcohol doesn't work that way.

It's a drug; one that acts as a depressant and retards the activity of your brain. As a result – even after just one drink – you'll experience a mild sense of euphoria and loss of inhibition as the alcohol acts on those parts of your brain that control your behaviour and the emotions you experience. This alcohol will also impair your judgement, memory, concentration and co-ordination. You'll overestimate your skills, your judgement won't be quite as sharp as it was before you had a drink and your reactions will be slower. All of this is *bad* for your presentation; you'll lose your pace, your cutting edge and maybe even your sense of timing and you'll do that just when you need them most. Worst of all, you won't necessarily be aware of that loss, you'll blithely 'soldier-on' as if all was well. If you feel that this paints too dismal a picture there are three things that you can do to test your conviction that 'just one drink doesn't do you any harm'. First, type 'effects of alcohol' into your website browser and then read the hard fact material about alcohol that it brings up. Second, remember that awful after-dinner speech that you heard when the speaker had had 'one too many'. Third, ask yourself – and get an answer to – the question 'why do you need the drink?' (*see* **a.9 anxiety, c.15 courage, n.1 nerves, s.6 stage fright**).

a.8   anecdotes

See **s.7 stories**

a.9   anxiety

> *The characteristics of anxiety as an emotion are that it is distressing, and that its sources are indefinite. In the latter respect it is unlike fear which has reference to a specific aspect of the outside world.*

> Derek Russell Davis

See **n.1 nerves, s.6 stage fright**

a.10   appearance

There's an oft-quoted proverb that tells us that 'appearances are deceptive'. But for the professional presenter this isn't true. For them, appearances aren't deceptive; instead they're a key contributor to the way that a presenter reaches out to his or her audience. When a presenter stands up in front of an audience she or he is making a statement to them. But this statement is different from your usual presentation opening (*see* **o.2 openings**). It's a statement without words, a statement that the presenter makes without opening her or his mouth. It's the statement that her or his appearance makes.

As far as the professional presenter is concerned there are three key factors that contribute to her or his appearance. These are:

- his or her physical appearance
- the way she or he dresses
- the way she or he moves or stands.

All of these are important; important enough to be covered in detail in separate aspects elsewhere in this book (*see* **d.6 dress, f.5 feet, h.2 hands, l.10 looks and form, p.9 posture**). Work hard at these, get them all right, and you'll be awarded the three Cs. That is, your audience will see you as confident, competent and capable.

Get any one or more of them wrong and you'll be seen as the three Is – improbable, inadequate and incapable. And, don't forget, all of this happens before you've said a single word or projected a single slide or overhead on the screen!

a.11   appropriate

In a world that's becoming increasingly concerned with political correctness, the word 'appropriate' – as in 'specially fitted, suitable or proper' – and its antonym 'inappropriate' seem to get used a lot. The presentation is no exception to this phenomenon. But for presentations it is easier to identify what's appropriate by taking a look first at what's *in*appropriate.

The word 'inappropriate' – as in unsuitable, unfitting or improper – throws its net in a wide arc. It can be used to describe either the whole of a presentation or any one of its parts. It can also be used to describe the style – as in 'this is the way she or he presents' – of that presentation or its structure, content or objectives. The language used in a presentation serves as a good example of the range of inappropriateness and its boundaries with appropriateness. For this language can:

- be formal as in 'Mr Jones will now make a statement', or informal as in 'Bill Jones has something to tell you'
- use taboo words such as swear words or obscenities, or use euphemisms for them or avoid them all together
- involve slang words and expressions as in 'apples and pears' for stairs, or use correct, accurate, conventional names and terms
- draw on jargon as in technical terms, acronyms or buzz words, or make use of plain, straightforward language
- use clichés a lot, or avoid using them.

For the professional presenter the touchstone for most of what is appropriate in the language of his or her presentation lies in his or her knowledge of the audience (*see* **a.13 audiences**). The only exception to this is the use of obscenities. It is never, ever appropriate for a professional presenter to use taboo words or words that are obscene, coarse or even vulgar. Beyond obscenities, the issue changes. It switches from whether or not to use to how much to use. For example, the limited use of colloquial language – as in 'cool' or 'cred' – can tell an audience that you're thinking along the same lines. But it can also be seen to be patronizing and thus alienate an audience. To a greater or lesser degree the same situation also applies to slang (*see* **s.4 slang**), jargon (*see* **j.1 jargon**), euphemisms (*see* **e.6 euphemisms**) and clichés (*see* **c.7 clichés**).

This issue of what is appropriate or inappropriate for a presentation is a key one for the professional presenter. Get it wrong and your audience will either be offended, even angered, by what you say or bored by a presentation that's so p.c. it's soporific. Get it right, and find the right balance between these extremes, and you'll have a presentation that's *appropriate* because it:

• is tailor-made for that audience,
• takes into account the needs, hopes, desires and prejudices of that audience.

a.12   are you receiving me?

If your presentations are going to be professional then you have to communicate with your audience. Getting this right can easily be forgotten in the rush to perform. But it's so important, it's worth repeating.

| no communication = no gain |

For you, as a professional presenter, this act of communication won't just mean talking at your audience or showing them outstanding visual aids. There's much more to it than that – you're going to have to reach out to your audience, share with them your passion, fun and vision.

Doing this and doing it well means that you'll have put yourself in their shoes in the earliest stages of your preparation. Doing it well also means that ideas, information and even feelings flow between you and your audience. This is communication in its fullest sense (*see* **c.12 communication**); it's about you:

- sending out ideas, facts or feelings, and
- receiving back other ideas, facts or feelings from your audience.

To achieve this level of communication you're going to need to:

- have a clear objective or target for your presentation (*see* o.1 **objectives and targets**)
- prepare well (*see* p.12 **preparing your material, r.1 rehearsal**), and
- present professionally.

You've got to get *all* of these right. Doing that is a key issue. Slip up or don't make the grade on any of them and you'll fail – both to communicate and to reach your objective.

a.13 audiences

Your audience is important. Without them, you don't have a presentation. With them, you do have a presentation – but one that will be professional only if you integrate or blend that audience into your presentation. To do this you need to have your audience foremost in your mind when you prepare, produce and perform your presentation.

But this audience may be strangers to you and as a result you may feel that you know little about them. But that's not true. You do actually know quite a lot about them. As a professional presenter you'll know, for example, that they:

- are likely to be experienced adults
- will assume – at least initially – that you have the authority and ability to speak on your subject
- will, normally, be friendly and sympathetic but will expect you to speak effectively
- will listen – but only if you capture their imagination and show them that the subject of your presentation is important to them.

But that's not all that you'll know about them. Your experience and knowledge will tell you that they:

- might have a disability (*see* d.3 **disability awareness**)
- can be reached through their senses
- have other things on their mind and are easily distracted
- will have ups and downs in the level of their concentration

- remember better when you repeat things or present them with a pattern or structure
- respond to variety
- hear and forget, see and remember, do and understand.

They can also turn out to be difficult (*see* **d.2 difficult audiences, h.3 hecklers**).

b is for ...

b.1 bandwidth

In the jargon (*see* **j.1 jargon**) of communications technology, the bandwidth of a transmitted signal is a measure of the range of frequencies that the signal occupies. Generally speaking, the broader this range, the broader the bandwidth. A wide bandwidth means higher rates of data transmission and a narrow bandwidth means restricted rates of data transmission. In a qualitative sense, the broader the bandwidth of a signal the more complex the data that can be transmitted. For example, on the internet it takes more bandwidth to download a photograph in the same time as it takes to download a page of text. Similarly the internet transmission of large sound files, computer programs, or animated videos needs even more bandwidth and virtual reality and full-length three-dimensional audio/visual presentations require the most bandwidth of all.

Fortunately, as human beings, we're all equipped to handle broad bandwidth transmissions from each other. We all have broad waveband antennae in the form of our ears and eyes and we all have brains that are designed to work as incredibly powerful signal decoders. This means that we can receive static and moving images, text and speech all at the same time.

However, for the professional presenter, the idea isn't to flood all this bandwidth with data. It's the *quality* and *focus* of the information sent – or presented – that counts rather than its quantity or rate of transmission. The professional presenter needs to 'hit the spot' rather than 'boost the bandwidth'. To do this you'll have to:

- really know who your audience is, rather than just know names and job titles (*see* **a.13 audiences**)
- be aware of and understand what pressures they're subject to
- design your presentation to answer their needs rather than yours (*see* **o.1 objectives and targets, w.4 why**)
- use limited bandwidth to send your message – keep it simple, clear and short
- maximize the quality of your message.

Doing all of this may mean that, during the course of your preparation, you throw out or reject some of what you think is your best presentation material (*see* **e.1 editing**). It may also mean that you don't use the video that shows a particular but minor point so well. Simple, clear and short – rather than complex, obscure and lengthy – are the key words that lead to making sure that you use your presentation bandwidth effectively. They'll also lead to you achieving the objective of your presentation.

b.2   beginnings

You stand up; you look at the audience – and they look at you. It's time to begin. But that's not all it is. It's also the start of the two or so minutes that you've got in which to grab the attention

of your audience. For the next 120 or so seconds you have their full attention. But beware – by the end of it they'll have made their minds up about you. After that everything you say or do will be filtered by the impression you made in that first two minutes. What this means is that getting the beginning of your presentation right is incredibly important.

Get it wrong and you'll be swimming against the tide for the rest of your presentation. But what does 'right' mean? Let's answer that by looking at your opening sentence. This, believe it or not, is the most listened-to sentence of your presentation. Most times this happens because you're an unknown to them. It can also happen if the last presentation you gave to them was a good one. If you're going to take advantage of this then your opening sentence needs to:

- seize their attention and interest
- tell them that it's going to be worth paying attention to what you have to say.

So, very early in your opening two minutes, you need to give them some answers; answers to questions such as:

- why are they there?
- what's in it for them?
- is it important?

If you get it right, your audience will pay attention and listen to what you have to say because they can see that doing that might just lead to an advantage for them. This advantage will have many shapes and sizes. It can, for example, be about material gain, management approval, gaining prestige, acquiring 'special' information, achieving peace of mind or just plain simple satisfying curiosity. Take a look at **o.2 openings** for some ways of beginning your presentation.

b.3 believability

Believability, and its close cousin, credibility, are key, must-have, outcomes for a professional presenter. You've *got* to be convincing, believable and credible if you're going to succeed in the world of professional presenting. It doesn't matter how brilliantly you've prepared and structured your presentation, how excellent your slides or overheads are or how well you've rehearsed – all these will be of little or no use if your audience doesn't see you as being either believable or credible. The audience's view of you is what's important. But when the audience views you they don't just look; they:

- see and hear you, and then
- interpret what they see and hear.

It's in the second of these – the interpretation – that the influence of a number of factors creeps into the equation. Your believability as a presenter will be influenced by:

- what the audience expects to see
- what the audience thinks they see
- what sort of situation the seeing is done in
- what the beliefs, attitudes and prejudices of the audience are.

When you think about this you'll soon see that it makes sense. For example, a young long-haired male presenter dressed in jeans and a sweatshirt will have limited credibility with an audience of conservative bank or finance managers – unless, of course, he's known to have made a billion dollars by launching internet companies. Similarly a female presenter who started up and runs her own successful company will have high credibility with an audience of business women. There's quite a range of factors at work here with the presenter's age, physical appearance, dress, gender, style of speech and posture and body movement all being significant (*see* **n.2 non-verbal communication**). Seeing people as fitting into preconceived and oversimplified models of appearance and behaviour, or stereotyping, can be responsible for a lot of confusion here. It tries to tell us, for example, that all university or college professors look or behave like this or that all fair-haired blue-eyed men are inspiring or that red-haired people lose their tempers easily. But these stereotypes aren't just nonsense, they also confuse the audience when the presenter doesn't behave in the way that meets the audience's expectations.

Confusing, isn't it? But all is not lost. Here are some guidelines that will reduce the complications and positively influence the audience's perception of you as a professional presenter:

- research your audience – find out all you can about their expectations, beliefs, experiences and prejudices (*see* **a.13 audiences, d.2 difficult audiences**)
- make sure that you take your audience into account at every stage of your preparation (*see* **p.12 preparing your material, r.1 rehearsal**)
- prepare your dress and appearance as carefully as you prepare your material (*see* **a.10 appearance, d.6 dress, l.10 looks and form**)
- prepare the presenting environment (*see* **c.1 can you all hear me?, c.3 chairs, l.1 laser pointers, l.4 lcd panels, m.2 microphones, m.4 multimedia projectors, o.3 overhead projectors, v.1 video conferencing**)
- prepare your audience by making sure that you are introduced accurately (*see* **i.10 introductions**) and that your opening (*see* **o.2 openings**) tells them what you're going to talk about, how long you'll take to do that, and when they can ask questions
- perform your presentation with care, skill and professionalism (*see* **a.5 ad-libs, a.7 alcohol, e.8 eye contact, g.4 gestures, u.3 using your voice**)

But even when you do all of these there's still no guarantee that you'll be believable to your audience. Professional presenters know this and they work hard to stay in touch with the audience because of this. It's key to their believability. The reactions, postures and facial expressions of the audience all provide information – telling the presenter whether she or he is in touch with and believable to that audience (*see* **f.4 feedback**).

b.4 black screens

Black screens aren't a fashion statement – they're a necessity. Professional presenters use them a lot. They are what they seem to be – black, without detail of any sort and very boring to look at. But they're also very useful. You can use them, for example, to:

- switch the audience's attention away from the screen and back to you
- provide a visual break point or boundary between different sections of your presentation
- enable you and the audience to concentrate on a question–answer routine without the distraction of an attention-grabbing visual on the screen

- enable you to leave an inactive projector on, thus avoiding a blank, white-glare, screen and minimizing the number of bulb-busting switch-ons and switch-offs
- provide the starting point for a visually dramatic presentation opening.

Remember, though, that if you're going to use black screens a lot then you'll need a quieter-than-average projector. Noisy projectors and black screens aren't a good combination; they'll irritate your audience rather than interest or stimulate them. Create your black screen by:

- masking your ohp transparency with a piece of card – paper isn't opaque enough (*see* **o.3 overhead projectors, o.4 overheads**)
- clicking on the 'black screen' item of the relevant pull-down menu of your presentation software when you're using an lcd display panel or a multimedia projector (*see* **m.4 multimedia projectors, o.3 overhead projectors, p.10 powerpoint presentations**).

b.5 boredom

When it comes to definitions the dictionary is a good place to start. If you look up 'boredom' there you'll find it defined as 'wearied, suffering from ennui'. It's a common enough condition, we've all suffered from it; we've all been bored by what we've been doing or by the person who we've been listening to. In the presentation situation, there are two sides to boredom:

• your audience can be bored by or with you, or
• you, as a presenter, can be bored with the presentation that you're doing or the audience.

 All of these are catastrophic. They're also, for you as a professional presenter, *totally* unacceptable. Boredom is, as someone once put it, the world's second-worst crime; the first is being a bore. Boredom wastes time, stifles creativity and even, it is said, causes revolutions. If you're boring your audience then you *aren't* a professional presenter. Doing something about boredom – and doing that before it happens – is a must for a professional presenter (*see* **e.3 enthusiasm, p.3 passion**).

Here are some tips to help you achieve this:

• If an oncoming presentation seems unexciting or even boring then find out why – and then do something about it, or get somebody else to do the presentation.
• If you're in a sequence of repeating a presentation to different audiences and it's beginning to feel stale or boring then review the presentation material to see if it could be improved or changed. Try to identify the parts of the presentation where you feel 'flat' and then see how you can change that part of the presentation.
• Get back in touch with the core message of the presentation and use that to reinvigorate or recharge your performance.
• Start your presentation in a different way.
• Get back to basics, get focused on your audience's needs.

b.6 breaks

The professional presenter knows a thing or two about breaks. The first of these is that if a presentation needs a break – because its time span has exceeded 20 minutes – then it's way too long (*see* **l.7 length**). The second is that when an audience is facing a lecture (*see* l.6 **lectures**) or a sequence of presentations (*see* **t.2 team presentations, t.6 training presentations**) then that audience will need breaks at strategically placed times in the schedule. Breaks appear to be about giving your audience the chance to use the washroom or toilet, have a cigarette, stretch their legs or make that important phone-call. But breaks have other less obvious – but just as important – purposes.

When the professional presenter takes a break it's not just about answering his or her audience's immediate needs. It's also about:

- having a personal 'time-out'
- preparing for what comes next
- allowing the audience to digest what they've seen and heard
- signalling a change in subject or pace.

For these and other reasons the professional presenter will:

- finish the pre-break lecture or presentation on an upbeat, with the audience wanting more and knowing what comes next
- tell the audience – clearly and audibly – what time the next presentation or lecture will start
- always – unless the building's on fire – start at that time
- begin the next presentation or lecture by reminding the audience where they'd left off before the break.

The duration of the break is also important. Too long a break and your grip on your audience will have begun to loosen; too short a break and somebody won't have had time for that coffee that they need so desperately. Ten to 15 minutes is a good length for a non-meal break, while an hour to an hour and a quarter will suffice for a well-organized lunch break. Do make sure that the back-up facilities – coffee, tea, lunch, etc. – are ready and available before you break and don't announce the break before they are.

b.7 brevity

Brevity isn't just the soul of wit; it's also – in professional presentations – a key factor in the way you gain access to your audience's hearts and minds. Brevity is *always* a virtue in presentations. Brevity sharpens the meaning of your message whereas verbosity clouds it, makes it diffuse and unclear. Brevity follows when you keep your sentences short, your verbs active and nouns concrete (*see* **s.3 simplify**). Here are some examples:

Use	Don't use
be	exist
go	proceed
know	comprehend
by	by means of
if	in the event of
near	in the vicinity of
to	with a view to
think	of the opinion that
will	take steps to
to	in order to

Brevity is good. It will leave your audience feeling that you've said just enough and no more, and left them with the last word.

To be effective brevity needs to go hand in hand with:

- directness
- lucidity
- simplicity
- vigour.

(*See also* **a.3 accentuate the positive, l.7 length, p.1 pace.**)

c.1   can you all hear me?

Being heard clearly and consistently by your audience is incredibly important. Seems obvious, doesn't it? But how many presentations have you sat through where you've strained to hear what the presenter was saying? Alternatively, how many have you sat through when the sound was too loud, out of balance or full of feedback? All of these situations place a barrier between the presenter and the audience. They limit the presenter's ability to reach, motivate or inspire that audience and they all, in their various ways, come together to make up what's called the presentation 'sound barrier'.

 Professional presenters bypass that barrier by having a sound rehearsal. When you think about this, you'll see that it's entirely logical. If you've ever sung a song or played a piece of music in public you'll know that you wouldn't consider doing it without adequate preparation or rehearsal. Nor should you consider speaking to an audience with any less a degree of preparation. However, conducting a sound rehearsal properly isn't something that you can do on your own. You're going to need help and the sort of help you'll need will depend on whether you are going to use a sound system to amplify your voice.

Sound systems are usually used in medium- and larger-sized rooms or halls. But size isn't the only factor that you need to take into account. Even small and medium conference or meeting rooms – the ones that don't usually need a sound system – can have acoustic problems. Not having curtains, drapes and even carpets can lead to echoes, while having them can swallow, attenuate or flatten your voice. What you must do is to test your voice in the room in order to check out its acoustics. Get somebody to walk around the room while you talk from the presenting position. Vary your voice level and the pace of your speech while they tell you – using simple, agreed hand signals – whether you can or can't be heard clearly. Don't forget, though, that the acoustics of the room will change when it is full of people. Their clothing and bodies will dampen the sound. While this will reduce reverberation and echoing, it'll also flatten or dampen your voice. In a room that has a 'flat' acoustic you may even find that an audience can absorb too much sound, making what you say difficult to hear. Avoid this, if possible, by visiting the room while someone else is presenting and adjusting the volume or pace of your presentation as needed. Alternatively, have somebody in your audience who monitors your audibility and signals you – subtly and discreetly – if there's a problem.

If you're using a sound system, there ought to be a sound technician to go with it. Call on him or her to help you with your sound rehearsal. If there isn't a technician, then make sure you get someone who knows what they are doing with a sound system. It's often thought that adjusting and operating a sound system is an easy task, just like turning the volume up or down on a radio. But sound systems are often very complicated creatures with as many as 30 adjustment controls for each channel. During your rehearsal, the sound technician can adjust the volume and mix levels for the main speakers that deliver sound to your audience. This is also the time to find out what sort of microphone you're going to use and to get used to it (*see* **m.2 microphones**).

If you are presenting in a very big hall or arena then the system will probably have monitor speakers. These are driven by a separate sound system and are designed to let you hear how you sound. Without this you'll have no idea whether you're speaking too loudly or too quickly. The only way the monitor system can be adjusted properly is by working with the sound technician during a sound rehearsal.

However you do your sound rehearsal it should have three targets. For when conducted well your sound rehearsal will:

- get you used to speaking in the room or hall that you're going to present in
- enable you to bypass the presentation sound barrier
- do away with the need for you to ask your audience 'Can you all hear me?'

c.2 cartoons

Cartoons are, by and large, good for presentations. You can use them in a variety of ways, for example to

- illustrate a point
- change the pace of your presentation
- lighten up an unremittingly heavy message
- break the ice with your audience.

But, like all good things, cartoons need to be used with discretion and care.

Too many cartoons or a cartoon at the wrong time or in the wrong place and your audience will see you as being too lightweight or frivolous or even lacking in concern or tact. Getting your cartoons right takes skill and practice; they have to be chosen with care and seamlessly integrated into your presentation. The key factors of the professional presenter's cartoon use are:

Why?

 You need to be very clear in your own mind about why you're going to use a cartoon. They are not add-on optional extras that are put in for a bit of light relief. If they are going to have a place in your presentation it must be because they make a significant and worthwhile addition to it. Be clear about what your cartoon is going to add and whether you *really* need that addition.

What?

The 'what' of presentation cartoons involves a number of crucial issues. You'll need to decide, for example:

- what your cartoon is going to be about
- what style of cartoon will be appropriate
- what's the reason for the cartoon being there?

While deciding these never forget that a cartoon is, by definition, a humorous or topical drawing. Its intention should be to:

- amuse your audience
- caricature something or somebody
- hold somebody or something up to ridicule.

By now you will have realized that this is where the care and discretion element of your cartoon use comes in. Cartoons – like jokes (*see* **h.5 humour**) – should be:

- chosen with both a specific audience and a particular presentation in mind
- capable of being easily understood and appreciated by that audience.

Your cartoons should not – under any circumstances – be gender biased, racist or ageist. Nor should they be – without prior permission – against a member of the audience or someone who the audience knows well.

Who?

Since it's your presentation, the 'who' of cartoons is primarily about who creates the cartoon. We all know someone who's a tyro cartoonist; you may even feel that, given the clip art resources available these days, you could create a cartoon. The answer is 'don't' – not just don't do it, don't even think about doing it! The reason for this is straightforward – your cartoons need to be professional in both drawing standard and in content. It's also actually quite rare for professional presenters to be professional cartoonists too. So get your cartoons from a professional (*see* **Taking it Further**). But don't steal or borrow them – respect your fellow professional and pay him or her for their use.

c.3   chairs

How many times have you sat through a presentation and found your concentration waning as the discomfort of your chair gradually made itself known, or struggled to see what's on the screen through the back of someone else's head? If you've ever encountered these situations then you'll know that chairs are important. Seems obvious, doesn't it? After all, your audience sits on chairs, don't they? But chairs are often treated as a mundane and unimportant detail – despite the fact that they can turn your audience off in as little as two minutes.

The professional presenter's approach to chairs asks three questions:

- how comfortable or uncomfortable are the audience's chairs?
- are these chairs in the right position?
- do I need a chair?

Let's look at each of these in turn.

Seat comfort

This is one of those things that's noticed when it *isn't* there – that is, when your seat isn't comfortable. Professional presenters check the audience seats before they present. They ask themselves 'Could I sit here for 20 to 30 minutes without becoming uncomfortable?' If the answer is no then a professional presenter will cut material and time out of his or her presentation. He or she will also stay alert for signs of audience discomfort, adjusting the pace and content of the presentation if and when it appears.

Seat layout

Seat layouts vary a lot. They reflect, amongst other things, the size of the audience, the formality of the meeting and whether your presentation is just one part of a bigger event or meeting. The upsides and downsides of the layout alternatives are given elsewhere (*see* **l.3 layout**). But whatever layout is used the professional presenter makes sure that all of the audience can easily see him or her and the screen on which the material is being projected.

Getting this right isn't always easy. You may have to contend with a unique room shape or geometry, the lack of power outlets, the shortness of the projector's only power cable or the fact that the screen available is bolted to the 'wrong' wall. Getting all this sorted out is important. It's important that your screen is in the 'right' position relative to your audience (*see* **s.2 screens**) and that your audience can see you (*see* **p.7 podiums and lecterns**). It's also important to sort all this out *before* your audience enters the room – the presentation that starts with a brief session of 'musical chairs' doesn't leave a good impression.

Seat for the presenter?

There are very few occasions when a presenter will need a seat. Even when a chair is offered professional presenters rarely use them and will often remove them from the presenting area. There are at least three good reasons for this:

- presenting from the sitting position can be seen as indicating a lack of enthusiasm, or even as being discourteous
- sitting in a chair limits the extent to which you can fill your lungs and this limits your speech volume and duration
- the audience's view of you is limited.

When you add to these the fact that a lot of what a presenter says to an audience uses body language rather than spoken words you'll see that sitting to present *isn't* a good idea. However, every rule has its exceptions and there are some situations when it's OK for a presenter to use a chair. These include:

- when the presenter's mobility is limited (*see* **d.3 disability awareness**)
- when the presenter is formally introduced by another speaker (*see* **i.10 introductions**)
- when the audience breaks up into discussion groups as part of a training exercise or a participatory presentation (*see* **p.2 participative presentations, t.6 training presentations**).

c.4   challenge

Presentations, like life, are full of challenges. The professional presenter knows this and uses those challenges as a launch pad from which to move his or her presenting to a higher level of performance. These presenting challenges generally arrive in three waves:

- *before* the presentation
- *during* the presentation
- *after* the presentation.

Pre-presentation challenges are about things like preparing a presentation on a new subject, getting geared up to present with a team of strangers, preparing a presentation for someone else – such as your boss – to perform, getting ready to do a presentation at short notice or creating a presentation for that *very* important sales pitch. All of these, and others, are challenges that can be answered and overcome by hard work, clear thinking and meticulous preparation.

During the presentation challenges are different because their arrival is more instant, more 'real-time'. You're on your feet speaking when someone asks that unwelcome question, you're in full flow when the disagreeable heckler raises his or her voice and you're onto the next slide when someone in the audience tells you that they disagree with your facts. Professional presenters take these challenges head on. They acknowledge and accept the audience's right to challenge – almost to the point of welcoming it – and they strive to answer the challenge in ways that are open, truthful and honest. But these aren't the only challenges you'll face during a presentation. There will be disasters (*see* **d.4 disasters and how to cope**), you'll find that you've been allocated that after-lunch 'dead' zone (*see* **d.1 dead zones**) or, for reasons that have nothing to do with you, your audience turns out to be preoccupied with other matters or just plain difficult (*see* **d.2 difficult audiences**). Again the key to handling these challenges lies in taking them head on rather than trying to avoid or ignore what's happening before your very eyes.

After the presentation challenges are as different again. For now it's over, now you've done what was planned and needed, now you have (or haven't) scored another victory. The challenge here is simple and straightforward. It lies in the way you answer the question that asks if you learned anything by doing that presentation. If the answer is yes and you can identify what it was then you've answered the challenge. If the answer is no, then the challenge changes to that of finding out *why* you didn't learn something. After all, presentations are full of challenges, aren't they!

c.5   charts

See **g.6 graphs and charts**

c.6   checklists

Checklists are used everywhere. Airline pilots use them before take-off, astronauts before re-entry and deep sea divers before going down. Professional presenters use them as well. This is because a checklist is, at its core, a 'ready means of reference, comparison, or verification'. As such a checklist is *very* useful. It'll remind you about things that you might have forgotten, tell you that things are as they ought to be and give you the confidence to move forward. Here are some examples for you to try out or add to before you start writing and using your own checklists:

Audience need checklist

(To be used before presentation material is prepared.)

- Who are the audience?
- Why are you presenting to them?
- Who are the key decision takers?
- What information do they want or need?
- Why do they want or need it?
- Who is going to be affected by it – who stands to gain or lose?
- What are the most important bits of this information?
- Why is this information relevant now?
- How did that situation come about?
- Will that situation change – if so, when?
- Are there any disability factors?

Screen checklist

(To be used before presentation.)

Is your screen height:

- about one-sixth of the distance from the screen to the back row of seats? or
- about half the distance from the screen to the first row of seats?

Is your screen width:

- no more than one-sixth of the distance from the screen to the back row of seats? or
- at least two-thirds of the distance from the screen to the first row of seats?

Is the base of your screen:

- at least 1.25 metres above the floor, so that people seated toward the rear of the audience can see it?

Is your screen's aspect or height/width ratio:

- 1:1 if you are using an overhead projector?
- 3:2 if you are using a slide projector?
- 4:3 if you are using an lcd projector?

Confirmation checklist

(To be used no less than a week before the scheduled date of your presentation.)

Previously agreed:			
Date:	– has this been changed?	Yes ☐	No ☐
Starting time:	– has this been changed?	Yes ☐	No ☐
Duration:	– has this been changed?	Yes ☐	No ☐
Location	– has this been changed?	Yes ☐	No ☐
Subject	– is this still as agreed?	Yes ☐	No ☐
Audience composition or size	– are these still the same?	Yes ☐	No ☐
Equipment to be provided	– will this be available?	Yes ☐	No ☐
Room layout	– is this as requested?	Yes ☐	No ☐
Rehearsal time	– is this available?	Yes ☐	No ☐
Room access prior to presentation	– can this be arranged?	Yes ☐	No ☐

Pre-presentation checklist

(To be used on day of presentation.)

- Check room and chair layout and change as required.
- Check sound system and adjust as required.
- Check projector/screen positioning – adjust as required.
- If no sound system, check audibility around room.
- Check slide carousel, order of slides or overheads and focus on projector.
- Make sure person who is introducing you has all information needed.
- Check disability factors – access, sound loops, etc.

- Check your appearance.
- Remind yourself of your objective.
- Relax – you're ready.

c.7 clichés

A cliché is a phrase or quotation that has achieved significant and major over-use. Clichés are amazingly common in the English language – the earliest recorded cliché dates back over a thousand years! More contemporary clichés include phrases such as 'bottom line', 'brand image', 'dizzy heights', 'tower of strength', 'back to basics' and 'trickle down'. Clichés – when chosen well – can convey the meaning of what you say in a way that's concise and efficient. They can also be used to advantage when tact, discretion or evasiveness is needed, as in 'gardening leave' or 'victim of circumstances' (*see* **e.6 euphemisms**). But there are disadvantages. An excess of clichés leads to sentences and statements that are almost devoid of real meaning; sentences that are, as someone once said, 'the sort of things that we say to one another to make sure we're still alive'. Yet this doesn't seem to limit the use of the cliché. Speakers who want to manipulate their audiences often use them to great effect. These speakers use clichés to deceive these audiences into thinking that more has been said than is the case and that significant words have been spoken when the reality has been wall-to-wall clichés.

 Professional presenters are very careful with clichés. They are aware that it's all too easy to slide down the slippery slope (yet another cliché!) that leads from the occasional use of a cliché to major over-use. So beware, for even a single well-worn cliché – when misused – can bring sudden death to an otherwise competent and well-crafted presentation. It will irritate your audience, sound trite and hackneyed to their once-receptive ears and stick out like the proverbial 'sore thumb' from the smooth flow of your polished presentation.

c.8 climax

One of the meanings of the verb 'to climax' is 'to ascend, to rise by successive steps, to come to a culmination or highest point'. For the professional presenter that 'highest point' isn't one that's stumbled upon or reached by accident or error. It's the outcome of an arranged progression; one that starts at the presentation's opening, takes the audience through a sequence of revelations and then, finally, arrives at its end point, where you'll find the climax of the presentation. It's that sentence, that image, that set of words that you want to 'burn' into the minds of your audience. It's those words that you want them to remember when all the rest have been forgotten.

Sounds dramatic, doesn't it? Well, climaxes are dramatic (*see* **d.5 drama**). After all, to get to an effective climax you'll have moved your audience. They'll have been on a journey; a journey that has taken them from disinterest to interest, from cynicism to commitment or from neutrality to engagement. It's this dramatic content that gives the climax its impact. A really effective climax reaches an audience – it can be greeted by applause, even stunned silence. But too many climaxes – as in a close chain of mini-climaxes or a completion that comes with a cloud of smoke – can result in climax 'over-kill'. When this happens your presentation will appear out-of-balance to your audience, they'll become confused, misunderstand your message. You'll get the same sort of result if you climax too soon. Your audience will be left wondering why you're up there, still talking. They may even feel that they must have missed a key point earlier in the presentation.

 The key to the success of your presentation's climax is to make sure that it's at the end of your presentation and that both you and your audience arrive at it together.

c.9   clip art

You can find clip art everywhere. It can come from:

- your own collection – the images, cartoons and pictures that you've clipped and scanned into your computer over the years
- the clip art collection that you purchase from your favourite software house
- the presentation or word-processing software that you use every day
- one of the many clip art collections you can find on the Web.

These give you an enormous range of images. They reach back into the early days of printed material and, of course, reflect not only the immense variety of drawing styles that have waxed and waned during that time but also an incredible range of subjects. You can, it seems, find clip art on almost any subject.

But wherever it comes from and whatever its subject or style might be, the problem is the same – it's pre-used, pre-owned, second-hand material. It has, by definition, been cut out of, extracted from, its original point of use. This tells you that clip art is material that:

• has been taken out of its original context
• often reflects the styles and fashions of other times and places
• is available to *everybody* else.

What this means is that when you use clip art in your presentation it can, despite your best efforts, leave your audience feeling that you're using images that:

• are commonplace and prosaic
• aren't appropriate to the subject of your presentation
• don't fit in with the style of your presentation.

Your audience may also feel that you've taken the easy or lazy route in preparing your presentation. None of this is good, either for you or for your hopes of achieving the objective of your presentation. Because of this it's best that you *don't* use clip art unless it's relevant, appropriate and *absolutely* necessary.

c.10   closing your presentation

The closure is *the* most important part of your presentation. It's where you do – or don't – hit your target; it's where you achieve – or don't achieve – the objective that you set yourself when you started out to prepare for this presentation (*see* **i.4 influence, persuasion or information?, o.1 objectives and targets, w.4 why**). If you're in 'sync' with your audience you'll realize – as you approach this closure – that you're going to get some answers to some important questions. Questions like 'Does the audience agree with me?', 'Will they take the actions I've suggested?' or 'Will they buy?' will all be answered.

Professional presenters realize that closure is a one-shot event – you've only one chance at it. Once it's done, that's it; there's no going back, no re-adjustment, no subtle re-alignment. The close is so important it's almost like you decide what it is and then build your presentation around it. But that's not all it is. Because from the audience's point of view, the close is what they came for. The rest of your presentation – opening, middle, visual aids – has been a build-up to, a preparation for, this close. Now – if you got all of that right – you'll be ready to deliver. This means that the way you close your presentation needs to be as full of impact and attention-grabbing as the way you started it. Professional presentations end on a high note and provide a clear indication of what you expect to happen next.

Your audience should also be left in no doubt that it is the end of your presentation, by both your manner and the words that you speak. A really professional closure will start some five or six minutes before the actual end; it will go through a sequence of subtle changes in the pace and tone of your speech, your gestures and posture and, of course, what you say. If you get it right, if you hit the spot, you'll have made a strong impression on your audience. If that does happen you may find that they sit quietly while they absorb what you've said and the fact that you've finished saying it. When this happens it's the ultimate accolade – you've really touched the hearts and minds of your audience. So when that does happen don't be anxious. Sit quietly and patiently, wait for them to catch their breath and for their reaction. What this reaction is will depend upon where you are and who your audience is. It might be applause, the beginnings of a discussion, a question or a thank-you. If these don't happen then don't worry; just recognize that it's:

• down to you to remind them that it's their turn to contribute
• time for you to check out why your ending didn't work.

Take a look at **e.2 endings** for some proven and reliable ways of closing your presentation with professional 'polish'.

c.11   colours

There's more to colour than meets the eye. Choose the right colour and your presentation will shout out your message, grab your audience's attention. Choose the wrong colour and you'll get exactly the opposite effect; your audience will turn away, they'll miss the point of your message altogether. Colour communicates, it speaks a universal language, one that bypasses the need for words. It's used in this way, for example, in signs, signals, maps and advertisements. Research tells us that colour:

- increases your willingness to read what you see
- has a substantial influence on your motivation and participation
- enhances your learning and increases what you retain of what you've learned
- accounts for most of why you accept or reject something
- is *the* critical factor in how you feel about what you see.

In the light of all of this you shouldn't be surprised when you learn that colour adverts for a product outsell black-and-white ones for the same product by almost 90 per cent. When it comes to presentations colour is just as powerful. Presentations that really use colour effectively, rather than are just colourful:

- make you, the presenter, appear more professional
- are better at getting your message over
- are remembered for longer.

All of this tells you that colour – and the way that you use it – can make a significant contribution to your presentation. Get it right and you'll liven up your slides and emphasize your message; get it wrong and your slide presentation will look a muddled, multicoloured mess. For professional presenters, the effective use of colour results from the choices they make about the background colour of their slides or overheads and the colours used for the material that's viewed against that background.

Background colours are important. They are the largest area of colour on your slides or overheads and as such they have considerable influence over the atmosphere you want to create for your presentation. Each of the eight basic colours will convey a different impression:

- **Blue** Probably the most popular background colour, blue is associated with peacefulness, contemplation, patience and competence.
- **Green** Green is said to promote audience feedback. It's also considered restful and refreshing and is associated with harmony, growth, money and relaxation.
- **Purple** A rich, impressive colour, purple is about spirituality and vitality. Dark shades of purple are good for backgrounds and lighter shades for accents.

- **Red** A hot, dominant colour, red calls attention to messages and also stimulates audiences into action – but don't use it in a financial presentation.
- **Orange** Orange is a cheerful colour that encourages communication.
- **Yellow** Yellow is bright, cheerful, enthusiastic, optimistic and warm.
- **White** White represents a blank canvas and communicates freshness, innocence, neutrality and purity.
- **Black** Black is associated with sophistication, independence, emphasis and finality.

Some of these colours – such as red, orange, yellow and black – are more suitable for the text and figures you'll need to locate against these backgrounds. These are 'warm' colours that are said to visually advance or 'pop out'. The remaining blues, greens, purples and whites are said to be 'cool' colours. These visually recede and as such are all excellent background choices. But the key to making sure you choose the 'right' colours for your text and figures lies in choosing colours that work well together. You can do this by using the colour wheel.

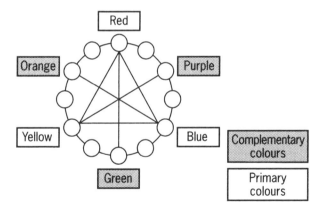

Each primary colour has a colour that it relates well to. These are called complementary colours and are as follows:

Primary	Complementary
Red	Green
Blue	Orange
Yellow	Purple

In addition to the complementary colours, each colour also relates well to a complex colour near its complementary colour, as, for example, orange and green-blue. You can use these colour combinations in different ways, for example a purple background with yellow for text or a blue background and gold for text.

 The colours that you use in your presentation should never be chosen in an arbitrary or subjective way. If your audience includes people with visual impairments, for example, you'll need to use maximum contrast in your visuals (*see* **d.3 disability awareness**). Using a colour because you like it isn't good enough. You need a plan, a presentation palette, if you're going to use colour effectively.

c.12 communication

Let's start with the obvious. Communication – or rather whether you get your communication right or wrong – is a core issue in *all* presentations. Get it wrong and both you and your audience will be, literally and figuratively, lost. Get it right and your audience won't just understand your message – they'll refine and add to it. But, time after time, books about presentation come up with a view of presenting as a one-way process. It's seen as a one-sided give-and-take – you give out the information and your audience *has* to take it. But this isn't real communication. Nor is it professional presenting. For both of these involve a two-way process; one that involves sending *and* receiving, talking *and* listening (*see* **f.4 feedback, l.9 listening**). It's no accident that you are born with two ears and only one mouth! Professional presenters use all of these as well as the rest of their bodies. As well as speaking, they listen, gesture, smile, whisper, wave, frown and point; sometimes they even shout or cry. As well as doing all of this they also:

- think their presentation through and plan it meticulously
- consciously choose its content, style and method with both care and due regard for their audience
- get clear about the objective of their presentation
- decide whether they are influencing, instructing or exchanging information
- anticipate and eliminate what might cause it to fail.

If there's one thing that all professional presenters have in common it's that they are, above all, good communicators.

c.13 conference presentations

Presenting at a conference can be a scary experience. When you do, it's not a small or medium group that you're presenting to – it's a huge crowd, a vast sea of half-seen anonymous faces. This often means an increase in pre-presentation nerves – almost in proportion to the size of the audience! There are very few presenters who don't have a difficulty of one sort or another with conference presenting. It's as if it is the Mount Everest of presenting. But, in reality, the nerves, stresses and strains that you suffer are much the same as those that you experience when you present in front of a smaller audience – they only *seem* to be different (*see* **a.9 anxiety, f.3 fear, n.1 nerves, r.2 relaxation**). Nevertheless, there are some features of conference presenting that are different and well worth taking note of.

Conference guidelines

Most conference organizers issue guidelines to potential speakers. These are usually about things like speech or presentation length, the use of slides or overheads, the type of equipment available and the way questions are to be handled. Take note of these but, if you decide to do something different, do check it out with the conference organizers – earlier rather than later.

Session title and purpose

Choose these with care. Most of your potential audience will get their first impression of your session from this title. When it appears in the conference programme it must catch the reader's attention and create a mental picture of what's going to happen in the session. The session's purpose or objective must be one that's attractive or interesting to conference attendees.

Session description

Make sure that the description you give to the conference organizers is clear, concise and accurate. This description isn't just about attracting any old audience, it should be about attracting an audience that's interested in what you have to offer. As these descriptions are often rewritten in the months before the conference, don't get worried if you are asked to revise your initial draft.

Session format

Conference session formats can vary a lot. Here are some of the commoner alternatives:

- a formal lecture followed by a question-and-answer session
- panel session involving short talks by three or four presenters followed by discussion among the participants, chaired by a session leader
- workshop session involving interactive participatory exercises
- roundtable session or a guided discussion of specific defined issues.

Make sure that you know what sort of format the conference organizers are proposing for your session. If you're not happy with their proposals say so – but suggest a constructive alternative.

Length

A typical conference session lasts for 75 minutes. If you're speaking to the formal lecture format allow about one-third of this for questions. If you're using the panel format with three speakers then allow 15 minutes for each presentation, leaving 30 minutes for questions and discussion.

Session handouts

Handouts are a good way of reinforcing the core message of your presentation. An effective handout fits on a single A4 or foolscap sheet. It gives a summary of the main points of this message, lists relevant resources, and suggests ways that audience members can use to follow up on what they've learned. Ask the conference organizer to copy this for you and arrange for these to be placed at the hall exits during – not before – your session.

Introductions

Make sure that you make early contact with the person who's going to introduce your session. It's often useful to do this before the conference – the organizers should be prepared to give you a name and contact telephone number or e-mail address. Make sure that they know all that they need to know in order to give you a good introduction (*see* **i.10 introductions**).

Help

If you've never spoken at a conference before it's worth talking things over with someone who has. Listen to and absorb what they say – they have experienced and survived all that you're going to go through.

c.14   copyboards

See **w.3 whiteboards**

c.15   courage

It takes courage to do a presentation. If you don't believe that then you're either an inexperienced presenter or, worse still, one of those over-confident, maybe even arrogant, presenters who think that the act of getting up to do a presentation is a 'breeze'. These attitudes are, at best, unrealistic and uninformed and, at worst, very risky – for both the presenter and his or her audience. The act of giving a presentation is, above all, an act of courage. There are no stunt people, no deputies or substitutes to stand in for you when it comes to *your* presentation. It's something that *you* do, rather than have others do it for you.

The courage that a professional presenter shows is a rare and special gift. He or she repeatedly immerses him or herself in the critical gaze of others, he or she persistently exposes him or herself to the judgement of an audience. It's a brave, courageous act, one that draws heavily upon the presenter's individual resources. But courage – as most of us know – is a virtue that you can never be quite sure that you'll have enough of until the time comes to use it, and you can't be certain that it will be there when the next presentation comes around. If you – like most people – have difficulty finding your courage here are some tips that might help:

- Recognize that being courageous doesn't mean being free from fear.
- Try facing your fear by working out what's the worst that's likely to happen – and then working out what you'd do if it did happen (*see* **d.4 disasters and how to cope, f.3 fear**).
- Don't cut corners on your preparation – do it thoughtfully, carefully and thoroughly (*see* **p.12 preparing your material**).
- Don't skimp on rehearsals – work hard to get it *all* right (*see* **r.1 rehearsal**).

- Know *exactly* what you're going to do or say when you first get up to speak (*see* **b.2 beginnings, o.2 openings**).
- Face your fear as yourself – and then put it aside.
- Be prepared to risk the known for the unknown, the familiar for the unfamiliar.

c.16   credibility

See **b.3 believability**

d is for . . .

d.1   dead zones

The dead zone or, as the seafarers of old called it, the graveyard watch, lay between midnight and 4 a.m. It was the time when the ship was silent, the time when disaster usually struck. But the presentation dead zone is different. It depends upon what comes before it and its disasters are presentational rather than nautical. The presentation dead zone lies in the slot that follows lunch or dinner. It's then that the physiological imperative that shifts blood from the head down to the stomach – in order to digest food – overtakes us all. As a result your audience will suffer from a torpor that would have been astonishing in an earlier slot and you – a professional presenter – will be prone to make mistakes that are worthy of a novice presenter. Alcohol can also have a role here. That extra glass of wine will play havoc with both your and your audience's concentration and reaction rates (*see* **a.7 alcohol**).

So what can you do if you find yourself presenting in the dead zone? The first action is one that you must take well before you arrive at the hall, room or office that you're presenting in. This action is really a straightforward and simple one: you must do all that you can to be given another time, to get this slot changed. But if that fails then your next action must be to review your presentation. Make sure that it has:

- a message that's straightforward and to the point
- a time-span that's limited
- a handout that contains the detailed stuff.

It's worth making sure that this handout is on your audience's seats when they return from their meal – even if you have to put it there yourself. It's also important that you let your audience know – in both your presentation and the handout – how they can follow up with you.

d.2   difficult audiences

Professional presenters *never* make assumptions about their audiences. It's a foolish (or arrogant) presenter who ever assumes that an audience is going to be 'easy'. Professional presenters integrate or blend their audiences into the presentations; they make sure that their needs and wants are taken into account from the earliest steps of that presentation's preparation (*see* **a.13 audiences**). Failing to do this isn't just foolish or short-sighted, it's also an act of discourtesy towards that audience; one that often represents the first step towards a failed presentation.

But the first step towards a successful presentation – one that really reaches your audience – is different. It lies in the recognition that *all* audiences have the potential to be difficult. It's also a step that opens up the potential to turn them into a great audience – one that you really feel in tune with, one that's really responsive and asks all the right questions. The key to all of this lies, of course, in your preparation (*see* **p.12 preparing your material, r.1 rehearsal**); preparation that will take your audience into account every step of the way. But even when you have done all of this you may still find that you've difficulties with your audience. This can

happen for a variety of reasons. Your audience will, for example, become difficult when you deliver your presentation without enthusiasm (*see* **e.3 enthusiasm, p.3 passion**), too slowly (*see* **p.1 pace**) or without audience interaction (*see* **f.4 feedback, l.9 listening**).

Any or all of these has the potential to turn the best of audiences into a mob that's after your blood. Professional presenters do all of these things from time to time – but always in the rehearsal room and never in front of a live audience! But even when you've prepared well and rehearsed until you're word-perfect there's still one other thing that you need to look out for – and that's your need to control your audience. Overdo this control and any vestige of normal give-and-take between you and your audience will disappear. You'll see even a normal question as an attack and consequently treat that questioner as a heckler (*see* **h.3 hecklers**).

What all of this tells you is that whenever you – as a professional presenter – come across a difficult audience you should first look to yourself to see if you've caused the difficulty. Only when you've done that – honestly and completely – should you look at your audience.

d.3 disability awareness

One of the things about an audience (*see* **a.13 audiences**) that isn't always obvious is that some of the people in it will have disabilities. In the UK it's currently estimated that around one in seven people is disabled in some way while in the United States there are said to be some 54 million disabled Americans. The range of these disabilities is considerable. They can be visible or invisible, congenital or the result of disease or accident, and can result in minor inconvenience or place considerable limits on the range and nature of everyday life. These days legislation gives people with disabilities a helping hand. In the United States, Section 504 of the 1973 Rehabilitation Act prohibits educational establishments from discriminating against disabled people. The Americans with Disabilities Act (1990) extends that prohibition so that it includes a number of other areas including private businesses. In the UK, the Disability Discrimination Act (1995) draws a similar boundary and requires institutions and businesses to make 'reasonable' adjustment to the services they provide – so that they become more disabled-user friendly.

In all of this there are two things for the professional presenter, namely it:

• confirms the need to answer your audience's needs *fully*
• adds another dimension to the way that you prepare and perform your presentation.

For the professional presenter, disability awareness exerts an influence well before the start of his or her presentation. It features high on the pre-presentation checklist (*see* **c.6 checklists**), it's there in the way visual aids and handouts are prepared (*see* **h.1 handouts, v.4 visual aids**) and it's important when it comes to setting up the sound system (*see* **c.1 can you all hear me?**). It's just not good enough to walk in and find that your audience has special needs – needs that *must* be answered if you're going to reach them. A professional presenter will have found out about and catered for these needs during his or her preparation.

Here are some of the things that could feature in that preparation.

Hearing impairment

Almost one in five adults suffers from a hearing loss. Of these, the majority are people over 50 years of age. This loss can range from the moderate – people have difficulty following what is being said without a hearing aid – to the severe – people have difficulty following what is being said even with a hearing aid and use lip-reading or sign language to communicate. The Royal National Institute for the Deaf (RNID), The British Deaf Association (BDA), the National Association of the Deaf (NAD) and the American Speech-Language-Hearing Association (ASHA) are typical of the many organizations who provide excellent information and advice on overcoming the problems that can arise when presenting to people with hearing impairment (*see* **Taking it Further**). Your preparation may have to include the provision of induction loops to help hearing aid users, a lip-speaker for audience members who lip-read, British or American Sign Language (BSL/ASL) interpreters or a speech-to-text reporter. Whatever you use, always check that the hearing-impaired people in your audience are able to understand you. Be patient and take time to communicate.

Visual impairment

The Royal National Institute for the Blind (RNIB) estimates that there are just over one million visually impaired people (VIPs) in the United Kingdom alone and it's estimated that some 75,000 Americans become blind every year. The RNIB, the American Council of the Blind (ACB), the American Foundation for the Blind (AFB), the Braille Institute of America and the National Federation of the Blind (NFB) are typical of the many organizations that provide excellent information and advice on overcoming the problems that can arise when presenting to people with visual impairment (*see* **Taking it Further**). Nearly half of all people with impaired vision can read ordinary print but only with great difficulty. Reading like this is slow and tiring. For many blind and partially sighted people, larger print is essential. No single size is suitable for everyone but most people prefer their large print in the range of 16 to 22 point (*see* **t.7 typography, v.4 visual aids**). If possible, ask your audience which print size best suits their needs. You can produce simple large-print handouts yourself, but more complex print jobs may need to be sent to a commercial printer. Handouts on disc or audio tape or in Braille are alternatives. Your visuals should use maximum contrast with black on a white or yellow background or white on dark blue being the most legible. Helvetica Regular and Arial 14 point are the most legible typefaces. Use semi bold, medium or black types rather than light alternatives. Always check that your audience can read what is on the screen.

Language impairment or dyslexia

It's estimated that between ten to 15 per cent of the US population is dyslexic and in the UK some two million people are said to be severely affected by dyslexia. Dyslexics have an inherited neurological condition, one that results in language, perception, processing and attention or concentration difficulties. Yet only five per cent of people with this condition are ever properly diagnosed and given appropriate help. The lack of literacy skills that the average dyslexic experiences can limit his or her ability to become successful, productive adults, find jobs, or function independently within society. Yet with the proper recognition and intervention, dyslexics do become successful, using their talents and skills to enrich our society. Examples of people who have done this include Leonardo da Vinci, Richard Branson, Agatha Christie, Tom Cruise and David Bailey. Organizations that can provide information on dyslexia and its treatment include the British Dyslexia Association (BDA), the International Dyslexia Association and the Dyslexia Research Institute (*see* **Taking it Further**). The social stigma attached to illiteracy often makes it difficult for people to go public with their dyslexia. All the more reason for the professional presenter to take care that his or her material is simple, straightforward and clear.

Mobility impairment

Failing to make reasonable provision for audience members with mobility impairment is not only unreasonable, it's also unlawful. Yet time and time again we read about the obstacle race that wheelchair users face on a daily basis. But using a wheelchair is a common enough situation – around one million people in the USA do it daily. A professional presenter makes sure that the people who are responsible for the presentation location are aware of their legal responsibility to provide reasonable access not only to the presentation room but also to associated services such as toilets, washrooms, lifts or restaurants.

d.4 disasters – and how to cope

First, let's be clear about what we mean by a disaster. When you look in a dictionary you'll find that a disaster is 'anything that befalls of ruinous or distressing nature; a sudden or great misfortune, mishap, or misadventure; a calamity'. Just about covers most things, doesn't it? But for the professional presenter there's a further detail. For presentation disasters can also be classified as being either minor or major. Let's look at these in turn.

Minor disasters are the most common of presentation disasters. They include those 'shooting-yourself-in-the-foot' situations that follow when you forget your overheads, find that you didn't replace that spare projector bulb that you used in Cincinnati or Newcastle or start your presentation to find that your slides are upside down. They also include situations in which the airline sends your baggage (and presentation materials) to Chicago – when you're in San Francisco. These and other similar situations are avoidable by taking care, by being systematic and by being professional. Professional presenters avoid them by accepting the probability that they will occur at some time in their professional presenting career, and then planning what they'll need to do to stop them happening or to limit their effects.

Here are three examples:

Minor Disaster 1: Half-way through your presentation you drop your overheads on the floor.

Resolution: As a professional presenter you'll have avoided this situation by making sure that the table you present from is large enough to accommodate your notes as well as the stack of overheads you're going to show and the pile of overheads that you've already shown. You'll also have numbered your overheads – clearly and legibly. You'll also make sure that this table top looks – and stays – neat and tidy.

Minor Disaster 2: You're about to reach your sales pitch's key points and the decision maker has to leave to take a phone call from his or her boss.

Resolution: As a professional presenter you'll have planned for this situation. You'll have structured your presentation so that it:

- told your audience what your message was going to be
- gave them the message, and then
- reminded them what the message was.

When you do this the decision maker will see and hear the core of your message during the first few minutes of your presentation. You'll also have to hand a visual aid showing this core message – so that you can make sure that this is the last thing that the decision maker sees as he or she goes out of the door. You'll also ask – with a smile – for a moment to summarize before she or he leaves and in one sentence give the decision maker the single key point that you want him or her to remember.

Minor Disaster 3: The key audience member or decision taker is delayed by fog in Fairbanks, Alaska.

Resolution: Professional presenters know how to handle this one – because they've planned what to do. You'll know that someone in the room can carry your message to that key audience member or decision taker. In your preparation you'll have prepared the single sentence that you want the decision taker to remember. Now, this sentence changes. It becomes the message that you want that person to deliver to the decision taker. This message should be: clear, short, sharp and positive.

It should carry with it the passion of your presentation's core message. It should enable the message carrier to say – with conviction – things like 'We should use this product because it's cost effective and meets our engineering requirements' or 'This product means that we can provide a better level of customer service'. Make sure that you repeat that sentence three times in your presentation, at the beginning, in the middle and at the end.

Major disasters are quite different to their minor cousins. They happen far less often and usually occur without warning.

Examples of major presentation disasters include:

- the sound system fails totally and can't be fixed
- the fire alarm goes off – and it's for real
- the power supply fails and there's no back-up supply
- the only road between you and the client is washed out.

When these and other major disasters occur there isn't much that you can do about them. As a consequence your disaster response planning will change its focus. It'll switch from being preventive – as was the case in your minor disaster planning – to being reactive. This means that instead of asking yourself 'what do I do to prevent this happening?' you switch to asking 'what do I do when this happens?' The answer has three parts:

- first, keep smiling – there's always tomorrow
- second, look after yourself – your presentation material or equipment can be replaced but you can't
- third, write off this presentation but make sure that you move quickly to re-arrange when and where you can give your presentation.

d.5 drama

There must be few of you who haven't, at some time in your lives, sat through a presentation that you later described as 'dramatic'. If you're not sure whether you have experienced this then ask yourself if you've ever seen a presentation that had you, literally, on the edge of your seat. You'll certainly have experienced this elsewhere – in the movies, watching your television and, of course, in the theatre. When it happens, you are transfixed, absorbed, drawn into whatever it is that you are watching. This sort of effect is just as real in a dramatic presentation. The audience is gripped by what they see or hear; they sit with bated breath, in the grip of emotion, waiting for what comes next.

Sounds great, doesn't it? But for the professional presenter, drama is a mixed blessing. While that drama is a very powerful device for gripping the audience's attention, it can also, when used to excess, undermine or even destroy the presenter's relationship with that audience. Using drama in a presentation, and using it well, isn't easy. It takes skill, experience, nerve and some talent. Get it wrong and you'll lose not only your audience but also your credibility.

Nevertheless, despite these risks, drama does have a place in the toolkit of a professional presenter. As such it can be created:

- by the content of the presentation, for example you're presenting a message that's really unexpected and sensational, such as a plant closure or a take-over
- by the way that content is presented, for example when you present your message with real passion and commitment or use sound effects such as fanfares or thunderclaps in a stage-managed setting.

The risks are high with both of these. Your audience may not want to hear that message delivered in a dramatic and exciting way and the special effects that seemed acceptable at rehearsal may take on a life of their own and become overwhelming when played out in front of an audience. For the professional presenter, drama is best used in moderation and with care, always remembering that, as someone somewhere once said, drama 'does not deal with truth but with effect'.

d.6   dress

Despite the demise of dress-down Fridays and dress-up Mondays, it's still difficult to know what to wear when you're visiting an unfamiliar office or workplace. Turn up in a business suit to find yourself facing a blue-jean audience and you're going to feel out of place and maybe even uncomfortable. Arrive in casual wear to be greeted by business suits and you'll find your audience viewing you with suspicion. Your appearance – and particularly the clothes you wear – are important (*see* **a.10 appearance, l.10 looks and form**). The clothes that you wear say things about you to your audience and they say them before you get the chance to open your mouth. That audience will draw conclusions about things like your personality, ambitions, job, role or rank, social class, attitude towards them – even your sexual availability – from the way that you dress. So getting your clothes right is a good first step on the road to giving a professional presentation. But what is right?

Here are some tips:

• Wear clothes that are appropriate rather than fashionable or copy-cat.
• Research your audience's dress codes. What's appropriate at the Bank of England won't be appropriate in Tin Pan Alley.
• Make sure that the clothes you wear add to, rather than detract from, the authority that your audience will assume that you have. Don't expect them to believe you if you turn up to speak on the world economic situation wearing a teeshirt and jeans.

• Don't insult your audience by turning up in scruffy, untidy or dirty clothes. They may dress like that but they won't forgive you for not being neat, clean and tidy.

- Remember that your audience has turned up to hear what you have to *say*, not to see how good your dress sense is – or isn't.
- Prepare your clothes well before your presentation. Leaving it to the night (or even the morning) before will only mean you have to wear an unironed shirt or blouse.
- Take a spare tie or pair of tights and a clean handkerchief with you – accidents do happen!
- Despite all of the above make sure that you feel comfortable in the clothes that you present in.

e is for . . .

e.1 editing

For most of us, the business of editing or revising something that we've written is a minor job. We tidy things up, correct our grammar or refine our punctuation. It's a process that polishes, adds a final gloss to what we've written.

But for the professional presenter the process of editing and revising the material of his or her presentation is quite different. It's far more radical and comprehensive. It cuts deep into the body of the presenter's initial draft or storyboard (*see* **p.12 preparing your material, s.8 storyboards**), pares away surplus material. Sub-objectives, sub-routines and side-tracks are cast aside until what's left, alone, is the core objective or key message of the presentation. It's a process that's aimed at creating answers to questions such as:

- how can I best get that key message across?

- how can I build a logical and relevant sequence?

- how can I build energy and momentum into my presentation so that it motors, smoothly and inexorably, to a single, clear-cut end point?

The editing process that will give the answers to these questions is a ruthless one. Concerns about grammar, structure and even precision are suppressed, chunks of your 'best' material are cast aside – all in the search for what some presenters call 'the beating heart' of the presentation. But even when that's found the pace doesn't slacken. You'll find yourself adding material, deleting it, bringing in new material to substitute for old, redistributing new and old material and collapsing together or consolidating material. The only rule about this sort of editing is that anything goes. It's quite different to the spit and polish of conventional editing. It's also different in that it takes place – once you've gathered together your pile of 'must-have' material – as an integral part of the process of creating your presentation (*see* **p.12 preparing your material**).

e.2   endings

 The way you end your presentation needs to be precise, clear and unambiguous. Done well, it will give your audience a high note to finish on, an indication of what you expect them to do next and a clear message that you've finished.

The way that you do all of this is vital to your presentation's success. If you're at all unsure about this then go back to **c.10 closing your presentation** to check it out. When you've done that come back here – to look at the following proven examples of the way you can bring your presentation to an end.

- **Summarizing your key points** is a way of ending that will concentrate your audience's attention on a small but vital number of key points. You shouldn't have more than three or four of these and they should be chosen with care. They are, after all, the last words you'll speak to your audience and, because of this, they're words that will be remembered. Craft these key points with care, remembering that if you try to emphasize everything, you'll end up emphasizing nothing.
- **Asking for a specific action** is a way of ending that urges your audience to actually do something. Example: 'If you want your sales force to be able to meet the competitive challenges of the future then it is vital that you introduce a new incentive scheme within the next three months.'
- **Presenting alternatives** is a way of ending that leaves your audience with a clear-cut choice. Example: 'It seems to me that we are left with three options: accept the consultant's recommendations; amend their proposals; or do nothing.'
- **Restating your objectives** involves you in reminding your audience what it was that you set out to do at the beginning of your presentation. Example: 'My aim today has been to try to convince you of the need for an increased and more professional marketing programme for our short course programme. I hope I have convinced you.'

- **Posing a rhetorical question** makes the audience think more deeply about the subject of your presentation. Example: 'So, ladies and gentlemen, let me leave you with this thought – how would you feel if you were told that you were HIV positive?'

- **Creating or injecting fear** is the sort of ending that should be used with great caution. Its aim is to give a warning to your audience about what, in your view, will happen if something isn't done. Never make an empty threat and always make absolutely sure that, during the presentation, you've backed your threat up with solid facts. Example: 'So, if we don't increase our productivity levels by at least ten per cent over the next six months and then maintain that improvement for at least two years, we might as well close the company down now.'

- **Using a quotation** needs you to choose a quotation that is relevant, concise and easily understandable. Example: End a presentation on manpower planning as follows: 'As the ancient Chinese philosopher, Kaun Chung Tzu, said: "If you wish to plan for a year, sow seeds / If you wish to plan for ten years, plant trees / If you wish to plan for a lifetime, develop men."'

- **Making an emotional appeal** is the sort of ending that's often used by politicians. Example: 'Doing this will require our best efforts. It will also require us to believe in ourselves and our capacity to perform great deeds; to believe that we can resolve the problems that now confront us. And why not – we are Americans!'

- **A cautionary tale** should provide a warning about what could happen if the audience doesn't do what you are suggesting. It should contain a tale that is true and relevant. Example: 'Let me leave you with this cautionary tale: In last year's promotion of their baby food Company A failed to specify that a proof of purchase of their special promotional pack was needed. As a result the response was overwhelming and the promotional budget was overspent ten times.'

e.3   enthusiasm

 Enthusiasm is good. It's the wind that blows the kite of your presentation into your audience's sky, it's the spice that converts 'commonplace' to 'cool' and it's that 'ingredient X' that enables a presenter to reach out to touch the hearts and minds of an audience. Professional presenters know this. They know that enthusiasm is a 'must-have' ingredient in *all* presentations. A presentation without enthusiasm is cold and uninteresting. But, surprisingly, you can have too much enthusiasm. In excess, enthusiasm is rather like a hurricane; it'll blow away even the best of presentations. The knack with enthusiasm is just the same as the one that you use with enthusiasm's close cousin, passion (*see* **p.3 passion**) – it's about getting just the right amount. Too little and you'll appear cold, unenthusiastic and disinterested, too much and your audience will become mesmerized by your antics rather than interested in what you're talking about.

You shouldn't need to be told about how to be enthusiastic. After all, it's something that you've been doing for most of your life. You know that you show other people that you're enthusiastic about something by your gestures, facial expressions, movements and posture (*see* **g.4 gestures, f.1 face, e.8 eye contact, n.2 non-verbal communication**). You also know that you can't pretend to be enthusiastic about something when you're not. If you're foolish enough to try this, you'll soon learn, to your cost, that audiences have a built-in enthusiasm detector – one that quickly signals whether the enthusiasm is real or not. Professional presenters know this. They start to make deposits in their enthusiasm 'bank' during the very early stages of their presentation's preparation and they go on doing that until the moment they begin their presentation (*see* **b.2 beginnings**). They also test the deposit level in that enthusiasm 'bank' several times during that preparation. They ask themselves how enthusiastic they are about doing this presentation. If the answer's 'not very' then it's time to take a good hard look at the preparation so far or even to consider whether they should be doing this presentation at all. For if you can't get enthusiastic about your presentation how will your audience manage to do that?

e.4   environment

The environment in which you present isn't really that different from the bigger 'whole-world' environment outside. This means that if it's going to encourage and enable the survival, growth and development of the ideas that you plant in your audience's minds then it'll need, amongst other things, enough space and light.

Here are some of the most commonly used environmental 'rules of thumb':

- Don't have too big a gap between you and the front row of your audience.
- Do make sure that your audience-to-screen distance is between two to six times the height of the screen.
- Limit your audience to three rows deep with no more than six in a row if you want lots of interaction with them.
- Get your audience's screen viewing angle right. This can be as low as 20 degrees or as high as 45 degrees depending on the material your screen is made from (*see* **s.2 screens**).
- If you're going to present from a stage platform to give your audience greater visibility, then make sure the ceiling height is 6.5 m or higher and free from obstructions, such as low-hanging chandeliers.
- If you're going for a participative presentation (*see* **p.2 participative presentations**) then choose a round or square table, with you seated as a member of the group, or set up audience chairs in a U-shape – so that the audience members face towards each other. You can also use banquet or café style seating with large groups, seating five to eight people on each of as many round tables as required.
- Don't dim the room lights – use a bright multimedia projector or a high-output overhead projector and leave the room lights on so that you can see the audience.
- Switch off any light that shines directly onto the screen or behind it. Both of these will 'wash-out' the images and text on your carefully prepared overheads or slides.

Take a look at **r.6 rooms, halls and caverns, c.3 chairs, l.3 layout, p.7 podiums and lecterns** for more points.

e.5   errors, mistakes and blunders

It's a rare presenter who hasn't, at some time, made a mistake or error while performing in front of an audience. Presenting errors, mistakes or blunders happen all the time and are incredibly diverse in their nature. Fortunately, they're also usually minor in nature and easily corrected (*see* **d.4 disasters – and how to cope**). So that you can reassure yourself that your worst-ever error isn't unique, here are some examples of presenting sins, errors and mistakes that have actually been committed, at some time or another, by experienced professional presenters:

- calling an important member of the audience by the wrong name
- forgetting the name of an important member of the audience
- telling the audience that they work in the Marketing Department when they actually work in Engineering or Design
- answering the question you *thought* was asked, rather than the one that was
- getting your facts mixed up or, worse still, wrong
- allowing yourself to get side-tracked by a question or a heckler
- forgetting where you've got to in your presentation.

For the professional presenter, recovering from a mistake involves running through a short and simple sequence of steps:

Step 1 *Don't* panic

Step 2 Decide whether your audience spotted the error or mistake

Step 3 If they haven't, continue with your presentation

Step 4 If they have, stop, put it right and apologize.

Never try to bluster or waffle your way out of an error – it won't work and you'll risk losing your audience.

e.6   euphemisms

Most of us use euphemisms a lot; they are those words or phrases that we substitute for something harsher or more offensive. Common examples include 'downsizing', which means getting rid of or sacking employees, 'senior citizen', which stands in for the old, 'pre-owned', which is used instead of second-hand, 'lost' as in 'I've lost my husband', which stands in for 'died', and 'less than truthful', which substitutes for lying. Euphemisms are almost always evasive. They use a vague word or phrase because a precise and clear one would be alarming, and they reject natural words because they might have unpleasant, embarrassing or non-p.c. associations. Euphemisms can – in some circumstances – avoid embarrassment or upset; however, like clichés (*see* **c.7 clichés**), their over-use leads to sentences and statements that are so evasive that they are almost devoid of real meaning.

Professional presenters avoid using euphemisms. They know that their use will confuse their audience rather than inform or intrigue them. They've also learned that most euphemisms have an in-built 'self-destruct' mechanism. It doesn't matter how subtle and well phrased the euphemism is or how well intentioned its use might be; the original masked 'unpleasant' meaning will seep through. What you're then left with is:

- a discredited euphemism
- the need for a new euphemism
- a puzzled audience.

Better by far that you don't use a euphemism. Use, instead:

- no more words than are necessary
- limited adjectives and adverbs
- words that are precise rather than vague.

Doing all of this and avoiding the use of euphemisms requires clear thinking, meticulous, thorough preparation, and a clear understanding of your audience's needs.

Take a look at **s.3 simplify** and **a.13 audiences** for more points.

e.7 expressions

There are three sorts of expression:

- those that use words
- those that appear on your face
- those that are a collection of symbols expressing a mathematical or algebraic quantity.

Despite their substantial differences, all of these expressions are used with one purpose or objective in mind – that of communication. In presentations, this objective is key. As a consequence, the first two – those based on words and those that appear on your face – are used a lot. These sorts of expression are – by intention or by accident – highly communicative. However, the last of these expressions – the algebraic one – is quite rare. Its appearances are usually restricted to presentations or lectures in the specialist language (or jargon) that you use when you are presenting to an audience of specialists (*see* **j.1 jargon**).

As a professional presenter, you need to be skilled in the use of all of these expressions. You need to be fluent in:

- **facial expressions** (*see* **f.1 face**) in order to read the many minor changes, relaxations and tensions in the faces of your audience and to change or adjust the mood, pitch and pace of your presentation in response to these

- **word expressions** (*see* **c.7 clichés, e.6 euphemisms**) that avoid the over-use of clichés and euphemisms, are precise and concrete, reflect clear thinking and thorough preparation, and demonstrate your understanding of your audience's needs
- **specialist expressions** (*see* **j.1 jargon**) only when *all* of your audience understand this specialist 'language', and *you* understand that specialist 'language'.

e.8   eye contact

 Professional presenters aren't just keen on eye contact – they're *mad* about it. Giving 'good-eye' and continuing to do that throughout your presentation can make a major contribution to its success. This is because eye contact is a key element in the way we communicate with each other. If you get your 'audience-looking' right then each of them will feel that you're talking to them, as an individual. They'll feel that you want to know whether they understand what you're saying. They'll sense that you're keen to know how they feel about what you're saying. If you get this 'audience-looking' wrong, your audience will see you as lacking in confidence, unsure and nervous. Lack of eye contact will lead them to feel that you're not interested in them, that you don't care about their reactions to what you say. But when you make eye contact with your audience you shouldn't subject them to a piercing, basilisk-like stare. Doing that will only make them nervous and unsure about you, rather than getting them on your side. Your gaze should be focused softly on your audience's faces and should shift occasionally to your notes or the screen.

Here are some useful tips and information about eye contact:

- Remember that most people look a lot while they listen but look far less when they talk, so train yourself to talk *and* look.
- Start by looking at the friendly faces – people you know or who you think are on your side.
- Scan the whole audience systematically but not mechanically.
- Try to look at every single person, but don't look too long.
- Remember that people who are scowling, looking unsure or bored have a message for you. Look at them, read the message, then do something about it!
- Make sure that you don't neglect to look at the edges or corners of your audience.

- Never talk to your notes or the screen – look at your audience while speaking.
- If you find it difficult to look people straight in the eye then look at their foreheads – the difference isn't noticeable at a distance.
- Remember that eye contact can be supplemented by a smile, and the more eye contact that you make, the more your audience will warm to you.

f is for . . .

f.1 face

There's a nursery rhyme that has a line that goes something like '"My face is my fortune, sir", she said'. But for most of us this isn't so and we have to exploit other attributes such as wit, intelligence, cunning or humour to make our way through the world. But our faces are, nevertheless, important. In your presentation your face will provide your audience with clues about what's coming next or about how you are feeling. But this isn't a one-way traffic for you can see whether your audience is interested, excited, bored or unhappy by the expressions on their faces.

However, facial expressions are complex and not always easy to read. Most of us have a wide repertoire of these expressions. Researchers tell us that there are around 30 basic expressions with some 45 possible positions for the lower face, 17 possible positions for the eyes and eight possible brow and forehead positions. Creating all these is quite a job! It involves you in co-ordinating movement of muscles in and around the eyes, forehead, eyebrows, cheeks, nose, jaw and lips. The facial expressions that result can be:

- deliberate and chosen, for example when you smile politely
- incidental or accidental, for example when you screw your eyes up in bright sunlight
- unconscious and spontaneous, for example when you react to sudden shock or surprise.

You're also able to fake facial expressions. You do this when you smile yet don't feel happy or laugh when you think you ought to. These and other faked expressions are used when you want to hide your true feelings or mislead others. However, many facial expressions are difficult to fake, particularly those involving small movements of lip and jaw muscles and the muscles around the eyes. Because of this, expressions involving these movements are more likely to provide genuine signals about, for example, how your audience feels about what you are saying. Facial expressions enable you to express a wide range of emotions, the most basic and easily recognized of these being anger, fear, surprise, sadness, happiness, disgust and contempt. These and other emotions can be expressed either separately or together as, for example, when you show your disgust *and* your anger about something or somebody. Nevertheless, despite all this complexity, it is possible to recognize emotions from a limited number of facial 'cues':

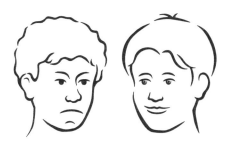

The face, with its ability to create hundreds of minor changes, relaxations and tensions, is able to portray changes of considerable subtlety and complexity in underlying mood. Being able to recognize and decode the facial expressions of your audience is a key skill for a professional presenter.

But the professional presenter never forgets that the audience is reading her or his face as well. What they see will tell them:

- how to respond to what you're saying
- whether you're concerned, happy, sad or excited.

Getting your facial expression right is an important part of your presentation. Altering your facial expression can enable you to change or adjust its mood, pitch and pace. Doing this well will take practice and experimentation – you'll have to rehearse your facial expressions and check out their effects if they are going to be successful. Here's a tip about how you can do that:

- Choose a topic or subject at random.
- Decide that you're going to, in turn, feel good and then bad about that topic or subject.
- Use that feeling, consciously and unconsciously, to drive or create your facial expressions.
- See if it worked using a mirror or an observer.

It may take some practice for you to get this right. You'll need to avoid being theatrical or excessive with your facial expressions. Subtle but obvious are the key words here. Once you've got it right you'll find that you've added a powerful tool to your presenting toolkit.

f.2 facts

A fact is something that has really occurred or is actually the case. For the professional presenter, facts form the bedrock of a presentation. Getting these facts right is a vital first step in the preparation of all presentations. To make sure that happens, professional presenters put *all* the material that contributes to a presentation through a veracity check (*see* **p.12 preparing your material**). This makes sure that what goes into the presentation is solid, verifiable fact rather than material based on inference, conjecture or speculation. Professional presenters don't take risks with this – nor should you.

But the resulting facts aren't information – yet. It takes the relevance test to convert a fact into a piece of information. Information is interesting, valuable and, above all, relevant, whereas a fact just is. You'll see the difference between a fact and a piece of information if I tell you that it's raining in London today. For some of you this is a fact; it's verifiable and true. But that fact will change into information when it's relevant to what you or somebody you know is doing in London today (*see* **i.5 information**). It's this shift from facts to information that converts a fact-rich presentation from the dozy side of boring to an inspiring and memorable experience. It's also a shift that professional presenters work at a lot when they are preparing their presentations.

f.3 fear

Fear is focused, it's attached or connected to something or someone (*see* **a.9 anxiety**). When you feel fear before or during your presentation, that isn't a random out-of-the-blue event. It's one that happens because:

- you haven't prepared your material well enough (*see* **p.12 preparing your material**)
- you're uncertain about your audience (*see* **a.13 audiences**)
- you're not clear about what you want to achieve with this presentation (*see* **o.1 objectives and targets, w.4 why**).

Because fear follows on from these acts of folly, it's an emotion that is deserved and arrives because of a lack of professionalism.

Professional presenters don't feel fear. Instead they get nervous or anxious and they work through these emotions and use them to give their presentations that extra cutting edge. There is, however, one exception to this and that is when a presenter suffers stage fright (*see* **s.6 stage fright**).

f.4   feedback

Feedback is a core issue when it comes to the way we communicate with each other (*see* **c.12 communication**). It's the other half of the communication process; we use it not only to tell each other that we've heard what's been said but also to announce how we feel about it. Professional presenters are sharp on feedback. They recognize it for what it is – the whetting stone on which they hone the cutting edge of their presentation skills – and they seek it out. There are at least three opportunities for feedback in the lifetime of a presentation:

- during the rehearsals (*see* **r.1 rehearsal**)
- during the presentation
- after the presentation.

Here are some tips to help you maximize the value of the feedback that you get on these occasions.

During the rehearsals your feedback needs to come be from an impartial observer and/or a video recording of your presentation. It's often useful to formalize the feedback process by using a questionnaire or checklist. Make sure that this covers all the relevant areas such as:

- body language – use of gesture, posture, movement, eye contact (*see* **n.2 non-verbal communication**)

- **visual aids** – clear, helpful for clarification, smooth operation (*see* **c.11 colours, v.4 visual aids**)
- **delivery** – tone, speed, projection, use of pauses, enthusiasm, pace and timing (*see* **e.3 enthusiasm, p.1 pace, p.4 pauses, u.3 using your voice**)
- **structure** – shape, logic, clear objectives, signposts (*see* **p.12 preparing your material**)
- **content** – clarity, relevance, use of language, level of detail (*see* **a.11 appropriate, c.7 clichés, e.6 euphemisms, s.3 simplify**).

Getting your observer to grade how you do on each of these – on a scale of, say, 1 to 5, with 5 being very good – often helps.

During the presentation it's audience feedback you'll be looking for. Watch, look and listen are the key words here. You need to be attentive to your audience, reading their 'body language' with care and attention (*see* **n.2 non-verbal communication**). For example, feet tapping, fidgeting and whispering can indicate either impatience, boredom or even confusion. Take care to read the whole face or body rather than a gesture or facial expression in isolation. For example, a frown may not mean disagreement, it could indicate concentration or reflection. Judging the mood of the audience as a whole is an important part of this feedback.

After the presentation your feedback can be:

- direct – as in 'yes, you've got the order' or 'no, we don't want to use you this time'
- conditional – for example, when your audience needs to ask you questions about the detail or implications of what you've been talking about
- indirect – for example, when your audience streams out to lunch or the coffee bar talking animatedly or when you're greeted with smiles and nods when you join them for lunch.

Sometimes it's appropriate for you to ask the audience to fill in a feedback form. This feedback mechanism is usually used after training presentations or lectures (*see* **t.6 training presentations, l.6 lectures**). The more effective of these focus on the objectives of the presentation rather than the way the presentation was made. Don't give it out before the end and do allow time for its completion.

f.5 feet

Your feet – or rather the way that you do or don't move them – can make quite a difference to the impression that you give your audience. Most of the time you move your feet when you want to get from one location to another. In your presentations you'll do this because, for example, you want to switch a piece of equipment on or off or because you want to get closer to the screen to point to an image or word. When you do this you make a conscious decision to move your feet and what follows is that marvellously smooth and interconnected sequence of muscle contractions and balance shifts that we call walking. But people walk in different ways; they shuffle, march, stride, stroll, hurry, skip or sometimes even hop to get from A to B. All of these carry messages to those who watch. You hurry when you're concerned about arriving and you stroll when you feel that you have all the time in the world. Trainee Customs Officers are told to 'watch their feet' when trying to detect smugglers as they pass through the Green and Red customs channels of airports. But most of the time, your walking is easy, natural and unselfconscious.

All of this changes, however, when your walking is done in the full glare of an audience's attention. For walking that seemed easy and natural off the presenting platform becomes stilted and awkward in front of an audience. Most of the time this shift is caused by your fear (*see* **a.9 anxiety, f.3 fear, n.1 nerves, s.6 stage fright**). You become anxious because of your concerns about whether the audience will understand or like you or whether you'll forget what you planned to say or whether you'll end up looking an idiot. What happens in response to these and other fears is that your body kicks in with a perfectly natural reaction. This is that in-built survival mechanism – the 'fight-or-flight' response. As a result your body finds itself battling to cope with the claims of opposing actions. Part of you wants to stay and face the threat of the audience while the other part wants to take flight, away from the presenting platform, to safety. The result of all this is the opposite of what you wanted to happen. You wanted to appear relaxed and easy when you walked – and here you are, awkward and stumbling. It even continues when you sit down, with that nervous foot tap or jiggle telling the audience about your anxiety.

But for the professional presenter – like the actors and actresses, barristers and lawyers, stand-up comedians and tv newsreaders who also appear in front of an audience of one sort or another –

all of this has to be coped with. Doing this is a real skill – one that's acquired, one that evolves as a result of training and practice. Video your rehearsals (*see* **r.1 rehearsal**) to try to spot how and when this inner conflict – between fight and flight – leaks out and shows itself. Work hard at overcoming your fear, find a way of walking on stage that doesn't look awkward or stilted. Work hard at this and you'll find that you'll be able to redirect the inward-turned energy of fear into a positive and outgoing energy that will help you reach out to your audience.

f.6 figures

It seems to be part of the natural order of things that in any collection of figures, the one most obviously correct, beyond all need of checking, is the one that's wrong. It also seems to be true that when you ask people to check your figures – find the mistake – they won't be able to see it. But all is not lost because the first person who stops by, whose advice you really don't want to hear, will see that mistake immediately. Professional presenters check their figures not just once but *at least* twice, and get a disinterested bystander to help them do that (*see also* **f.7 financial presentations, g.6 graphs and charts, t.1 tables, t.3 technical presentations**).

f.7 financial presentations

To say that financial presentations are full of figures is an understatement; there's no end to the amount of financial information that's available. This can be almost anything – the financial state of that organization, the costing of a new product, the performance of an on-going project or the ups and downs of the company's share price. This financial information is usually presented by experts of one sort or another. They can be cost or management accountants, financial controllers, market analysts, project controllers or finance directors. Faced with all this information and know-how, you'd have thought that financial presentations would be the best sort of presentations. The truth, however, is that they aren't. Audiences usually – but not always – leave financial presentations in a haze of numbers and without any real idea what the presentation was really about. There are three potential causes of this state of affairs. They are:

- the information – its complexity and quantity
- the presenter – his or her lack of skills and ability
- the audience – their lack of financial know-how.

 Getting all of these in balance is important. Get them in harmony with each other and you'll have a presentation that's great; get any one of them out of balance and your financial presentation will sink like the proverbial lead balloon. Let's look at each of them in turn.

Information

The key to getting the information level right in your financial presentation lies in simplifying that information and then focusing that simplified information on answering your audience's needs.

The professional financial presenter will sieve through thousands of pieces of financial data in order to find those 'special' few bits of data that are relevant and meaningful. These will be special because they will contribute to meeting the audience's needs and are relevant to the aims and objectives of the presentation (*see* **o.1 objectives and targets**). Once found, these bits of data need to be translated into a form that your audience can understand, and make use of. The first of these is, at least in part, dependent upon the way that this data is presented to the audience. The key here is to make sure that you:

- use graphs or charts in preference to tables (*see* **g.6 graphs and charts, t.1 tables**)
- keep the graphs and charts simple, clear and easy to understand.

Presenter

The skills that a presenter needs to make a successful financial presentation are just the same as those needed for any other sort of presentation. She or he must be able to:

- understand the audience's needs
- create a presentation that answers those needs
- perform that presentation in a professional manner.

In order to do that she or he will need to be not just familiar with the processes, procedures and conventions of the financial world but also able to understand them and translate or interpret them so that audiences without that specialist knowledge can understand them.

Audience

The audiences of financial presentations fall into three groups. They can be:

- a financially literate audience – with lots of know-how
- a mixed audience – with some people who have financial know-how and others who don't
- a lay audience with low or no know-how.

Each of these audience groups will have its own set of needs and expectations. The key to success in your financial presentations lies in finding out which group your audience falls into *before* you start your preparation. Knowing this will enable you to create a blend of words and visuals that will suit that audience. For example, if you are talking about operating costs you'd probably:

- not need to define these for a high know-how audience
- outline what you mean by 'operating costs' for a mixed know-how audience
- clearly define what they are for a low know-how audience.

In short, give your presentation in a language that your audience understands and in a way that answers their needs.

f.8 flip charts

The flip chart is a common tool in the world of presenting. It's a large – usually 85×60 cm – pad of paper, erected on a stand and bound so that each sheet (usually containing prepared information) can be turned over at the top to show the next one. If you hadn't guessed already, it's called a flip chart because you 'flip' a chart over the top of the board or easel that they're mounted on. They're also a remarkably effective way of presenting information. Flip charts are:

- easy to store and transport as a set of rolled-up sheets
- low on material costs – flip chart pad and marker pens
- easy and quick to produce – hand drawn or written.

But they do have disadvantages, including:

- the need for a bulky and not easily transportable easel
- their limited size
- restrictions in source material – you can't put a photograph on a flip chart and expect your audience to be able to see it

- limited visibility at a distance
- the need for graphic art skills in production.

As most of us have neither the neatness of hand nor the required flair in graphic design to produce really good flip charts you'll have to accept that you need to pay someone with these skills to produce them for you. As the use of shoddy or second-rate presentation material is not acceptable for a professional presenter, this means that the use of flip charts may have limited appeal to you. However, flip charts can be used during participative presentations (*see* **p.2 participative presentations**) – as an alternative to an ohp film roll – or under circumstances where the need for a presentation *now* overrides the need for professional-standard presentation material. If you find yourself in this sort of situation, here are some tips:

- Always print your text – joined-up writing, however neat, won't be legible enough.
- Keep content simple and limited – use bullet-pointed key words and no more than five lines of text.
- Use bold or dark colours as pastel or light colours will have limited visibility.
- Use large lettering and numerals – 20 mm high and larger.
- Number each sheet and staple them together.
- Practise 'flipping' – slow, smooth and easy is best.
- If you're going to repeat the presentation after the immediacy has faded then tidy it up and transfer it onto a more professional-looking medium such as overhead transparencies.

g is for . . .

g.1 gabble

Gabbling is a presenting trap that we can all fall into. It happens when you talk too quickly, when you don't pause to let your audience grasp the points you're making and when you don't wait for their reactions to what you've said. If you make a joke when you're gabbling your audience is too busy trying to catch up with you to appreciate it. The result – on your part – is panic, even fear, and a tendency to speed up or gabble even more. The result is almost always a disaster. Your audience will begin to make the shift towards seeing you as an inarticulate, incoherent gabbling idiot. All of this usually comes about because we're anxious or nervous (*see* **a.9 anxiety, f.3 fear, n.1 nerves**). But it can also happen when you become concerned about time and allow yourself to get caught up in a rush – to finish in time or to get in what you want to say before someone else interrupts.

While gabbling is often tolerated in everyday conversations it's certainly *not* tolerable when it comes to professional presenting. The gabbling presenter is about as *un*professional as a presenter can get. Presenters like this simply fail to communicate with their audiences. This means that you've little or no chance of achieving the objective that you'd chosen for your presentation (*see* **o.1 objectives and targets**). Allowing yourself to fall into the gabble trap also means that you've let your anxieties get the better of you. None of this will help your presentation. So don't gabble! Get tuned into the rhythm and pace (*see* **p.1 pace**) of your speech so that you pick up and stop the gabble when it starts. Rehearse thoroughly so that you know what comes next and how long it will take (*see* **r.1 rehearsal**).

g.2 gathering your material

Gathering potential presentation material is, for the professional presenter, rather like painting the Golden Gate Bridge. It's a non-stop harvesting activity that goes on all of the time. As such it appears, at least to the outsider, to be a random, almost indiscriminate, gathering together of cuttings and notes from almost everywhere. In fact, it isn't like that at all. If you've ever asked a really professional presenter where he or she got that fascinating story about so-and-so or where he or she found that amazing fact you may, if you're lucky, get shown what's often called their 'Bits and Bobs' or 'Odds and Sods' file. This, you will discover, is anything but what its title implies. Far from being indiscriminate or random, it'll be a structured data bank of files, cuttings, references and abstracts that have been gathered together over a period of time. The range of material it contains will be considerable – cartoons, newspaper and magazine articles and clippings, website addresses and print-outs, photographs and photocopied pages from books. The subjects covered by these won't only be wide, they'll also change as time passes, absorbing new topics or personalities as they appear.

This file is the well from which the professional presenter draws for the story, ad-lib, cartoon or fact that's appropriate to the particular audience she or he is about to face. But that's not its only contribution. It also acts as a guide book or road map to the more detailed sources of information that are used in the first step of the professional presenter's material preparation process – that of bringing together any material that appears to be relevant to the objective of the presentation (*see* **p.12 preparing**

your material). Start your own version of this file *now*. It's never too early and it will avoid you asking 'where was it that I saw that cartoon or story?' and not being able to give an answer.

g.3 gender

There is no such thing as a gender-free presentation. The gender factor is present in all your presentations – just as it's woven into everything else in your life. It's been there since the early days of human pre-history and it's still there when you do the basic ordinary things of life – such as laughing, talking, smiling, moving, sitting and looking at each other. Yet assumptions about gender have changed. Now, for example, it's no longer reasonable to assume that the person in charge of a team or an organization is male. Nor is it acceptable to presume that someone in a caring role is female. All of this means that the assumptions that used to be made about gender and roles are no longer valid. But the ogre of gender bias is still with us. We still have 'glass ceilings' – the invisible barriers that block the upward progress of women in organizations – and 'glass walls' – the horizontal barriers in organizations that prevent women moving between functional areas or from service divisions into line management. But these aren't the only situations in which gender bias raises its head. References to the chair*man* of a committee, rather than the chair*person*, and abstract examples given in a general debate that use the male gender, for example 'I thought *he* would . . .' rather than 'I thought *she or he* would . . .', are still with us.

For the professional presenter, gender bias – in any shape or form – isn't just unacceptable, it's also unprofessional. This is a general and absolute rule; one that even applies with single-sex audiences. As a result extra care must be taken when preparing material (*see* **p.12 preparing your material**) to ensure that:

- the examples given are balanced in gender terms
- the conclusions drawn are expressed in 'she and he' or 'they' terms
- the stories told are not sexist (*see* **s.7 stories**).

Similarly, care must be taken to ensure that the performance of the presentation is free from material that contains gender bias or can be described as sexist. This means that the professional presenter must have prepared and rehearsed her or his ad-libs, stories, answers to questions and responses to hecklers (*see* **a.5 ad-libs, q.1 questions, h.3 hecklers**). For in any of these situations, an ill-thought sexist remark or innuendo can antagonize an audience in a flash and thus destroy all hope of gaining your presentation's objective.

g.4   gestures

There's an old proverb that tells us that 'actions speak louder than words'. As a professional presenter you'll find that there are some of your actions that speak louder than others. Amongst these are your gestures. When you gesture you send signals – you 'semaphore' your intentions or feelings to your audience. Most of these gestures will involve using your hands and arms but the more complex ones will also involve moving your head or shoulders. These gestures are used for a variety of reasons. They can, for example:

- substitute for words, for example the 'goodbye' wave
- add to what you are saying, for example when you describe a shape using your hands or point to indicate direction
- act as markers in your conversations with other people, for example when you nod to say hello, indicate that you've heard what someone said and tell somebody that you agree to something.

As a professional presenter you'll use gestures a lot – to tell your audience about your:

- involvement in and commitment to the subject of your presentation
- intention to share what you know about that subject with them
- enthusiasm and passion for that subject (*see* **e.3 enthusiasm, p.3 passion**).

Some of these gestures will be consciously chosen and used to effect because you've rehearsed them and know that they work. But you'll also make other – unconscious – gestures, without prior planning, thought or choice. These will include the personal mannerisms that you've acquired over the years and the 'leakage' gestures that tell your audience about your inner or 'true' feelings.

We all have mannerisms (*see* **m.1 mannerisms**). They are those individual, idiosyncratic gestures, facial expressions or speech patterns that we use when we talk to each other. They get in the way of a professional presentation only when they are distracting in nature or used to excess. Once spotted it's usually a question of consciously using them less. Spotting your leakage gestures, however, is not so easy. These are the unconscious, spontaneous, 'of-the-moment' gestures that reflect how you feel in that moment. You'll use them when you feel tense, angry or frustrated. Crossing your arms over your chest, for example, is a leakage gesture that you'll typically make when you feel attacked. It's a defensive gesture; one that leaks your feeling of being attacked to your audience. But that's not all that leakage gestures can do. If you try to deceive your audience your leakage gestures – particularly those involving hand–face contacts and those that cover the mouth – will increase. These gestures will tell your audience that you either are trying to deceive them or are unwilling to speak the truth!

As a professional presenter your aim should be to use gesture rather than be driven by it, and to use it in ways that are purposeful and illustrative.

g.5 global presentations

The way things are these days if you're any good at presenting then you'll soon find yourself doing it abroad. Presenting globally – and getting it right *wherever* you are – is A1 professional presenting. Achieve that and you'll be seen not just as a professional presenter but as one of that rare breed – a *super* presenter. Get it wrong and the result often isn't just a misunderstanding – it's missed mega-sales, scuttled important relationship-building opportunities and scrambled cross-border training programmes that result. But becoming an effective global presenter doesn't happen overnight. It takes time, presents a real challenge and, some say, is one of those things about which you never stop learning.

Here are some key points to start you off on the road to success as a global presenter.

Keep your presentation material clear and simple

The challenge you'll face here is that of communicating more effectively. This means using simple sentences, making clear transitions, avoiding red herrings or digressions, using fewer potentially confusing pronouns and restating key points in exactly the same wording you used before (*see* s.3 simplify). You'll also need to limit your use of jargon, idiomatic expressions and acronyms (*see* j.1 jargon, c.7 clichés). Using phrases like 'barking up the wrong tree' or 'a shotgun approach' will only create confusion, misunderstanding and blank stares. Professional presenters get their text and visuals checked over by somebody who knows the local culture and language.

Do this before you leave, so you've got time for revisions, and do it thoroughly. Remember, disaster is only a word or phrase away.

Cut back on home culture related references and examples

Over-use of examples from your home culture can leave the impression that you're telling your audience 'We're No.1'. Even if the subject matter of your presentation or lecture necessitates using such examples, you still need to acknowledge that these might as easily have come from Madrid, Lyons, Haifa or Tokyo. You'll also need to remember that your audience's values, norms and prejudices will be different from yours. They may, for example, not understand references to baseball, football or golf and what you call nepotism may be, for them, the virtuous act of taking care of their family.

Stay off jokes

If you're really looking for a deep dark hole into which to drop your presentation, then tell a joke about French men when you're presenting in Paris, about Germans when you're in Berlin or an Irish joke when you're in Dublin. Few of us are able to accept an outsider trying to make jokes about our culture – even if we'd have laughed when the same joke was told by a colleague or friend.

Remember body language doesn't always travel well

Many of the gestures and facial expressions that you use at home will work just as well overseas. Examples include spreading your hands apart to indicate height or width, open palms for indicating openness or smiling when you are happy.

 But body language is by no means universal and many other gestures and facial expressions will be unacceptable overseas, and might even cause offence. Here are some examples:

- pointing your index finger is considered impolite in most Middle Eastern and East Asian countries
- the American 'OK' sign – a circle formed with your index finger and thumb – is considered obscene in Brazil

- the 'thumbs up' is a rude gesture in Australia
- a head nod indicates 'no' rather than 'yes' in Greece and Bulgaria.

Eye-contact habits can also be different. For example, direct eye contact can be considered impolite and an invasion of privacy in Japan or the Philippines, while strong eye contact is important in both Spain and Arab countries.

Review audience participation

Most presenters assume that audience participation is good. Case study or problem solving groups, question-and-answer sessions, even hecklers are all examples of this (*see* **p.2 participative presentations, q.1 questions, h.3 hecklers**). But professional presenters know that it's important to review this assumption when you're presenting overseas. In some cultures, for example, presenters and lecturers are seen as figures of absolute authority and an audience question would be seen as an improper challenge to this authority. Other cultures place different values on individualism. So exposing individuals to the spotlight of a role-play or a question-and-answer session, or allowing any kind of open debate involving disagreement could be seen as threatening and disturbing.

Formality

Professional presenters are also aware that there can be different rules about social standing and behaviour when you present overseas. In other cultures, lecturers and presenters are treated as figures of real authority and are accorded the respect due in that culture. As a result you may find that your presentation is received in total silence with audience members writing down or recording your every word. You may also find your audience becomes very uneasy when you crack that well-rehearsed joke. It won't be appropriate to turn up in casual dress and it may not even be appropriate to mingle with your audience during breaks. You may even get asked to pose for a 'celebrity' photo after your presentation. It's important that you make yourself aware of these *before* you leave and accept them for the courtesies they are when you arrive.

Icons, images and colours

Despite the fact that icons, images, cartoons and clip art often provide you with fast-track access to audience communication they do have to be used with care in overseas presentations. Many of these are specific to and appropriate for their culture of origin and their value may not survive the cross-culture passage. The same applies to colour use. Green, for example, is the national colour of Egypt and is considered a religious colour in Islamic countries. Purple is the colour of death and funerals in Brazil and Mexico and a lot of red in your visuals will bring back memories of Soviet domination in some Eastern European countries.

Handouts

Handouts and other paper-based take-aways are often well received by overseas audiences. It may be worthwhile sending out a master copy – for photocopying – ahead of your presentation. If your presentation is a technical one and you're presenting to a lay audience (*see* **t.3 technical presentations**) then include a glossary of key terms. You might want to consider using the Notes feature on PowerPoint (*see* **p.10 powerpoint presentations, Taking it Further**), which creates a printout with three screen graphics on the left side of the page and space for note-taking on the right side.

Despite all of these differences, it's worth remembering that, in the end, you'll still be presenting to an audience of real people rather than a group of cultural stereotypes. So, despite all your efforts to make sure that you and your presentation are compatible with their culture, you'll still need to reach out to them (*see* **a.13 audiences, u.2 using an interpreter**). Finally, it's also important to remember that there will be hardware and technology compatibility problems that need to be taken care of. 'Assume nothing and prepare for everything' seems to be the credo here. Remember that, apart from needing different plugs and adaptors:

- power supplies in some countries may not be as stable or as reliable as you'd like and may be different in terms of voltage and cycles per second
- when you're hiring equipment such as computers or multi-media projectors, you'll probably find that operating systems and instructions are foreign-language based, and available equipment has a different specification than your home equipment

- video systems could be different – many European countries use the PAL system, although France and Russia, among others, use a standard known as SECAM. A video made for one system will be unlikely to play on another system.

g.6 graphs and charts

To the professional presenter, a graph or a chart is a tool. It's a means to an end rather than an end in itself. If you get your graphs and charts right they'll enable you to explain something to your audience. If you get these charts and graphs wrong, if they're pretty pictures used to dress up your presentation, then you'll confuse your audience and turn them away from whatever your message is. Getting your charts and graphs right is important. To do that you have to:

- choose the right sort of graph or chart to use
- make sure that your graph or chart represents your data accurately and without distortion
- be *absolutely* sure that your graph or chart reaches your audience with the message that you want it to.

Choice

It's important that you choose the right sort of chart or graph for the data that you're explaining to your audience. Here are some guidelines to help you do that:

What are you showing?	Chart or graph to use
One thing, one time period	Pie chart or horizontal bar chart
Several things, one time period	Horizontal or double bar charts
One thing, many time periods	Vertical bar charts or line graphs
Several things, many time periods	Vertical bar charts or line graphs

Avoiding distortion

The key thing to remember here is that when your audience looks at your chart or graph it's not figures that they see. What stays in their mind is the scale of things. It's the relative heights, lengths or widths of the bars on your bar chart or the slope of your graph that they'll recall in the future. This presents a real challenge for the professional presenter. On the one hand he or she can create impact by altering the scales or adjusting the zero point of a graph or bar chart. On the other hand, he or she needs to make sure that the chart or graph truly represents what it claims to. If you get carried away by the need to gain impact you'll be creating charts or graphs that exaggerate the facts and mislead your audience. Remember that, in the end, your chart or graph is there to explain or compare something to your audience, not to pull the wool over their eyes.

Reaching your audience

If your graphs or charts are going to reach your audience then there are a couple of questions that you *have* to answer. So before you create your graph or chart, you must know why you're using it and what you want your audience to get from seeing it.

If you don't have clear-cut answers to these questions then forget about it – the graph or chart you create will be as muddled as your thinking. But even if you have got clear ideas about these there are still some other things that you need to do in order to make sure that your graph or chart will really reach your audience. Here are some of them:

• Make sure that your chart has a title.
• Make sure that this title is big, short and simple and located at the top of your chart/graph.
• Restrict labels to key words, abbreviated if necessary.
• Make sure that labels are big enough to be read.
• Use a legend box to tell your audience about the different colours or symbols.
• Limit your bar charts to no more than five bars; pie charts to no more than six slices and graphs to no more than six lines.
• Use different but contrasting colours for lines or bar and slice fills (*see* **c.11 colours**).
• Don't put more than one graph or chart on the screen at any one time.

- Remember it's the message that counts, so go easy on the 3D and other effects.
- Make sure your handouts contain the key charts or graphs (*see* **h.1 handouts**).

h.1 handouts

The questions that come up about handouts usually fall into two groups:

* when do you give the handouts to your audience?
* what should you put in those handouts?

But the answers aren't as straightforward or as clear cut as you might imagine. Here are some of the issues that you need to consider:

When?

The choices are before the presentation, during the presentation or after the presentation. Here are some of the things that you need to take into account when deciding which you're going to do:

Handout timing	Good points	Bad points
Before	Audience doesn't need to take notes which means you have their full attention.	May leave the audience feeling that they don't need to pay attention – it's all in the handouts.
During	Can create a 'natural' break or mark the boundary between one part of your presentation and another.	Disrupts the flow and rhythm of your presentation. Audience will lose concentration.
After	Provides real 'take-home' material to remind them of what you've said.	Can get lost or misplaced if your presentation is followed by a coffee break or meal.

What?

The choices here lie between key points only, copies of visual aids, and visual aid copies plus supplementary material. Here are some of the things that you need to take into account when deciding which of these levels of content you're going to adopt:

Handout content	Good points	Bad points
Key points only	Reminds your audience of the key issues.	Limited in content. Can leave an impression of a limited presentation.
Visual aid copies	Provides a take-home record of the most impact-full part of your presentation and provides the basis for additional individual notes.	Your commentary/ explanation is missing.
Visual aid copies plus supplementary material	Provides all of above plus other relevant information.	Risk of information overkill.

 Take care though, because some of these choices won't go well together. For example, handing out visual aid copies plus supplementary material before your presentation will tend to confirm your audience's feeling that they've got it all and don't need to listen to you. Views differ about which is the right way to do it. Some presenters argue that you shouldn't hand out any material before your presentation. Doing that, they claim, detracts from your presentation. Others argue that if you don't hand something out before your presentation all you'll see are the tops of people's heads as they scribble notes down as you talk. But, for the professional presenter, the answers to the when and what of handouts are always related to:

- what the presentation's objective is (*see* **o.1 objectives and targets, w.4 why**)
- what the audience is expecting (*see* **a.13 audiences**).

h.2 hands

Hands get used a lot during presentations. You don't just use your hands to pick things up, you also use them to communicate with your audience. Professional presenters know this and learn to use their hands in ways that complement, supplement and amplify their words (*see* **g.4 gestures**). But this doesn't mean that you – or they – wave your hands and arms about or semaphore messages to the audience. These hand movements are often small and subtle. Yet they convey a lot of information. Hand movements can be used, amongst other things, to point, indicate movement, trace shapes or curves and substitute for words. When they do, they:

- are often faster than the spoken word
- are visible at a distance
- have more direct impact than speech.

These movements are made with your right hand if you are right handed and with both hands if you are left handed.

But that's not all that your hands do – they also tell others about your feelings. When you're anxious, you interlock or wring your hands, open and close your fists, scratch your face or just fidget. But when you feel confident this changes. You then make hand movements that are fast, expansive and emphatic. Professional presenters use this 'emotion signing' to influence their audience. They use hand movements that convey confidence, self-assurance and enthusiasm, often to great effect. Use videos of your rehearsals to check out your hand signals (*see* **r.1 rehearsal**). Cut out those that you shouldn't be using and rehearse and build on those that give your audience positive signals. It's also worth watching experienced television presenters for the hand signals that they use. Turn the sound down and see if you can get the 'message' without the words.

h.3 hecklers

Hecklers come in all shapes and sizes and their heckling is just as diverse. They can talk loudly with other people in the audience, read a newspaper, make loud comments and ask lots and lots of questions. But whatever they do, it's always disruptive. It doesn't matter whether you're delivering a sales pitch, presenting a training seminar, running an employee information session or speaking at a conference, a heckler has the potential to put you off your stride, break the rhythm of your presentation and, worst of all, to annoy you. People heckle because:

- you're boring them (*see* **b.5 boredom**)
- they don't agree with what you're saying
- they don't think you know what you're talking about
- they want to be in control
- of a variety of other issues, such as union/management disputes, that you should have been told about – but weren't.

Here are some of the techniques that you can use when you have the misfortune to be heckled.

Ignore them and they'll go away

This approach is based on the assumption that your heckler either craves attention or is trying to provoke you. It assumes that if you ignore your heckler completely, he or she will eventually shut up.

Overcome them

This technique takes strong nerves and an extrovert personality – on your part! When the heckler begins, acknowledge them by looking right into their face, smile broadly and then launch enthusiastically into your next point. This tells the audience and the heckler that you are in control. The heckler will often then stop interrupting. Take care though, for he or she may be an inexperienced questioner rather than a heckler.

Involve them

You do this by asking your audience a rhetorical question during your presentation – when and if it's appropriate – and then singling out the heckler to provide the answer. If you're lucky, this will give them the attention they need and make them more willing to listen to the rest of your presentation. If you're unlucky they'll launch into a lengthy diatribe or rant, which you'll then have to cut short.

Limit them

One way of doing this is to break your audience into small groups. This way the heckler won't infect an entire audience. Another way is to walk over to the heckler and stand beside them. This will often silence them or cause them to hesitate for long enough for you to take control again.

Answer them

It's important that if you answer the heckler's question then you do so briefly and clearly, and then promptly move on.

Use them

This approach works if the points that the heckler raises are points that you were going to raise anyway. You then respond by saying either:

- 'I'm glad you've raised that point' and then launching into your prepared material, or
- 'That's a good point but one that I'll come to shortly.' Don't forget to acknowledge his or her question when you get there!

Use humour

Making a comment like 'Let's call it a draw' to a persistent heckler can get the audience on your side and close him or her down.

Confront them

This should be used only as a last resort, when all else has failed. It involves stopping your presentation and asking the heckler to speak with you privately. After listening to his or her complaint, you then ask for their co-operation for the remainder of your presentation. Another version also involves stopping but then asking the audience whether they'd like you to continue with your presentation.

 Professional presenters know that it's important to close your heckler down. If he or she continues your audience will see you as not being in control of your own presentation and hence not worth listening to. But, however you do it, don't lose your cool and get upset or angry and *never, ever* be rude to your heckler.

h.4   how does a presentation work?

Presentations – when they *really* work – create involvement, understanding and belief. They do this because they:

- have solid substance rather than fashionable style
- tell an interesting story with a beginning, a middle and an end
- reach out to grasp and hold the audience's attention
- show the sheen of thorough preparation and rehearsal
- are rich in conviction rather than reeking of certitude
- need to be performed rather than ought to be done
- are enjoyable for both presenter and audience.

h.5   humour

There's nothing to beat the warm wave of sound that can result from the combination of a good joke, told well, and the response of a receptive audience. There's also nothing worse than the total silence that follows an inappropriate or badly told joke falling on the ears of a 'cold' audience. These extremes illustrate the difficulty of using humour in the presentation. On the one hand, the skilful use of humour enables you to reach your audience; it tells them that you are human, too. On the other hand, however, a poor joke, badly told at the wrong time or to the wrong audience, can go down like the proverbial lead balloon, leaving you struggling with the tattered remains of what you thought was a good presentation.

The combination of humour and presenting is an uneasy, risky one even for the professional presenter (*see* **r.5 risk**). Get it right and humour will add to your presentation; get it wrong and you'll find that your attempts at humour have ruined your presentation. For many presenters, it's a combination that's explored in an improvised, rather than planned or premeditated, way. There's no prior decision to crack a joke at a particular point in the presentation – it happens on impulse or in response to the audience's mood. The results can, of course, be either very good or very bad. In either case you're left feeling not quite sure about what happened and, more importantly, why it happened. All of which isn't good for your future presenting and certainly isn't professional presenting!

For the professional presenter, the joke is a means to an end, a tool, something that can be used to: break down the barriers between he or she and the audience; signal either a shift in the pace of the presentation or a change of direction of the presentation; allow the audience to catch their breath. Whatever its purpose might be, the professional presenter rarely uses a joke in an unpremeditated way. Jokes are always chosen before rather than during the presentation. The jokes that you choose should be:

- chosen with both a specific audience and a particular presentation in mind
- capable of being understood and appreciated by that audience
- short and sharp
- practised and rehearsed
- used only if you feel relaxed and funny.

However, these jokes should *not* – under any circumstances – be gender biased, racist or ageist. Nor should they be told about a member of the audience or someone whom the audience knows well. Despite all of these cautionary notes, there is one set of circumstances where ad-lib humour can help (*see* **a.5 ad-libs**) and that is when the presentation is disrupted because you've messed up or the equipment has failed. Using humour here can reduce the tension felt by you and the audience. But it must be humour that's directed against yourself rather than the equipment or the technician. Try a brief humorous anecdote; one that starts 'The last time this happened to me was in . . .' – and don't panic.

i is for ...

i.1 imagery

Imagery is about mental rather than actual images. You use rhetoric and words rather than pencil, paper or paint to create imagery. When you do that you touch your audience's imagination. Professional presenters use imagery a lot. They use descriptions and comparisons that appeal strongly to the senses; they create mental pictures that affect their audience's imaginations and emotions. They do this in order to:

- illustrate a point and to bring it alive
- clarify facts and information that would otherwise appear dry or distant
- focus attention and emphasize messages
- make things more memorable.

One of us can remember a Spanish colleague's response to a question on how Spain was after the fall of Franco. She replied that it was like a bottle of champagne with the cork just taken out. This conversation was 25 years ago and the imagery invoked has meant the memory has remained clear!

But imagery is best used sparingly; over-use dulls its cutting edge. Professional presenters make very sure that their imagery makes a positive contribution to their audience's understanding rather than adding to their confusion. If you're thinking about using a particular piece of imagery, ask yourself if it does this. If it doesn't, leave it out. Remember, imagery should turn your audience on, not switch them off.

i.2 images

The image is a major item in the toolkit of a professional presenter. It's there because it's versatile and can be put to a wide range of uses. The professional presenter can:

- use an image to act as a substitute for words
- generate an impression of him or herself in the minds of the audience
- create an image in the minds of the audience by speech.

The contributions that images can make to your presentation are significant. This is because images – whether real or imagined –

 appeal to the audience's senses. They have the potential to focus attention, emphasize and underline messages and enable what is meant to be 'seen' better. But achieving those outcomes isn't either instant or easy. It takes skill, practice, planning and thought for the professional presenter to:

- choose and use the right pictures or clip art (*see* **c.2 cartoons, c.9 clip art, o.4 overheads, v.4 visual aids**)
- present him or herself to the audience in ways that enable him or her to access their minds (*see* **a.4 access, a.10 appearance, d.6 dress, i.10 introductions, l.10 looks and form, p.9 posture**)
- use similes, metaphors, analogies and allusions in such a way as to create images in the audience's minds (*see* **a.11 appropriate, i.1 imagery**).

But that's not all that's needed. Because, however the image is used, it will only reach its target, the audience, if it is apt, exact, compact and fresh.

i.3 improvisation

See **a.5 ad-libs**

i.4 influence, persuasion or information?

When deciding what your presentation's objective or target is (*see* **o.1 objectives and targets, w.4 why**), it's worth taking time out to reflect on the three significant 'doing' verbs that are associated with presentations.

Instructing

In its simplest form, instructing is about changing the ways in which people do things. It acts by providing 'this-is-the-way-it-ought-to-be-done' models:

- 'The nut A is now placed on the top of screw D.'
- 'I am talking to you today to ensure that we all know and understand the right way to start up this computer.'

Instructing can also be called teaching or lecturing (*see* **l.6 lectures, t.6 training presentations**). In these, the emphasis shifts from a single 'this-is-the-way-it-ought-to-be-done' model to a range of 'this-is-the-way-it-can-be-done' examples, which the audience may, or may not, use at its own discretion. Most presentations that instruct do so in training courses or programmes. Outside of these, most presentations don't instruct and professional presenters take care not to fall into the trap of appearing to instruct their audience on how to think or feel. Doing this will *not* win over your audience.

Informing

Informing presentations do the obvious – they answer the audience's need for information (*see* **i.5 information**). The information given might include:

- facts – 'Turnover was up by ten per cent last month'
- ideas – 'Why don't we do it this way?'
- interpretations based on facts – 'They are reacting to falling sales'
- feelings about all of the above: 'I believe that, based on the evidence available, it is time for us to move into a new marketing strategy.'

Presentations that inform are very common at conferences, briefing sessions, symposia and seminars. They also tend to be formal in style and structure with audience participation being limited to questions after the presentation.

Persuading

The verb 'to persuade' is commonly used when it comes to describing how we influence each other (*see* **p.6 persuasion**). When it works, persuasion generates a clear and identifiable change in someone else's behaviour. Your presentation might, for example, be aimed at getting your audience to:

- buy your products or services
- work harder or differently
- adopt a new approach
- support your project.

To do this you can give them facts and figures, interpret those facts and figures for them, and generate emotions such as fear or happiness.

When you think about these 'doing' verbs you'll soon realize that it's actually quite rare for a presentation to be locked into just one of them. Usually at least two are involved as, for example, when you inform your audience in order to persuade them to accept your viewpoint, or instruct them using factual information.

However, one of these 'doing' verbs is usually more important than the other – it becomes the key 'doing' verb while the other becomes the enabling 'doing' verb. Professional presenters work hard in the early stages of their preparation to get a clear understanding of which of these 'doing' verbs is key. Not doing that can only lead to confusion and confusion will lead to failure.

i.5 information

At some point, you're going to find yourself standing up in front of an audience that is looking to you for information. Let's assume that, as a professional presenter, you'd worked out that this was going to happen before you started your preparation. Your answer to the question 'why am I presenting to this audience?' was 'in order to inform them' (*see* **w.4 why**). Alternatively you may have decided that you wanted to persuade them or instruct them and do that by using information. In all these situations, the job that you face seems, at first glance, to be a simple and straightforward one. It is – or it seems to be – to furnish your audience with knowledge.

The first step on the road to doing this is to research, research and research. When a professional presenter starts his or her research she or he knows from experience that a lot of material is going to turn up – sometimes too much. This material can be already known to you or the people around you, come from library sources or be accessed through the internet, magazines or newspapers or on TV.

The next step that a professional presenter takes is the one that converts the mountain of material into something distinct and different – information. But the outcome of this conversion process isn't just any old information. It has to be information that's special – information that's accurate, credible and relevant to the audience's needs.

There is no room for half-truths, fables and figments of someone's imagination in a professional presentation; nor is there room for red herrings that divert the audience's attention from the presenter's objective. The ways and means of this conversion process are covered in more detail in **p.12 preparing your material**. It's worth reminding yourself though that it's a process whose outcome is facts. But facts aren't information. However, they can become information when you apply the relevance test. This is the one in which a professional presenter asks two questions about every fact. These are:

- is this fact relevant to my presentation's objective?
- is this fact relevant to the audience?

If you get 'yes' answers to both of these, then you've got a piece of information. One yes isn't enough, it has to be two. But that isn't all you have to do. You now have to take these pieces of information and find the way that brings out their essential quality or character, polish them until they are what they are. In short, you need to make them inspiring (*see* **i.8 inspiration**).

i.6   in-house presentations

In-house presentations are different. For one thing, you know your audience better than the audience at most of your presentations. It's an audience that consists of your colleagues and bosses, the people you work with. But this doesn't make it easier, for this audience is probably just as 'clued in' to the subject of your presentation as you are. It may even be that in the audience is the creative brain that first thought of the core idea of your presentation! All of this means that in-house presentations are stressful – even for the most professional of professional presenters. But with that increased stress comes the opportunity to excel, to do it better, to push back the boundaries of your presenting performance.

Unfortunately, not everybody sees it that way. There's often confusion about the relationship between you, the presenter, and the audience – after all, they are your friends, aren't they? Interdepartmental rivalries – 'not another Marketing campaign!' – can polarize attitudes before a word is spoken. But for the professional presenter, the in-house presentation is akin to the Olympics of presenting. It's an opportunity to push past all these communication barriers and achieve a gold medal presentation.

Here are some tips to help you do that:

- Get yourself into the state of mind that tells you that this isn't just any old presentation – it's *the* presentation.
- Do your homework. It's easy to assume that just because you work there you're up to date with regard to all the current key issues. You need to demonstrate that your knowledge of the business extends beyond your own area. Be able to show an understanding of other areas of the business, such as finance, marketing, information management or even manufacturing, if you want to make a favourable impression.
- Get urgent – but not frantic – about things. These days we all face tough deadlines, even for the most modest of projects. Respect your colleagues' lack of time, set clear objectives, speak concisely and get straight to the point.
- Keep it simple and make your main points obvious. Overly complicated or self-important presentations irritate, 'nice-to-do's' are secondary. Get to the point, fast, and say it out loud, no matter how obvious it seems.
- Be specific and direct. Contrary to rumour and myth, facts don't always speak for themselves. Explain what the facts mean and use them to generate recommendations for action.

i.7   insight

Insight is unusual. You can't make it, buy it, plan it or create it. It's elusive, ephemeral, it just happens. And when it does that you suddenly get a glimpse of what's beneath the surface of a situation or arrive at the solution to a problem. In presentations this can happen to the presenter or to the audience. For the presenter the insight experience often comes pre-presentation – for example, when he or she suddenly sees a new way of reaching the audience. For the audience the flash of insight comes when somebody puts 2 and 3 together and suddenly finds that they've got 7 or maybe even 10. In both of these situations insight is elusive and unpredictable. But it's well worth having. For as someone, somewhere, once said, 'A moment's insight is sometimes worth a life's experience.' But despite its value, there are no magic formulae or processes that will guarantee insight for the professional presenter's audience. But what the professional presenter does know is that if he or she works hard to put him or herself into 'the audience's shoes' then insight, for the audience, *might* follow. It's worth the effort; for as Peter Drucker tells us, 'Insight lasts, theories don't.'

i.8 inspiration

Professional presenters aim to inspire their audiences. They endeavour to do this by breathing or infusing something into the minds of the audience. Sounds like brainwashing, doesn't it? But it isn't. The audience is a willing participant in the process. For when it happens they willingly grasp the idea, the image or the dream that's presented to them and so become inspired. What happens then is that a feeling, an idea, an impulse or a purpose catches fire, becomes kindled, aroused, awakened in the hearts and minds of the audience.

But getting to this point with an audience isn't something that 'just happens'. It takes hard work, thorough preparation and real experience to get an audience to make the jump from 'interested' to 'inspired'. If he or she is going to stand any chance at all of getting an audience to make that jump then a professional presenter must make sure that she or he:

- 'wears the audience's shoes', all the time, through each and every stage of the presentation's preparation and performance
- becomes inspired, aroused and awakened by the subject of the presentation.

Doing the first of these involves a change in attitude. Instead of being concerned with what you, as a presenter, think about what's being prepared or done you have to shift into asking yourself what will or what does the audience think of this? This isn't a one-off or occasional question. For the inspiring professional presenter it's an ingrained habit – one that happens at regular and frequent intervals before and during the presentation. The second of these – an *inspired* professional presenter – is as different again. For when it happens it isn't a logical or systematic event. Nevertheless, it *does* happen and when it does you'll find, as you prepare your presentation, that its subject has 'caught fire' in your mind. This is a rare and precious moment. Make sure that you hold on to that feeling because with it you'll create a presentation that your audience will remember.

i.9   interruptions

Your presentation can be interrupted in a number of ways. As a professional presenter, you'll have to be prepared for these. You'll be ready for the unexpected question (*see* **q.1 questions**), you'll know what to do when someone starts to heckle (*see* **h.3 hecklers**). But there are other sorts of interruption – the fire alarm can go off, the lights (and your projector) can suddenly fail or a noisy machine can start up in the next room. You might even – in some parts of the world – feel the earth shake or the building roof blow off (*see* **d.4 disasters – and how to cope**). All of these can distract your audience and detract from the main message of your presentation. But, as a professional presenter, you'll have to be able to cope with these and the many other sorts of interruption that happen from time to time during presentations.

The key to doing this lies with you. Stay calm, don't panic, draw a deep breath and start to think about what you're going to do next. Here are some suggestions:

- Stay in touch with your audience.
- Involve them in coping with whatever's happening. For example, ask someone to go and see what's happening when the lights fail.
- Use humour to defuse the tension that you and they are feeling.
- If it's an evacuation situation as when the fire alarm doesn't stop after a few moments, tell everyone, clearly and calmly, what to do and where to go.
- If you're in someone else's offices and there is a noisy machine in the next room that's interrupting you, stop and ask if the machine could be switched off, and don't restart your presentation until it has been switched off.
- If you're in a public building or a hotel and there's an external noise that's distracting your audience, stop and ask whoever had organized the meeting if they could stop whatever's causing the noise, and don't restart your presentation until that happens.

- When you do restart, remember that both you and your audience will have temporarily lost the thread of what was being said. Backtrack, remind them how you got to where you were before the interruption, and then move off again.
- If the interruption takes some time to resolve and you hadn't gone too far into your presentation before it happened, offer to restart your presentation from the beginning.
- If the noise can't be stopped or the lights don't come back on, then you must apologize to your audience, tell them that it's unfair on them to try to continue, and offer to come back and do your presentation at another time.

i.10 introductions

Introductions are usually done *to* you rather than *by* you. For that reason professional presenters take steps to make sure that they are introduced in ways that are at least accurate and might even be done well. This involves spending time with the person who's

going to introduce you. The object of this is to make sure that they are clear about who you are, who you represent, the subject and aims of your presentation, how long your presentation will be and when you're going to take questions.

You might even want to summarize the key points of all this in a brief written note to be given to the person who's introducing you. Doing this over a cup of coffee or a drink also enables that person to get a preview of your enthusiasm and passion for the subject you are presenting. Remember that while this introducer isn't your audience, he or she can sell you to your audience with the right sort of introduction. You can also use these key points when it comes to framing the introduction that you make yourself.

The aim of all this is to influence your audience's expectations. If you get it right you can settle into the opening of your presentation (*see* **o.2 openings**) secure in the knowledge that at least your audience knows who you are and what to expect. Get it wrong and the impact of your opening, however it's done, will be lost while your audience grapples with such questions as 'Who is this?' and 'What's he or she talking about?'

j is for

j.1 jargon

There's almost nothing – except perhaps a sudden power cut – that can kill a presentation as fast as jargon. One of the definitions that a dictionary will give you for jargon is that it's talk or writing that is 'unintelligible or meaningless, nonsense or gibberish'. The jargon that you'll find in presentations isn't usually as bad as that. But it's still jargon, as you'll see when you look at another of the definitions for jargon – the one that tells you that jargon is 'speech abounding in unfamiliar terms, or peculiar to a particular set of persons'. If you let this sort of jargon creep into your presentation it won't be long before you'll be wondering where your audience has disappeared to. It'll alienate them, leave them wondering what you said and turn off whatever interest they had.

However, there is one situation in which your use of jargon will be acceptable. That is when you are presenting to an audience of specialists, all of whom understand and use the specialist language (or jargon) that you're using. But if this is the situation then here are two things that you must be sure of: first, that all – not the majority – of your audience understands this specialist language, and second, that *you* understand it well enough to use it in your presentation. If there's any doubt about either of these, then don't use jargon.

Here are some tips about jargon:

- Cut it out – from both your preparation and your presentation.
- Use plain English as much as you can.
- Get someone to come into your rehearsals and do a 'jargon-check' on you and your presentation material.

- Realize that trying to impress your audience by using – or rather misusing – jargon doesn't work.
- If jargon crops up, for example in a question from the audience, then explain it to those of your audience who don't understand what it means.

j.2 jokes

See **h.5 humour**

k is for

k.1 keystoning

This is the phrase that's used to describe the sort of image distortion that you get when the axis of light beam generated by your projector isn't at right angles to the screen. The result is an image that is noticeably wider at its top or bottom. To correct this, tilt either the screen or the projector until they are at right angles to each other and the image has straight sides. Some projectors have built-in keystoning correction functions – check these out *before* you buy or lease.

k.2 kinetic

Presentations are rather like the mobiles of kinetic art – they depend upon action and movement for their effect. These actions or movements can come from:

* video action clips using video tape, DVD or CD-ROM sources (*see* **v.3 videos**)
* animated software-driven presentations with screens full of bullet points that fly in, flash and then fly out (*see* **p.10 powerpoint presentations**)
* props that move or can be moved
* your gestures and walk-and-talk (*see* **g.4 gestures, h.2 hands, f.5 feet, m.1 mannerisms**).

But all of this can be overdone. You can stride to and fro wind-milling your arms or use a video clip that fills the screen with chaotic movement. Your presentation can be so full of features and cool effects that they overwhelm the core message. You might find yourself using props whose movements or presence dominate the presenting platform. In excess, none of these will help you to reach or inspire your audience. Rather the opposite – they'll antagonize, confuse, even turn your audience off. They also have another effect – they have the potential to highlight the faults, flaws and limitations of your presentation. As film producer Sam Goldwyn once put it, 'A wide screen just makes a bad film twice as bad.'

But despite all this, the professional presenter knows that action and movement can contribute to his or her presentation, for without them, you and your words will seem dead, uninteresting and certainly uninspiring. Actions and movements lift the words of the presentation off the page and give them a life beyond their dictionary meanings. As the Chinese proverb tells us, 'Action will remove the doubt that theory cannot solve.'

k.3   kitsch

The kitsch presentation lies beyond the boundaries of professional presenting. For the kitsch presenter, presentation is a mechanical process, one that operates by formulae and recipes rather than hard work, commitment and passion. Presentations like this are superficial, they rely on experience that's pretended and sensations that are counterfeit rather than drawing from real experience, inspiration and perspiration. Kitsch presentations are made up of material that's doubtful rather than verifiable. Presentations like this follow the winds of fashion rather than using solid proven techniques as their foundation. But despite their changefulness, kitsch presentations, at their core, remain the same – counterfeit and phoney. Professional presenters just don't do kitsch presentations.

k.4   knocking copy

The phrase 'knocking copy' comes from the world of advertising. In its simplest form, it describes an advert that focuses on criticizing another manufacturer's product rather than trumpeting the virtues and unique features of its own product. The presenting equivalent is just as bad. For presenting 'knocking copy' is there in the sales presentation that criticizes the competition rather than trying to convince the audience that your product or service will answer their needs. It raises its head when the financial or project presentation concentrates on whose fault it is that profits are down or the project is late rather than presenting answers to those problems. Knocking-copy presentations are destructive, negative and inward-turned. They offer no hope for the future, no solutions, no way forward.

Professional presenters don't do knocking-copy presentations. Their presentations are about inspiration, passion and solutions, they begin the process of drawing up the road map to success. Professional presenting – whatever its subject – has that 'can-we-fix-it-yes-we-can!' style and that, as they say, is about as 'un-knocking' as you can get!

l is for ...

l.1   laser pointers

Laser or laser diode pointers work by emitting a beam of visible radiation that generates a red dot or arrow shape wherever they are pointed. They are low cost, operated by AAA batteries and can be bought in office supply and electronics stores, by mail-order, or over the internet and are being used in more and more presentations. Small enough to be carried in the pocket or on a key chain, these pointers produce a beam of light that's easily visible hundreds of metres away and have power outputs that can range to above 5 milliwatts (mW).

They do, however, represent a risk to you and your audience. Because of this, high-power laser pointers are banned from sale in the UK and the US Food and Drug Administration (FDA) has advised caution in their use. This followed a number of incidents – in which laser pointers were misused – and test results that indicated that many laser pointers on sale failed safety regulations (i.e. they emitted above 1 mW). However, laser pointers with low power outputs – as specified in the relevant European and international safety standards – are still available.

 Professional presenters rarely use pointers of any sort (*see* **p.8 pointers**) but if you feel that you *must* use a laser pointer then make sure that you follow the following safety rules:

- Never use a laser pointer unless you're sure it meets the relevant regulations, particularly for power output.
- Never point any laser pointer at a person.
- Make sure that the room in which you're using the pointer *isn't* entirely blacked out.

- Check the room before your presentation to ensure that it contains no reflective surfaces that might divert the laser beam back into the audience or towards you.
- Never ever stare into a laser pointer and never view a laser beam through an optical instrument.
- Take the batteries out of the pointer when it's not in use.
- Be aware that some locations may require you to register your laser pointer before use. Check whether this is required *before* you get there.

l.2   laughter

Laughter is universal and powerful. Everybody laughs. We laugh when we meet the familiar or the unfamiliar, when we want to attract attention, express relief or announce uncertainty. But, most of all, we laugh when we find something funny. Genuine laughter is good for us. Not only does it make us feel better, more alive, it also boosts our immune systems and triggers off biochemical changes in our bodies that are the reverse of those that happen as a result of stress.

 But the humour that leads to this laughter doesn't always sit easily with presenting (*see* **h.5 humour**). The 'obligatory' opening joke almost always fails because it's being told by a presenter who thinks that it's expected of him or her and is probably more nervous or anxious than he or she is at any other time during the presentation (*see* **o.2 openings, a.9 anxiety**). As a result, the joke falls flat, the resulting laughter is polite, limited and anything but natural. Jokes like this give laughter a bad name. At best, they are obvious and often irrelevant attempts at audience manipulation.

But genuine humorous laughter is good. It's very different from laughter that's social, evasive, apologetic or derisive. It happens when we share our common responses to a joke, story or cartoon (*see* **c.2 cartoons, h.5 humour**). In the professional presentation it happens when you, as a presenter, tell a joke or show a cartoon that's relevant, timely, appropriate and supports your message.

Get all of these right and the audience will be on your side. The genuine humorous laughter that will follow contains the promise of your audience's future attention. It shows you what you and they share – rather than what divides you – and, above all, it's universal.

l.3 layout

The way you arrange your presentation room is important. Get it right and you'll be able to communicate and interact with your audience. Get it wrong or leave it until the last minute and you could find yourself fighting a losing battle to gain and keep their attention and interest.

Some of the things that influence the way you arrange your presentation room are fixed and unchangeable, such as:

- the shape of the room (*see* **r.6 rooms, halls and caverns**)
- the presence and location of pillars, windows, a fixed rostrum or fixed rows of cinema-type seats
- fixed-to-the-wall screens, whiteboards or chalkboards.

Finding out about these early is important (*see* **c.6 checklists**). If you leave it too late or don't check at all you could find yourself in the same situation as the presenter who turned up to give a presentation to find that he'd been allocated an L-shaped room that was too small! However, some of the limitations imposed by these fixed features can be overcome by moving the room furniture around. The list of 'moveables' includes chairs, desks or tables, projector, screen, flip chart board and whiteboard.

Most professional presenters agree that there are four basic arrangements for these.

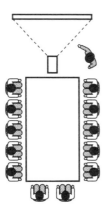

Around-the-table layout

Positive points: good for presentation that will involve a lot of debate and discussion. Can use a round table.

Negative points: limited in numbers – 15 maximum for rectangular table, 10 maximum for circular table. Some of audience may need to turn to see screen.

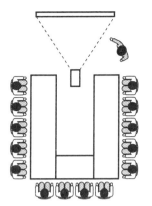

U table layout

Positive points: flexible arrangement – size can be adjusted to cope with up to 25 people. Helps/encourages discussion. Variant can be V-rather than U-shape. Presenter can use space within U or V.

Negative points: some of audience will need to turn to side to see screen. Variant of sitting inside U or V *doesn't* work.

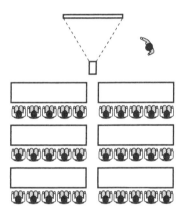

Classroom layout

Positive points: can handle large (25+) numbers easily. Tables give note-taking space. Good for some training presentations. Variant can be multiple small, round tables, as in a café or banquet.

Negative points: reminiscent of school days, discussion not easy, audience mobility (for work groups/exercises) limited. Needs higher-quality projection and graphics, might need sound system.

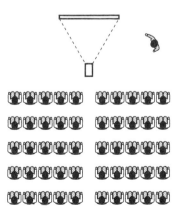

Theatre layout

Positive points: excellent for 'informing' presentations or lectures with large or very large groups.

Negative points: not good for participative presentations, needs good sound system, high-quality graphics on large screen and a raised podium or platform.

For many of your presentations the layout of your presentation space will – at least initially – be decided for you. It'll be the 'way we always have it' or the 'way the last speaker wanted it'. But that doesn't mean that you have to accept it, providing you:

- allow enough time for it to be changed
- are clear about what sort of layout will suit the audience you're presenting to and the aims and objectives of your presentation.

I.4   lcd panels

These are the liquid crystal display (lcd) panels that you connect into your computer and then lay on top of the overhead projector stage or platen (*see* **o.3 overhead projectors**). This then projects the image that your computer has generated on the lcd panel. These days the panels are compact, portable and easy to use but, because of changes in technology, are starting to seem a bit old fashioned. Nevertheless, they're still a powerful presenting tool and you may have one or come across one in your professional presenting travels.

Lcd panels come with various resolutions (VGA (screen resolution 640 × 480) or XGA (1024 × 768)) and have either active or passive matrices. The main difference between these is the refresh rate of the panel. Active matrix or Thin Film Transistor (TFT) panels refresh at a rate of 30–60 times per second while passive matrix, double-layer supertwist nematic (DTSN) or dual-scan lcd panels refresh much more slowly. As a result, you can't:

- play video or show animation through a passive matrix panel because the individual frames will ghost or blur
- keep track of movements of your mouse's pointing icon (mouse) on a passive matrix panel because you'll move it faster than it can be updated.

TFT or active matrix screens are also thinner than dual-scan lcd panels, making them lighter.

In general, the main advantage of both these display panels lies in their compactness and portability. They also share with their more modern cousin, the lcd or multimedia projector, the ability to change the image displayed. This means that they can be used for 'what-if' displays of spreadsheet data or graphs in which your audience's decisions or ideas are fed into a computer program and the outcome is then – almost instantly – displayed on the screen. Their major disadvantage lies with the fact that when used with an overhead projector with below 4000 lumens of power the projected image doesn't have sufficient brightness. As a result you'll have to darken the room – an action that will give your audience some difficulty if they want to take notes.

l.5 lcd projectors

See **m.4 multimedia projectors**

l.6 lectures

The lecture is a traditional way of imparting information – one that's been used in universities and other centres of learning for centuries (*see* **i.5 information**). However, because of this history, the lecture has acquired a bad image. It's often seen as somewhere where, as a member of the audience, you're talked *at* rather than *to*. As a result your average lecture is usually seen as being boring, long-winded and dry. But lectures don't have to be like that.

For you – as a professional presenter – the lecture is yet another opportunity to communicate with your audience. Do this well and your audience will be given the opportunity to 'tap into' information that would be difficult to access in other ways. Your lecture will not be a closed loop of knowledge or information. It will encourage or invite its audience to think imaginatively about its subject. It will impart information, provide a framework for future work or discussions on the subject in hand and leave the door open for the audience to pursue their own learning pathway outside the lecture.

So, if you find yourself with the opportunity to give a lecture at a university, college or conference grab it with both hands. That lecture will give you the chance to extend the range of your presenting experience; it'll present you with a challenge on which you can sharpen the cutting edge of your presentation skill. Here are some tips to help you do that:

- Recognize that an average lecture lasts 50 or so minutes and your average audience's attention span is limited to around 10 minutes.
- Limit your lecture content to between three and five core concepts.
- Tell your audience what you're going to tell them, tell them that and then tell them what you've told them.

- Develop each of your core concepts into five- to ten-minute mini-lectures, each ending with a mini-summary.
- Keep your sentences short and simple and your voice varied, but not too fast or too slow (*see* **u.3 using your voice**).
- Don't forget that, while you may have given this lecture before, it's the first and possibly the only time that your audience will have heard it.
- Present your ideas, initially, in a stripped-down, unqualified form and then use guided discussion to identify the detail and the qualifications.
- Give your audience time to understand and write down what your visual aids are saying.
- If audience interest is flagging, ask them to turn to their neighbour and talk about the core point that you've just presented.
- Always finish by reminding them what you've said.

I.7   length

When it comes to presentation length, short is better than long but too short is almost as bad as not at all. Audience attention is the key factor here. Audience members are, by and large, subject to far more stimulation than they can usefully use. There's much to draw their attention – the sound of the presenter's voice, the images on the screen, the coughs and rustles that come from other people in the audience and the noise of traffic that filters in through the windows. There's also the memory of what their partner said at breakfast, the nagging doubt about yesterday's decision and the growing concern about what needs to be done back at the office. Yet audience members – just like the rest of us – are consciously aware of only a limited amount of all this at any given moment in time. They filter these multiple sensations and events and let through only what they find relevant or interesting. Doing this enables them to cope with what would 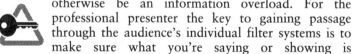 otherwise be an information overload. For the professional presenter the key to gaining passage through the audience's individual filter systems is to make sure what you're saying or showing is *interesting*. Doing this means being empathic towards your audience. You have to put yourself in their shoes, see it from their point of view and, above all, show them that you're doing that.

But, no matter how well you do this, you're going to have to recognize that you'll never overcome your audience's attention lapses. These are short breaks in attention that:

- don't have a known cause
- are called 'Bill's blocks', after the man (called A.G. Bills) who discovered them, and
- occur frequently – whatever we are doing.

The time between attention lapses is called the attention span. Estimates of this vary considerably, from two up to ten minutes, and it changes with the individual and the circumstances. Too long a presentation will cause your audience's attention span to plummet while too short a presentation will leave them wondering if they missed something. You have to accept that each member of your audience will have their own individual attention span whatever you do. So keep reminding your audience about the key points of your presentation – right up to the end.

l.8 lighting

Most of the time your presenting will take place under normal light conditions. This means that your audience can see you and – just as importantly – you can see them. Seeing your audience and getting your 'audience-looking' right is a key factor for a professional presenter (*see* **e.7 expressions, e.8 eye contact**). But this normal light level has its disadvantages because it will challenge the ability of your projector to project legible images. A typical slide projector, for example, will demand a darkened room if the images it projects are to be clearly seen (*see* **s.5 slide projectors**) and a multimedia projector with image brightness capability below 1000 lumens will struggle to reach an audience under normal light levels (*see* **m.4 multimedia projectors**).

There will also be some situations – at conferences or in large halls or when you're presenting to large audiences – in which you'll need stage lighting. This enables you to have different light levels in different parts of your presenting area. It means everybody in the audience will be able to see you at the same time as they can see the images your projector is generating. But the downside of this is that while the audience can see you, you can't see them. This means that you lose out on audience feedback (*see*

f.4 feedback) and eye contact (*see* **e.8 eye contact**). These are so important that it's worth finding a compromise between the clarity of stage lighting and the audience contact that comes with normal lighting. There are two steps in doing this:

Step 1   Getting your stage lights right

a Put on all the stage lights that will be on when you present.
b Turn the house lights off.
c Hold your hand up about 23 cm in front of your face, palm towards you.
d Starting in the dark part of the stage, walk forward until you reach the exact point where your hand is lit.
e Stop.
f Move backwards slowly, one step at a time, stopping when your hand becomes dark.
g Take one step forward, towards the light.
h Mark that spot on the stage. This gives you the position that you shouldn't go beyond – if you want the audience to see you.
i Make sure that you're happy with the stage lighting's:
  • colour or tint – red is hot and exciting, orange is warm but strange, yellow is cheerful, green is weird, blue is cool and sombre, magenta is warm and romantic, lavender restful and soothing and pink active and flashy. The more vivid the colour or tint, the more pronounced the effect; the more pastel, the more delicate and subdued the effect
  • direction – for best effect, ask for a warm tinted 'key' light source 45 degrees to the left and 45 degrees above you, coupled with a cool tinted 'fill' light source 45 degrees to the right and 45 degrees above you. Together these will yield a natural depth, free of harsh shadows, that flatters the facial features and gives you a pleasing appearance.

Step 2   Getting the house lights right

a Stand on the lit side of the above position with the stage lights on.
b Get two or three people to sit in different positions in the hall.
c Gradually increase the level of the house lighting.
d Stop when you can clearly see who's sitting where.
e Ask the people in the audience if they can see your face clearly.
f If they can't, adjust the stage lighting until they can.

If you can't do any of these because there's no lighting technician then you may have to cope with not seeing your audience. Try to overcome this situation by imagining that you can see your audience and making sure that you remember to scan this imaginary audience systematically but not mechanically.

I.9   listening

The way that presenters do, or don't, listen to what their audience says to them is one of the things that identifies professional

 presenters. Professional presenters hear, listen to, digest and respond to what their audience says, while not-so-professional presenters just hear and then retort. The difference between hearing and listening is more than just a matter of words. Hearing is a purely physical process, a reaction to the sound of noises and other people's voices. It's passive and involuntary. Listening, however, is active. It demands the presenter's voluntary participation, asks for her or his time and energy. Listening also gives you more than hearing. You'll get hints and signs about how the audience is feeling about you or the subject of your presentation. But that's not all that listening does. For when you really listen to, rather than just hear, what is said then you affirm, in a very real and tangible way, the value of what your audience has to say.

Here are the ten top rules for effective listening:

1 Indicate that you are listening – look, encourage by nodding, and reinforce – 'I see'.
2 Don't interrupt, unless it's to ask for clarification and stop others interrupting.
3 Listen for the theme of the question, focus on what the speaker is saying.
4 Concentrate on hearing 'what' is said, not 'how' it is said.
5 Maintain eye contact, lean forward, occasionally summarize – 'So you are saying . . .'
6 Don't rush to fill the speaker's pauses. If she or he stops, encourage them to continue – 'Go on' or 'What happened then?'
7 Listen in an understanding way, don't prejudge what they will say before they've said it!
8 Listen for the message between the words. Sometimes the essential message is contained in what is not said.

9 Listen for feelings as well as meanings.
10 Check your interpretation of the question or comment, ask questions if you don't understand or try to clarify by saying, 'So the situation is . . .?' or 'Do you mean . . .?'

I.10   looks and form

The way that each of us looks is particular and individual, almost unique. It's also, so psychologists tell us, an important factor in the way we appear to, or are perceived by, others. As such our 'look' is a key opening statement in any presentation (*see* **a.10 appearance**). But this is a statement without words, a statement that is built from our looks, the way we dress (*see* **d.6 dress**) and the way we stand and move (*see* **f.5 feet, n.2 non-verbal communication, p.9 posture**).

The factors that come together to make up your individual look are many and varied. They include, for example, the physical characteristics and bone structure that you inherit from your parents, the way you wear your hair, the jewellery and other adornments that you may wear and the colour of your skin, lips, hair and eyes. Some of these factors are controllable, others are changeable or modifiable and others you are stuck with. Some of them, however, are significant in that they influence the way that an audience perceives you as a presenter. Your height, weight and body shape are all factors that can have a considerable effect upon an audience's reaction to you. Tall people are literally looked up to, thin people are seen to be tense and nervous and fat people are thought of as warm-hearted, sympathetic, good-natured and agreeable – all without saying a word! But as most people's height, weight and body shape are primarily defined by their genetic make-up, the question for the professional presenter is whether these can be modified to advantage. The answer, of course, is a very personal and individual one. But there are, nevertheless, some general rules that can help us all to make the best of what we have and, in so doing, present a 'good look' to the audience:

- Everybody's hair – whether it's long, short, curly or patchy – looks best when it's clean, well cared for and cut or styled well.
- Grubby or stained hands with bitten or unkempt nails are very unattractive and off-putting.

- Beards need to be tidy and well trimmed, whatever their length.
- Bad teeth lead to bad breath and limited smiling, both of which will do little to help your presentation.
- A healthy, well cared-for complexion will help your audience to get 'turned-on' to what you're saying.
- Regular exercise leads to fitness and fit people look good. Use the Body Mass Index (BMI) or Ashwell Shape Chart to help focus the exercise that you take (*see* **Taking it Further** for more information).

m is for . . .

m.1 mannerisms

We all have mannerisms. They are those habitual peculiarities of action, expression or speech that we've acquired over the years. We use these gestures, facial expressions or speech patterns a lot – almost without knowing that we do – when we talk to each other. Without them we would appear robotic, almost inhuman. With them we send signals about the sort of person we are – or aren't.

The range of these mannerisms is enormous. They include:

- style mannerisms, for example a phrase such as 'if you like' or 'so to speak' that's used repeatedly
- physical mannerisms, such as hand-wringing, foot-tapping, touching your face or body and playing with loose change in a trouser pocket
- speech mannerisms, such as 'erm-ah', nervous coughs, grunts, sighs and unnecessary laughs.

 When it comes to presenting, personal mannerisms are usually quickly accepted by the audience. But they can sometimes get in the way, for example when they are distracting or over-used. When this happens, it's the mannerism rather than what you're saying that becomes the focus of the audience's attention. Videoing your rehearsals will help here (*see* **r.1 rehearsal**). If you turn the sound off during play-back you'll soon be able to see the gestures that go to make up your personal mannerisms. You'll also be able to see whether or not you use them to excess. Listening to the soundtrack without the picture or getting someone to listen to your presentation will help you to identify any style or vocal mannerisms that you have. Once spotted it's usually a question of consciously using them less.

m.2   microphones

If you're going to do your presentation in any more than a medium-sized room or hall (*see* **r.6 rooms, halls and caverns**) or present to an audience of more than 25 people (*see* **l.3 layout**) then you're going to need to use a sound system and a microphone (*see* **c.1 can you all hear me?**). Using a microphone well is a skill and one that will take quite a lot of practice to get right. It's also one that you'll need to acquire if you're going to become a professional presenter.

There are three basic sorts of microphone:

- omni-directional microphones that pick up sounds from all directions
- uni-directional microphones that pick up sounds from only one direction, usually in a cone-shaped pattern
- cardioid microphones that pick up sound in one direction but in a heart-shaped pattern, strong in the front, and about half as strong from the sides.

 Getting to know which sort of microphone you've been given is important. You can test this by speaking into its head, first from the front and then from the side. If the sound is fairly even from all sides, you have an omni-directional microphone. If your voice fades when you speak from the side, you have a uni-directional or cardioid microphone. Most of the time you'll be given a cardioid-type microphone. This will pick up the sound of your voice when you stand directly in front of it but ignore sounds from other directions. All of these microphones can be either a condenser type, which needs additional power to get its signal to the amplifier, or the dynamic type, which uses the sound source alone to generate signals sent to the amplifier. The signal that your microphone generates is sent to the amplifier by using a cable or an audio transmitter.

Cable-connected or hard-wired microphones have cables plugged directly into a sound control board or amplifier. Most of these are of the low impedance type (low resistance), which are resistant to interference and tolerate long cable runs. Wireless or audio transmitter microphones use tiny transmitters that send the sound of your voice to a receiver that's connected to the amplifier. They can be either hand-held or pinned or clipped to your lapel. These microphones run on batteries, which need to be changed regularly, and are sometimes subject to transmitter interference or 'dropout'. The lapel type leaves your hands free and doesn't have dangling cords to trip over, but its sound isn't as good as the sound you get from a larger, hand-held microphone and you can't control the volume by lowering and raising the microphone.

Here are some practical tips for using your microphone:

- If you're using a stand-mounted microphone use the gooseneck or boom to make sure that the microphone stays within 8 to 20 cm of your mouth.
- If you're using a hand-held microphone hold it about 7 to 10 cm under your chin.
- Speak across your microphone – rather than into it.
- Don't blow into your microphone to see if it's on, say something or tap it gently.
- Place a clip-on microphone over rather than under clothing.
- When you're not using a hand-held microphone always hold it in an upright position, lowered away from your mouth but ready to be used.
- Don't hold two microphones closer than 60 cm from each other or you'll get some unpleasant, unnatural sounds!
- Take care of your microphone. Don't drop or bang it or dangle it by the cable – you're a presenter, not a rock star!

m.3 multimedia

We live – whether we like it or not – in a world that's irrevocably multimedia. But this isn't new; it's always been like that. Our five senses – smell, taste, sight, hearing and touch – have always given us the potential for a rich multichannel relationship with the world around us. But the development of written language around 5000 years ago changed the balance of that relationship. Literacy spread, following in the train of changes in the technology by which the written word was created, reproduced and distributed. As a result, the written word became dominant, almost, but not quite, eclipsing the visual image. Creating visual images became a specialist occupation for artists – and the use of these images became limited to art and religion.

But technology never stands still. Lithography, photography and, nowadays, the digital encoding of images for use by electronic equipment, have begun to restore the balance of these senses. This will continue. For humankind has always had an innate bias towards the image. That's why they appear in newspapers, adverts, traffic signs, as computer screen icons and last, but not least, in our presentations. The reason for this is quite simple – the human brain is said to be able to process images 400,000 times faster than it can text. That's why we've been creating images for at least 20,000 years – far longer than the written word has been around.

But multimedia isn't just about images. You can now digitize music and sound effects ready for hi-fi reproduction at the press of a key. This means that your presentations are edging, or being dragged, into the multimedia arena. Already you can flood your audience with still or moving high-resolution images complete with soundtracks or sound effects. In time, no doubt, you'll be able to add touch, feel and taste effects, giving your audience a total multimedia presentation.

But multimedia doesn't automatically upgrade the quality of your presentation. Indeed, quite the opposite can happen with multimedia misuse damaging and downgrading the quality of your communication with your audience. The key to the *effective* use of multimedia lies in the skill with which it's used. As a professional presenter you'll need to acquire and maintain that skill. You'll need to become first, literate, and then second, fluent, in multimedia use. If you achieve this your presentation will have real and solid substance rather than fashionable style (*see* **k.3 kitsch**). Then it will, as Marshall McLuhan *didn't* say, be the message rather than the medium that counts.

m.4 multimedia projectors

These are small, self-contained and highly portable projectors that take the images that are generated or stored in your computer and project them onto a screen. They work with PC or Mac computers, usually without special software, messy set-up routines or special 'handshakes'. To generate those images they use either:

- thin film transistor (TFT) liquid crystal displays (lcd) or
- polysilicon lcd panels or
- digital light processing (DLP) technology.

Light from a halogen or metal halide lamp shines through these panels or displays and is then projected onto the external screen via a lens. Many multimedia or data projectors can also handle audio signals, such as sound effects, as well as signals from VCR and DVD units or memory cards.

Portability is good with weights ranging from 4 to 20 pounds. Projected image brightness ranges from 300 to as high as 2200 lumens. What you will need in your projector will depend upon:

- what you're using it for – training presentations in which your audience will need to take notes will need a projector that's bright enough to avoid having to dim the room lights
- what screen you're using (*see* **s.2 screens**)
- the number of people in your audience – large audiences need larger screen image sizes and the light generated by the projector is spread over a larger area, leading to lower picture brightness and lower visibility.

Here are some guidelines:

Projector brightness (lumens)	Suitable audience size	Ambient lighting level needed
less than 500	Small	Dark–dim
500–1000	Medium	Reduced
1000–1500	Large	Normal
1500+	Large–huge	Normal

Image resolution or sharpness is also important:

Presentation type	Resolution needed (column pixels × row pixels)	Projector rating	
Simple graphics, graphs, pie or bar charts	800 × 600	SVGA	Increasing resolution
Spreadsheets, detailed graphics	1024 × 768	XGA	
High-resolution graphics	1280 × 1024	SXGA	
Very high resolution	1600 × 1200	UXGA	

A top-of-the-range multimedia projector can cost you (or your company) a great deal of money so it's worth thinking about what features you need, such as portability, SXGA rating or multiple input/output ports, before you buy. It's also important that you feel easy using the projector. So set up trials, using the same presentation, with different makes of projector.

Here are some tips:

- Buy the highest brightness level you can afford. Brighter images leave a better impression than dull, dark, dingy ones.
- Zoom lenses are worth having – particularly if you need to use the projector in different-sized rooms.
- A remote control gives you the freedom to move about. Do make sure, though, that you know where the unit mounted control buttons are – batteries can run out!
- Image contrast – or the ratio between lightest and darkest areas – should be as high as you can afford. High contrast → clearer images. The higher the contrast ratio, the easier your projector will be to use in well-lit rooms, thus enabling people to take notes, etc. Typical contrast ratios range from 150 to 400.
- Switching your light source off and on too frequently will reduce bulb life. Leave the fan running for a while after you've switched the light off.

- Make sure you keep a spare bulb and practise how to change it without burning your fingers.

Remember that this sort of projector is still new technology. This means that there will always be a newer model – smaller, cheaper and brighter – coming on the market (*see* **t.4 technology**). Future projectors will not only keep pace with upgrades in laptop computer screen resolutions, they'll also use developments such as plasma displays. This may mean that it's worth considering leasing or hiring your multimedia projector rather than buying.

n.1 nerves

Nerves, or rather, nervousness, is built into the act of professional presenting. Sweating palms, increased heart rate, memory loss, difficulty in breathing are all common symptoms of what we call nervousness. Your body seems to be saying to you, 'Why are you here, doing this, in front of all these people?'

 In fact, presenting nervousness is *so* common that it's *normal*. As Mark Twain told us, 'There are two types of speakers: those that are nervous and those that are liars'.

Some of your nervousness will have its roots in a generalized and rather vague feeling that 'something will go wrong' (*see* **a.9 anxiety**). But as a professional presenter you know that this is unlikely. After all, you've prepared your material well (*see* **p.12 preparing your material**) and rehearsed yourself thoroughly (*see* **r.1 rehearsal**). You know and are confident about:

- what you're going to say
- who you're going to say it to
- why you're going to say it
- how you're going to say it.

But you're still nervous, although nervousness isn't really the right word to describe what you're feeling. What you're experiencing is better described as anticipation. And this is exactly how you *should* be feeling! It means that you are absolutely ready and raring to go, your body might even be twitching in its eagerness to perform. You're literally sitting on top of a huge reservoir of potential energy; one that's just waiting to explode into a *huge* presenting performance. The knack here is for you to side-step your dislike of or attempts to control what you call nervousness. Instead, regard it as a good friend who will look after you during your presentation. Presenters who don't do this, who hate their nerves, become overly nervous – a completely different physical and mental state, one that never, *ever*, leads to good presentations (*see* **s.6 stage fright**). So when you feel nervous, remind yourself that it's your nerves that'll give your presentation its cutting edge. Smile and relax in the knowledge that it means you're ready (*see* **r.2 relaxation**).

n.2   non-verbal communication

Actions *do* speak louder than words. Research tells us that the dictionary meaning of the words that you use accounts for as little as a tenth of all that you communicate. The professional presenter is keenly aware of this. He or she not only chooses these words with care, but also makes sure that:

- the way that they are said adds to their impact
- his or her gestures, facial expressions, gaze and posture support and complement these words.

All of these send non-verbal messages, though some of them, in particular features such as pace of speech, use of pauses and tone of voice, involve sounds. The most significant of these non-verbal messages involve what is commonly described as body language. This body language accounts for over half of your line-of-sight communication and uses your head, arm, hand, foot and leg movements, body posture, gestures, eye movements, facial expressions and appearance and dress.

If you doubt any of this then think back to the last time you were with someone who stood with his or her arms crossed, tapping his or her foot and looking annoyed, who then huffed, 'I'm fine.' Which did you believe – the words or the body language and tone of voice? The truth is that these non-verbal messages often send a much louder and clearer message than the words you speak.

Professional presenters use non-verbal communication to their advantage. They use gestures to reinforce and expand their spoken words (*see* **g.4 gestures**), dress and appearance to add to their authority (*see* **a.10 appearance, d.6 dress**), eye contact to connect with their audience (*see* **e.8 eye contact**), facial expressions to change and adjust the mood, pitch and pace of their presentation (*see* **f.1** face) and the movements of their hands (*see* **h.2 hands**), feet (*see* **f.5 feet**) and body (*see* **p.9 posture**) to add to the words that they speak. When you add all these to the pitch, speed, pauses and emphasis of the words that they speak (*see* **u.3 using your voice**) you'll see that it's a potent package. However, the professional presenter doesn't just need to be fluent in the *use* of non-verbal communication – she or he also needs to be able to read the non-verbal messages that the audience sends with equal fluency (*see* **f.4 feedback**).

n.3 notes, scripts, overheads or cue cards?

All presenters need notes of one kind or another. Presenting without any notes is rather like setting sail across the ocean without a chart or compass – fraught with risks and uncertainties. Even professional presenters don't do it. But what they do is to take balanced and realistic decisions about what form these notes will take. Here are your choices.

Scripts

Scripts are, literally, every word you say. They're often formal, stilted and awkward, though they can be written in a spoken or colloquial style. Even then it requires great skill to bring a script alive, to shift its emphasis so that you're talking *to* your audience rather than *at* them. Professional presenters use scripts only under circumstances where a formal statement – about, for example, a new project, an expansion or a take-over – has to be made or when what's being said is on-the-record. If you think about these, you'll soon see that they aren't presentations, they're announcements. As such their purpose is exclusively that of giving the audience information – it's one-way traffic rather than the two-way exchange of real communication (*see* **c.12 communication**). But even when you have to make a scripted announcement, there are some things that you can do to help make it sound natural:

- avoid the head-down mumble-mumble position
- lift your head up, look round, establish eye contact
- colour your voice by varying pitch, pace and volume where appropriate, such as before a key point
- pause before and after key points or when changing subject.

Notes

Notes are a condensed version of what you say. Most professional presenters who use these keep them on sheets of A4 or foolscap paper and in a ring-binder. That way they stay tidy and you don't lose your place. Guide lines for preparing and using your notes include:

- write the topic at the top of the sheet and key points below
- include references to slides, visuals and handouts as well as reminders, such as 'pause here', and links, such as 'So now let's move on to how we . . .'
- number the pages, so you know where you are
- use large type and double spacing, so you can read it at a glance
- highlight key points.

Cue cards

Cue cards are even more condensed than notes. They are plain postcards or small, stiff reference-type cards. Each of these will contain prompts about what you say next. These prompts usually take the form of single bullet-point key words but can also be visuals, for example a smiley face, or brief sentences or phrases, for example when an exact quotation or wording is necessary. Cue card guidelines include:

- print what's on them – so that you can read them easily
- make your printing big enough to be read at a glance
- number your cards
- keep them in order – punch holes and thread them onto a loop of string if necessary.

Overheads

You can also use overheads, slides and visual aids to prompt what you say (*see* **o.3 overhead projectors, o.4 overheads**). But doing this is not without its temptations and risks. You must avoid reading out the words on the overhead or slide or packing your overhead with too many words.

However, if you're using overheads there's a compromise. You can either write your bullet points on the cardboard frame of the overhead or attach a fold-over cue card or note sheet to that frame.

In the end it's up to you to decide which of these you use to provide the prompts that you need for your presentation. But, whichever you choose, remember to use them as a support rather than a crutch and to talk directly *to* your audience and *not* down at your notes or prompts.

n.4   numbers

The world is full of numbers – telephone numbers, fax numbers, personal identification or PIN numbers, security lock numbers, identification card numbers and car registration numbers. All of these are significant, in one way or another, in your life. But let's not forget that numbers and the world of work go hand in hand. They are used to define or quantify a wide range of things – profit, loss, sales figures, efficiency data, performance returns – in a wide range of organizations. Because of this, numbers and presentations come together quite often. While this happens most often in technical or financial presentations (*see* **f.7 financial presentations, t.3 technical presentations**) it can also happen to a lesser degree in other sorts of presentation (*see* **s.1 sales presentations, l.6 lectures**).

The presence of numbers in a presentation is something that sets the alarm bells ringing for the professional presenter. There are two major reasons for this. The first is that your average audience has a limited tolerance for numbers. What usually happens when you give your audience a screen of numbers to look at is that you lose them. The reason for this is simple; it's that for the average audience a screen full of numbers has an amazingly mind-numbing and soporific effect. Fill your screen with numbers and they'll lose interest, not only in what's on the screen but also in what you're saying. The second reason for the alarm bells is that deep in the hearts of many members of your average audience there lies an innate suspicion about numbers. As someone, somewhere, once put it, 'You can prove anything with figures'. So when you've put up a screen full of numbers what happens is that all of that trust or credibility you've worked so hard to achieve is put – at least for a while – on hold.

But there will always be audiences that are not 'average'. These will be the audiences that are well versed in some sort of technology – one for which numbers are the lingua franca – or audiences of accountants or financial analysts, for whom numbers are grist to the everyday mill. These, and other specialist audiences, will *expect* numbers in your presentation. What this means is that, in this day and age, achieving a number-free presentation is almost impossible. For the professional presenter, the challenge is then to find a way of presenting these numbers that doesn't turn the audience off. In short, a way of presenting numbers that works! (*see* **g.6 graphs and charts, t.1 tables**).

o is for

o.1 objectives and targets

As you make the move to becoming a professional presenter you'll realize that there's a factor that's common to all your presentations. It doesn't matter whether you're doing a financial presentation, a state-of-the-project presentation or a sales presentation because in all of these your aim, target or objective is to influence your audience. That is, you want to change their thoughts and/or feelings and/or behaviour or actions.

The 'and/ors' above are important. You'll rarely want to change only the way your audience thinks; you'll usually want to influence the way they think *and* act and you may even want to influence the way they think, act *and* feel!

All of this adds up to the objective or target of your presentation. Defining this clearly and doing it before you start your preparation is *very* important. You should be able to spell out your target or objective in a single, simple sentence. This should say, clearly and unambiguously, what you want your audience to do or believe or feel as a result of your presentation. This is your presentation's mission statement. It will tell you, or anybody else, exactly what it is that you want your presentation to achieve. But that's not all it will do. If your presentation is going to be a success then this mission statement must also be clearly understood by your audience and seen, by that audience, as being appropriate to them, their roles and the current situation.

Here are some examples:

- To get the Board's approval for the DCR project.
- To persuade the Steering Group to agree to and support your proposal.
- To sell the XYZ company a PDX computer.
- To alert this committee to the risk to humpback whales.

But getting that right, writing it down in big bold capitals, isn't the end. You'll need to keep referring back to this mission statement, for example when you are:

- deciding what material you're going to include in – or exclude from – your presentation (*see* **p.12 preparing your material**)
- preparing your visual aids (*see* **v.4 visual aids**)
- rehearsing your presentation (*see* **r.1 rehearsal**).

You'll also do that again – one last time – just before you get up to begin your presentation (*see* **b.2 beginnings**).

o.2 openings

The opening of your presentation is a significant event. As a professional presenter you'll open your presentation with impact and drive. That opening will be attention-getting and will tell your audience you're worth listening to.

If you're not sure about this go back to **b.2 beginnings** to check it out. When you've done that come back here to look at these examples of the ways you can open your presentation.

Make a thought-provoking or arresting statement

To succeed your statement needs to be true, simple, relevant, direct, to the point, and intriguing, even controversial.

Example: 'Over 60 per cent of all the Rolls-Royces ever built are still on the road.'

Ask a provocative question

Example: 'How many of you walked to work today?' or 'How many of you own a foreign car, camera, or watch?'

Use a quotation

This has to:

- relate to the subject of your presentation
- have impact
- be short enough to be understood.

Example: 'The best way to help the poor is not to be one of them' or 'The duration of the marriage is inversely proportional to the cost of the wedding.'

Generate emotional appeal

This can be done in a number of ways. You can, for example, ask a question, make a factual statement or begin a story. But it has to be delivered in an emotive way.

Example: Introduce a presentation on famine relief with the following words: 'It only takes 50p from each of your pockets to enable Joseph Umbala to live until next year's harvest.'

Tell a story or personal experience that relates to your subject

The story has to be relevant, powerful and brief. If you get it right you'll tell your story naturally and with conviction and enthusiasm. It'll also have the benefit of helping you to overcome the very natural nervousness that you'll experience at the beginning of your presentation.

Refer to an event or person

Your reference needs to be one that everyone in the audience will know about.

Example: 'Every one of you in this room today will recall the shock and pain that you felt on September 11th 2001.'

Pay a compliment to the audience's organization, profession, etc.

 This will only work if it is genuinely felt – rather than cynically used – and is genuinely warranted.

Get it wrong and you'll come over as dishonest, cynical and deceitful, and none of these will help your presentation. A variation of this sort of opening is to relate something in your background to the common denominator that brings your audience together. Done well, this will give the audience the impression that 'you are one of them' and, in certain circumstances, that you're all in this together.

Demonstration

This opening draws strongly on the audience's ability to see as well as hear.

Example: 'Here, ladies and gentlemen, is a series of fax messages received by our City branch in May [holding them up]. They ought to contain repeat orders – but they don't. Every single one of these is a complaint.'

You'll have noticed that none of these openings makes a statement about what the subject of your presentation is. The reason is simple – doing that is dull, uninspiring and likely to turn your audience off rather than on. Remember, the opening of your presentation is a golden opportunity for you to:

- capture your audience's attention and interest
- provide the audience with a clear answer to their question 'What's in it for me?'

Choosing the right opening is important. Make sure that the one you choose is right for you, your audience and the subject of your presentation.

o.3   overhead projectors

These are the Model Ts of the projector world. But if you dismiss them in favour of a hi-tech multimedia or a slide projector, you do so at your peril. Overhead projectors are reliable, uncomplicated and inexpensive. As a consequence, you'll find them almost everywhere. They work by shining light through an image you've prepared and then projecting this – via a lens – onto a screen. These images can either be:

- printed onto transparent film, or
- created by your computer on a separate liquid crystal display (lcd) panel (*see* **l.4 lcd panels**).

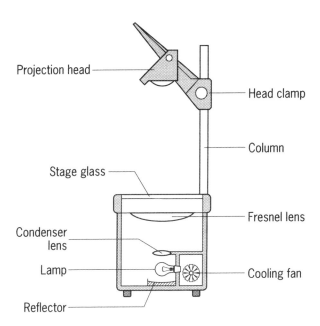

Projection head — Projection head

Head clamp

Column

Stage glass

Fresnel lens

Condenser lens

Lamp

Cooling fan

Reflector

Overhead projectors can have their light source in one of two places: the base of the projector or its head. The first of these is called a transmissive projector because the light shines up through the transparent image and then into the lens. The second is called a reflective projector because the light shines down onto the transparent image and is then reflected back up to the lens. Projected image brightness will range from 1700 to 11,000 lumens, depending on model. The image brightness that you'll need from your overhead projector will depend upon:

- what you're using it for – if you're using an lcd panel you'll need at least 4000 lumens (*see* **l.4 lcd panels**)
- what screen you're using (*see* **s.2 screens**)
- the number of people in your audience. Large audiences need larger screens with the result that the light generated by the projector is spread over a larger area. To maintain visibility and keep the room lighting at normal levels you'll need at least 2500 lumens.

The resolution or sharpness of the image you project will also depend on the quality of the lens on the projector. Here's what you'll need:

Presentation type	Lens needed	
Simple graphics, graphs, pie or bar charts	Singlet	*Increasing quality*
Spreadsheets, detailed graphics	Doublet	
High-resolution graphics	Triplet	↓

If portability is an issue for you remember that reflective projectors are generally smaller and lighter – and hence more portable – than transmissive projectors.

Using a powerful overhead projector – one that works well in a fully lit room – helps you to get in touch with your audience. It's located at the front which means that the audience can see you, and you can see them. Your presenting position will give you face-to-face and eye contact with your audience and this will help you to pick up non-verbal cues from them (*see* **e.8 eye contact, f.4 feedback, n.2 non-verbal communication**). If adaptability is going to be a key issue for you then remember that with an overhead projector you can:

• modify transparencies during presentation
• highlight important points with transparency pen
• write on blank acetate film
• change the sequence of your transparencies during presentation.

But don't forget that:

• overhead projectors aren't easy to move around – even the 'portable' ones!
• framed transparencies are awkward to store
• your audience may see your use of an overhead projector as 'less professional' than using slides or a computer/multimedia projector combination.

Here are some practical tips for using overhead projectors:

• Most projectors have a two-way position switch: the first position switches on the light and also starts the cooling fan; the second position increases the lamp intensity and therefore brightens the screen image. It also reduces lamp life.

- On many models the fan will continue to run after the lamp is switched off. This will be distracting and the audience may not be able to hear you.

  - You must *always* have access to a spare lamp.
  - Before your presentation, check that the projector table is at the right level, the screen is at the right angle for audience vision, the projector works properly and is clean, and a spare bulb is available.

- At least 15 minutes before the presentation switch on the projector – if the bulb is going to fail it's more likely to do so at start-up than any other time.

- If you need to replace the bulb remember that some types of bulb shouldn't be touched with bare hands, and there are safety systems that will stop the bulb being tested until the projector has been reassembled.

- During the presentation, remember to use a pencil or pointer, rather than your finger, if you want to emphasize a part of a visual aid, and lay the pointer on the top of the projector platen.

o.4   overheads

Overheads, or view-foils, transparencies or acetates as they are sometimes called, are what you put on the stage glass or platen of an overhead projector. The projector, when switched on, will throw the image that's printed on the overhead onto a screen or wall. Teachers and lecturers have been using the hand-written version of these for years – because they're cheap, easy to prepare and almost as easy to modify or change.

But the advent of low-cost, high-quality colour printers and copiers has changed all that. As a result the days of barely legible hand-written overheads have gone for ever. Now you can create overhead presentations that:

- are elaborate, polished and sophisticated
- exploit the use of colour
- include everything from complex graphs to colour photographs.

This change has taken place because the basic material of your overhead or transparency – its plastic film – has changed. What was once just a clear piece of plastic now has a special formulation or coating so that it can work with different makes of copiers, ink jet printers and laser printers. But take care! Some of these need a white strip on the leading edge of the film in order to ensure even feeding into your printer, while others need film with paper backing or special coatings to help ink dry or film that will tolerate high temperatures. Use the wrong type of film and you'll have a problem – one that can range from a smeared image to a jammed-up printer or copier. But the changes don't stop there. Now these overheads can:

- have cardboard frames to protect the edges of the film
- be in transparent sleeves to protect the surface of the film
- be hole punched for binder storage
- have paper flaps attached for your notes (*see* **n.3 notes, scripts, overheads or cue cards?**).

 Whatever proprietary film system you use for your transparencies make sure that it is scratch resistant – to stop your transparencies appearing dirty or becoming damaged – and will work with your printer or copier.

If you're using transparencies in participative presentations (*see* **p.2 participative presentations**) you can:

- write comments on or add to them by using water-soluble ink pen of a different colour
- use underlining, circles, arrows, stars, etc., to emphasize.

You can also use film, as a sheet or a roll laid on the projector stage or platen, to write on. This is then projected onto the screen where everybody can see it. This enables you to list points made in group discussion and use these points to focus further discussion.

p is for ...

p.1   pace

Professional presenters know that the pace of a presentation affects how it's listened to. Too fast – and your audience won't be able to take in what you're saying, they'll become bewildered and switch off. Too slow – and your audience will become bored and disinterested. But what *is* too slow and how fast is *too* fast?

There's some research that suggests that 'good' listening occurs in response to speech rates up to twice the normal rates that we talk at, but that 'bad' listening cuts in at only ten per cent below this rate. This tells you that faster is better than slower. But you can talk *too* fast and the same research indicates that above twice normal delivery rate 'bad' listening cuts in quickly. But the pace at which you talk is rarely constant – a steady, unvarying pace of delivery is boring. When you vary your speech rate it adds emphasis, variety and interest to your words. These changes in pace add intensity, emotion and meaning to your words (*see* **u.3 using your voice**). The professional presenter uses pace in the same way.

Changing the pace of your presentation is rather like changing gear in your car. But you'll do that when the material you're presenting needs it, not because you're in a rush or find you have too much time to fill. You'll change pace by slowing down – for emphasis on important words and by going faster – as in 'Here's a quick recap of the main points' or by speeding up for climaxes and moments of success and brilliance. You'll also use pauses (*see* **p.4 pauses**). But because you're a professional presenter you'll work out these changes in pace in advance, rehearse them until they are perfect, mark them in your notes (*see* **n.3 notes, scripts, overheads or cue cards?**) and then carry them off as if they were as natural as speech itself.

p.2 participative presentations

When you participate, you enjoy or share something with others. What's shared in a participative presentation is the role of presenter – it's shared between you and your audience. Participative presentations are more common than you might think they are – they often masquerade as discussions groups or hide under the title of case study or focus groups. However, all of these and many other types of participative presentations have one thing in common – they all have a presenter (or facilitator) who:

- manages the course of the presentation
- sets out and explains the ground rules for what will happen during that presentation
- makes sure it happens.

They also have an audience who take an active – rather than reactive – part in the presentation and create and present part of that presentation.

As a presenter you're going to find that participative presentations are much more demanding than an ordinary straightforward presentation. For example, you'll have to:

- decide and prepare for what sort of participation is going to happen – question and answer, case study sessions, problem solving or work groups?
- be flexible about timing

- control discussions, accept interruptions and handle awkward questions in a way that's acceptable to the majority
- be approachable, encouraging and nurturing.

You'll also have to do all of this with one eye on the clock!

Being professional in the way you handle a participative presentation takes meticulous preparation. This involves:

- anticipating questions and preparing answers
- making sure you've got any additional equipment or handouts needed
- deciding on and preparing for the process you'll use
- planning for the detail of that process – syndicate group composition, instructions, location and feedback
- deciding what form of feedback you want (*see* **f.4 feedback**).

Once you start the presentation you'll need to tell your audience right away what to expect. Delaying this will only confuse them and allow resistance to build up. You also need to make sure that they're actively involved within five minutes. During that time you need to:

- brief them clearly and concisely on what's expected of them – handouts are essential here
- check that they understand the brief
- make sure that they know where they're going to do it, how long they have to complete it, how they must present what they've done
- get them going and then, after a while, check that they are OK
- visit regularly to encourage and make sure that they keep to schedule.

It's very important that during the feedback session you make sure that each sub-group or team has the same amount of time and the key issues or questions are answered. Following this feedback it's often worth having an open session so that people can comment on each other's ideas. It's important that you build and maintain an atmosphere that enables your audience to forget that they are the audience and consequently break through the barriers that exist between presenter and audience. It's also important that you sum up at the end.

p.3   passion

Passion – like its close cousin enthusiasm (*see* **e.3 enthusiasm**) – is what converts a run-of-the-mill presentation into a presentation that's powerful, riveting, inspiring and memorable. But you can't buy passion in a shop, drink it from a bottle (*see* **a.7 alcohol**) or create it using computer software. Nor is it logical or planned. The passion in your presentation comes from only one place – and that's from within you. Sounds obvious, doesn't it? For if *you* don't feel passionate about your topic how can you expect your audience to? But the passion of your presentation has to be the genuine article. False zeal or pretend passion will make your audience wince.

So how can you get passionate about something? Here are some ideas:

- Choose a subject that interests, even intrigues, you.
- Prepare thoroughly so that you 'own' your ideas and become more committed.
- Engage first your own and then your audience's feelings and emotions.
- Care about what you're saying and show your audience that you do.
- Interact with your audience and keep them on the edge of their seats.

But remember that passion, like drama (*see* **d.5 drama**), can be overdone. You need to control your passion and use it to lead and fire your audience, so they will take away more than just words from your presentation. Doing this takes real skill. For the professional presenter, passion is like the chef's seasoning – best used in moderation – and used remembering that, as someone, somewhere, once said, passion is 'a good servant but a bad master'.

p.4   pauses

Pauses occur regularly in ordinary speech and conversations. They occupy around a third of the space of these, they're used spontaneously and they can be filled – with 'ums' and 'ers' – or unfilled and silent. Listeners interpret these pauses in different ways. Too many filled pauses and you'll be seen as anxious or bored; too many silent pauses and the people you're talking to will think of you as anxious, angry or even condescending.

 But, as a professional presenter, your pauses will be different. You'll see the pause as a powerful tool, an event that's created and used in a planned and conscious way. You'll use the pause, for example:

- as a lead-in to a key point
- to give your audience time to digest what you've said
- so that points don't pile on top of each other
- to highlight a consequence
- to give your audience time and space to digest what's being shown on a flip chart, slide or oht
- to observe the impact of a visual or a point you've made
- to flag-up an on-coming change of pace or subject
- as a moment of quiet and calm.

These pauses are rehearsed, prepared-for, events. You've planned them, rehearsed them and tested them to find the right duration. You've learned that, while your pauses may feel long to you, it's your audience's measure that counts – and they need space rather than wall-to-wall words.

p.5 personality

Personality is something that we've all got at least one of. It's that quality or collection of qualities that makes a person what she or he is. But is it really as simple as that? Our experience tells us that it isn't. For personality can be and often is a complicated, part learned, part innate, mixture of reflexes, reactions and choices. It's reflected in the way we behave towards each other, it's expressed or acted out in our roles and relationships. It involves our temperament, disposition and even that 'catch-all', our personal identity. As such it's individual, idiosyncratic and personal.

So, given all this, what has personality to do with professional presenting? The answer is quite a lot. For *your* personality is core to *your* presentation style. It's the engine that drives the stuff that your audience buys into – stuff like passion, commitment, enthusiasm, courage, honesty and credibility (*see* **c.15 courage, c.16 credibility, e.3 enthusiasm, p.3 passion**). But all of this doesn't mean that ace professional presenters are necessarily nice or even good people. After all, they're people and being a person involves being complicated, driven, ambivalent and often contradictory. This means that when you next take a look in the professional presenters' 'hall of fame' what you'll find is lots of different sorts of people – each with their own individual personality. Using your personality to effect in your presentations involves making sure that personality is:

- yours – and not one you've borrowed, stolen or copied from someone else
- comfortable – and fits in all the right places.

p.6 persuasion

Persuasion is a key element in the professional presenter's toolkit. Without it, your presentations will be limited to dry recitations of facts, cold statements of opinions or mind-stultifying monologues. It's persuasion and its close cousins, passion and enthusiasm (*see* **e.3 enthusiasm, p.3 passion**) that convert the cold to the bold, the dry to the dramatic and the boring to the extraordinary. But these days there's a lot of persuasion about. It comes at us through adverts, television programmes, radio programmes and newspapers, magazines and books. All of these are trying hard to persuade us either to buy or do something or to sign up to this particular set of values or to accept this particular point of view. As a result the average presentation audience has become turned-off by or desensitized to persuasion. Instead of being special and unique, attempts at persuasion have become commonplace and ordinary. But this doesn't mean that the art of effective persuasion is lost for ever. Rather, it means that for you, as a professional presenter, persuasion has to be refined, sharpened, transmuted; it has to change from being commonplace to become special.

At the core of this special persuasion there lies a particular point of view. It's one that recognizes and uses the four fundamental laws of effective persuasion. These tell you that:

1 Persuasion is an act of communication – as such it must be a shared two-way process to be effective (*see* **c.12 communication**).
2 Effective persuasion is a conscious act that respects and acknowledges the autonomy of all involved.
3 Effective persuasion is about attitude change.
4 Effective persuasion is an act that is done *with* someone rather than *to* them.

In short, effective persuasion is a dance that you and your audience do *together* rather than a solo performance for you. Getting to the point where that dance is effective and satisfying takes practice (*see* **r.1 rehearsal**), knowledge of the audience and their needs (*see* **a.13 audiences**), preparation (*see* **g.2 gathering your material, p.12 preparing your material**) and clarity (*see* **o.1 objectives and targets, b.7 brevity**). In the meantime, here are some points to start you off on the right track towards getting the skill of effective persuasion in your presentations:

• Make sure that you prepare and perform your presentation with your audience's needs foremost in your mind.
• Be up-front and open about your intention to persuade them.
• Tell them where your presentation is going to go.
• Prepare them for what's involved.
• Provide reasons for them – benefits rather than features.

- Be self-confident and honest.
- Tell them what their next step should be.
- Remember that they have the last word – and that can be 'yes' or 'no'.

p.7   podiums and lecterns

A podium – just in case you're not sure what we're talking about here – is a raised platform or dais that's sited at the front of a hall or stage. It's usually quite small with just enough room to stand on. Conductors stand on podiums so that all the members of the orchestra can see them clearly. A lectern, however, is a stand-alone reading desk. Lecterns often appear in churches or lecture halls. They are usually fixed in position and often also fixed in height. Church lecterns are the places from which readings are made and are often ornate, made of wood, metal or stone and sometimes in the form of an eagle with outspread wings supported on a column.

So how do podiums and lecterns fit into professional presentations? The answer is that they're both to do with presenter visibility. When the presenter stands on the same level as the audience, most people will have a limited view of her or him. At best, they'll only be able to see the top third or so of his or her body and, at worst, their view may be substantially blocked by the person in front. So if the audience is sitting in more than two rows of chairs there will be some people who can't see the presenter. The podium is one way of getting around this problem. It raises the presenter about half a metre or so off the floor; it increases your visibility. But the podium also severely restricts your mobility. You become marooned on a square platform with an ever-present risk that you'll fall off it. Most professional presenters avoid podiums – they are risky, inhibiting and they isolate you from your audience. Better, by far, to use a platform or stage. In the absence of these, use your mobility and move amongst your audience. This not only increases your visibility, it also makes you appear approachable and accessible.

Lecterns pose the same problem. When you stand behind the average lectern around three-quarters of your body is hidden from the audience's view. This means that using a lectern holds great attractions for the inexperienced presenter – their knocking knees or shaking hands are hidden from the audience's view. But, for the professional presenter, lecterns are also to be avoided. The fact that they conveniently hold your notes means that you're 'tied' to your lectern. It's more difficult to communicate when less of your body is visible and mobility helps you to express yourself. However, if – on your way to becoming a professional presenter – you must use one, then make sure it is angled 45 degrees to the audience and can be adjusted to your height.

p.8   pointers

Once upon a time, the commonest pointer used in lectures and presentations was a two-metre-long pointed wooden rod rather like a billiard or pool cue. These days, pointers come in all shapes and sizes. Now, for example, your pointer can be:

* integrated in your computer software and controlled by a remote radio frequency mouse, a trackball or a trackpad
* made of extendable metal tubing, like a car radio aerial
* laser driven.

 But, whatever the pointer type you've chosen to use, the key point remains the same: that is that you should only use a pointer sparingly or not at all.

The reason for this is that, unless you're very disciplined, you'll forget to put your pointer down or switch it off after you've used it. The result is:

* a software pointer that remains, irrelevantly and distractingly, on the screen
* a hand pointer that serves to amplify your arm and hand gestures
* a laser pointer that has your audience diving for cover when you gesture.

All of these will both irritate and distract your audience. They can also, if you're using a laser pointer, be dangerous (*see* **l.1 laser pointers**).

A visual that's been thought out carefully and created with care doesn't need a pointer. It should make its point without the need to have the audience's attention drawn to it by your pointer. Professional presenters will use pointers only in answer to a question about a very complex visual, such as a site plan, flowchart or wiring diagram. When they've used them they put them down or switch them off.

p.9 posture

Your body posture – or the relative disposition, position and carriage of your limbs and body – speaks volumes to your audience (*see* **n.2 non-verbal communication**). Professional presenters know this; they change, adjust and use their body posture as a powerful part of their communication with their audience. Some professional presenters take posture so seriously that they practise posture in front of a mirror! Finding the right postures for you and your presenting is important. Stand tall and you'll tell your audience that you're confident, alert and feeling positive. Stand with open arms and you'll send them messages about openness and acceptance. Stand with a balanced, relaxed and comfortable stance and you'll tell your audience that you're balanced and calm.

But that's not all that it will do for you. For standing correctly will help you breathe properly, it enhances the clarity and quality of your voice (*see* **u.3 using your voice**) and makes you feel more energized and alert. Try this exercise and see how it feels:

* Stand with your feet slightly apart.
* Ground yourself by imagining your feet as roots of a tree, reaching down into the ground. The top is flexible but the base is firm and steady.
* Working upwards, make sure that your knees are loose and not locked, the legs straight, your arms are hanging by the sides with hands and fingers relaxed, your stomach and bottom are held in but not too tensely, your back is straight, your shoulders are relaxed and back, not drooping, and your head is held high as if a piece of string in the middle is attached to the ceiling.
* Listen to how your body feels – if part of it hurts or feels uncomfortable, relax that bit and shift your posture gently until the discomfort passes. Hold the posture for two or three minutes then relax.

p.10 powerpoint presentations

The Powerpoint software package has been around for a while. In the years that have passed since its introduction it has:

* eliminated most of its rivals
* grown and adapted to changes in hardware technology
* evolved to become the only significant presentation package for both Apple Mac and Windows PC systems.

All of this has resulted in a software package that's powerful and all pervading. Now everyone's presentation uses Powerpoint. As a result they're all animated with screens rich in bullet points that fly in, flash and then fly out – all to an accompaniment of drum rolls, foghorns, race car sounds or Beethoven's Ninth. At their core, these features and effects are good. Having them readily available extends your ability to produce presentations that at least look professional and they provide an instant skill base for all of us. But that's not all they do – they also lead to presentations that all look the same and in which the outstanding features, the new cool effects, overwhelm the presentation's message.

Overcoming this, holding back the creep towards effect-dominated presentations, takes courage and skill. But if you're going to be a professional presenter then it's a must. For professional presenters are the ones who use these effects skilfully, with discrimination, and, above all, with good taste.

Here are some tips to help you do that:

- Master the software rather than letting *it* master you (*Teach Yourself Powerpoint 2000* and *Powerpoint 2000 Quick Fix* might help here).
- Try clicking on 'no' when that little icon asks 'do you want help?'
- Resist the knee-jerk click on the 'auto-content' wizard.
- Build your own presentations that say what *you* want them to say.
- Don't over-use transitions. Select just one or two, such as 'wipe-up', 'fade', 'cut through black' or 'uncover down', that aren't distracting and bring your audience's eyes back to the top of the screen, ready for the next slide.
- Use sound effects very, very sparingly and only when they are relevant and add *needed* impact rather than impact that's there for effect.
- Be aware that external sound sources – like audio tapes or CDs – can add to your presentation if you sort out and solve the 'techy' problems they often bring.
- Use animation sparingly. Don't fall into the trap of thinking that if it moves it must be good.
- If you must use animation then pick one sequence – like 'wipe right' – and then use it consistently.

'Practice makes perfect.'

Proverb

See **r.1 rehearsal**

p.12 preparing your material

If there's one thing that draws a line between the professional presenter and the talented amateur, then it's the way that they prepare their material. For while the talented amateur sees this sort of preparation as a chore or a have-to-do task, the professional presenter sees it as a challenge. Getting your preparation right is incredibly important. If you do it thoroughly, painstakingly and with an eye for detail then it's the first step on the road to presenting success. But if the material preparation is skimped or limited, if short-cuts are used or unproven assumptions made, then everything that follows is at risk. It won't matter how good your graphics are (*see* **v.4 visual aids**), or how well you've rehearsed (*see* **r.1 rehearsal**) – failure, in one form or another, will follow because the foundation of your presentation is flawed.

It's also a process that takes time. As Samuel Clements is reported to have said, 'It usually takes me more than three weeks to prepare a good impromptu speech.' But the first step in your material preparation process is one that, at first sight, seems to be remarkably indiscriminate. It involves you in bringing together *any* material that appears to be relevant to the objective of the presentation (*see* **g.2 gathering your material, o.1 objectives and targets**). Some presenters suggest doing this by asking questions about the six w's – who? what? where? when? why? and how? – of the presentation's objective. However it's done, it's thoroughness and attention to detail that count. The result can be, and for many presentations is, a mountain of material. But the next step will reduce the size of that mountain. It involves you in putting all this material through a veracity or truth check. As a result of this check you'll have three piles of material that are verifiable, doubtful or very, very doubtful.

It's worth being very tough here and making sure that what's left in the verifiable pile is *really* verifiable because that's the only material that goes on to the next stage. In this next stage you check the material for its relevance to the objective of the presentation. Done well, this will also result in three piles:

- 'must-have' material that's essential if you're going to meet your presentation's objective
- 'should-have' material that's important or valuable but not essential
- 'could-have' material that's interesting but not essential or important.

The last of these – the 'could-have' material – can be put aside, but not discarded, while the 'must-have' and 'should-have' material is now arranged in the best sequence for your presentation. You'll need to take care in choosing this sequence. Get it right and you'll upgrade the chances of your presentation being a success. Get wrong and your audience will become confused, bewildered, and finally disinterested. Here are some of the sequences you can use:

- chronological sequence – time based, usually runs from historic to present time
- psychological sequence – usually runs from known to unknown or safe to scary
- logical sequence – presents material in a rational way and finally draws to a logical conclusion.

Some presenters say that thinking of your presentation as a story that you're going to tell helps here. If you do this you'll need to create a storyboard for your presentation. You'll find the detail of how to do this elsewhere (*see* **s.8 storyboards**). Using this technique will enable you to sketch out exactly what you want to say one frame at a time and decide where you want to insert video footage or audio clips. When this is all done you've completed your material preparation and you're ready to move on to actually creating the material that you'll use when you do your presentation (*see* **v.4 visual aids**).

p.13   presentation powerpoints

- Your audience's minds can and do work faster than your mouth.
- Audiences remember what they see and forget what they hear.
- There's only one way to open – powerfully and well.
- Professional presenters close early, clearly – and ahead of their audience.
- Keep your language lively and colourful, your sentences short, your verbs active and your nouns simple, specific and concrete.

- Make sure that you're interesting, special – anything but boring and mediocre.
- Passion, fun, insight and vision – professional presenting has all of these.
- Insight lasts – theories dry out and blow away.
- Passionate presenters persuade their audiences; cold, dispassionate, rational presenters lose them.
- Presenters with conviction convince.

p.14   project presentations

Projects are very common these days. But, whatever their size and complexity, all of these projects:

- are about achieving change
- involve a wide range of people
- need managing and controlling.

The communication workload between these project people is considerable. As a result project meetings get held in order to:

- exchange information about the project
- exchange opinions, views and feelings about this information
- make decisions based on this information.

Presentations are an excellent way of making sure that your project information gets heard and seen. But to be successful your project presentation must be clear, understandable and time efficient. It must also tell the meeting about the project's progress, problems, difficulties and costs.

Progress

A project's time-scale and the order of its events or activities are usually planned, monitored and controlled by using specialized planning tools or charts, such as the Gantt chart and the various forms of the Critical Path network. Each of these has its own nomenclature, icons and format.

However, if your audience hasn't been trained in the use of these planning tools then using them in your presentation won't help. The answer here is to abstract the relevant information from the chart and present it in a simpler form. Avoid using jargon – your audience won't understand you or it (*see* **j.1 jargon**). Even when your audience is familiar with these charts there's still a problem – they're often too large and complex to be projected on the screen. Again, abstracting and summarizing is the answer. But be prepared to answer questions; if the question or the potential answer is too detailed then offer to discuss it outside the meeting.

Problems

Projects always have problems. There's always a late delivery or a task that's taking longer than planned. The first step towards helping the project meeting to solve these problems is to identify, during your presentation, the facts about the problem – size, cost, start point, duration – and its implications for the rest of the project. Brevity, clarity and accuracy are what's needed here, even if it's a 'don't-know-but-will-find-out' situation. Be prepared to answer questions – they won't be asked because people want to embarrass you but because they really want to know the answers. The second step towards solving a problem is to identify the options for its solution during your presentation. Again it is brevity, clarity and accuracy that are important together with a willingness to see your proposed options challenged and tested by your audience.

Costs

Money is the lifeblood of all projects. Making sure that your project's money spend and cash flow patterns are right is important. In your project meeting presentation you'll need to identify planned spend, actual spend and predicted spend. Use diagrams, such as S curves, pie charts and histograms, to do this. They're better than tables of data. Be aware that before you get into techniques like Earned Value Analysis you'll need to be very sure that all of your audience understands and is familiar with the technique.

p.15   projectors

There are three sorts of projector that you'll meet on your way to becoming a professional presenter:

- slide projectors
- overhead projectors
- multimedia or data projectors.

Used well, all of these can make a major contribution to your presentation. Used badly, they will create a barrier, an audio-visual moat between you and your audience. It's important that you find out – before your presentation – what sort of projector is going to be available. Making an assumption about this is an excellent way of courting disaster. You *must* find out what's available – down to the make and model – at the earliest opportunity and well before you start your preparation. Each type of projector has its own set of foibles, advantages and disadvantages. This means that a key part of your preparation should be making yourself familiar with whatever projector you're going to use. If you have a choice about this then there are a number of factors – audience size, lighting levels and your presentation's content – that will influence which projector is best for you. For further details *see* **m.4 multimedia projectors, o.3 overhead projectors, s.5 slide projectors,** and **Taking it Further.**

q.1 questions

The thought of a question-and-answer session is one that fills most presenters with fear and trepidation. It seems that, for them, when it comes to questions and answers the dictum is 'expect the worst'. But as a professional presenter you'll take a 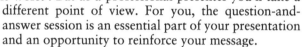 different point of view. For you, the question-and-answer session is an essential part of your presentation and an opportunity to reinforce your message.

However, getting to the point where this actually happens isn't always easy. You'll need to think ahead, anticipate the sort of questions that your audience is likely to ask and then prepare your answers to them. You'll also need to be able to handle 'loaded' questions. Sooner or later, someone is going to try to take you unawares, to blindside you. When that happens everyone in the audience will be watching to see how you handle it. It's worth remembering, though, that when your audience asks questions these will tell you whether or not they've been listening to you and whether they've understood and agreed with what you've said.

Sometimes there aren't any questions. You end on a high note; you've told your audience that you expect them to ask questions. But your audience sits quietly talking amongst themselves. It seems as though they don't have any questions. However, as a professional presenter, you don't make the mistake of concluding that this is so. There may be a whole host of reasons why your audience is reluctant to ask questions. They might, for example:

- be new to the idea of a question-and-answer session and unsure about how to start the session or phrase their questions
- think that their questions are stupid or not worth asking
- feel that their questions would be of limited interest to the rest of the audience
- be unwilling to ask a controversial or hostile question – it might generate hostility or criticism from you or others in the audience
- be reluctant to ask a question until they get some indication as to which way the political 'wind' is blowing from more senior or powerful members of the audience.

It's also possible that they might have understood your presentation so completely that they have no questions at all! The key to getting the questions rolling is to ask one yourself. But don't use the mundane 'Are there any questions?' If you've done your homework, you'll have planned provocative questions that stimulate, that call for your audience's views and opinions. Questions like this usually start with phrases such as 'What's your opinion of . . . ?' or 'What's the first thing you would do if . . . ?' or 'What do you think is the cause of . . . ?'

Once the questions get started you'll need to:

- look at the questioner and nod your head when appropriate. Doing this will encourage her or him as well as letting the audience know that you are listening (*see* **l.9 listening**)

- wait until the questioner has finished – don't jump in – even if you know the answer right away.
- avoid getting caught in a barrage of questions from one person – answer the first question, then move on to the next questioner
- restate the question in your own words before you answer. Doing this will make sure that everyone in the audience hears the question, clarify a confusing question or diffuse a loaded one, and give you time to develop your answer
- answer a question only when you're sure you understand it
- start by establishing eye contact with the questioner, then look at and speak to everyone in the audience, then finish your answer by looking back to the questioner
- use questions to restate and reinforce your key point. A slide or overhead from your presentation will help here; repetition raises retention levels

- be respectful to the questioner – acknowledge a good question but don't rubbish or ridicule a bad, aggressive or difficult one
- say so if you don't know the answer, but make sure that you offer to find the answer and follow it up with the questioner at a later date or give the question back to the audience by asking if anybody is more familiar with this issue than you are.

Questions are important. They let you know how effectively you are communicating your message (*see* **f.4 feedback**). They can highlight areas of misunderstanding, areas in which you've failed to reach your audience. If the questions are vague, or wide of the mark, then don't assume that your audience is stupid or has been asleep. These questions are telling you that you need to either:

- sharpen or polish your presentation
- spend more time in a particular area of your presentation
- think of a different way of presenting the information, such as using an analogy or a video.

q.2   quiet

The idea that success in presenting comes from being fast, flashy and, above all, loud, is a common one. But, for the professional presenter, fast, flashy and loud *aren't* good; they confuse and irritate the audience, their cataclysmic finales generate sighs of relief rather than rounds of applause. When you watch a really professional presenter you'll realize that quiet has a role to play in the presentation. But this isn't any old sort of quiet. It isn't, for example, the quiet that's there when you strain to catch the inaudible words of a mumbling presenter. Nor is it the sort of stunned quiet that follows when a gender-biased joke or comment is made or inappropriate language is used (*see* **a.11 appropriate, g.3 gender**). It's a special sort of quiet – one that's quite rare. It sometimes comes in pauses (*see* **p.4 pauses**). It throws its shadow over an audience when they realize that the person who they are listening to is saying something important. It's the sort of quiet that you get when a presenter actually engages with his or her audience rather than striving to entertain them. It's also a quiet that's about the calmness and inner stillness of a presenter, a calmness that comes from competence and capability rather than brash noisiness.

q.3 quotations

Quotations can be useful. You can use them to:

- open your presentation (*see* **b.2 beginnings, o.2 openings**)
- illustrate or validate a particular point that you're making
- close or finish your presentation (*see* **c.10 closing your presentation, e.2 endings**).

 The professional presenter will, however, also use quotations with care and sparingly. The reason for this is that quotations are, at best, second-hand wisdom, at worst, irrelevant, and are often taken out of context.

When used to excess, quotations bore; they leave your audience confused, not sure what you mean, adrift in a sea of clichés. They might even reach the point where they echo Ralph Waldo Emerson and say:

I hate quotations. Tell me what you know.

It's a quotation that's worth remembering every time you feel tempted to use one.

r is for . . .

r.1 rehearsal

There are very, very few performers of any sort who can perform well in front of an audience *without* a rehearsal. Singers, dancers, pianists, actors, comedians and even rock groups *all* need rehearsals. They use the rehearsal to exercise, train or make themselves more proficient. They do, in private, in rehearsal, what they intend to do later in public. 'Practice makes perfect' is the key phrase. The same applies to professional presenters. They rehearse until they are familiar and comfortable with everything about their presentation. Some will go as far as to tell you that it's impossible to rehearse too much. They argue that once you are *totally* familiar with your message and how to deliver it, then and only then can you be free to really interact with your audience.

So, how do you rehearse? There are, for most of us, three stages to rehearsing. These are:

- the stagger-through
- the walk-through
- the run-through.

In each of these stages you check, practise, change (if necessary) and polish your presentation's:

- beginning and end – so that you can look at your audience rather than your notes
- content – logic, clarity and brevity
- sequence – chronological, psychological or logical?
- spoken words – style, simplicity, directness
- visual aids – too many/few?, readability, effects
- timing – length, breaks, pauses.

You'll also be working hard on the way you use your voice – pauses, pitch, speed and articulation – and body language – gestures and eye contact.

You'll get quicker and smoother as you move up through these stages. At first, you'll stagger, then you'll walk, then finally you'll run. It's important to use observers and video yourself in each of the stages. Look for feedback (*see* **f.4 feedback**) and encourage constructive criticism. If you can, rehearse in the place you're going to use for the presentation. This will enable you to iron out any problems of equipment positioning, room layout and seating; you can decide where you're going to put your notes and where you're going to stand. If you can't do this then make sure that you know how the room will be laid out and rehearse in as similar a situation as you can manage (*see* **c.6 checklists**).

r.2   relaxation

Tension and relaxation lie at different ends of the spectrum of being. Shift yourself towards the relaxed end by trying this routine:

- Clench, then relax your muscles. Lift your shoulders, scrunch up your face, grip your hands in turn. Hold each clench for ten seconds, release suddenly, then repeat. Stretch your mouth and face, release and repeat. Shake your hands and arms vigorously.
- Stand with your shoulders relaxed and breathe in deeply through the nose. Let your breath out through the mouth. Check your shoulders haven't lifted! Put your hand on your diaphragm (just below the ribcage) and make sure this rather than your chest rises when you inhale.
- Breathe in and let out a long aaaaahhhhh on the out breath. Make your voice deep and resonant. If it's croaky, sip water. Practise a tongue-twister and run through the words, flexing your voice.
- Dab cold water on your wrists, inside the elbow joints and behind the ear lobes.
- Use lip salve inside your lips to stop them drying out and bite gently on the sides of your tongue to stop dryness in your mouth.

r.3   rhetorical questions

Rhetorical questions are special – they're asked without any expectation of an answer. Professional presenters use them, often to great effect. They might, for example, ask their audience

'Have you any idea why this has happened?' or 'Do we know when this will happen?' They are questions that are asked for effect, as a part of the rhetoric or flow of the presentation, rather than to gain an answer. However, to be effective, the rhetorical question must be answered. But it's the questioner – the presenter – who provides that answer. Here's an example of a rhetorical question-and-answer routine:

Presenter: 'Do we know when this will happen?'

Short, but not too short, pause followed by –

Presenter: 'No, we don't and that's why I wanted to talk to you today.'

Rhetorical questions, when used well, do a number of useful things. They can, for example:

- generate interest
- open an audience up to something new
- build links between different sections of the presentation
- nudge the audience back into wakefulness.

But, powerful as they are, rhetorical questions do need to be used with care and thought. Ask too many and you'll finish up with an irritated, testy, audience; ask the wrong question and you'll get an answer or even a heckle – neither of which you'll want!

r.4   ridicule

Ridicule and its close cousin, sarcasm, rarely appear in professional presentations. Why is this? Isn't the professional presenter allowed to make fun of other people or make sharp, cutting, remarks about them? The answer is, of course, that professional presenters are as allowed and able as the rest of us to raise laughter against people, things and ideas, just as they are 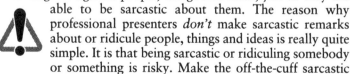 able to be sarcastic about them. The reason why professional presenters *don't* make sarcastic remarks about or ridicule people, things and ideas is really quite simple. It is that being sarcastic or ridiculing somebody or something is risky. Make the off-the-cuff sarcastic remark and you run the risk of upsetting or offending your audience. Ridicule an idea and you'll find that an important somebody in your audience thinks that it's the greatest idea since sliced bread. For the professional presenter, ridicule or sarcasm have much in common with jokes – they are never used in an unpremeditated way (*see* **h.5 humour**). This means that they should be:

- limited in use
- only used with both a specific audience and a particular presentation in mind
- capable of being understood and appreciated by all of that audience
- practised and rehearsed
- used only if you're comfortable using them.

Should you ever feel tempted to wield the sharp cutting edge of ridicule and sarcasm, try to remember what Giovanni Boccaccio, the Italian writer of the Decameron, said:

> *It often happens, that he who endeavours to ridicule other people, especially in things of a serious nature, becomes himself a jest, and frequently to his great cost.*

r.5   risk

Performing a presentation is a risky business. There's always the chance that things won't go as well as you'd hoped or planned for. But as a professional presenter there's a lot that you can do to reduce or limit the influence of risk on your presentation. When you do this you not only increase your presentation's chance of success, you also increase your ability to perform it well.

Presenting risk reduction involves:

- making sure that you know who your audience is and what they want (*see* **a.13 audiences**)
- being clear about what you want to achieve (*see* **o.1 objectives and targets, w.4 why**)
- gathering and preparing your material with care (*see* **g.2 gathering your material, p.12 preparing your material, v.4 visual aids**)
- making sure you're happy about your presenting environment (*see* **c.1 can you all hear me?, c.3 chairs, e.4 environment, l.3 layout, l.8 lighting, w.2 where**)
- getting your equipment ready (*see* **f.8 flip charts, p.15 projectors, w.3 whiteboards**)
- getting yourself ready (*see* **n.1 nerves, r.1 rehearsal, r.2 relaxation**)

You'll also have prepared your answers to the questions that you think the audience will ask (*see* **q.1 questions**), rehearsed your ad-libs (*see* **a.5 ad-libs**), thought out how you'll handle hecklers (*see* **h.3 hecklers**) and decided if you're going to use a joke or a story (*see* **h.5 humour, s.7 stories**). But, despite all of this, you'll still be at risk from those unpredictable calamities that always seem to be waiting to happen, so also take a look at **d.4 disasters – and how to cope**.

r.6 rooms, halls and caverns

You'll be surprised at some of the places you will be asked to do presentations in. Some of these will be like caves – small, dark and damp – others will be big and full of echoes while still others will be *huge* auditoriums in which your audience is a distant sight. But, as a professional presenter, you're aware that you say 'yes' or 'no' to presenting in these. Whether you do – or don't – present there will depend upon a number of factors. Key amongst these are:

Size and shape

The key issue about the shape and size of your presenting space is the number of people in your audience. Getting a space that's right for your audience is important. Obvious wrong space combinations include a concert hall with an audience of ten or an audience of fifty crammed into a small, even medium-sized, office. Big spaces tend to intimidate people and spaces that are too small mean that your audience will be preoccupied with personal space issues rather than listening to what you have to say. But it's not just size that counts here. You've also got to have a room that has the right shape. Accept a room or hall with an L shape, for example, and you've effectively halved your usable audience space.

Distractions

Some presenting spaces have built-in distractions. Large picture windows with panoramic views, thin walls that allow noise to intrude from adjacent rooms or areas, bad or no air conditioning so that the noise of traffic or the roar of planes taking off comes in through open windows, the smell of cooking from the restaurant next door – all of these will divert your audience's attention. Avoid presenting spaces like these. Their distractions won't just intrude – they'll also mean that you've got to battle for your audience's attention – and you'll probably lose.

Ventilation

This isn't an easy one. The way things are these days almost all of your potential presenting spaces are going to have air conditioning of one sort or another. But, however good that conditioning is, when you fill that space with people and close the doors you'll soon find that it develops a 'stale' or 'stuffy' feel. If this happens sooner rather than later and you can't find an alternative space then you'll have to:

- leave the doors open to ventilate the room
- plan breaks into your presentation to keep people awake and active.

Acoustics

Presenting spaces with sharp, clear acoustics – without echoes – are better than those in which the sound of your voice is swallowed up by the sound-attenuating properties of carpets, drapes and curtains. Remember that people absorb sound too and that your audience can take the edge off the echo or resonance that you heard when the room was empty.

s is for ...

s.1   sales presentations

Most, if not all, presentations have an element of selling in them. You can sell ideas, facts, information (*see* **i.5 information**) or even dreams in your presentation. For all of these, it's your knowledge of your audience that's key. Knowing them, being aware of their wants and needs, is what enables you to shift your presenting up a gear. This takes you from amateur to professional and lifts your presentation from adequate to superb. However, there are also presentations that aim, purely and simply, to sell.

Sales presentations are different. In these it's not enough to be aware of your audience's needs and wants and to take these into account when you design and perform your presentation. In sales

 presentations you need to move on beyond that. You need to convince your audience that you're able to *answer* those needs. This shifts the focus of your presentation. It's no longer good enough just to tell them how good your product or service is. Now you must aim to convince your audience that your product or service can and will answer their needs and do that in ways that are much better than your competitor's product or service.

Doing that and doing it well isn't easy. It's a process that starts well before you begin your presentation's preparation; it's a process that starts the moment that you pick up the telephone to make your first contact with them. Here are some tips that will help you to achieve success in your selling presentations:

- Know your product or service inside out, know and understand its features, benefits and pricing.
- Understand your potential customer's business, work out how they could use your product/service and identify the benefits that would result.
- Talk to someone who has already successfully sold into that company, or one similar, and tap into his or her experience.
- Remember that while your goal is the sale of the product or service, your potential client's goal is to use what you sell them to get something else that they *really* want. Find out what that something else is.
- Try to meet or at least talk on the phone with each member of the group you'll be presenting to *before* you arrive to present. If this isn't practical or possible then find out who the key decision-makers are and talk to them.
- Choose your sales approach:
  - closure approach: based on high levels of presentation skills, trial/test closure, overcoming objections then a final major closing sequence
  - problem-solving approach: involves probing for problems with open and closed questions and presenting solutions to these problems
  - value-added approach: used to overcome a price problem by adding on extras/incentives to the basic product/service in order to make up a difference in perceived value and price
  - consultative approach: aimed at proving that your product or service will lower the customer's operating costs or increase their revenue; needs a strong track record and good proof of results.
- Find out in advance how much time you'll have. Adjust your presentation length to 60 per cent of that time, thus giving enough time to sort out any remaining issues and, if possible, reach an agreement.
- Ask where they are in their decision-making process – do they have scheduled presentations with other suppliers after you or have these already taken place?
- Try to be the last presenter, the one nearest to the decision point; if you can't achieve that then schedule another appointment.
- Make sure that your presentation paints a bright, clear picture of the way things will be if they buy your product or service. Talk in terms of outcomes, results and, above all, achieving *their* goals.
- Finish with a flip chart, overhead or slide that gives at least three reasons why you are the customer's best choice; the more you have the bigger your chance is of winning that sale.

s.2 screens

Screens are important. A dirty, torn screen, a badly located screen or, worst of all, no screen at all will ruin the best thought-out and prepared of presentations. But the screen that you use in your presentation is often a 'given'. It's 'the one we've always used' or 'it

comes with the room'. So, if you're on unfamiliar ground, check the screen that's being provided and make sure that it's suitable for your presentation and in the right place for you and your audience (*see* **l.3 layout**).

Here are some of the screen factors that you need to take into account:

Screen type

Screens can be portable, wall mounted or ceiling mounted. They can also be either manual or electric. All of these have good points and bad points. A portable screen, for example, will enable you to site it where you want and rotate or turn it as you need, but will rarely be bigger than a 160 cm square. A fixed wall screen, however, can be as large as a 300 cm square, but will be fixed in position and orientation.

Fabric

Different screen fabrics have different 'viewing angles'. This is the angle over which your audience can comfortably see what's on the screen. This angle is as high as 45 degrees for screens made of diffuse fabric and as low as 20–30 degrees for those made of speculum or beaded fabric. Wide-angle diffuse fabric screens are appropriate for low ambient light conditions while beaded screens are the right choice for well-lit rooms.

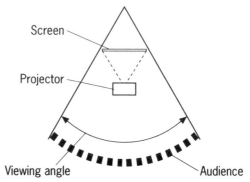

Size

It's your audience, rather than your projector or the material of your presentation, that will decide the size of screen that you use. See the screen checklist in **c.6 checklists**.

Image distortion

If you're going to avoid the 'keystone' effect (*see* **k.1 keystoning**) then you'll need to make sure that the tilt angle of your screen can be adjusted easily.

s.3   simplify

Simplifying what you say – before you say it – is key to reaching your audience.

Here are some of the ways that you can do this:

Word use

The sort of words you use will be influenced by:

- the subject of your presentation
- the type of presentation (*see* **f.7 financial presentations, t.3 technical presentations**)
- your audience (*see* **a.13 audiences**).

As a rule, you should avoid jargon (*see* **j.1 jargon**) unless you and *all* the audience know what it means. You should also try to use words that are straightforward – for example 'end' instead of 'terminate' or 'conclude'. Verbosity will confuse your audience as will polysyllabic, even eloquent, language (*see* **b.7 brevity**).

Sentence length

Long sentences can be hard work, for both you and your audience. Avoid tying your audience up in knots by dividing your ideas into separate thought groups. Put 'bracketed' information and additional bits and asides into separate sentences. Here's a before and after example:

Before: 'On that note, I'd like to thank Mr X for his illuminating presentation and suggest we finish there unless you have any questions which, speaking for myself, might help us to further our understanding of this exciting and innovative project.'

After: 'Thank you very much, Mr X. That was both interesting and informative. Are there any questions before we finish?'

Remove and avoid padding

We often use more words than we need to. When we do this we run the risk of losing or obscuring the main message contained in what we are saying. Reducing the padding allows your information to stand out more boldly. Here's another before and after example:

Before: 'If you'd just like to cast your eyes over this graph and see the increase this year in comparison to last year.'

After: 'Look at the increase this year' – followed by a pause while the audience engage and digest (*see* **p.4 pauses**).

Signposting

When you come across a signpost on the road it tells you where you're going to and, sometimes, where you've come from. It's the same in presentations. When you use a spoken-language signpost you tell your audience what you've covered, where you are going and how many parts there are. Verbal signposts are often used to round off a section and introduce the next one:

'Right, so we've seen how . . . What do we do?

'Well, we have three alternatives. One . . .'

They also keep your audience informed of progress:

'The second of my four points is . . .'

or tell the audience about timing:

'We've got five minutes left so I'll go through the key points. One . . .'

'My final point is . . .'

'And now to sum up . . .'

Signposts enable you to keep your audience informed.

s.4 slang

Most languages – English included – have a version that's highly colloquial in nature. It's one that's often thought of as being below the level of standard speech. This is called slang. Slang, like jargon (*see* **j.1 jargon**), is used by particular and limited groups of people but it's also one of the ways that new words or different ways of using existing words are added to a language.

For the professional presenter, slang offers a particular challenge. With some audiences, the use of slang can give you credibility; with other audiences, it can be upsetting and unacceptable. In general terms the best advice about slang is to use it only when it's appropriate (*see* **a.11 appropriate**) and only then if you are absolutely sure that you really understand what it means and your audience does as well.

s.5   slide projectors

These days, slide projectors are different. Gone are the days of noisy, manual-load, single-slide projectors. Now, slide projectors can auto-focus, overlay or dissolve images, project onto the front or rear of screens, auto-present timed sequences of slides, switch automatically to a standby lamp on bulb failure, project images with a synchronized audio output and carry trays or carousels of up to 140 slides. These slide projectors are also easily transported, readily available and easy to maintain.

As a professional presenter you'll need the professional rather than domestic model. This way you'll get all those easy-to-use features that will make your presentation look better. If you choose well you'll get additional features such as:

* easy-change lamp modules
* remote random access to slides
* digital interfaces
* built-in viewing screens for desk-top presentations and editing.

You'll also need to choose a lens for your projector that suits the material that you're projecting and the room or hall that you're projecting it in.

Flat-field lenses work best with glass, plastic non-embossed cardboard mounts and when you're rear projecting. While curved-field lenses work best with embossed cardboard mounts. The focal length of your projector's lens will determine how far you can project a readable image. Here are some examples:

Lens focal length	Approximate distance to screen
75 mm	4 m
100 mm	5.5 m
125 mm	6.5 m
150 mm	7 m
175 mm	9.5 m
200 mm	10.7 m

The advantages of a slide projector include:

• a wide variety of source material can be copied or captured
• audiences often perceive slides to be more professional than overheads
• slides and projectors are easy to store and transport
• slides can be used to focus the audience's attention.

Its disadvantages include:

• there is less contact with your audience as the room usually needs to be darkened
• the projector sits at the back of the room, well away from you if anything goes wrong
• you can't modify either your slides or the sequence in which you show them during your presentation
• there is a long lead time (two to five days) for slide preparation
• slides can be damaged easily during transportation or as a result of a projector slide jam.

Here are some tips to help you with your slide projector:

• Number each slide mount in the upper right-hand corner of the shiny film side
• To obtain the best results, insert slides with the emulsion side towards the projection lens, slide curve towards the light source
• Before loading the slide tray make sure you've got your slides in the right order and orientation by checking each slide's orientation (horizontal or vertical), arranging them in the order you wish to show them and then turning the slides upside down.
• Load your tray by inserting your first slide into the first slot so that its number is visible on the outer circumference of the tray, then inserting your second slide in the second slot with the emulsion (dull side) facing your first slide, and so on.

- If you're using auto-focus don't forget to focus your first slide manually.
- Make sure you are thoroughly familiar with the projector's control, both on the remote control and on the projector control panel.
- Rehearse clearing a slide jam before you have one.

  - Always have a spare bulb or bulb module handy and make sure you know how to change it.
  - When you remove your slide tray always make sure that the plastic lock ring is on the tray before you remove it – this stops your slides dropping out all over the floor.
  - Have a spare slide tray handy – in case the tray you're using gets damaged.
- Before your presentation, check that the projector table is at the right level, the screen is at the right angle for audience viewing, and that the projector works properly.
- At least 15 minutes before the presentation is due to begin switch on the projector. If the bulb is going to fail it's more likely to do so at start-up than at any other time.

s.6   stage fright

Stage fright is very different from nerves, fear or anxiety (*see* **n.1 nerves, f.3 fear, a.9 anxiety**). When it happens – frequently without warning – it's overwhelming, catastrophic and completely disabling. If you've ever seen somebody in the grip of stage fright you'll know how incapacitated they become. But it's not an illness; it's actually a perfectly natural reaction – on the part of our bodies – to a situation that we find threatening. When this happens our bodies automatically kick in with an in-built survival mechanism – the 'fight-or-flight' response. But the 'threats' that trigger stage fright are hardly ever real. They are about what we think *might* happen rather than what's actually happening. Most of the time stage fright is caused not by one single stand-alone fear but by a whole bundle of them rolled up together. However, these fears can be overcome by changing the way you see the situation.

Professional presenters do this in a number of ways:

- By thinking positively. They replace imagined catastrophic what-if scenarios by positive affirmations. This involves turning the inward-looking nervous energy of anxiety around, to look outward and so become enthusiasm and vitality that can work for you.
- By preparing thoroughly. Professional presenters make a religion out of being prepared. They take, in advance, every step of a presentation. They identify every possible unknown and make it into a known – often several times before they feel comfortable.
- By treating mistakes as opportunities. As a professional presenter you'll be no more immune to making mistakes than anybody else. What will be different, however, is what you do with that mistake. For mistakes are opportunities to learn, chances to change and improve, rather than career-impairing blunders.

Getting all of this right is important. When you do that you'll have harnessed your anxiety about stage fright so that it becomes a positive aid rather than a hindrance to your presenting.

s.7 stories

Professional presenters have a lot in common with the storytellers of old. But the stories that the professional presenter tells aren't about ancient heroes or historic kings; they're about life as it is today. To be a successful storyteller the professional presenter has to make sure that the stories he or she tells are:

- relevant to the aim of the presentation
- matched to the audience's experience, occupation, vocabulary, expectations and age span
- appropriate to the nature of the occasion.

But that's not all – they also have to be told in ways that are honed and polished and recognize that storytelling is a skill.

Here are some of the dos and don'ts of good storytelling:

- Do choose a few stories and practise telling them.
- Do learn your stories so that you can tell them without notes.
- Do tell stories that illustrate a key point in addition to telling the story.
- Do space your stories – leave a good interval between them.
- Do use stories to provide a change of pace.

- Do keep your stories short. Write the story out and then edit it until you've found the least number of words that you need to convey the message in an interesting fashion.
- Do specify a location for your story.
- Do use people, places and things that your audience knows – this helps them to get involved.
- Do put punch and emphasis behind the adjectives and verbs of your story.
- Do use true facts in your stories.
- Don't start your stories by saying things like 'That reminds me of a funny story' or 'I heard a good one the other day' or 'I don't know whether I should tell you this one' or 'A funny thing happened on the way to the meeting today'.
- Don't finish your funny story by saying 'But seriously, folks'.
- Don't use too many stories – either on the same topic or in the same presentation.
- Don't tell a story where you are the hero.
- Don't use terms that are foreign or unfamiliar to the audience.

s.8   storyboards

Storyboards first appeared in the early days of the film industry as a series of rough, hand-drawn, illustrations mounted on a large surface or board. These showed a scene-by-scene breakdown of the film, indicating where the camera was to be sited and what the viewer would see. These storyboards were used to:

- work out the content of individual scenes
- plan these scenes ahead of the shooting day
- shift and shuffle the sequence of these scenes.

They were also used to great effect by animators in the production of cartoon and other animated films. While the film world has moved on since the storyboard, the modern computer version of it – the outliner – still has its uses for the professional presenter.

Most presentation software packages have an outliner (*see* **p.10 powerpoint presentations**). You use it to:

- shuffle the order of the slides
- change the slide content
- specify the format of all your slides by using a master slide
- create audience handouts that contain reduced-size versions of the slides with explanatory text if required.

It all seems quite easy, doesn't it? But before the professional presenter gets to the point that she or he needs to use the outliner, there's some important preparation to be done off-screen.

One of the best ways of doing this is to create a time line, story-line or a sequence schedule for your presentation. Doing that goes something like this:

Step one

Define the duration (in minutes) of your presentation, making sure that it's for the presentation alone, not the presentation plus questions session. Draw a horizontal line to scale on a piece of paper to represent this duration, marking the scale on the line when you do that. You'll need space to write things against that line so use an A4 or bigger sheet with its long axis horizontal.

Step two

Split this line into six equal duration segments and label those at each end of the line as your opening and closing segments. Make sure these labels are on the top of the line.

Step three

Decide what the four key messages of your presentation should be and label each of the remaining four segments with one of these. Make sure that you order them in the way that you had decided to use when you were preparing your material (*see* **p.12 preparing your material**) and write the labels on the top of the line.

Step four

Start to make notes under each of these labels. Write them under the line and make sure that they are relevant and concise.

Step five

When you have completed all of the notes under each of your key messages, read them all through. As this will be the first time you'll see your embryonic presentation as a whole you'll probably have to do some editing (*see* **e.1 editing**).

Step six

Once that editing is complete, you'll find you have the initial draft of the text that you'll input into your presentation software. But before you do that it's worth spending time thinking about the format of your slides. Remember that there are important issues here about what colours you use (*see* **c.11** colours), the sorts of charts, graphs, figures and tables that you decide to use (*see* **g.6 graphs and charts, t.1 tables**), the way you convert your raw data into information (*see* **i.5 information**) and the way your text appears on the screen (*see* **t.7 typography**).

s.9   symbols

A symbol, in its broadest sense, is something that stands for something else. They are used a lot nowadays with symbols like the signs on men's and ladies' washrooms, no smoking signs or the big 'M' of McDonalds® being a part of our everyday lives.

Professional presenters also use visual symbols. They do this because these symbols can tell a story without using words, quickly and precisely.

But the symbols used need to be chosen with care. They aren't always as clear and unambiguous as they might be and the context in which they are used can be important. A wineglass symbol, for example, can be used to indicate fragile contents and 'this way up' when used on packaging or to indicate the presence of a wine bar when used on a sign in a public place. Symbols as basic and simple as the tick (✓) and the cross (✗) can have meanings that are subtly but significantly different when used in different contexts. A tick, for example, can be used to indicate approval, accuracy or acceptability – depending on its context.

The other factor that will influence the symbol that the professional presenter chooses is the knowledge and understanding that the audience has of that symbol (*see* **a.13 audiences**). The risk of the audience misinterpreting a symbol increases as the separation between the symbol and the conventional use of the object portrayed increases. Low-risk symbols include those that directly represent an object, such as a train or a bus, representing a rail station and bus depot respectively. However, some symbols, such as the dove of peace or the skull and crossbones, are almost universal. Despite all these difficulties symbols can make a significant contribution to the success of your presentation, providing you choose them carefully.

t is for ■ ■ ■

t.1 tables

A table is a practical way of summarizing or comparing a lot of data. But, like all of the images that you show your audience, tables appear on your screen for only a short period of time. This means that your audience *doesn't* have time:

- to study them in detail
- to assimilate what's contained in them
- to understand the comparisons that are contained in them.

This means that tables have limited use for the professional presenter. It's better, by far, to show your audience the data you've got by using line graphs, bar charts or pie charts (*see* **g.6 graphs and charts**). The benefits that you'll reap if you avoid using tables will be considerable. If you *don't* use tables, your audience will understand more of what you are showing them and will be more interested in what you're saying to them.

However, there will be presentations in which the conventions demand that you use tables (*see* **t.3 technical presentations, f.7 financial presentations**). If you find yourself having to use tables here are some tips for limiting or delaying the inevitable 'table turnoff':

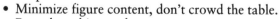

- Keep words to the minimum.
- Minimize figure content, don't crowd the table.
- Round out big numbers.
- Use tables *only* when you can't use graphs or charts.
- Limit table column labels to one word.
- If you use more than three columns and rows, you're in danger of losing your audience.

- Grey out everything except the column or row that matters.
- Circle the important figure using colours.
- Align columns by decimal points.
- Talk your audience through the table.

Here's an example:

	January	February
Sales A	1,100,000	1,200,000
Sales B	800,000	600,000

t.2   team presentations

Presenting in a team is probably one of the riskiest things that you – and the other people in the team – will ever do in your presenting careers. The risks are high, the potential for catastrophes substantial and the failures frequent in team presentations (*see* **r.5 risk**). As a result, professional presenters take early, firm and positive steps to reduce this risk level. Here are the basic minimum that you'll need to take:

- Decide who's in charge before you start your preparation.
- Make sure that the presentation team leader is known to, compatible with and acceptable with both your team and your audience.
- Choose team members who are experienced presenters, are compatible with each other and who know what they are talking about.
- Make sure that your team size is less than your audience size.
- Give each team member a clear role, a well-defined remit and an understudy role to cover for illness and accidents.
- Make sure that all presenting material is consistent and co-ordinated in terms of colour and style.
- Make sure that all team members dress appropriately.
- Rehearse, rehearse, rehearse and then rehearse again.
- Make sure everyone knows about the how and when of handing over to the next presenter and taking over from the previous presenter.

- Have an additional non-presenting team member who's responsible for making sure there are enough chairs for all team members, equipment set-up and testing, coping with and correcting equipment failures, prompts when somebody dries and carrying a back-up copy of everybody's presentation material.
- Agree and rehearse – as a team – the how and who of answering your audience's questions.

The best teams, whatever their task or job, are those whose members are loyal to each other and the team. They co-operate and collaborate with each other and generate outcomes and end results that are shared and meaningful. These are the teams in which 2 + 2 gets to equal 5 or more; they are the teams whose presentations are memorable and inspiring.

t.3   technical presentations

Technical presentations are different from other types of presentation. If you compare a technical presentation to an ordinary or business presentation you'll find that:

Technical presentations:	Business presentations:
• are very factual	• contain facts and opinions
• aim only to inform	• aim to sell or persuade
• present data/methods	• present views and opinions
• often use technical jargon	• use everyday language

The people who make technical presentations are usually specialists in one discipline or another. They can be biologists, chemical engineers, economists, statisticians, computer programmers, mathematicians or any other sort of specialist. But the audiences of these technical presentations aren't necessarily as specialized as the presenters. They can be:

- specialists – with the same or even higher levels of technical knowledge as the presenter, or
- lay people – with a lower level of technical knowledge than the presenter.

You'll find technical presentations being made to specialist audiences at conferences or seminars (*see* **c.13 conference presentations**) while technical presentations for lay audiences are often made at exhibitions, in educational establishments or even on television or radio (*see* **l.6 lectures**). Both of these have much in common. They both aim to inform their audience and the contents of both of them are fact-rich. But the way that these facts are presented is significantly different. The presenter who presents to a specialist audience will use words and phrases that have special meaning for that audience (*see* **j.1 jargon**) while the presenter who faces a lay audience will use simpler, more everyday, language.

 As a professional presenter, it's vital that you avoid the trap of assuming that your audience will understand the language or jargon of your specialism. Check it out, make sure you know what their level of technical knowledge is before you start to prepare your presentation. Don't make the assumption, however, that an audience that is familiar with the technical jargon of one specialism is necessarily familiar with the jargon of another. A chemist, for example, will be unlikely to understand the jargon used by an economist and an electronic engineer will have difficulty with the jargon of a medical doctor.

Another and equally important aspect of a technical presentation is the visual aids that you use (*see* **v.4 visual aids**). These are also different. The visuals used in a technical presentation are supplemented by the words spoken, while in a business presentation the reverse is true – the visuals are there to supplement the words spoken. This difference is reflected in the nature of these visuals. In technical presentations the usual charts, graphs and tables (*see* **g.6 graphs and charts, t.1 tables**) can be added to by:

- schematic drawings
- engineering drawings
- block diagrams
- videos (*see* **v.3 videos**)
- models
- photographs
- physical objects.

These can significantly add to the range and quality of the information that you're presenting, providing your words supplement what the audience is seeing and facilitate their understanding of that.

t.4   technology

Presenting technology has changed enormously over the last decade or so. Now there are faster, more reliable computers, better printers, more sophisticated projectors and software that will almost do your presentation for you. This has meant that:

- presentation standards – for how you design, create and perform a presentation – have risen
- audience expectations – about the sort of presentations that they have to sit through – have also risen.

This wave of technical change is unlikely to slow down or stop. If you believe all that you read, within the next five or so years, you'll be watching and performing presentations that involve the use of:

- large plasma display screens
- smaller and faster computers based on organic nano-transistors
- high data capacity internet 2
- display panels that use either field emission techniques or hybrid plasma and lcd technology
- screens of light-emitting polymers
- projectors using digital light processors
- 3D holographic screens
- Very High Bit-rate Digital Subscriber Line (VDSL) access to the internet.

But none of this technology – marvellous as it will be – will guarantee that your presentation will be professional enough to reach your audience. To do this, now and in the future, you'll have to:

- master that new technology, whatever it is
- learn to use it appropriately and effectively
- raise your presenting standards ahead of the arrival of new technology
- re-invent your presenting style so that it's in tune with new technology
- not be too proud to get re-trained when you need to.

But even when you do all of this it still won't be enough. Your presentation will only be *really* professional, whatever technology you use, when you perform it with passion (*see* **p.3 passion**), conviction and credibility (*see* **c.16 credibility**).

t.5 thank-yous

Thank-yous can be found in at least five places in professional presentations:

• before the presentation, when you talk to the person who's going to introduce you or interpret for you and thank him or her in advance for doing it well (*see* **i.10 introductions, u.2 using an interpreter**)
• at the beginning of the presentation, when you publicly thank the person who introduced you, the person who arranged the session and the audience – for turning up
• after a question has been asked, when you thank the questioner
• at the close of the presentation, when you thank the audience for their attention and remind them that you'd be happy to answer any questions that they have
• after it's all over, when you make sure that you thank the sound, lighting or television technicians who've been working with you.

All of these are important. But doing your thank-yous is more than just plain old-fashioned courtesy. It's also a good way of getting yourself remembered and making certain that you receive a warm welcome next time you present there.

t.6 training presentations

Training – as someone, somewhere, once said – isn't an event, it's an ongoing continuous process. It's also a process that often involves presentations. But presentations aren't the only training technique or tool you can use. You can also train people by giving lectures – with little or no audience involvement (*see* **l.6 lectures**), holding discussions – in which attitudes can be changed by a free exchange of views, running skill instruction sessions – in which people gain specific skills by practising them or doing role-playing exercises. In all of these the objective is the same: to develop and enhance the abilities of the people involved. What all of these and the presentation have in common is that, in order to be effective, they have to be a part of a sequence that goes something like this:

1 Find out what training is needed.
2 Decide how you're going to deliver that training.
3 Do it – and then, finally,
4 Check out whether it has worked.

The training presentation that you give can be one of a series of training sessions taking place over an extended period of time or a stand-alone session answering a specific and limited need. In both of these presentation situations, you'll need to communicate effectively with your audience and do this in a way that:

• engages them – by seeking and sharing information and ideas and drawing on their diverse backgrounds, roles and experience
• uses visuals – in order to effectively instruct, orient or motivate them
• takes account of both their learning needs and their learning abilities.

Here are some tips to help you do that:

• Check out the stated training need – make sure that it's real.
• Create training that's needed and job-focused.
• Work hard to get your audience to identify and understand the link between the training and individual needs.
• Make sure that your training has clearly stated objectives and measurable outcomes.
• Tell your audience exactly what the training session involves; do this before they arrive if it's a one-off presentation or at the beginning if it's a string of training sessions.
• If your training session lasts for more than a day, then encourage the use of 'learning contracts', have music playing before the first session to relax people, bring in another trainer for one or two of the sessions to give both you and your audience a break, use role plays, case studies and 'how would you do it?' sessions, and take care of yourself.
• Have 'how to apply this' discussion sessions and create a 'bright idea' list.
• Get feedback – encourage your audience to fill in feedback forms before they leave and follow up later in the workplace if you can (*see* **f.4 feedback**).

t.7 typography

The typography of your presentation – or the way its printed material looks – can have a significant effect upon the impact it has upon your audience. These days, we've all got personal computers with a wide range of font families. We are literally spoilt for choice when it comes to deciding what typefaces we use in our presentations. When it comes to making this choice the key words for the professional presenter are simplicity, subtlety, elegance and, above all, legibility.

If you adopt these – you should do if you want your presenting to reach professional standards – then it means that you're *not* going to be using the more unusual or specialized fonts. But that's not all. You'll also use a sans-serif font, such as Helvetica or Arial, for any presentation that involves a multimedia projector (*see* **m.4 multimedia projectors**). The serif is the fine cross-stroke that you get at the top and bottom of a letter. Fonts with it – serif fonts – tend to look fuzzy when displayed on a large screen whereas sans-serif fonts have a clean, simple appearance. Another key factor is font size. The size of your font is the distance from the top of the highest lowercase letter – such as k, b or d – to the bottom of the lowest lowercase letters – such as y, p or q. This is measured in 'points' – of which there are around 72 to the inch, or pica – each of which contains 12 points or millimetres. The rule here is to keep your font size in proportion to the size of your screen (*see* **s.2 screens**). A huge font on a small screen is almost as bad as a tiny font on a large screen. Some presenters suggest that you avoid using fonts smaller than 24 points and if you have to go down in size don't go below 18 points.

Here are some more tips that will help you with the typography of your presentations:

- Use one sans-serif font only.
- When you want impact, change your typeface colour, size or style, i.e. bold.
  - Don't use italics – they are difficult to read.
  - Clearly title each screen and use a larger font and/or a different colour to do it.
  - For maximum effect use white or light-coloured text on a dark – navy blue or black – background.

u is for . . .

u.1   unique

When two men do the same thing, it is not the same thing after all.

Publilius Syrus

You are, when all is done – just what you are.

Goethe

u.2   using an interpreter

The way things are these days if you're any good at presenting then you'll not only find yourself doing it abroad (*see* **g.5 global presentations**), you'll also find yourself using an interpreter. Interpreting well is a real skill, one that demands proficiency in two languages and involves a lot more than simple translation. For the interpreter interprets your message rather than just translates your words.

Here's how you can help the process:

- Get to know your interpreter. Thank them before and after the presentation. Find out where they'll be sitting and make sure you can see them when you speak.
- Hand over a copy of your script/notes and handouts ahead of time. Make sure that your interpreter has these in advance and spend time going through these with her or him to clarify subtleties and meaning.

- Speak to your audience. Once you're on stage, direct your speech at your audience rather than your interpreter. Smile, gesture and make eye contact with them, just as you would with an audience that speaks your language (*see* **g.4 gestures, e.8 eye contact**).
- Watch your language. Cut out jargon, clichés, puns and acronyms. These aren't easy to move across the language barrier (*see* **c.7 clichés, j.1 jargon, s.3 simplify**).
- Watch your pace. Speak slowly to allow time for your message to be translated and then received by the audience. Make sure you can see the interpreter in case he or she needs to signal to you to slow down, or you need to signal that you're departing from the script momentarily. Agree signals for these in advance. For simultaneous interpretations, it's worth writing 'Slow Down' at the top of every page or card of your notes to remind you not to speak too quickly. In consecutive interpretation, where you and the interpreter take turns speaking, try using ideas rather than the number of words or lines as a pace measure.

u.3   using your voice

If you're going to be a professional presenter then there's a key issue about voice that you've got to get hold of early on. It's not just *what* you say in your presentation that counts, the *way that you say it* is just as – if not more – important. Using your voice well and with effect is a key skill in professional presenting. Get

it right and you'll really reach your audience. Get it wrong and they'll strain to hear you, become bored by your monotone or feel that you're shouting at them. Professional presenters use pitch, emphasis, projection, articulation, speed and silence. Here are some practical tips to help you do that.

Pitch

Varying the pitch of your voice will keep your audience interested and attracted.

Try this: Pretend that a friend has told you a piece of gossip about someone you know. Try saying 'Really' out loud to show disinterest, real interest and surprise in turn. Your voice probably slightly sloped down for disinterest, scooped up and down for real interest and started higher and then plunged for surprise. If yours were different it doesn't matter, the main thing to notice is that differences in pitch produce differences in meaning. For example, low, flat speech indicates boredom and disinterest, an even lower pitch speaks of anger and a higher, varied pitch conveys anything from interest to hysteria. The pitch of your voice changes and colours what you say. A professional presenter uses this to his or her advantage, for example raising the pitch of her or his voice slightly when introducing a new topic.

Emphasis

Try saying these sentences, stressing or emphasizing the words in bold:

- **Sales** have risen this year.
- Sales have **risen** this year.
- Sales have risen **this** year.

A shift in emphasis can completely alter the way your audience hears what you say. When you emphasize a word, you expel more air through your mouth and lips. This automatically raises pitch and slows speech down. Using emphasis and pauses together puts a 'highlight' around what you're saying (*see* **p.4 pauses**).

Projection

Projecting your voice isn't about shouting. It means making sure that you use the resonating cavities in your mouth and nose. Try the following exercises to maximize your voice projection.

First, relax your neck muscles, then:

- nod, tilt and circle your neck
- raise and drop the shoulders, circle them forwards and backwards
- stand comfortably upright.

Second, breathe deeply, then:

- put your hand on your diaphragm, just below the rib-cage central join, and breathe in through the nose. Concentrate on making your diaphragm move in and out rather than your chest
- make a sound or say a word as you breathe out through your mouth. Feel the sound resonate

- try saying . . . aaaaaahhhhh . . . on the out breath, then . . . mmmmmm . . . also on the out breath. Once you get the feel of this resonance, you can drop the aaaahhh and mmmmm and feel the vibration of your words as you speak them. Increase your awareness of this resonance by using the exercise of building humming into your speaking.

Articulation

Poor articulation will make your voice sound throaty or muffled, either because your tongue is pulled too far back or because you don't move your tongue enough when you speak. Professional presenters articulate well. They practise this; they position their tongues towards the front of their mouths and they use them to enunciate their words clearly. They also slightly exaggerate the use of their lips to slow their speech and to help the listener to see the shape made. Try relaxing your tongue by stretching it out and moving it from side to side. Relax your jaw by moving it up and down (not side to side) and massaging the lower jaw area. You can also warm up your lips and tongue by reciting tongue-twisters with all the sounds fully articulated.

Speed

Speak too quickly and you'll lose your audience, speak too slowly and they'll go to sleep. Check out your natural speech rhythm, get feedback if you're unsure. If you generally speak quickly, speak slower than usual, particularly when you're making an important point. If your speech is usually on the slow side then make sure that you vary its pitch and pace, especially at a change of topic (*see* **p.1 pace**).

Silence

Silence can be just as powerful and effective as words. Silence can be used, for example, to allow your audience time to digest or reflect upon what you've said or to signal a new topic. Learn to live with three seconds (at least) of silence and remember how you appreciate it (*see* **q.2 quiet**).

v is for . . .

v.1 video conferencing

Video conferencing is growing in popularity and sooner or later you're going to have to face doing a presentation using a two-way video link. The technology that enables you to do this – such as ISDN (integrated service digital network) or ADSL (asymmetric digital subscriber line) linkages – is advancing rapidly and becoming more commonplace. Video conferencing systems are currently:

- satellite-based – in the form of 'interactive television', i.e. one-way video, two-way audio
- medium to high bandwidth 'by wire' systems using digital picture and sound compression technology and giving two-way video and audio.

These can be point-to-point, where just two sites are linked, or multi-point, where one main site is linked to a number of other sites simultaneously.

But presenting down a video conference link is very different from presenting to an audience in the same room. In the video conference presentation, technology interposes a filter or screen between you and your audience. You see and hear each other but only by courtesy of that technology. The sort of connections that you make when you're in the same room as your audience *don't* happen. This means that it's vitally important to become familiar with both the technology and the process of video conferencing. To do this you should:

- talk to an experienced user
- sit in on someone else's video conferencing presentation
- book a practice session and ask someone to observe you and give feedback

- visit the room from which you'll be presenting, with a technician or an experienced user
- familiarize yourself with the controls and equipment. This may take more than one visit.

Before your video conferencing presentation you'll need to:

- meet with the technician in advance to discuss your plans in detail
- make sure the technician knows what visuals you're going to use so he or she can then make requisite adjustments to cameras or other equipment
- make sure that you've got a far-end facilitator who can cope with the technology to make sure it runs smoothly, give out handouts, etc., and encourage questions and discussion
- plan and discuss this far-end facilitator role with the person who is carrying it out – don't just leave it to 'happen' on the day.

During your video conferencing presentation you need to:

- forget you're on-camera, just behave and talk naturally

- try not to wear small patterns, checks, fine stripes or highly saturated colours such as bright red or green, as they can dazzle your audience or make your image appear blurred
- remember that the camera cannot move as fast as you, so don't wave your arms about or make sudden movements
- show you are listening when the people at the remote locations talk – look at the camera rather than the monitor on which you can see them, leaning forward, nodding
- cope with the response delay between you and your audience at the remote site by pausing when you expect a response from the far-end site and waiting until the person at the far end has finished talking before you reply.

v.2   video presentations

There are some circumstances – like distance, time constraints or the need to release or present a message at a number of disparate locations simultaneously – that will lead you to consider prerecording your presentation. But doing this has a number of significant disadvantages including inflexibility, lack of participation, expense and, last but not least, the fact that not many of us are video stars!

Video conferencing (*see* **v.1 video conferencing**) is almost always a better alternative to pre-recording your presentation, particularly when audience participation or questions are important. Nevertheless, despite its drawbacks, a pre-recorded video presentation is better than no presentation at all. It can also be an effective way to communicate ideas consistently, pass on information uniformly and generate interest which can then be carried forward by support people on the ground.

 Producing a pre-recorded video presentation – and doing it well – requires professional skills and experience. Because of this, and despite the fact that digital technology has given us all the opportunity to be movie directors, you should strongly resist the temptation to direct and produce your own presentation. You'll need to work with a top-class professional producer or director, someone who'll work with and guide you through the stages of:

- pre-production – research, finding locations, booking facilities, writing the outline and 'shooting script'
- shooting – shooting the material
- post-production – recording narration, adding any graphics, video effects or music required resulting in a master tape
- duplication stage – when the master tape is copied onto its final format.

Once it has gone through all these stages, your video will be difficult and costly to change. So make sure that you really do need a pre-recorded video presentation and, if you do, also make sure that you've got a delivery-point facilitator who knows the content and background of your presentation as well as you do and can give out handouts, etc., and handle and encourage questions and discussion.

v.3 videos

Videos are a mixed blessing for the professional presenter. When you ask your audience to watch a video you also often expect them to:

- accept a reduction in room lighting level
- adapt to looking at a small television screen instead of the big one that you've been using with your projector
- shift their attention from you to the video
- shift their attention back to you once the video is over.

All of this will reduce your audience's attention levels and detract from the main drive of your presentation.

But, despite all this, a video *can* make a contribution to your presentation. You can, for example, use a video to change the rhythm, pace or subject of your presentation or, in long training sessions (*see* **t.6 training presentations**), use them to give your voice a rest and your audience a break from seeing you at the front. But, as a professional presenter, you're going to need to plan, confine and control the contribution of your video. Get this right and you'll be able to integrate a video into your presentation in a way that adds to and supplements your message.

Here are some tips to help you achieve that.

• Make sure – before you choose your video material – that you know what video equipment is going to be available.
• Keep your video clips short.
• Make sure that the clip you intend to use is compatible with available equipment, high quality, relevant and supports your message.
• Limit 'talking head' clips to one minute or less.
• Other video clips, such as product-demos, activity, building or place shots can be longer but never more than two minutes.
• Source your video clips from clip-media collections, DVD, CD-ROM, websites and commercial videos.
• Never, ever, use amateur videos.

• If you're using material created by somebody else always check out the copyright situation and acknowledge your source.
• Make sure – before your presentation – that you're familiar with the technology, know what to do if it doesn't work, have your video source cued up correctly and know when and how to shut that source off.

v.4   visual aids

The visual aid is an everyday, ordinary, tool of the trade for presenters (*see* **o.4 overheads**). As such, it pops up in every presentation. Part of the reason for this lies with the electronic tools that we use. The personal computer, the scanner and the photocopier have all contributed in the shift from material that was hand-written or hand-drawn to material that's copied, scanned or downloaded from a clip art or graphic art website. As a result, the visual aid has truly become 'illustrative matter designed to supplement written or spoken information'.

But that's not all the visual aid is. For the professional presenter, the visual aid forms a key link between her or his message and the audience. Without it your presentation would become a speech or a lecture, in which your audience would be talked *at* rather than talked *with*. But visual aids aren't automatically good. Use too many or project over-elaborate badly-thought-out visual aids and you'll have an audience that's confused and has lost interest in what you're saying. Professional presenters avoid that sort of visual aid over-kill by making sure that their visual aids work. Visual aids like this will lead your audience to both the sense and the substance of your message. Here are some tips towards getting to that.

- Maximize the message and minimize the medium.

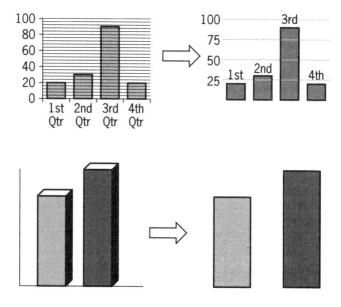

- Make your graphics truthful and self-explanatory – no false zeros or out-of-scale comparisons.
- Prune the detail – it's going to be viewed at a distance.

- Run words from left to right and in upper and lower case.
- Put your graphics in landscape mode – horizontal and wide.

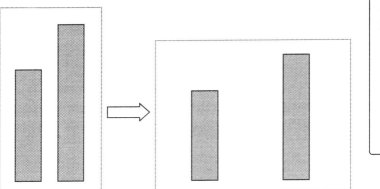

- Make sure that a text-only visual contains no more than seven lines and a maximum of six words per line.

For other tips see **c.2 cartoons, c.11 colours, f.8 flip charts, g.6 graphs and charts.**

w is for ... ■ ■ ■

w.1　when

When it comes to the 'when' of your presentation you're often, at least initially, at the mercy of others. They'll tell you what day and time of day that they want you to present on. If you're lucky there may be a number of alternative days and/or times. But for the professional presenter these are just the opening offers in a negotiation – one that's aimed at identifying a date and time that are acceptable to *both* the presenter and the organizer, and maximize the presenter's chances of really reaching his or her audience.

Achieving success in this negotiation will take skill and patience; it's also a process that is discussed in detail elsewhere (see **Taking it Further**). But however you do – or don't – negotiate about the when of your presentation you do need to be aware that there are days and times that you should avoid. Here are some of the more obvious:

- any 'after-lunch' slot (*see* **d.1 dead zones**)
- the Friday afternoon 'after 3 p.m.' slot
- the 9 a.m. Monday morning slot, particularly when the majority of your audience has a distance to travel.

Professional presenters are never reluctant to try to negotiate out of slots like these. But if this fails and you find yourself stuck with a slot that puts your audience's attentiveness or attention span at risk then you need to do something about your presentation. Restructure it to take into account your audience's state of mind. Split your message up into a limited number – no more than five – of clear, short and impactful linked sub-messages. Remember that your audience's attention span has probably decreased to five or so minutes. Try to put yourself in their shoes and adjust the pace and style of your presenting accordingly.

w.2 where

The 'where' of your presentation – like its 'when' – is often decided by somebody else. If you're presenting to a client, they'll want to use their meeting room; if you're presenting at a conference, the organizers will have 'set the stage' and if you're giving a lecture, you'll have to use the 'usual' lecture theatre. In all of these and other situations, factors such as equipment availability, ease of audience access, audience size or room availability will have taken precedence over your presenting needs. When this sort of thing happens the result is a presenting environment that's less than ideal.

Despite this, all isn't lost. It's never too late to do some of the things – even quite small things – that will upgrade your presenting environment. This doesn't just benefit you, it also benefits your audience. A professional presenter will start this process about a week before the scheduled date of his or her presentation. This is when she or he will ring the contact and confirm the basic facts of the presentation. Information such as when? where? how many people? how long? what equipment? will be confirmed or changed. Professional presenters often develop and use simple checklists to make sure that nothing is missed (*see* **c.6 checklists**). They also use this opportunity to arrange pre-presentation access to the location. You'll never find a professional presenter presenting in an environment that they haven't seen, checked out and tried to improve before the beginning of their presentation. Time is needed to do this, time to visit the location before it's too late, time to change things, time to put them right. Access to someone who can put things right will also be needed. If this visit can't be made before the day of the presentation then arrive at least three-quarters of an hour before the scheduled start time. Once there, check out the basics – are there enough chairs? is the layout OK? does the sound system work? (*see* **c.6 checklists**). This will do several things for you. It will:

- reduce the probability of a presenting disaster taking place
- increase your presentation's success capability
- put your mark on the presenting environment.

However, really professional presenters avoid all of this by getting themselves into the planning loop for the presentation. This means that they are able to make sure that all of the key environmental issues are dealt with well before the event (*see* **e.4 environment**).

w.3 whiteboards

Whiteboards are those large, often grubby, expanses of off-white surfaces that hang on the walls of many conference rooms or lecture theatres. They are positioned so that you can write on them – if you can find the dry-wipe pen that you're supposed to use! Most people don't or can't find it and as a result the surfaces of most whiteboards are covered in the ill-erased residual graffiti that results from using the wrong sort of pen.

But, despite all this, whiteboards do have their uses, particularly in participative presentations (*see* **p.2 participative presentations**). Here you can use them as a bigger and easier-to-use alternative to sheet or roll film on an overhead projector platen (*see* **o.3 overhead projectors, o.4 overheads**) when you 'chalkboard' your audience's comments or suggestions. Using a whiteboard like this is easier than writing on the small area of an overhead projector platen. It also enables you to interact more easily with your audience and list points made in group discussion more fully.

You can also answer these needs by using a digital whiteboard or copyboard. These digitally capture what you write on them. They use dry-wipe pens but save what you're writing on the hard disk of your computer or print it out using a built-in printer. This enables you to edit, print, fax or e-mail what you wrote on the board. This provides you, your audience and anybody else who needs to know with identical and accurate notes of the meeting. It also allows your audience to focus on what's going on in the meeting rather than on note-taking. Currently digital whiteboards differ in the way that they detect what pen you're using and where that pen is on the whiteboard. They can detect what colour pen you're using by:

- storing pens in special trays
- interacting with software
- interacting with the pen.

They can also detect where that pen is on the board's surface by:

- listening for the ultrasound that the pen emits
- tracking the pen's movement on a resistive membrane that's built into the board's surface
- picking up a magnetic field emitted by the pen
- using lasers built into the board's frame to scan for barcodes on the pen.

Each of these systems has its own set of strengths and weaknesses. Some need special dry-erase pens, others use special pen holders for standard dry-erase markers. Other boards have soft, damage-susceptible surfaces or need you to press hard when you write. The computer software packages that come with them are just as diverse – some can create thumbnail views of whiteboard images, others can recognize your handwriting or export whiteboard images into standard graphics file formats.

Here are some tips if you're thinking about buying or using a digital whiteboard or copyboard:

- Make sure the software is simple enough to enable you to focus on what your audience is saying rather than the computer.
- Try them all out before you select one to buy or hire.
- Hire one for a limited period if you're still not sure after a short trial.
- If you're going to buy then make sure that the board has a warranty that covers you for failures, replacement, etc.
- Make sure you *really* know how to use your board before you use it in front of an audience.
- Make sure that it's all working – set-up is usually simple – *before* the start of your presentation.
- Try covering the digital whiteboard with stick-on flip chart sheets that you'll write on. Instead of erasing the board after saving a page, peel off the sheets and stick them to the wall. This way you and your audience can always see what you wrote as well as having it stored on your hard disk.
- Print off and distribute your board notes at the end of the meeting – it creates a good impression and helps your audience remember and retain what was said.
- Send the captured notes as an e-mail attachment to others who couldn't make it. Do this on the same day as the meeting – it'll create quite an impression!

w.4   why

If you've been reading this book alphabetically, then you'll have had some clear hints about the answer to this question already. Nevertheless, the question 'Why am I presenting?' is so important it can't be asked too often. For the professional presenter, a key first step in the process of preparing that presentation is deciding what the aim or objective of a presentation is (*see* **o.1 objectives**

and targets). That aim or objective will also be high on a professional presenter's pre-presentation checklist (*see* **c.6 checklists**), thus making sure that the presenter launches his or her presentation with a clear understanding of its desired outcome. In all of these situations it's the four Is that loom large. For the professional presenter's answer to the question 'why?' will be that he or she aims to finish the presentation with an audience that has become:

- inspired and
- influenced – to do something or feel something, or
- informed – on a particular subject or issue, or
- instructed – on how to do something.

The last three of these Is can sometimes overlap. For example, you can inform your audience – by giving them information – and thus inspire them. You can also show them how easy it is to do something that they thought was difficult and thus influence their views about whether to do it or not (*see* **h.4 how does a presentation work?**).

If your answer doesn't fit into any of these, then you've got a problem. Answers such as 'I aim to entertain them' or 'Because I've been told to' will *not* lead to a presentation that will inspire any audience. Similarly, answers such as 'To fill in a free slot' or 'To stand in for someone else' can only lead to presentations that are boring and totally uninspiring. If you want to get your presenting up to professional standards then you have to realize that such answers – which some people will describe as 'pragmatic' or 'realistic' – are actually second-best and unprofessional. Get focused on what your real aim is and do that before you start your preparation (*see* **p.12 preparing your material**).

x, y and z are for . . .

x.1 -xtras

The secrets of professional presenting

Professional presenters are always:

- interesting
- passionate
- convincing
- prepared
- believable.

The Tale of Three Stonecutters

Three stonecutters were asked what they were doing. The first one, who stopped cutting to answer the question, said, 'I'm making a living and providing for my wife and children.' The second one kept on hammering away at the stone and answered, 'I'm trying to be the fastest stonecutter on this job.' But the third one – who stopped cutting, stood up and thought before he answered – looked at the questioner with a visionary gleam in his eye and said, 'I'm building a cathedral.' Professional presenters are like the third stonecutter, except that their aim is to set an audience on fire rather than build a cathedral.

Japanese proverbs

- You do well what you like well.
- You can change your clothes, not your character.
- Others are others; I am I.
- Sooner or later you act out what you really think.

Cool quotes

You cannot achieve the impossible without attempting the absurd.

Anon

. . . security, certitude, and peace do not lead to discoveries.

C. J. Jung

Whether you think you can or can't – you are right.

Henry Ford

In making a speech one must study three points: first, the means of producing persuasion; second, the language; third, the proper arrangement of the various parts of the speech.

Aristotle (384–323 BC)

Speech is after all only a system of gestures, having the peculiarity that each gesture produces a characteristic sound, so that it can be perceived through the ear as well as through the eye. Listening to a speaker instead of looking at him tends to make us think of speech as essentially a system of sounds; but it is not; essentially it is a system of gestures made with the lungs and larynx, and the cavities of the mouth and nose.

Robin George Collingwood (1889–1943)

taking it further

Books

Body language

Argyle, M., *Bodily Communication*, 1988, Routledge, London

Morris, D., *People-watching*, 2002, Vintage/Ebury, London

Ribbens, G. and Thompson, R., *Understanding Body Language in a Week*, 2000, Hodder & Stoughton, London

Wainwright, G.R., *Teach Yourself Body Language*, 1999, Hodder & Stoughton, London

Communication

Hargie, O. (ed), *A Handbook of Communication Skills*, 1997, Routledge, London

Culture

Hickson, D.J. and Pugh, D.S., *Management Worldwide*, 2002, Penguin, London

Hofstede, G., *Cultures and Organizations: Software of the Mind*, 1994, HarperCollins, London

Lewis, R.D., *When Cultures Collide*, 1996, Nicholas Brearley, London

Negotiation

Baguley, P., *Teach Yourself Negotiating*, 2000, Hodder & Stoughton, London

Powerpoint

Kirk, R., *Teach Yourself Powerpoint 2000*, 1999, Hodder & Stoughton, London

Peppitt, E., *Teach Yourself Powerpoint 2000 Quick Fix*, 2001, Hodder & Stoughton, London

Other subjects

Auger, B.Y., *How to Run Better Meetings: a Reference Guide for Managers*, 1986, McGraw-Hill, New York

Craze, R., *Teach Yourself Relaxation*, 2001, Hodder & Stoughton, London

Cresswell, J., *The Penguin Dictionary of Clichés*, 2000, Penguin, London

Tufte, E.R., *The Visual Display of Quantitative Information*, 1983, Graphics Press, Cheshire C.T.

Tufte, E.R., *Envisioning Information*, 1990, Graphics Press, Cheshire C.T.

Websites

There are websites on almost every subject that you can imagine. Here is a by-no-means exhaustive list of websites that you may find useful:

Cartoons

http://www.tedgoff.com

http://www.planetcartoonist.com/poptoon

http://www.nfx.com/com/toonsites

http://www.100topcartoonsites.com

Clip art

http://www.gardenartbysandpiper.com

http://dgl.microsoft.com

http://www.100000freecliparts.com

http://www.graphicmaps.com/clipart

http://www.clipart.co.uk

http://www.100clipart.com

Disability awareness sites

http://www.rnib.org.uk/

http://www.dyslexia-inst.org.uk

http://www.dyslexic.com

http://deafness.about.com

http://www.britishdeafassociation.org.uk

Hardware and equipment

Computers

http://www.apple.com

http://www.compaq.com

http://www.dell.com

http://www.h-p.com

http://www.sony.com

Copyboards

http://www.panasonic.com

http://www.brother.com

Multimedia projectors

http://www.epson.com

http://www.hitachi.com

http://www.mitsubishi.com

http://www.nec.com

http://www.sanyo.com

http://www.sonypresentation.com

http://www.toshiba.com

http://www.3m.com/meeting/multi

Overhead projectors
http://www.3M.com

Screens
http://www.da-lite.com

Slide projectors
http://www.kodak.com

http://www.braun.com

Presentation tips and techniques

http://www.3M.com/meetings

http://www.presentations.com/

http://www.presentationskills.com/

http://www.presentersuniversity.com

http://www.public-speaking.org/

http://www.speaking.co.uk

Software

http://www.adobe.com

http://www.apple.com/quicktime/

http://www.microsoft.com

http://www.shockwave.com/

Weight control sites

http://www.cambridge-diet.com/statistics/ashwell.html

http://www.cambridge-diet.com/statistics/findyourBMI.html

acknowledgements

Both of us are experienced enough to realize that much of what you learn in life comes from the people that you meet along the way. For that reason we owe thanks to many – if not all – of the people that we have presented to, with and for in the past. They've all contributed, in one way or another. The list of their names is, of course, far too long to be published here. However, special mention must be made of:

- our respective partners – Linda Baguley and Tony Benton – whose patience has been considerable
- Peter Graves – for the walks, read-through and encouragement
- Katie Roden and Jill Birch at Hodder – for their contributions to the process of getting this book to you, its reader.

Phil Baguley and Janet Bateman

Brighton, England

your notes

Afrikaans
Access 2002
Accounting, Basic
Alexander Technique
Algebra
Arabic
Arabic Script, Beginner's
Aromatherapy
Astronomy
Bach Flower Remedies
Bengali
Better Chess
Better Handwriting
Biology
Body Language
Book Keeping
Book Keeping & Accounting
Brazilian Portuguese
Bridge
Buddhism
Buddhism, 101 Key Ideas
Bulgarian
Business Studies
Business Studies, 101 Key Ideas
C++
Calculus
Calligraphy
Cantonese
Card Games
Catalan
Chemistry, 101 Key Ideas
Chess
Chi Kung
Chinese
Chinese, Beginner's

Chinese Language, Life & Culture
Chinese Script, Beginner's
Christianity
Classical Music
Copywriting
Counselling
Creative Writing
Crime Fiction
Croatian
Crystal Healing
Czech
Danish
Desktop Publishing
Digital Photography
Digital Video & PC Editing
Drawing
Dream Interpretation
Dutch
Dutch, Beginner's
Dutch Dictionary
Dutch Grammar
Eastern Philosophy
ECDL
E-Commerce
Economics, 101 Key Ideas
Electronics
English, American (EFL)
English as a Foreign Language
English, Correct
English Grammar
English Grammar (EFL)
English, Instant, for French Speakers
English, Instant, for German Speakers
English, Instant, for Italian Speakers
English, Instant, for Spanish Speakers

English for International Business
English Language, Life & Culture
English Verbs
English Vocabulary
Ethics
Excel 2002
Feng Shui
Film Making
Film Studies
Finance for non-Financial Managers
Finnish
Flexible Working
Flower Arranging
French
French, Beginner's
French Grammar
French Grammar, Quick Fix
French, Instant
French, Improve your
French Language, Life & Culture
French Starter Kit
French Verbs
French Vocabulary
Gaelic
Gaelic Dictionary
Gardening
Genetics
Geology
German
German, Beginner's
German Grammar
German Grammar, Quick Fix
German, Instant
German, Improve your
German Language, Life & Culture
German Verbs
German Vocabulary
Go
Golf
Greek
Greek, Ancient
Greek, Beginner's
Greek, Instant
Greek, New Testament
Greek Script, Beginner's
Guitar
Gulf Arabic
Hand Reflexology
Hebrew, Biblical
Herbal Medicine
Hieroglyphics
Hindi
Hindi, Beginner's
Hindi Script, Beginner's

Hinduism
History, 101 Key Ideas
How to Win at Horse Racing
How to Win at Poker
HTML Publishing on the WWW
Human Anatomy & Physiology
Hungarian
Icelandic
Indian Head Massage
Indonesian
Information Technology, 101 Key Ideas
Internet, The
Irish
Islam
Italian
Italian, Beginner's
Italian Grammar
Italian Grammar, Quick Fix
Italian, Instant
Italian, Improve your
Italian Language, Life & Culture
Italian Verbs
Italian Vocabulary
Japanese
Japanese, Beginner's
Japanese, Instant
Japanese Language, Life & Culture
Japanese Script, Beginner's
Java
Jewellery Making
Judaism
Korean
Latin
Latin American Spanish
Latin, Beginner's
Latin Dictionary
Latin Grammar
Letter Writing Skills
Linguistics
Linguistics, 101 Key Ideas
Literature, 101 Key Ideas
Mahjong
Managing Stress
Marketing
Massage
Mathematics
Mathematics, Basic
Media Studies
Meditation
Mosaics
Music Theory
Needlecraft
Negotiating
Nepali

Norwegian
Origami
Panjabi
Persian, Modern
Philosophy
Philosophy of Mind
Philosophy of Religion
Philosophy of Science
Philosophy, 101 Key Ideas
Photography
Photoshop
Physics
Piano
Planets
Planning Your Wedding
Polish
Politics
Portuguese
Portuguese, Beginner's
Portuguese Grammar
Portuguese, Instant
Portuguese Language, Life & Culture
Postmodernism
Pottery
Powerpoint 2002
Presenting for Professionals
Project Management
Psychology
Psychology, 101 Key Ideas
Psychology, Applied
Quark Xpress
Quilting
Recruitment
Reflexology
Reiki
Relaxation
Retaining Staff
Romanian
Russian
Russian, Beginner's
Russian Grammar
Russian, Instant
Russian Language, Life & Culture
Russian Script, Beginner's
Sanskrit
Screenwriting
Serbian
Setting up a Small Business
Shorthand, Pitman 2000
Sikhism
Spanish
Spanish, Beginner's
Spanish Grammar
Spanish Grammar, Quick Fix

Spanish, Instant
Spanish, Improve your
Spanish Language, Life & Culture
Spanish Starter Kit
Spanish Verbs
Spanish Vocabulary
Speaking on Special Occasions
Speed Reading
Statistical Research
Statistics
Swahili
Swahili Dictionary
Swedish
Tagalog
Tai Chi
Tantric Sex
Teaching English as a Foreign Language
Teaching English One to One
Teams and Team-Working
Thai
Time Management
Tracing your Family History
Travel Writing
Trigonometry
Turkish
Turkish, Beginner's
Typing
Ukrainian
Urdu
Urdu Script, Beginner's
Vietnamese
Volcanoes
Watercolour Painting
Weight Control through Diet and
  Exercise
Welsh
Welsh Dictionary
Welsh Language, Life & Culture
Wills and Probate
Wine Tasting
Winning at Job Interviews
Word 2002
World Faiths
Writing a Novel
Writing for Children
Writing Poetry
Xhosa
Yoga
Zen
Zulu

available from bookshops and on-line retailers

project management
phil baguley

teach yourself

Teach Yourself Project Management is a practical introduction to the craft of project management. With diagrams, useful ideas, appropriate methods, checklists and tools, it explains and illustrates the what, why, when and how of this form of management. The ultimate guide for all who wish to develop the skills of effective project management.

This book shows you how to:

- manage, plan and organize your project from start to finish
- create an effective project team
- estimate and manage your project budgets
- solve problems, and monitor and control the activities of your project.

Phil Baguley is an experienced business writer and lecturer. He has held senior management roles in multinational corporations and worked as a management consultant in the UK and Europe.

teach
yourself

negotiating
phil baguley

Teach Yourself Negotiating is an important book for all professionals. The need to negotiate effectively exists at all levels in all organizations. Whether you are dealing with colleagues, suppliers or customers you need to be able to negotiate – and do it well.

A book you cannot afford to be without,
Teach Yourself Negotiating:

- shows you how to prepare for, carry out and complete your negotiations
- helps you decide what strategies and tactics to use
- illustrates how to use the bargaining process to generate a successful outcome
- guides you to a successful implementation of that outcome
- provides a checklist for assessing your own negotiating skills.

Phil Baguley is an experienced business writer and lecturer. He has held senior management roles in multinational corporations and worked as a management consultant in the UK and Europe.

surviving your organization
phil baguley

This essential guide is for anyone who wants to survive their organization and have a successful, stress-free working life. Arranged in a dip-in, dip-out alphabetical order for ease of use, this is a book you will use every working day.

From ADAPTABILITY to JARGON, BOSSES to LISTENING and LAUGHTER to ZEN, you'll find everything you need to raise your survival rating and maximize your potential and performance.

Phil Baguley has been a successful business consultant and is now a widely published author.

Confessions of a VAT Inspector

Dawn Fallon

Dedicated to all my Civil Service Colleagues
without whose positive input into my working life
this book would not have been possible.

The taxpayer

- someone who works for the government

but doesn't have to take the Civil Service examination.

Ronald Reagan

CONTENTS

FOREWORD

I was thrilled to be asked to write the Foreword for 'Confessions of a VAT Inspector'. I was a contemporary of Dawn's in the Central England 'Collection' in the early 1990s and our paths crossed at Coventry VAT office towards the end of our respective times in Customs & Excise.

Reading this lovely memoir was like a visit with old friends. The experiences Dawn describes were my experiences and those of so many inspectors from that time. One of the first things I was told after joining the department was: "the traders are not your friends!". Whilst that bleak warning made sense, if it was intended that I should therefore view every visit as a meeting with the enemy, that wasn't how it seemed in reality. As Dawn describes so wonderfully, what we often found during visits were small businesses owned by people who were struggling to make a living, often in very difficult circumstances.

Here is a story of the visits to small corner shops, inspecting records in gloomy back rooms; calculating mark-ups on orange juice when inspecting the books of milkmen; and even visits to undertakers where 'inspection of premises' could be particularly challenging when some of their rooms were 'occupied'.

This is a record of a time when the world was on the cusp of the computer age. In these pages you will discover an era of painstakingly handwritten ledgers; hundreds of invoices in plastic bags and occasionally, and memorably, ill-conceived fraud. But more than anything this is a book about the lives of ordinary people, both traders and inspectors, thrown together in strange circumstances with each trying to make the best of their day and find their route through life.

When reading Dawn's book, I was reminded of L. P. Hartley's famous quote: *"The past is a foreign country: they do things differently there."* Enjoy the journey.

Glyn Edwards

VAT Director, MHA

PROLOGUE

This collection of stories about VAT visits is based on my work experience as a VAT Control Officer during the 80s and 90s when I was appointed to do the job through the Civil Service promotion process. I'd originally trained to be a pianist and music teacher, but after finishing my music studies at Birmingham University, the whole course of my working life changed when I entered the Civil Service as a clerical officer in January 1981.

VAT Control was a job I struggled with on many levels - from trying to understand business accounts and VAT law to interviewing and interacting with traders. However, the work gave me a unique insight into business people and places - from multi-million-pound high street bakeries to small inner-city grocers selling rotting vegetables. Some VAT visits were funny, some were not. But some were unforgettable.

Woven around these stories is an individual and historical account detailing my personal journey as a civil servant working for HM Customs & Excise in a day and age that no longer exists.

NOTE

ON THE USE OF REGIONAL DIALECTS

The book is set in and around Birmingham, UK. I speak in a Birmingham accent, so all my speech would be in that dialect, along with several (though not all) of my colleagues.

However, I have occasionally written some speech in dialect - particularly in Chapters 1, 2, 10, 13 and 23 - because many people in the 1980s spoke in an older dialect which no longer exists.

For example, using the word "her" instead of "she" (or vice versa depending on which part of the country it is), or in the Midlands, the pronunciation of the word "lost" as "lorst", "backwards" as "backerds", "baby" as "babby" and so on. In Cornwall, there is the use of the word "they" instead of "those" and the word "ee" for "'you" - which is from the old English word "thee" (with the "th" dropped). Likewise with the Irish accent, "th" is spoken as a "t".

These dialects all sing of a way of speaking that is disappearing, if not now all but gone, and the essence of the rhythm, pace and charm of these interesting regional pronunciations is impossible to convey using standard written English.

I have included them in my stories because they reflect the era I write about, as well as having had an impact on me with the quality of their distinctiveness.

PART ONE – THE RELUCTANT VAT INSPECTOR

'Typical of Customs and Excise - they do everything cloak and dagger.'

Chief Inspector Japp in Poirot, Hickory Hickory Dock

1. FARMERS AND PLUMBERS

'**D**oes sheep semen have VAT on it?' asked the farmer as we made our way to the farmhouse where I'd be inspecting his VAT records. I wasn't sure if he was having me on or trying to wind me up, but I had to give him the benefit of the doubt,

'I'm not sure to be honest, but I'll find out and let you know,' I puffed, breathless from trying to keep up with his stride as I lugged my heavy briefcase over farmyard gunk in a pair of high heels and a pencil skirt. If only female officers were allowed to wear trousers.

'Are you selling sheep semen then?' I probed in an attempt to keep up the illusion that he was being serious. But he was serious.

'Not at the moment,' he picked up a stick and threw it across the yard for his sheep dog, 'but I'm thinking about it. I've got to try and make more money somehow.'

It had never even occurred to me that sheep semen could be sold at all, let alone be a source of lucrative revenue for the government, and I was clueless as to whether sheep semen was liable for VAT, exempt from VAT or outside the scope of VAT.

It was being asked oddball questions like that, and others such as 'what's the VAT liability of a Geiger counter?' or 'can I claim the input tax back on my guard dog's ashes?' that I decided VAT Control was a bit of a strange job. Besides, who in their right mind would want to be a VAT inspector anyway? It's hardly the sort of job any young person would aspire to, unlike noble professions such as being a vet, or a doctor.

It was September 1989 and I was thirteen months into my VAT training in and around Birmingham learning something new every day. Every week I was visiting all kinds of different businesses and met a variety of business people who were so diverse that I began to believe I'd lived my 28 years of life on the planet like a hamster in a tiny cage. Becoming a VAT inspector broadened my whole vista of life by bringing me into contact with the trading community and showcasing a vibrant city throbbing with a multitude of industrious people and productive firms. It had opened up a panorama of the business world along with its opportunities, difficulties, struggles, successes and - where VAT was concerned - temptations......

The temptation for businesses to fiddle their VAT returns continually lay at their door. To that end, VAT inspectors were trained to be suspicious. In reality, there are only two basic ways that traders can fiddle their VAT returns -

(1) by suppressing their taxable sales, or

(2) by inflating the VAT they reclaim on their business purchases and expenses.

The temptation was particularly alluring for farmers for the simple reason it was normal for some farms to reclaim large amounts of VAT on their expenses, and add to that the fact most farms generally only received a VAT visit once every 5-8 years, it was easy to falsify some of their returns and never get caught.

It was even more of a temptation if a farm was in financial difficulty, and my line manager, Kay, told me about a visit she once did to a dairy farmer who'd falsely claimed over £75,000 in VAT over a four year period to keep his failing farm afloat. He did this by reclaiming VAT on orders that he later cancelled.

'And you need to know about red diesel,' she added.

'Red diesel? What's that?'

'It's a rebated fuel which can only be used in off-road vehicles like tractors. It's illegal to use it in cars or vans, or sell it to the public.'

'I've never even heard of it. But surely most farmers are honest?'

'They are indeed, but an officer up north found a farmer using red diesel in his Landrover, and also selling it as fuel to hundreds of customers. He charged VAT on it which he then used to line his own pockets to the tune of nearly fifty thousand pounds.'

'How did the officer discover it?' I probed, hoping for some clues.

'He got a sample using a dipstick to check for the red dye in it.'

Dipstick? Crikey I wouldn't have the nerve....

So I was on my guard when I visited the sheep farmer and was on the lookout for false purchase claims, suppression of taxable sales, and red diesel fraud. But I had no intentions of using a dipstick, a syphon, or any intrusive method to physically check out red diesel malfeasance. I just hadn't got the bottle to do that, so if he was on the fiddle he got lucky having me as a VAT inspector.

'Do you use red diesel?'

'Yes, but only for the small tractor which I use to shift stuff around,' was his reply, and when I inspected his records it appeared to be the case and there was nothing which raised any alarm bells. In the end, after sifting through all his paperwork, I didn't find anything amiss other than two small arithmetic errors amounting to just over £150, and if I missed anything big, then he'd be having a laugh at my expense.

ΔΔΔ

Her Majesty's Revenue and Customs (as it's now called - HMRC for short) these days have a name-and-shame 'Current List of deliberate tax defaulters' on the 'My News Desk HMRC' website revealing eye-watering amounts of revenue stolen by traders, and details of how they stole it. If I'd had that resource at my fingertips as a VAT inspector I might have been a bit more savvy in my job. But in the 80s and 90s, we only had our own in-house stories of VAT mischief to keep our suspicious minds ticking over, exposing the lengths which some traders will go to in order to steal public money.

In reality the majority of businesses we visited were trustworthy, hard-working people who were trying to make an honest living, and major fraud was rarely found. And even if we did have suspicions, proving them was quite another matter. I once visited a trader called Plumb-Rite where a Mr James Satchwell was the sole proprietor of his small plumbing business registered from his home address in Erdington. He worked alone doing odd plumbing jobs, and used a small van. He'd been trading just over seven years, and the previous visiting officer had found everything in good order, noting there were no employees apart from the trader's wife who was paid a small wage to be the bookkeeper. So I made the appointment with Mrs Satchwell as she was the one who kept the accounts and would be able to assist me with my inspection while her husband was out working.

The house where Plumb-Rite traded from was in a part of Birmingham that, back in the 1930s, had been a smart middle-class suburb, but by the late 80s time had eroded its elegance. As I approached the house I was mesmerised by the telegraph cables stretching overhead - a veritable cat's cradle of black wires crisscrossing from brown fingered telegraph poles. The air was tinged with the earthy scent of golden autumn leaves which adorned the pavement like giant crispy cornflakes, giving me the joy of crunching them underfoot. A broken gate hanging off its hinges gave access to an overgrown front garden. I tapped the front door firmly using my knuckles as the knocker was missing, and an elderly, rotund gentleman answered the door.

'I'm Miss Smith from Customs and Excise, I've got an appointment with—'

'Oh-ar, come in luv. We're expecting yer,' he said in a broad Birmingham accent, leading me through to the living room.

'Sit down will you, and I'll go and fetch me daughter. Her's in the garden her is. Just wait a minute will you luv.' I sat down as commanded on a chair at the dining table which was littered with newspapers, comics, cans of pop, and - strangely - two screwdrivers, a hammer and a bradawl.

The room was a disarray of magazines, unboxed videos, and scattered toys. Clothing lay draped over the back of the settee, and a pair of socks were stuffed in the top of an old jug on the mantelpiece. Although it was all a bit of a jumble, there was a lived-in, homely feel which gave it a relaxed family warmth. It reminded me of my grandmother's home where everything was out of place, yet everything could be found.

Mrs Satchwell entered the room and greeted me before I could say a word,

'Hello Miss Smith, would you like a cuppa tea luv?'

'Not just yet thank you, maybe in a moment, I just need to ask you a few questions first before I check the records and accounts.'

'Yes luv, fire away.'

'Is the legal status of the business still sole proprietor?'

'Yes luv.'

'And is this address still the principal place of business?'

'Yes luv.'

'And is the financial year-end still the 30th June?'

'Yes luv.'

'Does your husband have any employees?'

'No luv, only me to do the books.'

'Is he still using the same van?'

'Yes luv.'

...I recited my tiresome queries - a VAT mantra - from my shopping list of questions which I'd jotted down in my official A4 notebook beforehand. All VAT visits began by interviewing the trader about the business and records, and I was rubbish at it. It was an area I was to struggle with throughout my career. I tried hard to make the interview sound casual and pleasant, but it just didn't come off. It was more like an inquisition, though Mrs Satchwell seemed blissfully unaware of how dire it was. I was glad when it came to an end and I could get down to checking the figures.

The accounts and business records were very well kept, and Mrs Satchwell had even produced her husband's work diaries and job sheets for me. These subsidiary records were a useful tool to assess the credibility of the business. She brought me a cup of tea and left me to it.

Mrs Satchwell's father came back into the living room and sat in a rocking chair in front of the window overlooking the street. He began talking to me as though we were old buddies and I'd just popped round for a friendly cuppa. His monologue went something like this:

'Cor my back don't half hurt. Now, I said to that woman - y'know her that lives round the corner - I said, they shouldn't allow that to happen. Lorst me balance I did and fell backerds. I couldn't help it - I tried to grab hold on the doings, but it blummin' well slipped. Arse about face I was. Didn't half hurt meself! Of course it's them kids y'know, that's what it is,' he held up a finger pointing at them in his mind's eye, 'I told them what for I did! I told them get out of it the pair on yer,' he stabbed the air with his finger, 'but do y'know what they did? They just turned round and stuck two fingers up at me. Well what d'you make o' that? Terrible innit? My grandson, God luv him, he wouldn't do nothing like that he wouldn't,' he concluded, 'anyway - I'm Alf by the way, and you'll never guess how old I am? I'm eighty-five I am. Eighty-five! I'll be eighty-six next wik, and I don't feel a day over thirty, mind you when I was a lad...' ...he continued his intriguing soliloquy in similar manner while I niddle-noddled along to be polite as I attempted to concentrate on my work.

After about an hour, Mrs Satchwell entered with an enormous bacon sandwich for her father, and more tea all around.

'Would you like a bacon sandwich?' she offered, all friendly and warm.

'Well, actually I've almost finished and I'll be going soon - thank you anyway. Everything seems fine so far. I've just got to look at the Annual Accounts, then I'll be on my way,' I smiled back at her.

She left the room and I continued with the final part of my

inspection. Suddenly there was a blissful silence from Alf who was totally engrossed in devouring his elevenses, and I carried on checking the Annual Accounts which appeared 'all fair and above board'. It had been a textbook visit.

The only thing I couldn't prove was the odd cash job that I suspected Mr Satchwell might be doing but not declaring. VAT inspectors developed mistrustful minds, and we often suspected that certain traders might occasionally be tempted to do cash jobs 'on the side' squirrelling away the money where neither Customs & Excise nor the Inland Revenue would find it. We'd been primed and conditioned like Pavlovian dogs to try and sniff out these off-record cash jobs, and we'd been made aware of the 'I-can-do-it-a-bit-less-for-cash' offer which some traders might bring to their customers. It would be easy for Mr Satchwell to offer any of his customers 'I can do it a bit less for cash.' But how could I possibly uncover that? Mrs Satchwell's accounts were immaculate and she was an excellent bookkeeper. All the jobs in the diary matched the invoices. And all the invoices matched the bankings. The audit trail was exemplary. Any cash jobs which Mr Satchwell might have done were very tidily put away and Customs & Excise would never know about it. Not even the Satchwell's lifestyle betrayed any cash stashed away. There was no evidence they had any other property, owned an expensive car, or had lavish holidays (I looked at some of the photos dotted around, but there was nothing to suggest they even went abroad) - even if they did, they wouldn't be so stupid as to leave evidence for a VAT inspector to discover would they? So if Mr Satchwell *was* doing the odd cash job he didn't seem to be a greedy man and all I could think was '*good luck to him.*' There was nothing more I could do.

As I finished writing my notes, the sound of snoring rose from the chair in front of the window. While Alf slept, an opportunist moment presented itself to me and I took a quick, sneaky look under all the stuff on the table. Maybe there was a secret diary somewhere showing Mr Satchwell's 'I-can-do-it-a-bit-less-for-cash' jobs, or statements from a secret bank account… but all I could see were old newspapers, puzzle books, gas bills, and Beano comics. We were trained to 'protect the revenue' which included employing any reasonable means of discovering undeclared tax and my conscience didn't flinch as I rifled through the assortment of paraphernalia. But there was nothing.

I packed my briefcase and finished my tea which had been made with sterilised milk - something I hadn't tasted since my 1960s childhood and it made the tea taste sickly-sweet, which although unexpected, wasn't unpleasant. It was strangely evocative of visits to my grandmother when I was small and it sparked one of my frequent daydreams. I had a besetting tendency to reminisce and the taste of the milk evoked a thumbnail memory of family teas at my Nan's house in Birdbrook Road, with soggy sandwiches of Nimble bread soaked through from tinned salmon squished to a pulp in vinegar, after which cheap Battenburg cake, all pink and yellow, wrapped in sickly marzipan was consumed along with the tea, always the tea made with sterilised milk. Or 'sterra' as we called it.

Alf then woke up with a bit of start and finished off eating his sandwich, which was no easy feat as they were doorsteps along with brown sauce mingling with egg yolk which oozed and trickled down..... I got up and called Mrs Satchwell to let her know I was ready to leave. She came into the lounge, her cheeks flushed from the heat of the kitchen.

'Everything's fine. Thank you for the tea.'

'Oh good! I'm glad everything's OK. Only I've never had to do bookkeeping before I met me husband. Me sister learnt me how to do it, cos her does it for her Dad like, and me accountant said I was doing it all right an' all,' a smile broke out on her pleasant face, which I interpreted as genuine relief after the concern she must have felt with a government official inspecting the business records.

'I just need to use your loo before I go if I may,' two large mugs of tea having taken their toll.

'Of course luv - upstairs, first on the left.'

Now even in my short time as a VAT inspector, I'd seen many different sorts of toilets. But Mr Satchwell's toilet was unusual to say the least. It was in a fairly large room with a slightly sloping floor so that you felt a little drunk when you walked into it. The toilet itself was mounted in the corner on a small podium which you had to climb up by stepping onto a sturdy old wooden box. How it got to be like that was baffling, especially as Mr Satchwell was a plumber. Surely he hadn't plumbed his toilet up in the air? Perhaps he was testing out his plumbing skills since it looked like the room had once been a bedroom which Mr Satchwell had converted into a bathroom, as many people did with those old houses.

Back downstairs, I collected my briefcase and handbag and took my leave. I breathed in the cool autumn air, dank with city fumes. It was nearly noon, so I decided to head back to the office to finish some other work.

I'd only taken a few steps when I heard shouting.

'Here! Here! Wait a minute luv!' It was Alf shouting after me waving something in the air.

'Is this your'n?'

Crikey! My notebook! It must have got covered over when I was rummaging around for secret records. I went back up the garden path and I could have kissed him, brown sauce, egg yolk and all, for his innocent honesty.

'Yes it is. Thank you very much,' and took it from him calmly.

'I thought it was your'n y'know. Good job you weren't gone long luv. Ta-ra then.' He waved and went back indoors.

It was indeed a good job I wasn't gone long, because to leave one's notebook at a trader's premises was a very serious offence, and one of the biggest sins a VAT inspector could commit (apart from receiving bribes that is). Our blue-covered A4 notebooks were 'official documents', and they had to be numbered and kept as official records. My book was nearly three-quarters full of notes from previous visits - confidential information. If I'd left it at any other business it might have all ended so differently. It didn't bear thinking about. I headed back to the office through the city centre. I was hungry and couldn't wait to get a bacon and egg sandwich with lashings of brown sauce...

Sitting in the café watching the anonymous shoppers bustling by, I reflected on the VAT visit I'd just undertaken and couldn't help wondering: why *did* Mr Satchwell plumb his toilet up in the air? What *was* inside that podium under the toilet? Some cash loot maybe?

2. NEWSAGENT SHOP

T he next day my visit was to a small newsagent shop and I wasn't sure I knew what I was doing. I'd never done a VAT visit to a newsagent before and my line manager, Kay, had given it to me so that I could build up my VAT expertise and repertoire. The afternoon had started badly getting lost in Nechells - an area of Birmingham I was unfamiliar with. My job involved working in parts of the city that were alien to me. Even though I'd been born and bred in Birmingham, it was a sizeable city and I'd only ever known the small pocket where I'd grown up in Northfield. Each suburb had its own aura, and Nechell's aura was a strange mix of old and new. It sang of a close community cocooned in a curiously disjointed atmosphere - a phenomenon only possible in large cities.

I was fifteen minutes late as I approached the shop. The weather had changed overnight; heavy rain had soaked the crispy autumn leaves and they now resembled soggy cornflakes in the bottom of a cereal bowl instead. I had a job wading through them, drenching my suede shoes in the process. Plus I was pigged off because it was a Friday afternoon and it was unheard of for VAT inspectors to undertake VAT visits on Fridays which were always an 'office day', but it was the only time the trader would agree to see me.

Mac's Newsagent was the husband and wife partnership of Mr & Mrs MacIntyre, and the shop was nestled between a launderette and a chemist. As I opened the shop door a gentle tinkling bell greeted me and I immediately stepped back in time to my 1960s childhood. The candied scent of sweets, fused with the pungent aroma of tobacco, mingled discordantly with the acrid odour of newspaper print.

Mrs 'Mac' was behind the counter sporting a pale pink twinset and pearls - something I hadn't seen for many years. Her hairstyle faithfully replicated the Queen's, with two large curls high above each eyebrow. I guessed she was in her early seventies.

After introducing myself, I launched into the interview using my 'shopping list' of questions as trigger notes, which went something like this:

'Is the legal status of the business still a partnership?'

'Yes, me and me husband luv, but he's not very well he isn't, not well at all,' she hooted in a nasal Birmingham accent.

'I'm sorry to hear that.'

'He's in very poor health, he is. I have to do everything in the shop meself. I do all the buying and tot up all the takings at the end of the day.'

'You must miss his support.'

'Jim always asks me how I've got on bless him. He really misses working in the shop and—'

'Yes, we can so take our health for granted. Erm, is the—'

'That's certainly true. Heart trouble he's got. It was a real shock when he had his heart attack I can tell you. All in a flap I was. He was taken away in an ambulance. Spent three weeks in hospital he did—

'It must have been a terrible shock.'

'It was, him getting ill gave me a lot of anxiety. He's never been right since, and—'

'Well hopefully resting will help him regain his strength. Is the—'

'The kids keep an eye on him while I'm working here in the shop, popping in and making sure he's all right and...' *Just my luck to have a chatty trader on a Friday afternoon when all I want to do is get on and get home.* Normally my interviews were over in a matter of minutes, but time was ticking on and we weren't passed the first question.

'Is the financial year-end still the 31st January?'

'Yes, still the same. January was a cold month this year wasn't it, the tree got blown down in our garden, and I had to call someone out to chop it up and take it away and—'

'Yes, it was very stormy, I remember it well, my dustbin lid blew off somewhere. Erm, are you—'

'Mind you, not as bad as the terrible storms we had a couple of years ago. The weathermen got that one wrong didn't they?'

'They certainly did. Are you—'

'What a mess it made everywhere. Our neighbour's shed roof got blown off and—'

'Yes, it was all a bit scary. Are you still using the same retail scheme?'

'Yes, still the same, nothing ever changes here luv.'

'Can you show me how the till operates and talk me through how you cash up at the end of the day?'

...and so it went on. I reflected on how much better the interview was when the trader was gifted in small talk - a skill that I lacked. Mrs Mac was a friendly, down-to-earth woman and the interview took a good 45 minutes - one of the longest interviews I'd ever done. I brought the interview to a close by asking about the overall mark-up, and requested permission to inspect the shop,

'Yes, no problem at all. I'll go and put the kettle on while you take a look around.'

I explored the bijoux shop crammed to the corners with greeting cards, newspapers and magazines, plastic toys, confectionery, packets of biscuits, a few tins of peas and soup, stationery, and tobacco. I made a note of selling prices to test out the mark-up. The most expensive items in the shop were cigarettes, cigars and a couple of large boxes of Black Magic chocolates. The cheapest items in the shop were the Pick'n'Mix sweets and chews at one or two pence each. I recognised many of them from twenty years ago: Black Jacks, Fruit Salad, Drumsticks, liquorice pipes and red liquorice 'shoe laces', jellied snakes, pink candy shrimps, sherbet saucers, cola bottles - and many others - all on display in square plastic tubs, where the grubby fingers of children could dip in, bagging their favourite sugary treats.

Along the back of the shop were several shelves of candy jars full of sweets sold by weight: pineapple chunks, pear drops, mint humbugs, chocolate limes, aniseed balls, to name but a few. Nostalgia shone from every jar, sparking memories and I slid into one of my frequent episodes of daydreaming. It was the jar of JuJubes that triggered it: there they were, small multicoloured gums - like jewels, all red, yellow, green, pink and orange - fruity and flavoursome. I loved the lime ones. I could even feel the presence of my father by my side, holding my small hand in the sweet shop in Northfield where he used to take me every Saturday morning; he always bought me JuJubes - they were my favourite. I was tempted to buy a bag.

I was bounced back to the present by Mrs Mac popping her head around the door,

'Would you like tea or coffee luv?'

'Tea please, milk no sugar, thank you very much. I'm ready to look at the accounts now.'

She sat me down at a small table and placed in front of me all the business records, a cuppa and a plate of assorted biscuits - Rich Tea, Bourbons and Custard Creams - and left me to it. I inched my way through the 'Daily Gross Takings' (DGT for short) which were all the 'Z' totals on the till readings. I also scrutinised many purchase invoices, noting how much Mrs Mac paid for her goods. She only used two wholesalers to buy her stock from - 'Nurdin & Peacock' and 'Booker'. I ploughed through the figures for several quarters, and the tedium was palpable. Fatigue crept over me and I had to take some deep breaths to stop myself from nodding off. The cold calculus of figures does not communicate anything: no emotions, no feelings, no sentiments - nothing. They are soulless sums and sterile, starving the heart of energy, but I had to carry on. I checked the annual accounts, but there was a problem with the mark-up and I hadn't got a clue what it was. Mrs Mac had told me the mark-up was 'round about 25%', but the annual accounts showed 22% - and neither matched my figure of 30%. My mind began to get muddled and fuddled with percentages and I lost my way with the visit. I'd been at it for over two hours becoming demotivated, and I needed a shot of adrenalin to keep me going, but there was nothing to draw on. It was one of those visits where nothing appeared to be wrong, yet something wasn't quite right.

I also began to wonder why Mrs Mac didn't just shut up shop and retire. It didn't seem worth the effort to keep it going and the drawings out of the business were pitiful. I knew the mark-up on newspapers was pathetic - just a few measly pence profit per paper - about 5% gross profit, and the items she sold at a higher mark up such as the two-penny sweets, and the boxes of chocolates didn't seem capable of making her a lot of money. I made a sensible guess that she'd have to sell tens of thousands of them to make a decent profit. Even if Mrs Mac was suppressing her sales somehow by popping a few quid in a pot somewhere instead of putting it through the till, I still couldn't see how in a shop that size she would be defrauding the public purse of much money - and how was I to prove it if she was stashing cash away? Mind you, I did take a sneaky look under the till, but I couldn't see any pots or victuals to stuff money in. The shelf under the till was full of boxes of the twopenny sweets, ready to refill the tubs. So I leaned towards giving Mrs Mac the benefit of the doubt. Added to that, I'd noticed that apart from half a dozen school children who'd come into the shop to buy Pick'n'Mix sweets, there'd only been a handful of elderly customers buying a newspaper, the TV Times and a few biscuits.

Mrs Mac chatted amiably to all her customers - both young and old - for several minutes. She related well to all ages, asking the children what they'd been doing at school, and asking about the health and well-being of her more mature clients, and the goings-on in the latest episode of Crossroads. I realised then why she kept the shop open: it was her only way of keeping connected to people. Retirement would have meant isolation for her, and Mrs Mac was a sociable person - she needed her customers. The shop gave her a sense of belonging in the Nechells community.

She re-appeared from the small kitchen out the back, which doubled up as a stock room, with another cup of tea,

'Thank you very much, that's kind of you.'

'You're very welcome, luv. It's getting cold outside now isn't it?'

'It certainly is, yes, autumn has definitely arrived. While you're here, I'm, erm, I'm having a bit of a problem with the mark-up, and I need some more information from your accountant.'

'I can ring him now if you like,' she offered, eagerly. I summoned up a twinkle in my eye and pointed at my watch, 'not at five o'clock on a Friday afternoon,' I said, smiling in an attempt to diffuse any concern she might have, 'it can wait, I'm sure it can be resolved.'

Mrs Mac closed up the shop by flipping around a sign on the door and locking us in just as I was completing my final checks. She disappeared out the back as I packed away my bits and bobs: calculator, pens, VAT leaflets on Retail Schemes, and my blue A4 notebook - I didn't want to leave that behind again.

I popped my head around the door to let her know I'd finished and needed letting out of the shop, my eyes falling on two slices of brown bread which she was gently flattening with a rolling pin. Noticing my open mouth struck dumb at the peculiar sight, she explained,

'It's for me husband's lunch tomorrow luv, he can't stand thick sliced bread he can't, but it's all I could get, so I'm mekkin' it thinner.'

'Good idea,' I nodded in support as Mrs Mac gave me a knowing glance,

'He'll never know,' she concluded in a semi-whisper as if he might have been eavesdropping.

I smiled at being let in on the conspiracy, approving of her resourcefulness,

'It'll taste the same that's for sure. I've finished now, and thank you for all your help and hospitality, and I'll contact your accountant next week.'

'You're very welcome luv, safe journey home. Toodle-pip.'

In the end, I never did find out why there were three different mark-ups, so I put it down to my bad, Mrs Mac's bad, and that the accountant was right, and I just winged it in my report. Why waste any more time trying to get to the bottom of a small problem on a shop which turned over a trifling £20,000 a year?

3. HAULIER

A round this time I did a joint visit with my line manager, Kay, to a fairly large trader - a haulier who forwarded freight for clients nationwide. They had a fleet of lorries and various vehicles, and its registered office was in a far-flung corner of our Local VAT Office (LVO for short), so we enjoyed a pleasant drive in Kay's car into the autumnal countryside.

I was relieved when Kay decided she'd be the lead officer for the visit and I didn't have to blunder my way through a poor interview, plus I was always flummoxed by the tachographs that hauliers used and was clueless as to how they tied in with VAT. We arrived ten minutes early so we sat in the car in our coats, gloves and scarves while our breath misted up the windows as Kay showed me the printout of the quarterly VAT returns and highlighted some dodgy-looking periods that we'd be looking at.

We were met by one of the directors, Mr Brown. He and his brother had set up the business about ten years ago and since then it had grown to a sizeable company. He was one of those people who - to use a popular 80s phrase - had 'verbal diarrhoea' and he happily talked and talked as he showed us around the premises, describing how he and his brother had set up the business with just one lorry, but now had a fleet of over fifty. After the interview, we were brought the obligatory tea and biscuits by Karen, the general 'do-it-all' clerk who also did filing, typing, and kept some of the accounts. We began our work and Kay got out a packet of her favourite mints. We checked the records. We checked the Annual Accounts. We looked at the tachographs and mileage records. We tested the credibility of the business. We ate lunch. We ate the mints. Then Kay instructed me to check some of the larger purchase invoices of which there were several in every quarter - just to make sure they were all bona fide.

The biggest invoices were for packing materials which was not an unusual item for a freight company to buy and to be expected, but I thought I'd better check them anyway. They were all from the same company 'Pac-Rite Ltd' and were for significant amounts totalling around £15,000 worth of VAT reclaimed every quarter for the past five years - nearly £300,000 in all. I decided I'd like to see the packaging stock, even though the invoices looked all good and proper. It would also get me up off my backside and help to wake me up a bit. I'd hit one of my familiar drowsy spots where I could have happily dropped off to sleep. I found Karen washing up the mugs next to her tiny chaotic office and I asked her where the packaging purchased from Pac-Rite was stored and could I inspect it, please?

'Oh Mr Brown doesn't buy packaging from them anymore - the customer packs their own goods. Saves us a job, and a lot of time'

'Good idea, yes, well makes sense,' I hedged with a degree of insouciance, deciding not to mention all the invoices I'd found and wait to talk to Kay about it, 'and how long has that been happening?'

'About four years now I think. Pac-Rite went out of business, so it was a good job the customer packs their own stuff.'

'I see, well that's helpful to know, thank you.'

'Another cuppa?'

'Ooh yes please, that would be lovely.'

'I'll put the kettle on.'

This new implication was as plain as could be: it was clear that the trader had been claiming VAT back on false invoices from a company that was no longer trading. I headed back to Kay to tell her about my chance discovery.

'Crikey. Well, we'll have to take this to the fraud office. There could be more to investigate. We'll finish our inspection, and take all the invoices from Pac-Rite with us. Write out a receipt for the invoices and give it to Karen.'

So there it was in plain sight - wrongdoing uncovered by simple checks where no great VAT knowledge or expertise was required. Kay heard later that the trader had gone to quite sophisticated lengths to acquire Pac-Rite's blank invoice pads by arranging a break-in to Pac-Rite's premises and stealing them just after they went bust. Sentencing Mr Brown to prison the judge hadn't minced his words, Kay said, describing him as a brazen and greedy predator stealing public money by wilfully creating phoney purchase invoices to line his own pockets.

......mind you I was still none the wiser about the link between tachographs and VAT, and I suspected Kay wasn't that clued up about it either.

4. ANTIQUE DEALER

In late autumn, after an uneventful weekend spent hacking overgrown Russian vine which had smothered my shed, I did a visit to a dealer in antiques near the Jewellery Quarter in Hockley. There was a definite whiff of winter from a frosty sun seeping through a thin cloudy veil. I arrived at the premises which were suspended on the corner of a quiet back street. It was 'Closed' but I roused the owner, a Mr Barrington Grey, who appeared like Fagin out of a cloud of smoke coming from an enormous cigar, complete with fingerless knitted gloves. He was the sole proprietor of his business, and after introducing myself, his tall and slightly stooping frame beckoned me to follow him 'this way through here please.'

We shunted through a long, dim and very narrow corridor into a fairly spacious room out the back with a paned window nosing out onto the street. Or was this the front? I'd lost my bearings through the Alice-in-Wonderland hallway and I wasn't sure where I was. The shop had the temperature of a sauna, and its Dickensian aura seethed with clocks of all shapes and sizes, along with piles of fanciful crockery, and wonky cabinets full of antiques, boxes of coins and medals.

'Take a seat m'dear.' Mr Grey had the air of a benevolent grandfather, looking every bit the part with wispy grey hair, pince-nez and sporting a checked waistcoat adorned with a pocket watch, which he got out.

'You're three minutes late.'

'Sorry about that. The traffic was very bad,' I lied, truth be told I'd arrived early but had popped into the office just a mile up the road for a cuppa first and a sausage roll I'd picked up on the way.

'Well, I've got everything ready for you here.'

Squinting from the blazing haze created by the bright sunlight and cigar smoke, I sat down in tandem with Mr Grey, prompting a burst of fine dust particles to explode, which sparkled like a million miniature diamonds hanging in the sunny smog. I coughed.

'I've just got a few questions to ask first before I look at the records and accounts.'

'OK fire away. Then I'll make us coffee.'

I worked my way through my list of questions and my interview was over in five minutes flat. Shortest ever. I'd never visited an antique dealer before and wasn't sure what questions I should be asking, but there would be more to ask as the visit progressed. I was in no doubt about that. With Mr Grey's permission, I inspected the premises - always my favourite part of the visit - to have a good nose around. His shop was full of unusual items. What stories could these artefacts tell if they could speak? Instinctively I picked up a strange looking long scoop, intrigued by its shape.

'Do you know what it is?' Mr Grey peered at me over the top of his pince-nez.

'No idea. Is it a medical instrument of some kind?'

'It's a marrow spoon. Sterling silver, made in Birmingham. 19th century.'

'Marrow spoon? I never knew such a thing existed. My father would have liked it. He loved marrows and grew them every year. Not one of my favourite foods I have to admit.'

'Me neither. Tasteless vegetable. But it's not that sort of marrow the spoon is for - it's for scooping marrow out of bones.'

Recoiling at the thought, I put it back quickly, 'Oh,' was all I could say.

I made a list of the various things he sold - medals, coins, clocks, crockery, cutlery, glassware. Gold. And stamps. Many used stamps. Some of them had been imported. *Drat. Gold and imported stamps are all I need.*

Mr Grey then showed me to a storeroom out the back (or was it the front?) which was cold, musty and dank, but it didn't appear to be harbouring anything suspicious, though I wasn't in the mood to ferret around too much despite enjoying some relief from the stifling heat in the shop. Might it be concealing some gold bullion stashed away somewhere? But all the 40-watt bulb revealed were piles of mouldy books, some rusty garden furniture, broken crockery, and myriads of bits of clocks.

I asked Mr Grey about what seemed to be his double-entry shop as we made our way back.

'Oh the entrance you came in was the pawnbroker bit'. Wincing at my lack of observation, I guessed that pawnbroking had its own peculiar VAT laws which I knew nothing about. I could be in for a long day in sweltering heat and cigar smoke.

After bringing me a coffee, which looked and tasted like watery gravy, he plonked himself into his dusty chair and fiddled around repairing a carriage clock. Just then an explosion of synchronised sound jangled from clocks all jingling at the same time on the quarter of the hour. I'd never heard such a sweet yet savage cacophony of microtones before, and for a trice, I felt slightly dizzy.

I got out my VAT leaflet on Second Hand Margins, pawn-broking, gold and philatelic supplies and began the inspection of Mr Grey's records and accounts. I'd done a bit of 'prep' for the visit and discovered he'd been trading in antiques and second-hand goods as a VAT registered business for many years, and his last VAT inspection had been nearly eight years previous. The last visiting officer had found everything in order, but the scanty VAT reports didn't fully paint the complex picture of the business.

Sweating profusely, I took off my jacket and opened the neck of my blouse, making an excuse to go to the loo to dab myself with some water to cool down, while trying to process all the VAT implications involved in Mr Grey's interesting business.

Accounting for VAT on second hand sales was simple - if you buy a second-hand watch for £20 and sell it for £30, you pay VAT on the £10 profit, but Mr Grey's dealings in gold, pawn-broking and imported stamps brought a multi-layered complexity to the business I hadn't foreseen. It was four VAT visits all rolled into one. Plus it was one of those visits where I learnt as I was going along. The scope of VAT and VAT law couldn't prepare an officer for every area of fiscal knowledge which might be required on a visit. It was a good thing that VAT visits weren't medical procedures and if an officer made a mistake there was no real harm done. We didn't have the luxury of the 'see one, do one, teach one' principle for surgeons - for us, it was often a case of straight in and do one.

All dealers in antiques and second-hand goods had to keep a detailed Stock Book and Mr Grey's was immaculate in every way. It was not only beautifully bound, but its contents were top-notch - every required legal detail was recorded in beautiful copperplate handwriting. He was a man of few words, but very fastidious. His Margin Scheme invoices were also impeccable, and his paperwork reflected the intricacy and precision required in his clock-making and repairs. Maybe it was just a front though? Was the benign Mr Grey a smuggler of gold perhaps? Was this just the sort of joint that could harbour such a sinister practice? I'd have to check how he sourced his gold - any whiff of smuggling and I'd have to call on Customs to get involved. Might this turn out to be an exciting VAT visit after all? Any smuggled gold - even if Mr Grey was an innocent buyer - was liable to forfeiture under the Customs and Excise Management Act. For a fleeting moment, I imagined his little shop swarming with Customs officers, police and sniffer dogs with the gold being seized as all the clocks went off.

Snapping myself out of my reverie, I worked my way through a drudge of documents to the accompaniment of the clock chimes every 15 minutes. At noon the jangles rang out for nearly half a minute - some clocks sang the Westminster Chimes tune.

'I shut up shop at one for an hour. The last officer had finished his visit in two hours and fort-five minutes.'

'That's fine, I'll go and get some lunch, but I'll have to come back afterwards I'm afraid. Everything appears to be in order, but the paperwork for imported stamps, and the gold and the pawnbroking side of your business is just making the visit a bit longer than normal.'

'OK.'

By 12.30 I was jiggered and could have dropped off to sleep. I gazed out of the shop window but the street was dead, in sympathy with the deadness of the VAT accounting checks. It was hard to keep motivated.

Like most VAT visits, it was uneventful in the end. Everything was squeaky clean - including all his dealings in gold, so far as I could tell.

'I never import gold,' Mr Grey had told me emphatically, 'you never can tell where it's come from.' *Very wise man.*

The discomfort from the heat and smoke combined with the boredom of checking numerous bits of paper was indelible, branding my memory with its peculiar vibes of a visit you never quite forget.

I did unearth one thing though (by being a nosey parker and looking at the *back* of Mr Grey's Stock Book) - I discovered that no VAT had been accounted for on 'payments received in advance' for certain second-hand goods which Mr Grey sourced for some of his clients. I was convinced that a 'tax point' had been created when Mr Grey received the deposit (a tax point being the date the VAT is due). But had it? When was a tax point not a tax point? I had no idea. Why hadn't his accountant picked it up?

'These payments received in advance at the back of your stock book Mr Grey - when do you account for the VAT on these deposits?'

'They're not deposits,' he protested, 'I can't work out the VAT until I've bought the item and know what I paid for it.' By now Mr Grey had switched to a pipe which bobbed up and down in his mouth as he spoke.

'Have you ever spoken to your accountant about this income?'

'Yes and he said they're not deposits. He said they're deferred payments and no VAT due until I know my profit margin.'

Bump. It was an interesting point and I didn't know the answer, but I couldn't help thinking the accountant had chosen to ignore the issue by classing them as 'deferred payments'.

'I won't spend time hunting down an object unless the customer gives me an advance payment. I return the money if I can't find what they want,' continued Mr Grey with an air of authority, his bobbing pipe nodding in support.

Bugger. What a mess. I can't brush this one under the carpet like I did Mac's Newsagents.

Some of his 'deposits' were substantial and were held for three or four months. I delved into my VAT law manual but there was very little - I'd have to get help from my line manager with this issue. When was a deposit not a deposit?

'Well I take your point, but a tax point will have been created when you received the payment - but I'll find out about it and let you know. I'll have to make a note of all the deferred payments you received in the last quarter and it might mean I have to issue an assessment, but I'll check it out first. You may have to pay the VAT on the full deposit - erm, I mean deferred payment - and then make an adjustment afterwards when you know what your profit margin is.'

Mr Grey grunted and muttered something under his breath, emptied his pipe with several bangs on an old tin dish, and stuffed it with fresh tobacco.

I finished the visit at 4 pm and headed home to write up my report. I stripped off my smoke-ridden clothes and stuffed them in the washing machine, washed my smoke-drenched hair, and ran a bath. I found two bottles of Babycham left over from the previous Christmas to drink while soaking in a bubble bath up to my neck. Then, for the first time since I'd been appointed a VAT inspector in just over a year, I mused about it all. How on earth had I ended up in a job like this? It had been an epic megillah of a journey. I never chose to be a VAT inspector, it seemed to choose me: Customs and Excise put in a 'bid' for me in a recruitment drive. *Rotters!* No wonder they had to recruit in such a mercantile fashion. It's hardly the sort of vocation anyone sets out to pursue as a career. And there, amid the bubbles in the bath and in the Babycham, I spooled back nine years, replaying the long, bureaucratic expedition I'd trekked which had landed me a job I didn't want, ruminating on the series of rather strange shenanigans bringing me to this point in time......

5. BECOMING A VAT INSPECTOR

*'Women however, were not allowed to compete
for jobs in the open competition
which had been introduced for men.'*

(Michael Coolican, *No Tradesmen and No Women
- The Origins of the British Civil Service*)

T he question 'so how did you come to be a VAT inspector then?' is one to which every VAT Control Officer will have a different answer. For me, it wasn't an easy one to answer because the process was so long and convoluted it was hard to know where to begin, especially as I'd set out to be a musician.

Lack of Ambition

I drifted back to November 1980 when my long journey started. The gentle whistle of the kettle from the kitchen accompanied the aroma of freshly baked pastry filling my friend's warm, cosy flat as she prepared a high tea for us. An icy grey drizzle descended from the Birmingham sky onto the sprawling council estate below. I enjoyed my occasional visits to Barbara, who was over twice my age, happily single and like an aunt to me. She was always so calm and serene, full of wisdom and experience - I always valued her worldview.

As she prepared our feast, I sat down at her upright Bentley piano and played the slow movement from Beethoven's Pathétique Sonata, bringing the piece to a close with the final gentle chords.

'Beautiful Dawn, let's eat,' cooed Barbara in her gentle voice. We sat at the table under the window as Barbara poured the tea from her beautiful bone china teapot.

'Tell me, what are you going to be doing now that you've finished your music studies?'

'Well, I applied for a job as a clerical officer in the Civil Service, and I've got an interview in a couple of weeks,' I chirruped, selecting several dainty sandwiches.

She stopped pouring the tea, put the teapot down, and stared at me, 'you mean to tell me you're not going to be a musician? Or teach music?'

'Well, it's not that easy,' I felt my cheeks colouring up.

'Do you realise that it's working people like *me* who have paid for your further education?'

Momentarily made speechless by her change of tone, and the hardness in her voice, I continued to help myself to a plate of the immaculately prepared food in the frosty silence.

'Well, it's quite difficult making a living as a professional musician.'

'So you're just giving it all up? Throwing away three years of study at taxpayers' expense? That's such a waste!'

'Well, I'm not that good at teaching either. The kids always seem to play me up, and the hours are long with lots of prep and marking to do, so I thought I'd get a steady nine to five job and see how it goes.' I popped a bite-size sausage roll into my mouth. Barbara picked up the teapot and continued pouring the tea. We changed the subject.

For all of Barbara's seniority and wisdom, I decided at that moment she was wrong about one thing: nothing we do in life is ever wasted.

△△△

Two weeks later I sat facing three men dressed in suits firing questions at me.

'Where do you see yourself in five years' time?' asked one of the interviewers.

'I don't know, I just take each day as it comes really. I haven't got a long term plan.'

And it was that line that got me the job as a clerical officer in the Civil Service. My lack of ambition, along with my shorthand and typing skills, fitted the bill: the interviewer who'd asked the question was the Regional Director of the Central Office of Information (COI for short) and he needed a secretary. He later told me my answer had been perfect - he didn't want anyone who had plans or aspired to get a promotion; he wanted a secretary who wasn't going to be flitting off to another job any time soon.

The COI was a government press office on the fifth floor of a smart office block - Five Ways Tower. It was a shiny black monolith of glass and red brick as if it was a spaceship that had landed from outer space. This twenty-floor tower block was gorged with hundreds of civil servants working for various government departments. It reflected the full and fat Civil Service of the early 80s when money was abundant, no one counted the cost, and it was all 'spend spend spend'. I even had my very own office - unheard of for a lowly clerical officer - complete with the latest electric typewriter, trendy office furniture and an expansive view over the city from an enormous window. My chic office was annexed to my boss's which was three times the size of mine. Although I had a low-grade job, it had a high end feel to it, and I was lulled by the superficial accoutrements into kidding myself it was a great little number, even though my annual salary was £3800 per annum, gross.

My work at COI was simple and stable. The mornings began with the ritual of opening the post and I was helped by a clerical assistant; armed with our HMSO letter openers and a mug of tea, we ploughed through the pile of envelopes for at least 30 minutes. But we had to be careful. Parcel bombs were being sent in the post to random government officials, and no one knew who might be the next victim. My boss was convinced he could be a target. And when one day I walked into the office to find my desk had been ransacked by petty crooks, it did feel a tad spooky. Mind you, the fact that they hadn't stolen anything but had scattered the contents of my tampon packet all over the floor seemed to suggest it was just a prank.

At first, the clerical job wasn't too bad, and I felt quite the part of a posh secretary, but it didn't take me long to realise that the staffing structure of COI meant there was no ladder of promotion for any of the clerical grades. I was in a dead-end job. As the months rolled into years, I became bored with shorthand, typing, filing, stuffing press notices into envelopes, and making endless cups of tea and coffee for my boss and his visitors. I knew I was capable of doing a more complex job.

It was good fortune I worked in a government press office because it meant that information was at my fingertips, and I discovered I could get a promotion to a different government department if I took the 'Civil Service Executive Officer Examination'. I hadn't got a thing to lose, so I applied to sit the exam.

The Examination

In his book *No Tradesman and No Women - The Origins of the British Civil Service,* Michael Coolican details the interesting history of the rule that male civil servants were to be appointed on 'merit' and through 'open competition', rather than through patronage. The Executive Officer entrance examination I applied to sit for was part of that process instigated in the 1850s.

Often we are clueless as to how our lives have been shaped and affected by the whims and quirks of dead politicians. The open competition for entry into the Civil Service is one such example (though the motive for it was originally dubious) and it took until 1925 before women were allowed to sit the entry exam. Had I been born a hundred years earlier there would have been no Civil Service job for me at all.

If I wanted to have a more interesting job and a higher standard of living then I had to go for it. As an Executive Officer (EO for short) I could rise up the Civil Service ladder to become a Higher Executive Officer, and who knows maybe even a Senior Executive Officer, before retiring comfortably with a good pension at some point in the distant future.

So in April 1985, I sat the EO exam. I took the day off work and all the candidates were duly seated at separate desks and invigilated like school children. I completed as many questions as I could in the time allowed and hoped for the best.

I failed. This meant I had to sit the exam again, but the examination could only be taken once a year. So in April 1986, I sat the exam a second time. And failed again. By now I'd worked out what my problem was: the exam required a speed of mathematical logic which I simply did not possess. So, undaunted and with the resilience of youth, in September that year I signed up for a night school class to take 'O' level maths. If I could elevate my mathematical skills and reasoning, I might just pass the third time around.

In April 1987, I sat the Civil Service exam a third time. I just about scraped through obtaining 218 marks out of 300 - the pass mark being 202. It had taken me three years to pass the Executive Officer examination.

The next hurdle was to get through the interview scheduled in the autumn.

The Interviews

Lacking confidence that I'd pass the interview stage, I'd scanned the job columns in the many newspapers that arrived every morning at COI, and I spotted an advertisement by the Halifax Building Society - they were training up Branch Managers. It was a job I didn't really have a heart for. I didn't fancy working with money and figures, and as for being a 'Manager' I seriously doubted I could manage people at all. As a clerical officer at the COI, I'd been granted a 'Responsibility Allowance' to manage two typists and a clerical assistant, and I was rubbish at it. I was quite incompetent at facilitating group dynamics in the working environment, even though we got along well together on a social level. But I'd heard that people who worked for building societies got a useful discount on their mortgage and I liked the idea of that. 'Bigger and better' was the 1980s meme. It was big everything - big hair, big shoulders, big car, big house, big salary.

The house I'd bought in Redditch for just £14,500 had been a council house that the previous owners had bought under the Thatcher scheme allowing tenants to buy council properties. It wasn't really what I wanted, but it was all I could afford on my low wage, but if I got the Halifax job maybe I could get a bigger and better house. The Halifax invited me to attend an interview - this was my Plan 'B' and who knows where it might lead? I waited to hear.

My Civil Service Executive Officer interview came a week later, and the interview panel - again three men dressed in suits - were curious about one thing in particular:

'We see that you've taken the exam twice before?'

'Yes, that's right.'

'We see that there's a bit of difference in your exam marks, can you explain that?'

'Yes, after I failed the second exam I decided to do 'O' level maths night school and it's made all the difference to my marks.'

Afterwards, on the way home, I mused about their question. Did the panel suspect I'd substituted someone else in my place to sit the exam for me? I'm not sure they believed my night school story. Good job I have the 'O' level maths certificate to prove it……..

The Letters

Often in life, we come to a fork in the road - a bifurcation forcing us to make a choice that we know will alter our future forever. In late November 1986, I received a letter from the Halifax offering me the job to train me up as a Branch Manager. *What should I do now?* If only I could split myself in two and walk both forks in the road for ten years, make my choice, and rewind the time. I wasn't completely sure I wanted to leave the Civil Service - I felt safe working there. I had to make a decision: should I play safe or should I take a gamble? But which decision was safe and which one was a gamble?

I followed my instinct, and I turned down the Halifax job. I've often wondered how my life would have turned out if I'd taken that job. I'm sure it would have been completely different - but I'll never know.

Then, on the 4th of December 1987, a letter from the Civil Service Commission in Basingstoke dropped through my letterbox and three years of waiting were finally over:

"Dear Miss Smith,

I am pleased to tell you that today's Board recommended you for an Executive Officer appointment......we will write to you again in 3-4 weeks time about your assignment..."

The relief was physical and I had to make myself a cup of tea with a tot of whisky in to steady my nervous energy. With a shaky hand, I filled out the 'Preference Form' they'd sent with the letter and I made it clear I wanted a post in the Birmingham area. *Let the promotion adventure begin.* I'd made the right decision in turning down the Halifax job. What a trade-off. I poured myself a port and lemon to celebrate, then, curled up on my sofa next to the radiator with my cat curled up to me purring away, I watched an episode of *Cheers*.

In January 1988 another letter arrived as promised, but with an unexpected message,

"Dear Miss Smith,

Following your success in this scheme of recruitment I am sorry to tell you that there are no Executive Officer vacancies in any of your preferred locations. There are, however, vacancies in other parts of the country and if you would like to consider an alternative location please telephone me and I will give you details of the vacancies available......"

I stared at the letter and had to read it again to make sure it was really telling me there were no Executive Officer vacancies in the Birmingham area. *Really? None at all? In a great big blummin' city like Birmingham?*

I flopped on my sofa, choking back the tears, stroked my cat, and calmed down. I picked up the telephone,

'I've received the letter informing me there are no Executive Officer vacancies in Birmingham and to call you.'

'Yes that's right, we only have two vacancies available - one in Ipswich and one in Guildford, both are with the Home Office.'

'But I don't want to move to Ipswich or Guildford. There must be some vacancies in the Birmingham area surely?'

'You have to take one of the vacancies you're offered, otherwise you'll lose the post,' came the blunt reply.

'But surely you make allowances for an officer's personal circumstances as indicated on the Preference Form?' I asked, suddenly realising that the 'Preference Form' was a complete sham and waste of time.

'No. You have to accept what's offered within six weeks or lose the post.'

The words sounded cruel. I'd just turned down a good job with the Halifax, and it had taken three and a half long years to get to this point, and now a mudslide was carrying me down a blind alley to nowhere. There was nothing to stop me from moving to Ipswich or Guildford. I was single. I could sell up. But I liked living in Birmingham near my family and singing soprano in a world-renowned city choir.

'I'll have to think about it. I'd like to work for the Home Office but is there nothing at all I can do about the location?' The pleading desperation in my voice seemed to prompt a modicum of sympathy -

'The only thing you can do is to write to all the government departments in your area asking them to put in a bid for you. But if no one puts in a bid within the required time you'll lose the post.'

'OK, thank you,' was all I could muster in a hoarse whisper as I put the receiver down, staring absently at the pile of dirty crocks in the kitchen, waiting to be washed up.

Bid? Put in a bid? Is that how they treat new recruits? Like a piece of blummin' furniture at the auctioneers? But at least there was a glimmer of hope, and I wrote to every single Civil Service department in and around Birmingham, asking them to put in a 'bid' for me with the Recruiting Office. It paid off - Customs & Excise and the Home Office both put in a bid for me. I was well pleased about the Home Office and I rang Recruitment,

'The Home Office has put in a bid for me and I'd be delighted to accept.'

'I'm sorry, Customs & Excise got their bid in first so that's where you'll be going,' came the terse reply.

At least I got a 'sorry' this time.

'But surely if both have put in a bid for me then I can choose which Department I prefer?' I said incredulously, my eyes widening in dismay at the implication of this unintended consequence.

'No, the Department that gets its bid in first is the one to which you'll be allocated,' said the toneless voice at the other end.

Customs and Excise? What did they do? The disappointment was palpable for several minutes. *Maybe it won't be so bad.* Perhaps I'd end up working somewhere really interesting and glamorous in Customs? In a plush office at Birmingham Airport? As for Excise, what was that? I hadn't got a clue. 'Excise' sounded like some kind of surgical procedure. Might it involve some kind of interesting detective work?

6. THE RELUCTANT VAT INSPECTOR

My visions of a glamorous job at Birmingham Airport were annihilated with the arrival of yet another letter. This time it was a missive from Customs & Excise itself informing me I would be working on something called 'VAT Control' which involved visiting businesses to check their VAT accounts. The logic being (I was to learn later) that if you can do VAT Control, you can do any job.

But I didn't want to be a 'VAT Control Officer'. I didn't like working with figures. Or accounts. I'd turned down the Halifax job partly for that reason. *Is this what they called Sod's Law?* And I had no desire - or confidence - to deal with accountants and business people. In addition to that, the job of VAT Control demanded that VAT officers not only 'protect the revenue' but also 'identify fraud' and 'interpret VAT law'. What kind of a job was this? Did they want a bookkeeper, accountant, lawyer, public relations officer and a sleuth all rolled into one? Five jobs for the price of one?

Then within seconds, I realised I could wriggle out of it because I couldn't drive. They wouldn't want an officer who couldn't drive doing VAT visits now would they? I mean, what use is a VAT inspector who can't drive? I'd be given a nice little cosy office job instead - or better still they wouldn't want me at all, and I could go to the Home Office.

'I don't drive, so I can't do VAT Control work,' I told the Customs Training Officer, my phone bill rising with each call I made.

'That's OK,' she said cheerfully, 'don't worry, you can do it on public transport.'

'Public transport?' *Is she joking? She cannot be serious?*

'Yes, several officers do the job on public transport. You just keep all your bus and train tickets and you'll be reimbursed the cost from the office,' she concluded happily.

And with that, my fate was sealed. VAT Control it was and there wasn't a thing I could do about it if I wanted that promotion.

But there was one last hurdle I had to jump. Another letter arrived. I was informed that I'd been allocated to the Birmingham North 'Local VAT Office' (LVO for short) which covered postcodes up to 80 miles away from where I lived in Redditch. *Do they really expect me to do a job on public transport covering up to 80 miles?* I rang again,

'I live in Worcestershire, but I've been allocated to Birmingham North LVO. Would it be possible to work in Birmingham South especially as I'll have to use public transport?' It wasn't like me to get palpitations, but I could hear the blood pulsing in my ears.

'I'm afraid there aren't any vacancies in Birmingham South LVO. When we bid for you it was for a post in Birmingham North. You might be able to get a transfer there at a later date or a transfer to Droitwich LVO in Worcestershire.'

There was only one thing for it: I'd just have to learn to drive and buy a car.

In July 1988 I was summoned to a 'career interview' with a Career Development Officer (CDO for short). I still had anxiety about the VAT job, and I didn't try to hide it. But they must have been desperate for new recruits to work on VAT Control and the CDO put a positive spin on the interview in her report:

*"**Miss Smith** admitted that she had some reservations about the work since one of the staff currently employed by another department was an ex-VAT officer who had apparently taken a*

drop in grade to escape HM Customs and Excise. After our discussion her fears were somewhat allayed but no doubt she will remain a little apprehensive until actually undertaking the duties. The idea of visiting the trading community quite appealed to her but it will be a complete change of routine for her. Note taking and report writing after the visits should be no problem due to her shorthand/typing skills. The fact that she is a very organised and self-motivated person will help her become an effective Control Officer. We discussed the training programme, together with probation requirements, staff report completion and promotion opportunities. Miss Smith does not own a car so will use public transport to conduct official business.

Signed ....
CDO"

.....and by the time I'd raked over all that in my memory, the bathwater had gone cold and the last dregs of my Babycham had gone flat, so I got dried, got cosy in a warm dressing gown, got a mug of hot chocolate and watched the Bond movie *Octopussy.*

△△△

Other VAT inspectors will have completely different experiences and stories to tell about their recruitment journey and unique pathway into VAT Control. But for me, I felt as if I'd been commandeered and snookered into a job I didn't particularly want - but then officialdom has a cold manner of bluntly making things black and white. I eventually decided to embrace the opportunity of being a VAT Control Officer and give it my best shot.

7. MURPHY'S LAW

Not long after my VAT visit to Mr Barrington Grey, Kay arranged for me to do a joint visit alongside a more experienced officer to a larger business to give me some experience working with double-entry bookkeeping. It was a pet food wholesaler and we met at a warehouse near the city centre where the inspection was to take place. James, the officer I was accompanying, had been on VAT Control for seven years. We were greeted by Mr Swanson, one of the partners, and shown into a chaotic office with piles of files and two noisy typewriters clacking away.

James did a superb interview, and he got a clear idea of mark-ups that would help us with our credibility checks. Mr Swanson introduced us to his wife, who was the other business partner as she did all the bookkeeping and VAT returns. We then inspected the premises where we discovered 'pet food' wholesaler was a bit of an understatement because the business had recently expanded to include a vast array of victuals for pets from goldfish to horses, from peanuts to cages, and much more.

We then settled down to do our checks along with two cups of steaming tea and a plate of biscuits brought to us by Tracy, one of the typists.

Everything added up and matched the figures on our VAT print-out (the 'D1507' report as it was called), and as we delved further into the records, James used it to teach me about the delights of double-entry bookkeeping. He explained the different sources of credit and debit entries in the VAT control account such as sales, cash, petty cash, credit notes, purchases, and journal entries, paying particular attention to those which were a liability as this was money owed to HM Customs & Excise.

'Journal entries?' I probed, 'what are they?'

'Sure, these could be debit or credit entries depending on the reason for the entry such as recording the VAT on the write-off of an irrecoverable debt - which would be a debit entry.'

'I see,' I lied, none the wiser. We both took a gulp of our tea and dunked our biscuits.

'Now, which side of the ledger will the VAT on credit notes sent to customers appear - the debit or the credit side?' He asked with a mouthful of chocolate digestive biscuit.

Crumbs. I hadn't got the foggiest idea, but had to take a stab at an answer.....

'Well, if it's a credit note sent to a customer, erm that is,' my mind went blank, 'let me think,' *(come on Smith, you've only got a 50-50 chance of getting wrong)* 'it will be shown on the, erm,' ....*bugger, what is this? Some kind of accounts quiz? ....think think think....* I tried to think it through in my own muddled manner: *credit notes on a sales return will reduce VAT liability, and to me, credits are really debits and debits are really credits.....* I took a sensible guess: 'it will be shown on the debit side?' I said hopefully, posing my answer as a question to minimise any embarrassment if I was wrong.

'Correct.'

I do not lie when I say I inwardly collapsed with relief.

As we worked through the audit trails, nothing seemed out of place, and the credibility checks we undertook all indicated that the mark-ups were correct. James asked me to do more in-depth checks by looking at the sequence numbers of sales invoices and also test the arithmetic of selected quarters in which the 'input tax' (that is the VAT reclaimed by the business) was higher than normal. *Now I know why he likes taking out trainees - he gets us to do the boring donkey work.*

By now the day was wearing on. We'd eaten our lunch and I was on my fourth cuppa of the day, working my way through the purchase day book, picking out higher than normal figures, stifling several yawns as the ennui crept over me like a blanket. I could have quite easily had forty winks.

Just as I was closing my eyes to take a sneaky power nap, it was then that I spotted it: there was a figure which stood out on a purchase invoice of Bonios and it was the fact that they were Bonios that woke me up somewhat because I used to eat these tasteless dog biscuits as a child (I kid you not!). It prompted one of my many daytime reveries as the memories came flooding back, giving me a second wind: I was transported back in time to when I was six, visiting my Aunt Ann's pub *The Three Horseshoes* in Sheldon. I could see myself stroking her guard dog - a long-haired fluffy Alsatian called Shandy who was as daft as a brush and completely rubbish at guarding anything; I was helping myself to one of his Bonios, nibbling my way through the hard-baked bone-shaped biscuit.

Back to the reality of the moment, the figure in the ledger read:

Gross.   £2041.25
Net.   £1775.00
VAT   £662.25

Now, even with my limited mathematical skills these figures shouted out - no way could the VAT be that much, so there was nothing for it but to source the original invoice and sure enough the VAT on the invoice was (of course) £266.25 - not the £662.25 which the trader had claimed. Mrs Swanson had claimed nearly £400 too much on just one invoice due to a transposition error.

I showed James my find without saying a word by just pointing to the Purchase Day Book figure and the figure on the invoice, as the typewriters clacked away behind us incessantly.

'There could be more,' he muttered, 'we'd better go through each quarter with a fine-tooth comb.'

By now it was four in the afternoon, and it was clear this was a problem that needed further investigation and we would have to do a return visit at some point. Two weeks later we were back to complete our inspection and we weren't surprised to uncover many more transposition errors - at least two or three a quarter for the past five years resulting in a sizeable assessment for James of over £25,000.

'Oh dear, my dyslexia,' was Mrs Swanson's excuse when confronted with the errors.

And so it was that the most basic of checks could uncover the most blatant of wrongdoing, and no great knowledge or in-depth understanding of VAT accounting or law was needed: just simple mathematical common sense.

After the visit, and feeling rather pleased with myself, I stopped off in the city centre to do some shopping before going on to choir practice. I'd decided to treat myself to something nice as I had some spare cash - a rare occurrence for me. I was always teetering on the verge of being overdrawn, and at the end of every month, without fail, I did a bank reconciliation to see if I had any 'disposable income' to spend and had been pleasantly surprised to find I was in credit by £72 - so I splashed out on a pair of stylish leather boots half price in a sale costing £60, reduced from £120. A month later when my bank statement came I discovered I was £72 overdrawn......a transposition error I made when I did my bank rec was the culprit, along with a nice £12 'unauthorised overdraft' fee to boot......

They say things come in threes, and certainly my nemesis did concerning transposition errors. Two months later my Surveyor rejected my travel expense claim - 'spot the error' he wrote on a Post-It note. I'd over-claimed the grand sum of £1.80 by transposing £6.80 as £8.60; then a week later the hat trick was completed when I accused a cashier of short-changing me 45 pence because I'd transposed figures on my till receipt of £3.05 as being £3.50. .....*Mrs Swanson, maybe you were innocent after all, who knows?*

8. TRAINING

'What about flambé?' The whole class of trainee VAT inspectors erupted into laughter at Andrew's question. But the question wasn't as oddball as it sounded. Andrew, a University graduate, had wanted to work for the Inland Revenue but he'd had to settle for VAT Control work instead. He had a tax-searching mind and was way ahead of the rest of us; while we were grappling with how to work out VAT on restaurant takings, he was already thinking about VAT liability and VAT credibility. In his mind, meals might involve flambéd food, and flambé meant alcohol, and alcohol meant tax. The course tutor congratulated him on his astute observations, and our laughter stopped as quickly as it had begun.

A confessional wouldn't be complete without some reference as to how VAT inspectors were trained back in the 80s, not least for the quaint quirkiness of the departmental rules and antics. Shortly after joining Customs & Excise, all trainees began a six-week training course broken up into two-week blocks in between which we accompanied more experienced officers on VAT visits. It was designed to give us an elementary understanding of Value Added Tax so that we weren't totally clueless when we joined our colleagues on a visit. We were on 'Probation' for two years and we had it in black and white that,

"the purpose of probation is to see whether an officer establishes by his performance his fitness or otherwise for a permanent appointment: only on successful completion of probation will the appointment be confirmed. During the probation period a close watch will, therefore, be kept on the officer's performance......"

The reference to '*his* performance' and '*his* fitness' was likely a historical hangover from the days when Customs and Excise had been a uniformed fraternity (before VAT was even thought of). As for the obscure and unwritten rule that female VAT officers were required to wear a skirt for work, it was never quite understood where that idea came from, though it was likely a dress code issue to do with accountants and business practices. VAT inspectors often had to deal with accountants, sometimes conducting VAT visits at accountants' premises, and it wouldn't do for female VAT officers to breach the 'skirt and heels' policy for women which was in place at many accountancy firms during the 80s, so we just fell into line with this regulation without questioning it.

As trainees, we all knew we would be watched closely during our Probationary Period and that we'd have to work hard to maintain our Executive Officer grade. But if we were successful, we would be rewarded with a safe and successful career. No threat of redundancy would ever hang over our heads. A job in the Civil Service was a job for life. VAT Control Officers would always be needed in Customs & Excise. Forever.

Value Added Tax
As ordinary citizens, all the trainees had paid Value Added Tax on goods and services as customers, but we were all clueless as to how that revenue was controlled, collected and passed on to the government by the businesses we paid it to. It's not something that most consumers think through, or need to know about.

Our course tutor, Mike, was nearing retirement and he told us that he used to be an inspector for the old 'Purchase Tax' back in the 50s and 60s. Purchase Tax was introduced in Britain during World War II to reduce the wastage of any raw materials. The Purchase Tax rate was originally a whopping 33.33%, and at one point rose to a staggering 100%, but 'purchase tax' was a rather deceptive name in that it was added at the manufacturing and distribution stage, rather than at retail outlets.

Purchase Tax was replaced by Value Added Tax in April 1973 when the UK joined the European Economic Community (EEC) - in that sense, VAT is a continental invention. On behalf of HM Treasury, the officers of Customs & Excise were empowered to levy various indirect taxes such as Landfill Tax, Insurance Premium Tax, as well as Customs and Excise duties. And because VAT is an 'indirect' tax, it was allocated to HM Customs & Excise (rather than the Inland Revenue - much to their chagrin).

In 1973, the standard rate of VAT was 10%. In 1974, the Labour government dropped the standard rate to 8% (but introduced a higher rate for some luxury items and petrol). In 1979, under Margaret Thatcher, the higher rate was dropped but the standard rate of VAT at 8% almost doubled to 15% - possibly to pay for the slash in income tax she gave to the most wealthy, cutting tax from 83% of earnings to 60%, and cutting common rate tax from 33% to 30%.

Then there was the issue of the VAT registration threshold. The threshold for VAT registration was so low in the 1980s that tens of thousands of small businesses all over Britain had to register for VAT by law. Small shops, window cleaners, milkmen, and other tiny businesses were required to register for VAT if their annual turnover was above £20,000. The knock-on effect of this was that the government had to employ an army of VAT Control Officers to visit every VAT registered business in the country to inspect their records and accounts. Most businesses could expect a compliance check every three or four years, although some 'low risk' traders would receive a visit every six or seven years. VAT was a booming business so to speak, and many officers were recruited and trained to undertake these routine VAT inspections.

Our tutor Mike had enjoyed being an inspector in the old Purchase Tax days - the job being much simpler back then. I sensed it had been a rather cushy little job compared to VAT Control.

Getting Equipped

The training course took place at Alpha Tower near Birmingham city centre. A windowless common room was furnished with bright orange 1970s sofas along with a machine that served watery tea and coffee, thin tasteless tomato soup, sickly sweet hot chocolate and an array of sugary snacks to keep our spirits up.

Apprehension bound us together as we all tried to grasp what the work might involve. We'd all had interesting pathways to VAT Control and were a bit dazed to find ourselves in this strange corner of the Civil Service which none of us had chosen or wanted, but had somehow been commandeered into by the Recruitment Office.

Mike taught us about tax points, VAT inclusive prices, VAT-exclusive prices, VAT liability, VAT exemptions, mark-ups, interpreting annual accounts, and the VAT fraction (being $^3/_{23}$ for a VAT rate of 15%), plus we were instructed in the basics of single-entry bookkeeping and the delights of double-entry bookkeeping. To my un-mathematical mind, double-entry bookkeeping was completely 'arse about face' (as Alf would have said) where debits seemed to be credits, and credits seemed to be debits, and I never really did completely comprehend it.

One morning towards the end of the course we walked into the lecture room and a colourful array of gin and whisky bottles were lined up on a table. Was this going to be a farewell party with a bang? We went up to them as if drawn to a magnet, but they were all empty. Mike used them as props to alert us to spot the difference in the duty-free bottles - an essential piece of VAT knowledge when undertaking VAT visits at pubs and restaurants with bars. I liked the Gordon's gin bottle best where the duty-free version was of crystal clear glass, with a vibrant yellow and red label that looked like a traffic warning sign. I'd be able to spot that one anywhere.

THE ORIGINAL

GORDON'S

LONDON DRY GIN

37% ALC/VOL   700 ML

We learnt that Value Added Tax is a vast source of revenue, raising billions of pounds each year and so our job was essential to ensure the government received the correct amounts of VAT due and that the 'public purse' was not defrauded. Despite our misgivings about becoming VAT inspectors, learning about this peculiar indirect tax had whetted our curiosity and Mike primed us well about the vagaries and complexities of Value Added Tax. We were ready to go out into the VAT Control field and put what we'd learned into practice.

We were equipped with two fat A5 volumes of 'VAT Law' which fitted snuggly side by side in a briefcase, along with an assortment of essential VAT leaflets, and in due course, we received our 'Commission' from the Commissioners of HM Customs and Excise, bound in an embossed leather wallet.

Inside, was a quaintly worded document that folded out. It was set in a strange mixture of type fonts and most peculiar language in what must be one of the longest sentences ever to be written - all 228 words of it:

To all to whom *these Presents shall come*

Greeting.

We the Commissioners of Her Majesty's Customs and Excise

pursuant to the powers in that behalf vested in us **Do Hereby**

appoint

— — — — — — Dawn Lesley SMITH — — — — — -

....

to be an **officer** *of Customs and Excise and to be employed on any Duty or Service which We may from time to time direct and approve with full power and authority to do and perform all such matters and things as are by any Act of Parliament in force relating to the Revenues of Customs or Excise or any other matter assigned to the Commissioners of Customs and Excise directed or authorised to be done and performed by an officer of Customs and Excise and to enforce all laws, regulations, penalties and forfeitures as directed by the Commissions of Her Majesty's Customs and Excise in all which premises she is to proceed in such manner as the law directs hereby praying and requiring all and every Constable and member of Her Majesty's armed forces or coastguard and all other whom it may concern to be aiding and assisting to her in all things as become the said*

— — — — — — Dawn Lesley SMITH — — — — — -

....

to observe and obey in such orders instructions and directions as she hath received and shall from time to time receive from the said Commissioners and to hold the office to which she is hereby appointed during the pleasure of the said Commissioners.

In Witness *hereof I the undersigned being one of the Commissioners of Her Majesty's Customs and Excise have hereunto set my Hand and Seal at King's Beam House, London. This day of......*

The Commission informed the reader in no uncertain terms about the considerable powers of Customs and Excise which included those conferred upon them by the VAT Act 1994, plus the powers contained in the Police and Criminal Evidence Act 1984 and the Customs and Excise Management Act 1979. These powers included the search of premises and persons, seizure of documents and goods, and arrest. As an officer of Her Majesty's Customs & Excise, I had the power to call upon the police to assist me if needed. In reality, woe betides any officer that did …..unless they were the fraud squad.

The course came to an end and we were all discharged back to our various Training Districts where we would continue learning the ropes of VAT Control for at least another 12-18 months.

First, however, we had to make known to Registration District any family member who was registered for VAT. It was not allowed, for obvious reasons, for a VAT officer to undertake an inspection of a VAT registered relative, and to this end, I declared my interest in a cousin who was VAT Registered as a publican in Birmingham, and then I was good to go.

9. THE ROOKIE

After I'd finished the training course, I joined the Training District in the Birmingham North LVO where two senior officers - Joan and Kay - took me under their wing. They were my mentors and would be supporting me throughout the next leg of my VAT Control journey. Joan had a continually smiling face with an extraordinarily calming personality. She would have made a magnificent nurse, and she exuded an aura of warm, caring authority. Kay - who was not much older than me - was also calm and caring, and was prone to spontaneously sharing random personal details, such as where she and her husband bought their underwear from (Marks & Spencer). These playful disclosures were all told with good humour, and I immediately felt at home in my new surroundings. Kay was appointed as my 'Line Manager' having overall responsibility for my continued learning.

Joan and Kay made the Training District a pleasant place to notch up VAT experience, along with various bits of light-hearted chat, and the occasional treat of assorted cakes to accompany our many cups of tea when at the office. I enjoyed working under these two women and was reassured by their example. I was still feeling jittery at being thrown into a job I didn't have a heart for, but they had a serene effect on my apprehensions. On the flip side, I soon learnt that VAT inspectors had to develop a bit of a hard side to cope with some of the more difficult aspects of enforcing VAT law.

Birmingham North LVO was situated in an office block above a huge Tesco supermarket at Five Ways in Edgbaston not far from the city centre. The offices were pleasant and open plan with plenty of light, and our grey desks were grouped in formats of two or three, in spacious areas.

Each District had a 'Surveyor' who was the District's boss - they were 'Senior Executive Officer' grade and were tucked away in their own private offices situated along the corridor. Why they were called 'Surveyors' I never did find out.

The Surveyor of Birmingham North Training District wasn't interested in us recruits. I can't even remember his name - his anonymity bearing testament to the fact that he was nearing retirement, just idling along until his departure. We rarely saw him, and he was content to leave us in the capable hands of Joan and Kay. Under their supervision, I built up my knowledge of the job. He had no input whatsoever.

I discovered that VAT visits were a bit like the sea - always different, yet always the same. The type of business would be different each day, but the basic accounting checks were stolid, unchanging, and monotonous.

I learnt the protocol for visit preparation including 'pre-credibility checks', and practised how to write up the '465a' and '465b' reports which had to be updated and completed after each visit. I learnt how to issue 'Assessments' for under-declared (or sometimes over-declared) VAT. It was rare, but occasionally we found some businesses had overpaid VAT. Those were happy times when a VAT inspector could inform a trader they would be receiving a cheque for overpaid tax.

The weeks turned into months as I accompanied Kay, Joan, and other experienced VAT officers on inspections to various businesses. I observed how they conducted a VAT visit, and I assisted them in the accounting checks. Soon Kay decided I should take the lead on a visit under her watchful eye. A small engineering firm cropped up for a routine VAT inspection in Sutton Coldfield. Kay lived in Sutton, it was her 'neck of the woods' as she called it, and she arranged to pick me up outside the cinema at 9.15 am. I arrived half an hour early, with the freezing November fog penetrating my bones and numbing my feet which I tried to lure back to life by moving from one foot to another like a lizard on hot sand. With each passing minute, a feeling of dread permeated the boredom of waiting, with my nerves jangling as I anticipated having to interview the trader while Kay looked on.

We arrived at the business and after introducing ourselves, Kay informed the trader the reason that there were two inspectors was because I was in training and she explained I would be conducting the inspection. The disclosure that I was a rookie drooped my already flagging self-belief. I began the interview using the trigger notes in my notebook,

'Erm, is the business still a limited company?'

'Yes.'

'And is this address the principal place of business?'

'Yes.'

'And, erm, is the financial year-end still the 30 June?'

'Yes.'

…..and so on went the discourse in a similar manner, stilted and awkward, shining a Super Trouper on my lack of skill as an interviewer with every passing monosyllable. The inspection was as Kay had expected - simple and straightforward - but my inability to conduct a reasonable interview left me feeling like a failure. Kay noticed my poor interviewing technique, and it was an area of weakness I was to battle with throughout my career.

Stressful and taxing were the visits I did under Kay's supervision, even though we got on well together and she was a very helpful line manager. Then Kay decided I could undertake some simple VAT inspections on my own. And was I glad.

10. GOING SOLO

'**W**ant a fag do 'ee my handsome?' asked Mrs Hoskins in a rich Cornish brogue, offering me a cigarette from a packet of Silk Cut.

'Er, no thank you, I just need to—'

'Want a ham sandwich do 'ee?' came the swift response.

'It's very kind of you to offer, maybe a little later.'

'Well, here, have a drop of hot in your tea my handsome,' she topped up my mug with the refreshing brew.

Although Mrs Hoskins's dialect and warm hospitality conjured up Cornwall and its friendly ethos, I was actually in Saltley - an inner-city suburb of Birmingham - conducting my first VAT inspection on my own. The business was a limited company selling industrial vacuum cleaners and parts. Mrs Lily Hoskins, and her son Vivien Hoskins, were the Directors of Vac-Rite Ltd. Yet another 'Rite' - a popular 80s word. They'd been trading for nearly 18 months and had never had a VAT inspection before. VAT registered traders always received a visit within the first 12-18 months of setting up a business to check for compliance. During my preparation for the visit I'd examined the figures on my printout and they'd all looked fairly reasonable.

Any preconceived ideas I'd had of limited companies being posh businesses with a receptionist, executives, plush offices and high flying salespeople with mobile phones and company cars had been completely eradicated during my training. We soon learnt that a limited company could comprise just two individuals bearing the grand title of 'Director' working from some run-down shack in a back street, with a very low turnover. Vac-Rite Ltd was barely turning over £25,000 a year - a small amount for a business in the late eighties. Traders often preferred to set up a limited company (rather than a partnership or sole proprietor) because it meant that if the business went bankrupt they wouldn't lose their home. It was less of a personal risk.

The business was registered from a private home address 20 miles away from where I lived and I had to get there on public transport. I was learning to drive and couldn't wait to take my test which was due the following week - if I passed it would save me many hours of travelling. It was still dark when I'd left home in Redditch at 7 am for my long journey into Birmingham on unreliable public transport. The bus was late, so I missed the train, and by the time I reached the city centre, I was behind time and feeling tense.

When I got off the bus in Saltley, feeling rather queasy because the driver seemed to take delight in throwing his passengers around by braking sharply, I had trouble finding the address and '9a Skeldale Road' was mighty hard to find. Was the business a spoof and trading under false pretences? Perhaps it was involved in a 'missing trader fraud'? Should I call the fraud squad? I decided I ought to telephone the trader first which involved a five-minute hike to a shop to get some small change for the public phone box. I was well and truly late for my visit by the time I rang Mrs Hoskins who told me that the entrance to 9a Skeldale Road was down a back alley in Ashley Avenue. When I finally arrived I felt as if I'd climbed Snowdon and that my arm wielding my heavy briefcase was about to break off.

'Miss Smith from Customs and Excise,' I announced, breathless, as Mrs Hoskins opened the door.

'Come in my handsome.'

I'd never been called 'my handsome' by anyone before, but after the perplexing and tiring journey, it was a comforting welcome.

'I apologise for being so late.'

'Don't you worry my handsome,' soothed Mrs Hoskins, 'come

in and have a cup of tea.' She led me through a narrow, dimly lit hallway into a cosy, warm kitchen with a verandah opening out onto an overgrown garden.

Mrs Hoskins' kindly welcome immediately melted away the stresses of the last three hours. She made two mugs of steaming tea as I got out my notebook to jot down details about the business during the interview. Her warm hospitality had helped to put me at ease, but it didn't help to improve my abysmal interview technique.

'Is the legal status of the business still a limited company?'
'Yes, my handsome.'
'And are you and your son the only directors?'
'Yes, my handsome.'
'And is this address the principal place of business?'
'Yes, my handsome.'
'Does your son have any other business premises?'
'No my handsome.'
'Does he keep any stock?'
'Only in his van and a bit in the spare room.'
'Have you appointed an accountant?'
'No, not yet my handsome.'

......and on it went in a similar vein, filling in the answers in my notebook as the replies came. It was at times like this I wished I could emulate the interviewing technique of Joan whom I'd accompanied on several VAT visits. She had a unique interviewing style which reminded me of a doctor interacting with their patient - there was definitely a medical feel to her interview technique with a soothing bedside manner. But try as I might, it just didn't work for me.

I asked to see the bit of stock in the spare room, and 'a bit' was an accurate description - there were just two boxes of spare parts comprising hoses and pumps for industrial vacuum cleaners.

Sales and Purchases
Mrs Hoskins told me that she was the bookkeeper and kept all the business accounts and that her son Vivien, who was out

working, did all the buying and selling. I'd detected during the interview that Mrs Hoskins had seemed a little vague when I'd asked about a 'Sales Day Book' (that is, a book where the sales invoices are listed) and a 'Purchase Day Book' (a book where the purchase invoices are listed) - so I didn't press any further, and thought I'd wait and see what turned up.

She presented me with a Tesco bag along with the words 'everything you need should be in there my handsome,' and then, after offering me a 'fag', a 'ham sandwich', and a 'drop of hot,' she went back to her ironing.

Being presented with a bag of invoices and accounting records was not unusual. We'd been warned on the training course that smaller businesses often kept their stuff in a carrier bag - or worse - not at all. I looked in the bag for books listing the sales and purchases, but there weren't any. Without a list of the invoices, I had no audit trail to trace the figures back to my printout.

'Mrs Hoskins, I'm sorry to trouble you, but do you have any books - or lists - of the invoices? I need to check the figures on the VAT returns.'

'Oh, aren't these no good?' She pointed to the photocopies of the VAT returns that I'd fished out of the Tesco bag.

'No, I have that information already on my printout. I need to see how those figures are reached. Can you show me how you work them out please?'

'Oh yes my handsome, I write them down in this here book, see, and then I work out a figure like what I was told to and write it in them there boxes,' she produced a Woolworth's exercise book from a large letter rack on the dresser.

'Thank you that's very helpful. Also, there aren't any sales invoices? Where are the sales invoices?' I asked while the going was good.

'Well what are they things there then my handsome?' she asked inquisitively pointing to a bunch of purchase invoices for vacuum parts that her son had bought.

'They're purchase invoices - they're what your son buys, Mrs

Hoskins.'

'Oh. Oh, I see. But they're things like what's been sold to my son aren't they?'

In a flash I knew what she was going through because we'd all been through it on our six-week training course: it was so easy to confuse sales and purchases.

'Yes, but what I need is the bit of paper your son gives to his customers when he sells them a vacuum or vacuum parts.'

Her face brightened as she understood what was required, 'Oh!!! Of course, yes, I have those things in here my handsome.' She went to a drawer and pulled out a rather battered duplicate book and gave it to me.

'Thank you, I'll see if I can check the figures now.'

She went back to her ironing while I looked through the sales invoices. Some of the pages were missing which disrupted the consecutive numbering of the invoices. Some were blank, and none of them had dates on them. One page was a shopping list written in loopy, spidery writing. I looked in despair at the pages which were supposed to be legal documents. None of the invoices had any of the required elements: date, VAT registration number, name and address of customer, item sold, price, VAT, VAT inclusive price.

I looked at the time - 10.45 am. The records were a complete mess - or so it seemed to me. Somehow I had to wade through these bits of paper for sales and purchases and make the figures add up and match the ones I had on my printout. I didn't know where to start. Most of the visits I'd done with senior officers in training had been straightforward, and I hadn't come across anything as messy as this. I felt I couldn't go back to the office just yet as it would look a bit odd: my first solo visit and I wasn't able to complete it on my own without help? So I decided to stay a bit longer and struggle on trying to make some sense of the figures.

Human Paradigm

Mrs Hoskins busied herself ironing and watering the many

plants around the kitchen while I attempted to make the figures add up. Physically and mentally I felt I'd done a day's work already: what with nearly three hours of city travelling, getting lost, interviewing without skill, the stress of a first solo visit, bad records - I felt whacked.

But I pressed on attempting to construct my own 'sales day book' but with no dates on the invoices, it was virtually impossible. There were no Annual Accounts available either. The financial year-end hadn't even been decided, so there was nothing to help me.

There was a knock at the door.

'Who's that then?' asked Mrs Hoskins in an intensely inquisitive voice as if I should know. Without waiting for an answer - not that I could have given one anyway - she went off to investigate and returned with a lady of similar age who, it turned out, was an old friend of Mrs Hoskins.

'Come on in Pat, have a cup of tea. I knew you were coming up country some time. What a lovely surprise. This here lady is Wot's Name from the Customs and Ex-er-cise,' said Mrs Hoskins by way of introducing me to Pat. Her mispronunciation of 'Excise' as 'Exercise' was a surprisingly frequent error by traders.

'Hello my handsome,' said Pat with the same Cornish affability as Mrs Hoskins, who poured yet another cup of tea.

'Sit down Pat, let's have a bit o' chat shall we? Want a fag do 'ee?"

The two women sat on a small sofa several feet away from me just inside the verandah. Mrs Hoskins offered Pat a cigarette, the first of many for the two Cornish comrades, who settled down to have a good natter while I tried to continue my VAT inspection. It was evident that this room was the main living room, even though it was a kitchen. Quite often VAT officers were put away in quiet corners, cold front rooms, or derelict offices, but here everything seemed to happen in the kitchen: meals, ironing, tea, 'a bit o' chat' - even VAT visits.

While the women chatted about the weather, I wrestled with the figures but got nowhere. I couldn't match the sales invoices with anything near what was on my printout. I'd succeeded in matching the first quarter of input tax (that is the VAT reclaimed on purchases) and at least the purchase invoices had dates on them so I could form some sort of list, but then the conversation of the two women became somewhat distracting, and my focus on the job in hand began to slip.

'How long have 'ee been up-country then Pat?'

'Oh about a week.'

'How's your son doing then and where's he to?' enquired Mrs Hoskins.

'Oh, he's all right. Doing well. He's settled and married, living in Redruth.'

The smoke from the cigarettes came wafting over in waves under my nose as if I was some sort of smoke magnet. Jaded and sapped, irritated with the smoke, my concentration was at a low ebb and I began to stare at the figures abstractedly while the two companions began to reminisce about old friends in Cornwall,

'How's old Rainsford Hocking then?' enquired Mrs Hoskins.

'Oh, he's gone,' replied Pat in a matter of fact tone.

'Has he?' asked Mrs Hoskins as if it couldn't be possible.

'Yes. Died last year he did.'

'Did he?' asked Mrs Hoskins in amazement.

'Yes. Heart attack he had.'

'Well I never.'

There was another pause while the women puffed away at their cigarettes. I kept my head down pretending to work, and occasionally shuffled the papers, but it was no use trying to make sense of them any longer.

'How's old Railton Retallick then?' asked Mrs Hoskins.

'Oh, he's gone.'

'Has he?' came the flabbergasted reply.

'Yes. Died two years ago he did.'

'Did he?' exclaimed Mrs Hoskins as if it couldn't be true.

'Yes - had a bad fall and never recovered, poor old soul.'

'Well I never! What a shame. We had some good times together we did, didn't us?'

'We did, yes.'

Another pause. By now my mind was becoming not only fuddled with figures, but the conversation also filled me with a dull realisation of the ephemerality of life and my impending mortality. I began to feel quite depressed.

'How's old Wot's Name from St. Ives then?' asked Mrs Hoskins.

'Who's that then?'

'Y'know.......her that makes lovely star-gazy pies.'

I could guess the reply, but I was hoping, just hoping........

'Oh she! She's gone,' came Pat's swift reply.

'Oh no! Has she?'

'Yes. Died about nine months ago she did.'

'Did she?'

By now I felt like saying to the two women, 'for goodness sake, can't you two talk about something else?'

'Yes. She never did recover from that stroke she had.'

'Oh, what a shame.'

'Yes. Nice fooneral she had mind. The singen' was lovely,' said Pat in her lilting Cornish dialect.

The two lit up another cigarette.

'And how's old Ernie from Trelawny Place then?' asked Mrs Hoskins.

Here we go again.

'He? Oh, he's in Bodmin, he is,' replied Pat.

'No! Is he?' said Mrs Hoskins with such passion in her voice that I feared whether being 'in Bodmin' was a fate worse than death.

'Yes. Been in three years he has. Found him wand'ring half-naked on the beach at Hayle,' continued Pat.

'Oh poor old soul. Nice chap he was.'

I gathered from this twist in the conversation that there was some kind of psychiatric unit in Bodmin. The realisation brought little comfort, but strangely my mood began to lift.....the tendrils of dark humour changed my emotions and I suddenly felt like laughing, as the incongruity of it all hit a funny spot and I had to stifle a giggle.

Again the women sipped tea and dragged on their cigarettes for a while as I waited for the next question, which wasn't long in coming.....

'And how's old Wot's Name from Lelant then?' asked Mrs Hoskins. (It seemed Mrs Hoskins called anybody 'Wot's Name' if she couldn't remember their proper name, but she said it in such a friendly manner you couldn't take offence).

'Married a girl from Nancledra he did,' replied Pat.

'Oh,' said Mrs Hoskins, softer now, and pensive.

I mused as to whether marrying a girl from Nancledra might be a fate worse than death or being in Bodmin, and I waited...... Mrs Hoskins spoke first,

'Better my son had married a girl from Nancledra. Divorced three times now, my son. They city girls aren't no good at all Pat. Better he'd stayed home in Cornwall and married a Cornish girl. All they city girls care about is theirselves and their careers. That's why I'm up here Pat,' she paused for a long drag on her cigarette, 'I had to come up and look after him. He wouldn't open his mail, nor pay his bills nor tax his car nor nothing. Bailiffs kept coming after him. Wouldn't get up in the morning he was so depressed. This last girl nearly wiped him out of house and home she did. And took the baby away. But I kept telling my son if you do right you'll end up right. I just hope he gets back on his feet soon.'

Pat was silent as her friend spoke, nodding in sympathy. Slowly the penny dropped for me too as I realised that, for Mrs Hoskins, keeping business records wasn't a legal responsibility at all - it was just part of being a good mum, helping her son at a difficult time in his life. Her lack of bookkeeping skills wasn't a consideration when they set up the business together. It was hard to ignore the human story behind the mess of the records, but I had to. And even though I was one of 'they city girls' I couldn't take offence at Mrs Hoskins or her perspective of what had happened to her son. I could only feel her sadness.

'Anyway Pat, how's that little dog of your'n?'

'Oh he's gone,'

'Oh, what a shame. Nice little thing he was, dear of him. Want a few chips do 'ee?'

'Lovely, yes, let's have a few chips shall we.'

'Have a few chips will 'ee my handsome?' Mrs Hoskins asked me in a manner I couldn't refuse.

'Well, if you're making some, thank you, that would be very nice,' my stomach by now rumbling from lack of a decent breakfast.

Light Bulb Moment

I was relieved that the conversation had come to an end and the two women disappeared further into the verandah where the cooker was. While the chips were being prepared and cooked, I tried to gather my thoughts together, as well as all the bits of paper. I looked blankly at the bank statements and all my training seemed to go out of the window. Nothing added up apart from the first quarter of input tax (for the purchases) but after that everything had gone to pot.

I decided to add up the bankings to see if they matched the sales figures shown on the printout and I was in the middle of this when a plate of steaming chips arrived. They were freshly fried and seasoned to perfection with salt, white pepper and vinegar. I never knew chips could taste so delicious. It was accompanied by a thick slice of juicy ham, two slices of bread and butter, and yet another cup of tea. As I ate the meal, I carried on with my work. The figures began to be a blur and it was no use - I just couldn't make any sense of it.

I admitted defeat: I'd have to ask Mrs Hoskins to sign a receipt so that I could take all the records and accounts back to the office and ask Kay to help me.

'Mrs Hoskins, I'm afraid I'm not able to trace the figures on the invoices through to the printout and I need a lot more time to look at everything. I'll need to take all these records back to the office.'

'That's OK my handsome.'

'The problem is that most of these sales invoices have no date on them. How do you work out the VAT if they have no date?' In a flash, I realised this was a question I should have asked three hours ago. *What an idiot I've been!*

'Well now I just add up the money like from this here list' (she opened the Woolworths book at the **back**) 'and work out the VAT on the cheques received like I was shown and put it on this here form.' Mrs Hoskins held up the next VAT return due in a few weeks.

No wonder I couldn't match the figures! Mrs Hoskins had been calculating the VAT on some sort of ad hoc cash basis instead of the invoice date.

'But what about the tax points?' I asked, suddenly quite relieved that at least I'd cracked half the problem.

'Tax points?' Mrs Hoskins frowned. 'Tax points?' she repeated to herself, as if it would trigger something, 'I've never heard of they things before my handsome.   Here, have a drop of hot in your tea. Want a fag do 'ee?'

'Er, no thank you. A tax point is the invoice date for this type of business.'

'Oh, oh I see.'

'The VAT has to be paid at the invoice date, not when your son receives the money.'

'But how can my son pay the VAT over if he hasn't been paid?' asked Mrs Hoskins with conviction.

At last!!! We were on the same page - and it was a good question she asked. I tried to give a simple answer.

'It's the law that your son has to pay the VAT at the invoice date even if he doesn't get paid the money.'

'That doesn't seem fair.'

'Well, the good news is that there's a new scheme called the Cash Accounting Scheme which allows you to pay the VAT when you get paid, but you need to apply for it as certain conditions have to be met. Until you have special permission to use the scheme, you have to account for VAT at the invoice date I'm afraid. Also, you can only reclaim the VAT on your purchases when you pay your bills - it works both ways.'

'Oh. Oh, I see,' said Mrs Hoskins, scratching her head. After all the warm hospitality she'd shown me, it was an uncomfortable task to inform her about the mistake.

'By accounting for the VAT when your son receives payment, rather than at invoice date, there's probably an underpayment of VAT and I'll need to work out how much it is. I'll give you a receipt for the records and let you know when they're ready for collection.'

'OK my handsome, you got to do your job,' she said without malice.

I'd also noticed that VAT had been reclaimed on a new TV and a vet bill for a cat which would have to be disallowed, and no apportionment for the private use of petrol had been made. These errors involved relatively small amounts of VAT which VacRite had over-claimed, and they were frequent errors found at many traders, but multiply such amounts to the whole country and it could add up to a fair amount of revenue for the government.

I explained to Mrs Hoskins about the VAT on the TV, vet bill and petrol, and I wrote out a receipt for the records and accounts.

'Here,' said Pat to Mrs Hoskins, 'I just remembered, I got some lovely saffron cake for 'ee.'

'Ooh, lovely. Can't get that up-country and I do love a bit of saffron cake.'

Pat got two large cakes out of her bag. Mrs Hoskins promptly took one, opened it and cut off two generous slices which she wrapped in cling film.

'Here my handsome, take this here bit of saffron cake. Nice with a cup of tea it is.'

'Thank you very much, that's very kind of you.'

We'd been warned in training not to accept any gifts from traders as they could be seen as bribes, but I recalled how Joan had once accepted some home-grown runner beans from a trader, so I accepted the saffron cake - so innocently given - as a genuine gesture of pure human kindness.

I gathered up all the records and accounts into the Tesco bag and gave Mrs Hoskins a receipt. It was getting on for two o'clock. Officers were allowed to go home to write up the reports after the visit (unless the visit finished unduly early) but I didn't even know where to start writing about this visit as it was all such a mess, so I decided to go back to the office to get some help from Kay.

'I'll write to you about everything we've discussed.' I had the urge to give Mrs Hoskins a hug, but it was out of the question. I wanted to tell her how much I admired her for the support she was giving her son, but all I said was 'thank you very much for your kind hospitality.'

'That's OK my handsome. Want a fag do 'ee?'

11. CAN OF WORMS

C an of worms. That was Kay's favourite phrase for the type of visit I'd experienced with Vac-Rite Ltd. Mrs Hoskins and her son weren't deliberately defrauding the public purse, it was just that the accounts were totally inadequate through ignorance and incompetence. I was relieved to find I wasn't totally incompetent myself when Kay agreed they were a total mess and would take some sorting out before I could issue an 'Assessment' of underpaid VAT along with a strong letter slapping the trader's wrists for using the 'Cash Accounting Scheme' unofficially.

The records were indeed a 'can of worms', but I confess that on an emotional level I sensed that Mrs Hoskins was a caring, compassionate, honest-as-the-day-is-long sort of person. It wasn't her fault she hadn't got a clue about VAT and bookkeeping. Why should she have? As far as she was concerned she was helping her son at a difficult time in his life. But officialdom has no level for such subjective nuances.

It wasn't the first time I'd felt sorry for a trader. It had happened on a joint visit with Kay several weeks earlier. An essential part of the training was to understand how retailers account for VAT and to this end, Kay arranged for me to accompany her on a visit to a Mr Kahn, who was the sole proprietor of a small, inner-city grocery shop. The initial inspection took place at the accountant's premises because they did all the bookkeeping as well as producing the Annual Accounts for their client.

The offices were plush and spacious, with marbled floors, adorned with planters and fancy leather chairs in regency style.

The accountant politely answered Kay's questions on behalf of Mr Kahn, who was working in his shop, because his English was poor, and in that sense, the accountant was acting as a sort of 'in loco cauponarius'. We spent a pleasant morning at the accountant's luxurious offices examining the business records, enjoying frequent refreshments of coffee and biscuits served on exquisite crockery.

Like most grocery shops Mr Kahn sold a mixture of vatable and non-vatable goods. His vatable (standard-rated) goods were things like toilet rolls, bleach, washing powder, sweets and tobacco, and his non-vatable (zero-rated) goods were milk, bread, tinned foods, fruit and vegetables. So to account for the VAT correctly, Mr Kahn was using 'Retail Scheme D' which was specially designed to work out the VAT on the vatable goods.

Everything seemed to be going well until we looked at the Annual Accounts which are a very useful source of information for VAT inspectors. All businesses have to have them for Inland Revenue purposes and nearly all businesses have them prepared by a qualified accountant because it is a complex document.

The problem with Mr Kahn's Annual Accounts was the closing stock figure in the Balance Sheet - it was very high. Now, a high closing stock figure to a VAT inspector's mind meant only one thing: it had been unduly inflated by the accountant to reduce the profit margin for Inland Revenue purposes. But it was also a very important figure for VAT in Retail Scheme D because - by some mysterious means that I almost once grasped like a piece of slippery soap in the bath only for it to disappear again - the closing stock figure affected the amount of VAT paid, requiring an 'annual adjustment'. So without any further ado, Kay announced there and then that we had to visit Mr Kahn's shop forthwith and do a stock take to check out whether the closing stock figure was feasible.

The accountant insisted on dogging along with us because Mr Kahn's English was not good. So off we all traipsed to the shop which was about a mile away. Mr Kahn looked morosely glum. We knew nothing of his background - how long he'd been in England, or how or why he came to be here, and it was none of our business, but I was interested and wished I could have known something of his personal story.

The shop smelt like all Asian grocery shops: a distinctive mix of aromatic spices with an earthy tinge of unusual vegetables. We set about doing our stocktake while Mr Kahn and his accountant looked on in silence. It was a fairly small shop and not very well stocked and I followed Kay around like a meek sheep, making a list while she counted:

Toilet Rolls - 3 packets x 75p
Washing-up Liquid - 5 bottles x 35p
Soup - 8 tins x 25p
Basmati Rice - 10 packets x 50p
Ginger Biscuits - 2 packets x 30p

….. and so on. Mr Kahn watched us from under black bushy eyebrows with his arms crossed in front of his chest, unsmiling. By the end of our little 'stocktake', it was clear it was nowhere near the figure on the accounts. So something was not quite right.

Despite Kay's youthful vivacity, sense of fun and pleasant personality, I glimpsed an iron thoroughness in her approach to VAT Control. It was evident she was convinced of the accountant's duplicity and she firmly challenged his figures right there in the shop - good job there weren't any customers around. I couldn't make head or tail of Kay's challenge and I stood behind her like a mouse while she did all the haggling. The evidence before my eyes told me Mr Kahn was unsettled by our intrusive visit; his shop location was isolated, and his half-empty shelves sported several out of date items along with a meagre supply of wrinkled vegetables. And added to that, he sold all his milk and bread at a loss. These 'loss leaders' (as they were called) were a popular ploy for many retailers - both small and large - to lure customers into the shop in the hope that they would buy other goods which were over-priced. But during the time we were there doing our stocktake - nearly 40 minutes - he didn't have a single customer, so clearly his 'loss leaders' weren't leading anywhere.

As Kay wrangled on with the accountant, my mind drifted to wondering how I would feel if I lived in a strange country where I couldn't speak the language, let alone write in a different alphabet, away from home roots, trying to make a living by selling rotting fruit and vegetables and out of date goods, in a cold climate, in a run-down part of a large city with graffiti everywhere. I wanted to go up to Mr Kahn and say, 'Hey look I'm sorry about all this - we're just doing our job you know. Something doesn't add up with the closing stock figure, but we'll sort it out somehow.' My eyes briefly met Mr Kahn's but I quickly averted my gaze. I was rather embarrassed by it all.

Kay stuck to her guns and issued a small assessment of £45 based on the fact that the accountant had used an inflated closing stock figure to calculate the annual adjustment of VAT on Retail Scheme D. She was probably right to do so and maybe with more experience, I would have done the same because as a civil servant you have to stick to the rules - you can't bend them to trader's personal circumstances, or say, 'let's forget about it this time, you're having a tough time but don't do it again.' But I couldn't help asking the question: was it worth nearly five hours of our time - let alone the accountant's time and trouble - for a measly £45? To Mr Kahn, that amount would have bought him a decent supply of fresh stock which he badly needed.

The reason the assessment was such a teensy amount was that most of the goods which Mr Kahn sold were zero-rated and had no VAT on them (such as foodstuffs). Only a small proportion of his takings were vatable. But to me it was a pyrrhic victory for Customs and Excise, costing the taxpayer a lot of money to employ a couple of officers (albeit one in training) to faff around in a shop selling loss leaders and rotting vegetables.

Apart from the confrontational element of arguing with a competent accountant over past-the-sell-by date stock, it seemed distasteful to issue an assessment to a small trader trying hard to make a living. We would have been better employed looking at bigger, higher risk traders. But I was trapped and couldn't do anything about it. I didn't do confrontation well and I hoped I'd never have to do a visit like that. Ever.

12. THE PUBLIC PURSE

I frequently travelled with other officers in their cars to VAT visits and it was during times like this they often told me about some of the cases they'd encountered in the past giving me an insight into VAT fraud and naughtiness. These random conversations alerted me to the lengths some traders would go to line their own pockets with VAT from the public purse.

One frosty morning Kay picked me up at Wylde Green station and we tootled off to visit an Italian restaurant in Tamworth. On the way there, as I thawed out in her toasty car, she told me about a visit she once did to a very upmarket restaurant when she worked on VAT Control in London. The charming owner had won Kay over with his helpful manner, showing her how the till worked, and giving her a guided tour around his plush restaurant while it was closed, quiet and calm, then showing her around the immaculate shiny kitchens.

'Did the restaurant do flambé?' I asked, remembering Andrew's question in our VAT training class, hoping to glean how to discover any VAT monkey business regarding food cooked in alcohol.

'No, it was famous for its seafood dishes mainly, and all the food was cooked by chefs in the kitchens.'

Kay went on to tell me how she began the visit in the normal manner reconciling the VAT returns to the trader's ledgers and everything was looking good as she worked her way through all the usual checks. She was there nearly all day because the restaurant hadn't had an inspection for over 6 years, and there was a fair bit to get through.

As the afternoon wore on, staff arrived to get the restaurant up and running in preparation for when it opened later that evening. The owner informed Kay that he would leave her in the capable hands of his senior waiter should she need anything further help, while he nipped home before coming back on duty later that evening.

Kay spotted the senior waiter behind the bar stocking up on booze and on a whim, as VAT officers do, she decided to ask him how the staff worked the till. Even though the owner had already shown Kay earlier, she wanted to stretch her legs and have a mooch around. The waiter informed Kay that only the owner or the restaurant manager operated the till, and it was while he was telling her this that she noticed a small green book under the counter. Boldly, she picked it up and asked 'What's this?'

'Oh I believe that's his petty cash book, you'll need to ask him about that.'

It turned out that the 'cash' recorded in the book was far from 'petty'. Inside, large amounts were recorded revealing suppressed restaurant takings to the tune of £500,000 which the owner had squirrelled away into a private bank account. He owed over £65,000 in under-declared VAT.

'What happened to him?'

'He was prosecuted for tax evasion, got a suspended prison sentence and some of his goods and chattels were seized to pay off the debt.'

'Didn't his accountants know about it?'

'The green book was never given to them, but the bookkeeper was complicit and in on the swindle. With this kind of cash in hand cash in pocket fraud, not even accountants will find it out. The bookkeeper in the end gave evidence for the prosecution, but she was also jailed.'

'So it really is that easy to make sales vanish.'

'Absolutely.'

'I'll be looking under the counter for little green books while you check how the till works then.'

'Definitely.'

The take-home from this story to me as a rookie VAT inspector was to be bold, be cheeky, be intrusive, be sneaky, and be suspicious. Five things that did not come naturally to me on VAT visits, as I always wanted to believe the trader was honest. And most of them were.

As it turned out the visit we did to the Italian Restaurant was uneventful and there was no little green book, or books of any colour for that matter, to be found under the counter - even though I dropped my notebook deliberately to have a sneaky look as I bent down to pick it up.

All that we found on the visit were two arithmetic errors and the fairly common mistake that no scale charges had been applied for the personal use of petrol resulting in a tiny assessment of just over £250.

'Ladies, ladies!' announced the Italian restaurant owner with a charming, expressive Italian accent, 'please please 'ava some pizza!' He handed us a box each containing a generous portion just as we were about to leave, 'and a good journey home ladies! Arrivederci!!'

13. OFFICE DAYS AND PINEAPPLE CREAMS

'**M**orning!' I said brightly with a mug of steaming tea in my hand.

'Morning Dawn' chorused Joan and Kay looking up at me from their work, smiling.

After a rough start to the week at Vac-Rite Ltd, it now was Friday. I liked Fridays because they were nearly always an 'office day' for VAT inspectors. I sat down at my desk and took a sip of my brew. It tasted foul. *I really must buy some fresh teabags.* Teabags got very stale in VAT Control offices. It was only once a week that officers were around to make themselves tea at work. When I examined my packet, it was two months out of date.

It was 7.35 am and more colleagues arrived, making salutations, with mugs of stale tea in their hands, some yawning. Nearly all officers made an early start on Fridays and I fell into line with this routine because it avoided all the congested city traffic before the school runs got underway, plus we would all be headed home by 3.00 pm. Early start, early finish. What was not to like? Fridays were only an eight hour day, rather than an eight-and-a-half hour day. As for overtime - what was that? Overtime was a rare beast in VAT Control. In Birmingham, we were required to work 42 hours a week (gross, including meal breaks) which was plenty of time to complete casework.

Within minutes of arriving at the office, our desks were awash with green folders as we all began working on our caseloads. Every VAT registered trader had a green folder that contained all their VAT details and history. Some folders were thick and some were thin, depending on how long the business had been trading and how many visits they'd had in the past. Our casework was varied ranging from writing letters (which we wrote by hand then sent to a typing pool) to issuing assessments of under-declared VAT and researching any complex areas of VAT law.

Most Fridays Kay would give me a bunch of green VAT folders. I quickly scanned them to see what sorts of businesses I'd be visiting. I found this to be rather fun - a bit like a child opening a lucky bag. I also looked to see where they were, hoping none of them involved hours of travelling as I was still using public transport.

After making a few phone calls to book VAT visits, I got underway working on the chaotic accounts of VacRite Ltd, with Kay helping me to make sense of them. I was in for a long morning. After trawling through the Tesco bag, I eventually issued an assessment for £200 accompanied by a stiff 'standard' letter instructing the trader to either account for VAT at the invoice date or apply for the special Cash Accounting Scheme. Poor Mrs Hoskins. How I wished I could have given her that hug.

Dave, from the VAT Enquiries section, popped into Training District with a pile of VAT leaflets. He was married to Jenny who also worked in VAT Enquiries. They'd just had a baby and we all congratulated him.

'My missus didn't half have a rough time of it though,' he lamented, shaking his head as the horror of the experience came back, 'the babby got stuck, and they had to call in some bloke to get it out with a pair of tongs. My poor Jenny was in agony. Bloody 'ell, I never want to go through that again! Then the bloke who pulled the babby out of her had to sew her up and put stitches in. I couldn't believe me eyes - not even I get that close!'

.....and so it was you never could tell what the topic of conversation would be from one Friday to the next.

But I'd discovered something about myself since starting

work as a VAT inspector: I enjoyed working on my own rather than as part of a 'team'. I always was a bit of a loner. For me, VAT Control work was solitary, but not lonely, and working on my own was something I'd warmed to. Yet even I found it was good to have a break from being out on the road, and so on office days, I enjoyed the company of my colleagues. It's true to say I was more the fly on the wall rather than a participant, but I liked listening to their banter and jokes.

Lunchtime approached and I nipped down to the supermarket below the office for a sandwich, doing a bit of shopping at the same time. Most of us worked through our lunch hour, or took only half an hour, making the working day even shorter.

During the afternoon, various official forms began to replace the green folders. Expense claim forms, diary sheets, and last but not least our VAVOPS forms. VAVOPS were 'work return forms' and had to be completed at the end of each week. For some strange reason they had to be completed in red ink and red pens invariably seemed to go missing on Fridays. Filling in VAVOPS required the use of certain coded numbers which showed how our 37 working hours each week had been spent. We were encouraged to put as much time on 00 or 01 (time spent at the trader's premises), whereas 06 or 08, which was 'non-productive' time - such as keeping up with any new VAT law or enjoying some banter and a pineapple cream - was kept to a minimum. However, it was easy to be creative with the tacit approval of our Surveyors. And I never did assimilate what the acronym VAVOPS stood for: it was something convoluted like 'Visit Analysis and VAT Operational Planning System'. To my mind, VAVOPS became synonymous with the word Cyclops, and the concept of a giant one-eyed creature scrutinising our work returns probably wasn't far off.

Our diary sheets got frantically filled in before home time. These showed all the details of our whereabouts the following week. They were important for the safety of the officer, as well as a useful tool for management to keep tabs on work schedules.

Filling in my VAVOPS work return sheet would certainly show a lot more '00' and '01' time because I couldn't deny that doing visits on my own took me much longer than when I was accompanied by a senior officer. I'd done three more visits on my own during that week: a small steelworks, a small manufacturer which produced nuts and bolts, and an electrician. All three had been relatively easy visits and all of them were 'invoice traders' using single-entry bookkeeping. I'd found some under-declared VAT on the sale of an old van that the electrician had sold, and I'd also found errors in arithmetic at all three traders. Although the mistakes were small, it was good that I'd found them because it proved to Kay I was being thorough in my checks.

To demonstrate to Kay I was developing a nose for 'credibility' I'd attempted a 'credibility check' at the electrician. I worked out how many plugs he'd purchased compared to how many jobs he'd invoiced. I reckoned a small domestic electrician would use at least one new plug every other job and his jobs exceeded his purchase of plugs by 1:3. However, over a cup of tea and pineapple cream (Kay's favourite sweet treat which she often bought for the District), she smashed my credibility check to pieces by pointing out that very clever traders suppress their purchases to match their suppressed sales, and I would need to think of better ways to test credibility. To this day I still can't work out my ridiculous reasoning behind my 'credibility check', and it was right that Kay brushed it off so skilfully without ridiculing me as a person.

Despite that, I felt my first week going solo had gone quite well and Kay thought so too. In the following weeks, I continued to accompany experienced senior officers on their visits but I was also given visits to do on my own to traders with a little more complexity to expand my knowledge of VAT further.

14. MORE WORMS

One dismal foggy day in late November, I was travelling with Ranjit, a senior officer experienced in large traders, to a fabric firm. As usual, when travelling with another officer, I tried to pick their brains about any significant cases they remembered. Ranjit told me how several years previously he'd visited a large company that had claimed over £100,000 in VAT by submitting fake invoices pretending they had renovated some of their business premises.

'How did you pick that up?' I asked, hoping to glean some clues detecting VAT waywardness.

'Well it was basically that the fake invoices looked, well, fake,' Ranjit laughed as he recalled the scene, 'they were very unprofessional, and even had spelling mistakes on them, and that's how I got suspicious.'

'What a nerve!'

'And when the fraud guys went to inspect the renovated premises which were up north near their sub-office, they were in such a state of dilapidation that it was clear there was foul play. No renovation work had been done at all and the premises were just four run-down garages on an industrial estate.'

'It's unbelievable that they think they can even get away with it.'

'It's rare, but yes there are traders who think stealing VAT is a legitimate way to do business, unfortunately.'

We arrived at the fabric business and we were met by one of the three directors, a Mr Lynch. I was as meek as a kitten looking on as Ranjit superbly conducted his interview, inspected the premises and quizzed the director about imported goods. Then, once we were ensconced in an office with the relevant accounts and the obligatory tea and biscuits, Ranjit said in serious undertones,

'Something seriously wrong here.'

'In what way?' I whispered back, confessing I hadn't picked up anything was wrong at all.

'Well did you see how shifty his behaviour was when I asked about the imports of yarn - something seems very wrong.'

'Erm...' I tried casting my mind back.....crikey, what did I miss?

'Something doesn't add up.....see here....' Ranjit began to show me the figures on the D1507 VAT print-out and talked me through the very thorough pre-credibility checks he'd done before the visit. The penny began to drop - it seemed there was an irregularity with the purchases of imported yarn and Ranjit suspected the business had undervalued their imports meaning they had not paid the correct VAT.

As we went through the records more discrepancies became apparent, and the financial accounts produced by the accountants didn't match the VAT returns. Ranjit was cagey with Mr Lynch when we left, telling him we needed more time to complete our inspection, and he confiscated the Annual Accounts.

On the way home in the car, we both knew he'd uncovered a major VAT scam where he'd have to get the fraud squad involved,

'Frauds like this syphon off millions, and all fraud undermines and harms law-abiding competitors because it puts companies like this at an unfair advantage,' was Ranjit's eloquent summary of the effect this kind of misdemeanour has on society in general.

To cut a long story short, this routine inspection by Ranjit - along with his hunch that something was amiss - uncovered quite a complex and sophisticated conspiracy to steal public money by the three directors. By declaring only half the price of imported yarn they avoided paying just over £200,000 in VAT and, in addition to undervaluing their imports, it was also found that they'd set up a string of bogus companies and unrecorded bank accounts. The directors produced hundreds of false invoices to cover the discrepancy between the trifling amounts of VAT they were paying on imports and the full amount of tax they received from selling their goods to wholesalers. They'd made huge profits by not passing on the VAT they received on sales.

I never did hear what their fate was, but likely a prison sentence and orders to pay compensation, and I made a mental note to check the value of imports at any future visits.

15. THE DRIVING TEST

The day of my driving test arrived. For nearly four months I'd done VAT visits spanning two or three counties using buses and trains which were invariably grimy, often smelly, unreliable, too hot or too cold, always time-consuming, with the number of hours spent travelling almost equalling a day's work at times.

I booked three driving lessons a week to give me the best chance of passing. Being able to drive would give me so much more freedom, a lot more time, and a little more money - I'd be able to claim 'travel expenses' at 32 pence per mile. I bought an old banger - a bright blue Datsun Cherry - in anticipation.

Calm, composed and determined, the test went well even though during my three-point turn a juggernaut pulled to a stop a few feet from my driver's door. I stalled. But I just restarted the engine and carried on as if nothing had happened. The lorry would just have to damn well wait.

Parked up at the Test Centre afterwards, the examiner quizzed me with questions about the Highway Code right there in the car. He was urgent, Magnus Magnusson-style, and I ping-ponged my answers back at him just as fast, Mastermind-like, '…..and no passes.' The last question came,

'Finally Miss Smith, what do street lamps indicate?'

Street lamps? I was stumped. *I don't remember reading anything about street lamps in the Highway Code.* I made a sensible guess,'They indicate a built-up area,' I said confidently.

'No. Try again.'

'Erm, they indicate to watch your speed?'

'No. Try again.'

'Erm....' I stalled in speech, struck dumb by a prick of panic - *surely I'm not going to fall at the last hurdle? Is he asking me a spoof question just to throw me off track?* Seconds stretched into a time warp of what felt like minutes before I decided to own up - it was no use bluffing,

'I'm afraid I don't know, I'm not sure, to be honest.'

The examiner was silent as he made notes, and I stared unblinking ahead through the misty windscreen. He was still writing when he spoke,

'I'm pleased to tell you that you've passed,' he turned and looked at me, 'but do get more familiar with the Highway Code,' he said in a tone of voice that reminded me of Q ticking off James Bond.

'I will, thank you, yes, I will,' I spluttered, sweating and for some strange reason salivating like a dog, trembling, and wobbly-legged with relief. We got out of the car and went into the Test Centre where he wrote out my pass sheet and handed it to me. I had to sign for something which I just about managed - my hands were quivering, and the calm control I'd harnessed during the test deserted me.

I must have been the only learner driver who was more nervous after their test than before.

△△△

The next day I drove to work in my old banger using the M42 motorway. I'd never driven on a motorway before. Vaguely excited at the prospect, I unconsciously upped my speed in tandem with the fast pace of other vehicles in front and behind me, and I revelled in Velocity. The thrill of speed didn't take long to set in.

The newly constructed M42 was a bumpy ride, however, particularly in my old car with poor suspension. It was a strange motorway - a kind of giant path laid with giant slabs, rather than smooth black tarmac.....diddum, diddum, diddum,

diddum......went the monotonous rhythm of my tyres rattling over the uneven surface. My car's rotting bodywork not only had poor suspension, but water ingress created musty smells, and its broken radio offered me no company. But the engine was excellent and purred sweetly.

Then the heavy sky slacked a grey aquatic blanket, veiling my windscreen with sheeting rain, reducing visibility to a pea-souper. Fog lights began to glow red on the vehicles in front. *Where are my fog lights?* I tried to find the switch, button, knob - anything - for my fog lights - but gave up. I hadn't a clue how to switch on my fog lights; I'd never had to use them before. I began to feel a tad vulnerable, forced to overtake convoys of sluggish juggernauts spritzing spray outwards soaking the overtaking cars. My wipers squeaked at full speed, out of sync with the diddum diddum of my tyres while my hands gripped the steering wheel tighter - not that it would have helped if a lorry had collided with my rusty tin car.

I slipped off the motorway after squeezing through two enormous lorries, onto a main road, shocked at how slow 30 miles an hour felt. If only I could get a transfer to Droitwich LVO I wouldn't have any of this rabid city driving to do.

△△△

'I passed!' I announced on Friday as I waltzed into the office with a mug of stale tea. Everyone cheered. I was eager to get my bunch of green VAT folders: what businesses would I be visiting and where would they be? Would I get lots of farmers out in the country to clock up some decent mileage at 32 pence per mile? Kay handed me my pile and I had to look at it twice - it was twice the size it normally was. Then I remembered. There would be several '301' visits for me to do and Kay had told me about them a while back. '301' visits were VAT inspections to tiny traders with trifling turnovers - so tiny in fact that any officer with a car is expected to do two '301' VAT visits in a day. So being parked up in my car, writing up the report after a morning visit, munching a sandwich, with my notebook balanced on the steering wheel, would soon become a familiar routine. ......not much fun in winter though. For how can one write wearing gloves?

Travel Expenses

On the plus side, my pay packet would increase by around £80 a month for using a private vehicle. Visits to the furthest outposts of the LVO were distributed fairly between VAT officers with cars, so I needn't have worried about not getting my fair share of miles. And I had the bliss of at least an extra hour and a half in bed every morning.

I frequently got lost doing visits on the north side of the city and I often did a mile or two more than necessary before finding the premises. I wasn't gifted in reading a map.

At the end of the month, a feeling of yuppie-ness pervaded as I filled in my expense claim form using the mileage record I'd kept in a notebook. I also qualified for a bit of 'subsistence' - I'd been entitled to claim the grand sum of £3.50 for a morsel of lunch on the occasions when I'd conducted two '301' VAT visits in a day. I was determined to make a profit out of this £3.50 and on those days I often just bought a crusty cob for 10p, a portion of paté for 25p, and a bag of crisps - I was left with a whopping £3 surplus.

I looked forward to a bit more income and I saw it as quite a perk on top of my salary. I didn't think too much about vehicle 'wear and tear', though in reality the 32 pence per mile probably only just about covered it.

First, however, my Travel & Subsistence claim had to pass the scrutiny of my Surveyor and was I shocked when he bounced it straight back at me. He'd rejected it and wanted it amended because I'd over-claimed by the grand sum of £2.56 - eight miles more than I was entitled to. I'd forgotten that our Surveyor was famous for possessing an A4 size 'A-Z of Birmingham & District' along with a box of pins and a piece of wool. These accoutrements he utilised with religious fervour to accurately measure the mileage from the office to the place of business recorded on our travel claims. It was a familiar end-of-the-month spectre: snatching a glance at him through his open office door, crouched over his A-Z with his pins and wool. I'd stupidly forgotten that no allowance was made for one-way streets, or getting lost. *Cripes, I never thought I'd end up feeling like a fraud as a VAT inspector.*

As the months passed it was as though I'd driven a car forever, and city driving became second nature.

Mind you, I never did find out what the presence of street lamps indicated.

16. MILKMEN AND BUTCHERS

As the months passed, I was sent out to more diverse types of businesses with derisory turnovers involving simple VAT accounting checks. These small 'low risk' traders were good training fodder - I couldn't do much damage on these visits since the figures involved were so paltry that if I did miss something it wouldn't be significant. They were perfect for unsupervised visits while building up my knowledge of different areas of Value Added Tax.

I was given a visit to a milkman, Mr Terrence Green, the sole proprietor of his milk round business registered from his home address. He'd been a milkman for eleven years and his last VAT visit had been over six years ago. Kay had given me this visit to do because milkmen were 'repayment traders' - in other words they did not pay Customs & Excise anything, but rather Custom & Excise paid *them*. Sort of 'arse about face' (as Alf would have said). This was because the goods they sold were not liable for VAT (things such as milk, certain foods, children's clothing, or anything that was 'zero-rated' or 'exempt' from VAT, or 'outside the scope' of VAT). However, these businesses were entitled to reclaim the VAT back on their business purchases and expenses - things such as fuel, assets and vatable services. Some repayment traders with large turnovers received huge cheques from Customs & Excise every quarter.

Mr Green however only sold milk, cream, some orange juice and a few loaves of bread. It was a simple visit and all I needed to check was that the VAT he'd reclaimed had proper receipts, was allowable, and was claimed at the right time. I also had to check for any sales of assets or goods which would be liable for

VAT. The figures for his business on the 'D1507' printout were typical of a milkman in the 1980s - nothing was untoward, and like many VAT visits, it proved to be uneventful.

Mr Green was still out on his round when I arrived and his wife, who did all the bookkeeping, greeted and escorted me to a long, spacious through-lounge where the accounts were neatly arranged on an oval dining table. She answered all my questions, supplied me with tea and biscuits and left me to it. The faint whirring of a washing machine and music from a tinny radio wafted through an open door. While I munched on a biscuit, I had a good nose around the room, baulking as I took a sip of my tea which tasted awful - the milk had curdled and it had gone off. *Stale milk at a milkman's house? Surely not?*

I always enjoyed being left alone to inspect the accounts in private homes, snatching a few moments of stillness. After studying the titles of about a dozen videos on a nearby bookshelf to see what sort of things they watched - which included *A Fish Called Wanda* and *Who Framed Roger Rabbit* - I decided I ought to begin leafing through the accounts.

The audit trails were all good and in order. There were only two things I found: a mathematical error where Mrs Green had read a number one as a number seven and in doing so had claimed £60 too much on the purchase of some new milk crates, and another error where she'd claimed the VAT on a new TV (a common occurrence - many traders tried this one on) so I had to disallow it and we both played the game in the 'mopping-up' session at the end of the visit: me the polite VAT inspector giving her the benefit of the doubt, and she the dumb bookkeeper promising she wouldn't claim the VAT back on any luxury items again. I'd completed the visit in an hour and a half during which time I'd been through every bit of paper there was for the previous five years.

It was nearly midday when I left, and after mooching in some of the local charity shops for clothes and shoes, then buying a sandwich, I parked on a side road and wrote my report in the car while I ate my lunch. It was one of those days when I was doing two '301' visits back to back. My next '301' visit was at 2pm at another small 'repayment trader' - a butcher - near the city centre. As I entered the busy shop the stench of sickly meat mingling with cheese and bloodied offal almost caused me to gag. Mr Midcalf was the sole proprietor of his business and employed two staff. The shop was rowdy with vibrant chatter and jovial banter between Mr Midcalf and a steady conveyor belt of his regular customers.

The premises were so small that there was nowhere for me to sit down, so I had to flick through the accounts on top of a chest freezer whilst standing up, with my feet strangled in my high heeled court shoes which throbbed in time with the butcher's chopping rhythms. There wasn't much to check. Mr Midcalf (a suitable name for a butcher I mused) had claimed the VAT back on the usual purchases of fuel (which had been apportioned for private use), some new butcher's knives and implements, and one or two other things. I checked all the arithmetic and it was spot on. The Annual Accounts were all in order and I'd finished the visit in just over an hour by 3.10pm. I hobbled to my car with my feet pulsating in my stilettos.

It was too early to go home, so I went back to the office to write up the butcher's report and prepare for my visit the next day. These were the days before words such as 'performance indicators' and 'performance-related pay' were even heard of, and sometimes one could just idle away an hour or two by leisurely writing up a report in one's best handwriting.

The afternoon drew to a close as I prepared for my visit the next day which was to a jeweller's shop in Handsworth where violent riots had raged a few years previously. I'd never felt unsafe anywhere in the city before, but unrealistic fears began to take an irrational grip and I didn't want to do the visit. Now, by the 1980s the Civil Service was way ahead of many of its counterparts regarding gender equality. Women received the same pay for doing exactly the same job as men. I got the same salary as my male colleagues. But equality works both ways and in VAT Control female officers were expected to do the same type of visits as male officers in the same parts of the city, so there was no way I could wriggle out of it. Besides, I didn't want to show I was timid.

An added safety net was that every officer had to complete a weekly diary sheet to be left on their desk detailing the trader's address and phone number. This had recently come into operation in VAT Offices since the disappearance of the estate agent Susie Lamplugh in 1986 (though quite how leaving a diary sheet would have prevented a similar crime is uncertain). But I couldn't shake off feeling unsettled about the impending visit in Handsworth and I couldn't stand it any longer, and casually asked Kay, who sat opposite me sipping a cuppa and munching a pineapple cream,

'Has any officer ever been attacked or mugged on a visit?'

'No?' came the swift response posed as a question, accompanied by an expression on her face as if to say 'What did you ask that for?'

'Oh, I just wondered.'

Eighteen months later Customs & Excise offered all VAT Control Officers a device that could be worn around the neck that emitted a high-pitched sound when pressed in the event they were attacked. To my knowledge, no one ever requested one, and neither did I.

17. TEARS AND TRIBUNALS

B eing cooped up in a car with a colleague whilst travelling to a visit was a good opportunity to pick their brains about VAT shenanigans and naughtiness without intruding on their work. One Spring morning, I drove to the office where I met Niall, a senior officer, to travel with him to a large waste disposal company so that I could continue learning about double-entry bookkeeping. On the way there we chatted about our journey into VAT-land and I learnt that - amongst other things - Niall had in the past been a waiter, a postman, a tiler, and a maths teacher (which probably explained why he sailed through the Executive Officer exam and passed the first time), but he told me his job on VAT Control was like no other job he'd ever done before.

'What's the strangest business you've ever visited?'

'A sex toy shop in Ladywood,' he said in a completely deadpan manner, 'very good mark-up on the goods, one of the most profitable businesses I've ever visited.'

Wide-eyed and my cheeks colouring, I quickly changed the subject and asked him if he'd ever come across any VAT wheeling and dealing. He told me about a business he once visited - a partnership between a husband and wife - where over a period of five years they'd set up several companies selling catering goods which they later closed, but not before pocketing the VAT they charged their customers amounting to nearly £100,000.

'How did you discover it?'

'It was partly just instinct as is so often the case uncovering this type of fraud. I picked up on my inspection that the company had registered for VAT too late.'

Me: slight shiver. I was clueless as to how I should check whether a new company had registered for VAT at the right time.

'How did you pick that up?' I asked, hoping for some pointers on how to verify VAT registration dates.

'Can't remember exactly. It was several years ago, but it was to do with the bankings.'

Niall related how one thing had led to another like dominoes falling and it ended up with the fraud squad investigating. They discovered that the couple had set up several other catering equipment companies which had charged their customers the VAT, but then closed the companies down without handing over the VAT to Customs & Excise.

'What happened to them?'

'Well apparently the wife broke down in tears in court and they both pleaded guilty to the fraud, but the judge went full psycho on them. He told them they were cheats who'd abused the tax system by deliberately stealing public money. They were both sentenced to several months in prison, and ordered to pay tens of thousands of pounds in compensation. Can't remember the exact details, but they got the full whack. It was a bit of a sad case in some ways because they had three small kids. Goodness knows what happened to them while their parents were serving time.'

I made a mental note to take more care verifying VAT registration dates at new businesses, but I confess I was shocked at the severity of the sentence, particularly where there was a negative impact on the welfare of children.

△△△

Several weeks later I found myself joining a senior officer on a visit to a large manufacturer of moulding tools. I met Donna at the trader's premises in Sutton Coldfield, and like many visits, it turned out to be uneventful. We only found a fairly small assessment of around £2000 for the VAT due on the sale of an asset which we discovered when checking the sequence numbers of sales invoices - one was missing. When the sales clerk located it, for some reason it hadn't gone through the ledger and no VAT had been paid over to Customs and Excise.

Donna invited me to drive back to her house in Water Orton for a cuppa before my long journey home to Redditch. While we sipped our tea and nibbled Garibaldis I asked her if she'd ever been a witness at a VAT Tribunal and she told me that a few years back she'd been involved in a case where her findings on a VAT visit had indeed led to a VAT tribunal.

The case involved a trader who owned more than one company. While there was nothing wrong with that in itself, Donna explained, in this particular case, one of his companies had been formed in order to evade paying VAT.

'The trader had artificially separated his business activities and formed another company within the Group. It was a big plumbing and heating firm working for industrial businesses. But they began expanding to do work for upmarket private homes and mansions, and rather than put all the sales through the existing business they started a new company that they didn't register for VAT. It was sneaky because they didn't have to charge VAT to customers that aren't registered for VAT. So it was classed as fraud,' explained Donna.

'Golly, no one's ever mentioned that scenario to me, I wonder if I've missed anything?' I confessed, 'how did you pick it up?'

'It was because they'd claimed the VAT back on radiators for domestic homes through the main business, but when I tried to trace the purchase through to sales, that's when I discovered they'd set up a separate business, even though they tried to say the radiators were for small industrial units.'

'What was it like being a witness at a Tribunal?'

'Well, it was all very official. And a bit intimidating I must say. The barrister working for us gave his opening statement, and then the trader's barrister gave a statement, and at one point I remember we were all sworn in. I was the only witness for Customs. I was petrified, but I needn't have worried because I was thoroughly prepared with my evidence and able to back up all my figures. That's the key thing if you ever get called as a witness - make sure you can support your assessment and pay attention to detail because the burden of proof is always on us.'

'Did you win?'

'We did, yes, but I had a gruelling six-week wait before the judge issued the written decision. I hope I'm never called to give evidence again, to be honest - it's too nerve-racking, even though my Surveyor backed me up and helped me write the witness statement.'

Me: decides to keep more detailed notes in my notebook from now on.

'Mind you, we don't always win,' continued Donna as she poured another cup of tea, 'has anyone ever told you about the ridiculous saga of the restaurateur who won his Tribunal case because the evidence from Customs and Excise was so pathetic?'

'No. Never heard anything about that, what happened?'

'Well, it was back in the days when some VAT officers could get a bit of a bob on themselves. You know, the jobsworth types. I honestly don't think it would happen today,' she said munching a Garibaldi, 'we're much more evidence-based these days......'

......Donna went on to tell me about a Tribunal case in the late 70s involving a restaurateur on the south coast who was issued with an assessment for several thousand pounds for suppressing his restaurant sales. She couldn't remember the exact details, but basically, Customs and Excise lost the case because their evidence was so feeble and fanciful. The 'evidence' was a concoction of complex columns of figures showing the mark-up on dozens of items of food and drink served in the restaurant. These figures were so detailed that they included ludicrous items such as how many prawns were put into a vol-au-vent, how many portions of carrots were served from a tin, and how many peas were dished up in a portion....and then there was the issue of wastage from the fat trimmed off the steaks.

The trader won his case, Donna said, because the VAT

inspector failed to take into account that a tin of carrots contained several fluid ounces of liquid.

'And you'll never guess what?'

Me: casts a quizzical sideways glance to Donna.

'The court had to be adjourned because the VAT officer insisted on getting a tin opener and a tin of said carrots to satisfy himself that just under half the contents of the tin was fluid.'

'No way! You're having me on!'

'Nope, the whole thing turned into a farce and the Department were criticised by the judge for being legalistic and pedantic, and the trader's MP slammed Customs & Excise for adopting a Soviet-style manner of inquisition which smacked of tyranny.'

We both burst out laughing at the language she used to describe the Department we worked for. Thank goodness it wasn't like that anymore……

PART TWO – IT SHOULDN'T HAPPEN TO A VAT INSPECTOR

'In this world nothing can be said to be certain,
except death and taxes.'

Benjamin Franklin

18. IT SHOULDN'T HAPPEN TO A VAT INSPECTOR

One bright but bitterly cold and windy April morning I had a glazier to visit. I wouldn't have been surprised if the business had been called 'Glaze-Rite' but it was called ClearGlaze instead. It was a partnership - two brothers with a small glazing firm in Ward End. They were trading from rather rundown premises on the corner of a row of shops. The turnover was mediocre and their last visit was nearly five years ago. I'd read the previous officer's report and it was all good.

On arrival at the premises, it was clear I was an unwelcome visitor. It was my first experience of encountering overt hostility where I was greeted with suspicion and dislike. I knew VAT inspectors were generally despised (who likes a VAT inspector?), but up until this visit, the reception I'd had from traders was generally very welcoming.

At ClearGlaze I sensed I was perceived as an impostor. The trader was unresponsive during the interview (not that that was anything unusual due to my abysmal interviewing technique), and I was shown upstairs into a cold cubbyhole of a room to inspect the business records and accounts. It resembled an interrogation cell for criminals. It was poorly lit with a single low wattage bulb flickering above a small table, a hard chair, and oddly - despite the trader being a glazier - the room had a broken window from which gusts of freezing wind blew in. This pattern of behaviour with traders was becoming commonplace: the plumber's toilet plumbed up in the air, the stale curdled milk at a milkman's house and now a broken window at a glazier? *What is it with these traders? Can't they appropriate the skills and victuals of their own businesses?*

It took me three lingering hours to go through the accounts and I stuck it out, doggedly completing all the necessary checks. I kept my gloves on as much as I could, but using a calculator in gloves is impossible, so my right hand got chilled to the bone. I'd never been so cold in all my born days. Misty vapour from my breath condensed onto the end of my nose, which dripped onto my notebook if I wasn't quick enough to catch the drips on the back of my hand.

By the time I'd completed the visit, I was chock-a-block with cold, had a headache from eyestrain, and was desperately thirsty as no drink had been offered during the inspection. I never took drinks with me on visits - there wasn't any need normally. I sensed I'd been deliberately placed in an uncomfortable room as some kind of ploy to literally freeze me out. *Why are they doing this to me? Do they want me to rush through the visit and so overlook some vital mistake?*

I never found any errors or anything suspicious. All the audit trails matched up and there wasn't a banking out of place. I felt sure I'd missed something but I had no idea how I could undertake any credibility checks to assess for cash jobs. I knew they might be doing the odd cash job but the records and accounts betrayed nothing. As Kay had taught me, a clever trader will suppress purchases to match suppressed sales, and the purchase of glass to sales all looked good. I strongly suspected that the trader might have an unrecorded bank account for cash jobs, but I couldn't prove it. So all I could do was pack up, take my leave and move on.......all in a day's work. And the lack of refreshment meant I didn't even need the loo.

I informed the trader everything was in order and left. Stepping outside after being cooped up in the dim room, I was blinded by the yellow-white sheet of sunlight which for a moment blurred the street into a hazy mirage, and I had to cover my eyes with my hand until they adjusted to the brilliant sunshine. It was warmer outside than it was in the draughty room and I basked for several moments in the April sun before driving home with the heating full on. Parched and famished, and to cheer myself up after such a horrible visit, I decided I'd go to the shopping mall in Redditch. I could defrag and thaw out with a nice nosh up in the restaurant at Owen Owen, and offload my mild misery doing some retail therapy. I drove home along the A441 which was much prettier than the A435.

After driving through the quaint village of Alvechurch my eye caught my speedometer - I'd crept up to 60mph. It wouldn't do for a VAT inspector to get caught speeding and I slowed down. Approaching Redditch town centre, I couldn't face parking in the dark, dismal multi-storey car park where a woman had been brutally stabbed to death in 1986. I wasn't in the mood, so I decided I'd park free of charge on a side road near the town centre instead.

I'd just bought myself a second-hand Maestro - all shiny and silver. It was only five years old and looked as good as new and I was well pleased with it. My old Datsun Cherry hadn't lasted very long where on my way home from work one night I'd stopped off at the garage to get a strange noise checked out,

'Drive home very, very carefully,' said the mechanic, 'the engine is hanging on a thread.'

I parked my Maestro along a pleasant street lined with trees, the young budding leaves still unfurled in rebellion against the lingering cold. After strolling about twenty metres I looked back to take a peek at my new car. But where was it? I could see a silver car like mine, but where was mine? I stopped and began walking back at a brisk pace to take a closer look, and it was there all right: but the wheel hubs had gone. Someone had stolen them. *Rotters!!* Did the trader nip out and nick them while I was tucked away upstairs inspecting his records? Or did some other despot in Ward End nab them? I would never know and there was nothing I could do about it. As my mother would have said 'if that's all that happens to you in life, you'll get by' but I did leave a note in the trader's file advising the next visiting officer to remove their wheel hubs. I wouldn't want it to happen to another officer.

△△△

As for tricks being played on VAT inspectors one of the most bizarre things I ever encountered when I worked for Customs & Excise was not on a VAT visit at all. It happened when I was leaving work one Friday afternoon after an 'office day.' I was laden down with my handbag, briefcase and several VAT files under my arm and as I made my way down the steps at the back of the office into the staff car park, I was stopped dead in my tracks.

In the middle of the step below was a pile of excreta that had been deposited spherically like the top of a giant cupcake (I kid you not!). I stood and stared at it for several seconds, my right foot suspended over it in mid-air. I was trying to work out what kind of creature could deposit such a vast turd and decided it could be neither human nor beast, but rather some grumpy trader had deliberately planted it there as revenge (using a giant piping bag maybe?) so that some unsuspecting VAT inspector would put their foot in it. Good job I spotted it in time. I wonder if they were watching from a distance?

19. COMPUTERS AND DOGS

C ustoms & Excise were slow at becoming computerised. It wasn't until the beginning of the '90s that officers were issued with primitive bulky laptops on which to write up reports - and only then if they wanted one. I once accompanied a senior officer to a large corporate manufacturing business in Birmingham and after we'd inspected the factory floor, the Accounts Manager proudly showed us the many different computers in his accounts department with much enthusiasm and delight, including one in particular which could communicate with their other offices by 'electronic mail'. He told us this would be the future of all correspondence, prophesying that even VAT returns would one day be submitted by 'email'. My colleague shot me a discreet glance that said 'he's off his rocker' and we both thought the Accounts Manager was talking poppycock. How wrong we were.

Many traders were ahead of Customs & Excise with technology, and even small businesses were beginning to use computerised records in the late 80s. A popular accounting software programme was called 'SAGE' which was liked and respected by VAT inspectors because it was well designed with good audit trails.

One soggy September morning, the sort where the smell of wet wool lingered in the air, I visited a small removal company - a husband and wife partnership - called MoveRite! (complete with exclamation mark). Mrs Hamilton kept the business accounts for which she was paid a small wage, while her husband did the removals with the aid of one employee. It was registered from their home address in Great Barr, and when I arrived I had a warm welcome from Mrs Hamilton who showed me into a bright, cosy kitchen diner, which housed many attractive plants, and where the accounts were neatly piled up on a table ready for my inspection. I conducted the interview in my usual wooden manner, concluding with questions about her accounting system. Mrs Hamilton told me that in the past nine months she'd switched to using a computer for accounting purposes,

'What software do you use?' I asked.

'I 'ave 'usband,' came the swift response (I kid you not!)

Now, there are times on VAT visits when not even the interviewing skills of Robin Day or Jeremy Paxman could extrapolate the right answers. I wasn't quite sure how to come back at her and was momentarily speechless. *Should I laugh? Is she joking?* But she appeared to be deadly serious in her answer: there was not a smirk or any indication she'd deliberately answered the question in a manner that had meant to be funny. So I decided to move swiftly on, and try a different tack,

'Erm, so what's the name of the computer you use?' Technically the computer was the 'hardware', but I decided to avoid the word 'hardware' with Mrs Hamilton, and eventually managed to establish she was using SAGE software for accounting purposes. I commenced the inspection and she disappeared into the kitchen to make some tea. Returning with a steaming brew she said she was cooking a 'little bit of breakfast' and would I like some?

'Thank you, yes that would be very nice if it's no trouble,' grateful for the offer because as usual I'd not had anything to eat and was hungry. Twenty minutes later the most delicious breakfast arrived with perfectly cooked eggs, bacon, sausages, mushrooms, tomatoes, beans, and hot buttered toast. I'd never had such a beautifully prepared breakfast banquet.

Near the end of the visit, Mrs Hamilton brought another cuppa and a plate of biscuits,

'Our dog needs a piddle, do you mind if I let him out through here? He doesn't bite.'

Now - unlike some of my colleagues - I'd never had any issues with dogs at traders at all. This was the first trader I'd visited who'd even had a dog - or at least required it to enter my presence.

'Of course,' I lied, having been bitten on the backside by an Alsatian once. She disappeared out the back to release the dog for its toilet break and the sounds of angry vicious growls, barks and snarls came nearer and nearer……I braced myself grabbing my briefcase as protection as Mrs Hamilton came back into the room with a small pug dancing angrily round her legs, barking at her and making his protestations.

'He won't hurt you luv,' Mrs Hamilton reassured me, 'it's me he's mad at for abandoning him and leavin' him shut up in the back room. Behave yerself, Dennis! Stop it you daft apeth!' She let the dog out where it promptly forgot its wrath and frantically sniffed the lawn for that special spot to relieve itself.   An involuntary laugh escaped,

'Well I've never seen anything like that before - he never even noticed me,' I remarked, 'he really was furious with you.'

'I know, he's as daft as a brush really, terrible as a guard dog he is.'

Just as well - good job Dennis wasn't an Alsatian.

△△△

Later that week I picked up a letter from the Assistant Collector out of my pigeon hole dated 25 September 1989:

"Dear Dawn,

I am pleased to inform you that your appointment in the grade of Executive Officer has been confirmed, following satisfactory completion of the period of probation.

I would like to take this opportunity to wish you every success in your future career with the Department.

Yours sincerely ......"

It was reassuring to know that my appointment had been confirmed - a permanent post. My starting salary as an Executive Officer was £8907 (just £1093 short of that magic £10,000 a year salary we all craved in the 80s). My status was no longer 'unestablished' - it was now 'established'. Even if I married and had children, maternity rights in the Civil Service were sound, and women's jobs were secure for those with families. The 'Marriage Bar' (which had demanded that single women resign from their posts when they married, and prevented married women from applying for vacancies) had been abolished in the Civil Service on 15 October 1946.

Raising the Marriage Bar, Cartoon from Red Tape Magazine, 1946

I now had a job where I could rise in the ranks until I retired at the age of 60. For a few fleeting moments, I pondered on the year 2019 - my retirement milestone. Where would I be? What would I be doing? Would I still be alive? I was brought back to the present by Kay,

'Would you like pineapple cream Dawn?'

20. SPOTTING THE DIFFERENCE

New Decade

1989 drifted into 1990 like a damp squib and a sense of foreboding hovered over the Civil Service; the 1980s spending party had come to an end and the champagne fountain of wealth was drying up. The bottle was empty and there was nothing to trickle down to us at the bottom of the pile. And it wasn't just the Civil Service, everyone was feeling it. Inflation was soaring and it was no longer possible to be in denial about it. Words such as 'cutbacks', 'cost-conscious' and 'recession' were being bandied about. The years of fiscal plenty were over. Now for the years of fiscal famine.

Not many traders were keen to have a VAT inspection over the festive season, so I went into the office and spent Twixmas drinking stale tea and catching up on casework.

All civil servants had Christmas Day, Boxing Day and New Year's Day off as paid leave, and although being single could have its advantages, over the past couple of years I'd become somewhat isolated, fuelling my natural introversion. I had no friends my own age to socialise with, and the Christmas season had been drab, with a distinct lack of hope. Even the Christmas Number One song in the charts *Do They Know It's Christmas?* by Band Aid II was depressing and disempowering. The lilting memorable chorus 'Feed…. the….. world……Let them know it's Christmastime…….' had a hollow ring to it, yet in a frenzy of truncated grief over witnessing the distressing scenes of famine on my TV I'd purchased the disc to ease my conscience a little. At least we had food on our tables.

Apart from a brief visit to see my parents and sister - who'd entertained us in spectacular style by tripping up some steps in the pub while doggedly hanging on to her glass without losing a drop of wine - I'd spent Christmas alone. The most exciting thing I'd done was to buy a 4ft plastic Christmas tree with all the trimmings from a posh garden centre in Studley on my way home from work on Christmas Eve.

I hadn't put a Christmas tree up for many years, but I'd stopped off at the garden centre to buy a Poinsettia plant and been smitten by the sparkling display of Yuletide glory in the shop foyer. I'd fallen in love with the realistic plastic foliage bedecked with baubles and pretty things - all in the traditional Christmas palette in vogue that year of red, green and gold. So I bought tree and trimmings, the lot: bows, bells, baubles and beads, and some red fairy lights.

I enjoyed a happy hour on Christmas Eve setting it all up, finishing off my tree with the beads and a big gold star on top (tinsel and fairies were out). It gave a warm, fuzzy feeling and I spent the festive season reclining on my sofa admiring it, listening to Bach Christmas Cantatas on my new CD player, sipping sherry and nibbling Wotsits and Twiglets. I felt I was going up in the world.

I loved the tree because although it was plastic it looked like a real pine tree with its mock pine needles and fronds. I was enamoured with it. I'd recently moved into a small semi-detached house which was a notch up from the first terraced house I'd bought on a council estate a few miles away. Although it was only a glorified two up two down, the previous owners had kitted it all out in 'olde worlde' style with white artexed walls and black wooden beams strewn across the ceiling and walls. It resembled a cosy old cottage. There was even a realistic electric log fire to top it all off which glowed orange and red, set into an olde worlde fireplace. But it was all fake. Fake black beams. Fake log fire. Fake fireplace. Fake Christmas tree. Still, I liked it and was well pleased with it all. The new decade seemed full of promise despite a lacklustre atmosphere.

So it was with a spring in my step that I did my first VAT visit of the new year on Tuesday 2nd January 1990. It was a glorious morning, bright and sharp with cold like a dagger stinging the eyes and nostrils. I was visiting a new business called GlamourPuss Ltd where a Mr & Mrs Pendleton were the directors. They'd only been trading for just over 12 months, but the visit had flagged up because they hadn't paid Customs & Excise a penny in output tax, yet the business had reclaimed over £40,000 VAT in input tax, so it was down to me to see if this was all legitimate. The figures on the D1507 print-out painted something of a puzzle, so I was sent to check out what was going on.

The business was registered from a private home and the address wasn't too far from the Chester Road in posh 'Royal' Sutton Coldfield. I pulled up outside a very smart detached house set back off the road. Turning into the large drive I poodled up in my Maestro and parked next to a Porsche. I made my way gingerly along the icy path in my stilettos, trying to balance my heavy briefcase. I climbed up three wide semi-circular steps embracing a wide front door that opened as if by magic where Mrs Pendleton stood to greet me. She was young and elegantly dressed in a flowing kimono.

'Miss Smith from Custom & Excise,' I said slightly breathless from the effort of trying not to go a pearler. She smiled broadly and put out her hand for me to shake,

'I'm Carrie one of the directors, come on in,' inviting me into a palatial hallway where a grand staircase opened up and out like a fan.

To the left of the staircase was an immense and magnificent real Christmas tree about 10ft tall, fabulously adorned with turquoise, silver and white trimmings, glowing with myriads of soft white fairy lights. I felt a pang of something. It was hard to know what the pang was - a strange mixture of feeling vaguely puerile, and an unrealistic sense of shame at the fatuous pleasure I'd had with my mock tree and mock home, all of which seemed rather pathetic compared to the scene before me.

I was shown into a spacious lounge, radiant with yet another resplendent Christmas tree. And a real log fire, warm and glowing, with glorious patio doors heralding a garden the size of a small park. I'd never been in such a grand dwelling before. I sat at the end of a vast shiny marble dining table where all the records and accounts were neatly placed ready for my inspection. I conducted my 'interview' with Mrs Pendleton in my usual stilted style, made worse by the fact I had to probe a bit deeper with this trader.

It was true to say that after spending over a year in the Training District I'd imbibed the VAT inspector's suspicious mind, yet it was at war with my innate desire to believe that all traders were good, honest citizens. The end product of this inner dissonance was a diffidence in my interview technique. I felt a sense of unrealistic guilt - as if I was prying into the trader's private business affairs - even though the powers in my 'Commission' gave me every right to do so. And although I had a natural tendency to be a nosey parker, I was more of a secret rummager than a detective who would ask pertinent questions.

But there were two moments in the interview which registered as a bit 'off', though I couldn't quite put my finger on what it was. I'd probed about the sales not generating any output tax and the simple answer was that all the goods sold were exported to South Africa, and therefore were zero-rated for VAT. *Exports?* A shimmer of a shiver passed over me. I knew nothing about exports or export evidence.

Certain words in VAT control work seemed to have that shiver effect, giving me the jitters. Words such as 'Disbursements', 'Reverse Charges', 'Self-Billing' and even 'Credit Notes'. They all set off a nervous edge, presenting dodgy areas where traders could get things wrong, either deliberately or innocently. And I lacked faith in my detective abilities to ferret out mistakes. What if I missed something big?

Then when I'd asked about stock, where it was kept and could I inspect it, I instinctively felt something was adrift in the reply,

'We don't really keep stock. We're using our double garage for now if we do store anything until we buy warehouse premises. We haven't got any stock at the moment, it's all been shipped abroad.'

She looked me straight in the eyes and smiled. *I wonder if I could start up my own export beauty business, make a bomb and live in a nice posh house with a Porsche?*

She brought me a cup of freshly ground coffee presented in an elegant cafetière along with a plate of Bahlsen biscuits and left me to it.

I dug out my VAT leaflet on exports from my briefcase. We always carried certain core leaflets with us, along with our two volumes of VAT Law. Exports were one such leaflet - just in case. I decided to start my inspection by getting to grips with the export evidence. But how could a piece of paper truly confirm that certain goods had left the UK, arrived in a foreign country and were correctly zero-rated for VAT purposes?

I began by examining the export invoices which all seemed good. They were very nicely produced documents on good quality headed paper with all the required legal information, stating shipping method, port of loading and final destination, and these were backed up by 'Pro Forma' invoices. But that was where the audit trail seemed to end. How could I be sure that the goods had left Birmingham and ended up in South Africa by a shipment from Dover to Port Elizabeth?

I got up to call Mrs Pendleton. *Crikey, I should have asked these questions half an hour ago.* I sighed at my incompetence as I popped my head around the door,

'Hello-o!!!' I called. Opposite me was a marble sideboard sporting several beautifully framed photos, and on the wall above was an enormous black and white print of the Pendletons on their wedding day, posing under a blossom tree - a very handsome couple.

Carrie appeared with a tiny fluffy dog in her arms which emitted a sweet little growl at the sight of me, baring its tiny teeth like a row of white needles.

'I'm sorry to trouble you, but I need to ask a few more questions about the export documentation.' We went back into the lounge, 'it's about the export evidence. Do you have any seaway bills or certificates of shipments to prove the goods have left the UK?'

Carrie shook her head, 'I'm afraid my husband deals with all those sorts of things, but he's up north at the moment. I don't have anything to do with that side of the business, I just do all the buying.'

'Well, do you have any supplementary evidence or documents to show the transaction has taken place at all, such as customer order, or sales contract?

'No, sorry.'

'I notice that on your export invoices there aren't any order reference numbers?'

'Mark deals with all the sales side. We're still in the process of setting up the business, but I'm sure he can sort that out.'

'How about customer correspondence or advice notes or packing lists?'

'No, sorry, that's all I've got.' She pointed to the files on the table, revealing a beautifully manicured bright pink nail. The little dog gave another sweet little growl.

'Do you use a freight agent?'

'Erm..... I don't know. No, I don't think so. Well, I'm not really sure. Mark will know but he's up north and won't be back until Friday.'

'OK, well not to worry. I'll just have to do a return visit to verify the export evidence when he's back. It's just that without satisfactory evidence of export the business will become liable for the VAT due, but I'm sure it can all be resolved,' I smiled, in an attempt to diffuse any tension. *Haven't they read the VAT leaflet on exports?*

'I'll just carry on for now - it shouldn't take me too long as there are only four quarters to check.'

'Would you like another coffee?'

'Oooh yes please, that would be lovely.'

I carried on with my checks examining the Sales Day Book and Purchase Day Book which all matched the figures on the VAT return, though the bank statements didn't reflect any income from foreign currencies. But what did I know about such things? There were no Annual Accounts either because the business hadn't been trading long enough and they hadn't even appointed an accountant. There wasn't a lot to check, unlike some visits which seemed swamped under a quagmire of accounting records and documents.

GlamourPuss only used two suppliers to buy beauty goods from, but the invoices from one of them caught my eye because there was something 'arse about face' about them. But what was it that was bugging me about the invoices? I took a second, third and fourth look and then I clocked what it was. GlamourPuss had bought hair styling products from a company called 'Style Rite' - just four invoices, one each quarter, reclaiming over £15,000 in VAT in input tax.

On the surface, the purchase invoices looked good. They were very professionally produced and printed in colour on good quality paper, with all the required legal elements but the VAT registration number of Style Rite began with the digit 112. Now, to the uninitiated, the first three numbers of a VAT registration number would be meaningless, but a VAT officer would know that a VAT number beginning with 112 indicated the company had been trading for a long time - probably from the 1970s. Yet the company name 'Style Rite' had a late 80s ring to it, though it's possible that the company might have changed its trading name. Nevertheless, I made a note of the VAT registration number, including the company number, to check it out later back at the office.

The other purchase invoices - for makeup and cosmetics - seemed good but I made a note of the details anyway, just in case I was missing something. I packed away all my gear, slurped down the last of my delicious coffee and called Mrs Pendleton again, who came with the cute pooch in her arms, which growled at me sweetly once more.

'I've finished now, but rather than do a return visit I'll take all these export invoices back to the office with me - here's a receipt for them, and then your husband can send me the necessary export evidence when he gets back, and I'll marry them up at the office, and I'll let you know when they can be collected.'

'Oh, okay, I'll let him know.' I was certain her face turned a slight shade of red.

'I'll write and let you know what documentation I need to be sent in. Thank you very much for the coffee, and you should receive a letter in the next week or so.' I didn't mention the issue of the dodgy purchase invoices from Style Rite so as not to spook the trader any further. I'd check the details out at the office first. I might be up a gum tree about it and didn't want egg on my face.

On Friday that week, I mentioned to Kay my concerns, and she told me to pop down to Registration District to check out the VAT registration number of Style Rite. My suspicions were confirmed: Style Rite didn't exist. The invoices were fake with a fake VAT registration number. Kay told me to put it all in the hands of the fraud squad. They had a small office down the corridor, with five guys working as a team, and I visited them.

The fraud office was one section of the LVO that was all-male, and they seemed quite a different animal to the rest of us VAT inspectors, but they were always very helpful and willing to assist with any concerns. I explained to Rhys, one of the Executive Officers, what I'd found and he took the whole matter out of my hands, export evidence and all, and I had no further dealings with GlamourPuss Ltd. Not that I was sorry - confrontation wasn't my thing. They would investigate they said, 'leave it with us.'

△△△

It was less than a month later that I came across another business where there was something very wrong, but couldn't quite work out what it was at the time. January was nearly over and that year it had felt strange: it was like being in limbo between years, seasons, past and future. And it was cold. Always so very cold. The frosts in Redditch had been ferocious most mornings, and I'd had to get up extra early to scrape off the ice from my windscreen. The frosts caused the A435 out of Redditch into Birmingham to be treacherous, often causing accidents early in the mornings. On the day of my visit, there'd been a very bad accident so the road was still blocked when I left home at 8.30 am.

I was visiting a building firm in Lichfield, a pleasant city on the very outskirts of Birmingham North LVO. It was nearly an 80 mile round trip from Redditch and due to the accident, I arrived 20 minutes late.

I liked Lichfield. To me, it seemed to be a city in the country with a unique sense of history, and I developed something of an emotional connection with it. I could have happily lived there. Plus it was a good number for my Travel and Subsistence claim form - a couple of visits to Lichfield each month was an extra £25 or so in my pocket at least.

The premises were located in a small office above an estate agent, and Mr Jackson - one of the directors - was waiting for me as I climbed the stairs. I didn't even need to introduce myself,

'Come on in, come in and take a seat. I've got everything ready for you right here. Would you like a drink?' He was a small, rotund man, with round glasses, and a round cropped hairstyle. He would have made a good monk. He exuded a jolly, avuncular aura, shaking my hand firmly bobbing it up and down for several long seconds.

'Maybe in a moment,' I responded, my voice shaking in tandem with my hand, 'I just need to ask a few questions before I look at the records?' I intoned my remark as a question, hoping it sounded more friendly.

I got out my notebook and began my interview, doggedly working my way through my list of questions to establish all the usual facts, and probe about the business accounts and how it was run. It had been trading just over five years and at the last inspection - nearly four years previously - the visiting officer had found several errors where Mr Jackson had reclaimed VAT on entertaining business customers, which had to be disallowed. He'd also claimed VAT on all his rail fares, but rail fares were zero-rated, so that had to be disallowed as well. Otherwise, it all seemed good. As I ploughed through the purchase invoices most of them were for building supplies, which was to be expected, and they all appeared to meet the legal requirements.

However, there were three from a consultancy firm in Doncaster called DonCon Ltd which flagged up a little blue light and at first I had no idea why. Mr Jackson had reclaimed over £5,000 in input tax from them over the past two years - not a huge amount - but why were they bothering me? They all looked fine and nicely printed with everything in order. I homed in on the itemised fees on DonCon Ltd's invoice to Mr Jackson -

    Consultancy Fee (plus VAT)   £3000
    Travelling Expenses (Rail 0% VAT)   £105
    Hotel Accommodations (plus VAT)   £300

......and it was the zero-rated VAT on the rail fare under 'Travelling Expenses' which jangled a bell, though it seemed a logical thing for the consultancy firm to do - after all, rail fares were indeed zero-rated. Passengers didn't have to pay VAT on rail fares. So why charge VAT on rail fares when recharging them to customers? But human memory can have an amazing capacity at times and something from my training course bounced up, and then I remembered: it was a curious thing about travel costs for firms like DonCon Ltd that no VAT could be reclaimed on rail or air fares because they were zero-rated, but when these expenses were recharged to clients VAT had to be charged at the standard rate because the travel had been 'consumed' by the consultant. Another 'arse about face' issue. When is a zero-rated supply not a zero-rated supply? Answer: When it has been consumed and recharged to one's customer.

Maybe that's why I remembered it. The curiosity factor

about the complexities, quirks, whims and fancies of UK Value Added Tax sometimes came in very handy. *Surely any consultancy firm worth its salt would get the VAT liability of recharges right?* I made a note of DonCon's details to alert the Doncaster VAT office about the error. They would need to send out an inspector to investigate. If it was a big consultancy firm that was failing to account for VAT on hundreds of pounds worth of recharged rail fares, then it could amount to quite a sizeable sum of underpaid VAT.

I continued scrutinising the purchase invoices for building supplies where tens of thousands of pounds of VAT had been reclaimed for new builds. It was a laborious task, but made a bit more exciting when I found several amounts of VAT, just over £10,000, had been reclaimed twice on the same supplies - once on actual invoices, and then again on 'Statements.' I also found that VAT had been reclaimed on insurance which I had to disallow because insurance was exempt from VAT. At least I'd found a decent under-declaration.

It seemed Mr Jackson had learnt his lesson from his previous VAT visit and no VAT had been reclaimed on business entertaining or rail fares. Even so, the responsibility of checking these figures and documents made me go a bit funny in my tummy - what if I'd missed something? How could I possibly verify everything? The Annual Accounts all looked credible, but it was at times like this when the weight of my inexperience felt very heavy.

At the end of the visit in the washing-up session I broke the bad news to Mr Jackson about disallowing the double portions of VAT he'd claimed on the statements, and also the VAT on insurance totalling £15,000. He took it well I thought. He had what my father would have called 'a bit of a bob on himself' but he was very polite, chirpy and upbeat, often cracking jokes with his typist who sat tapping away at the desk opposite me, and who kept me topped up with tea and biscuits throughout the visit.

I'd been unsure whether to mention the DonCon Ltd

invoices, but in the end, I decided not to mention them. After all, it wasn't Mr Jackson's fault the consultancy firm had made an error. I packed up all my gear and left, and on Friday that week on my office day, I alerted Doncaster LVO to investigate the rail recharges at DonCon Ltd and left it at that.

△△△

Some months later one Friday lunchtime I was in the large Tesco supermarket beneath our VAT offices with my arms full of tins of beans and packets of pasta, and I was trying to find where I'd left my shopping trolley. I thought I'd left it by the biscuits, but it wasn't there, so I marched round to the crisps aisle but it wasn't there either. *Where the heck I have left it?* After wandering up and down the store I eventually found it at the end of the drinks aisle, plonked my heavy load in the trolley, and then went off to get some cereals.

With my arms full of boxes of cornflakes, bran flakes and rice pops, plus a bag of cat litter I'd picked up along the way, with a bottle of washing up liquid, a bottle of bleach and a bag of rice balancing on the top, I made my way back through the drinks aisle and dumped it all in the trolley just in time - any longer and it would have all gone crashing to the floor. *Why the heck don't I take my trolley around with me?* So I pushed my trolley up the drinks aisle towards the cheese counter, and bumped into Rhys from the fraud squad, doing his weekly shop.

'Hey Dawn! How's things? Stocking up on your weekly quota of vodka and gin then?' he teased.

'One trolley wouldn't be enough!' I teased back, 'so are you on the lookout for duty-free bottles stashed away in the aisles then?'

'No joke - we've had a run of them would you believe. Several pubs in the city have been found out, we've had to get Customs involved.'

'Any news about that GlamourPuss case?'

'Yeah, they printed fake purchase invoices for the hair products, and printed fake export sales invoices for the beauty products.'

'No way! When is an export not an export eh?'

'In this case when it gets no farther than Milton Keynes.'

'Oooh, a bit naughty that! And I thought butter wouldn't melt.'

'By the way, I see that you visited J&J Builders, his file landed on my desk several weeks ago.'

'Yeah? What about him?'

'Well, turns out that consultancy firm you raised the alarm about was a fake company with puppet directors. Your discovery has launched a big investigation into his whole business shebang.'

'Crikey! Who'd have thought it.'

'Yeah, and to cut a long story short, Jackson had set up two other bogus companies that he'd claimed input tax on, but no transactions had ever taken place. It's all fake, a real can of worms. We'll have a ball with that one.'

'The naughty man! Yet he was so nice and respectable. How do they think they can get away with it?'

'You'd be surprised what some people will try on. Sometimes we never catch them - they de-register soon after the scam and disappear, but others keep trying it on for several years in the hope they'll never get caught. All for making illegal profits.'

'The barefaced gall of it.'

'Well done anyway, not bad for a fresher Dawn, keep up the good work, and don't drink too much gin this weekend! See you around!'

Well, stone the crows......maybe I'm not too bad as a VAT sleuth after all.

21. LEARNING CURVE

By the time I'd spent nearly 18 months in the Training District I'd visited a diverse range of businesses including civil engineers (though I never quite discovered exactly what they did), hairdressers (sometimes tricky because they rented out 'chairs'), chemists (very tricky), accountants, solicitors (interesting), schools (quirky from a VAT angle), vets, garages, skip hire firms, rag and bone yards (can of worms), taxi firms, coach hire firms, property companies (more worms because it often involved something called 'Partial Exemption' - an area of VAT which caused a cold sweat to break out in even the most experienced VAT inspector), tour operators (more cold sweat trying to suss out the 'Tour Operators Margin Scheme'), and construction companies (even more cold sweat as it could involve Reverse Charges and Self-Billing for VAT purposes).

I also picked up in Training that there was a sort of coded language which VAT inspectors used with traders, a form of unwritten speech, and we soon grasped the VAT lingo when communicating certain things to traders, such as…..

'You might wish to discuss it with your accountant,' which was code for 'I've got to send you an assessment, but I feel really bad about it.'

Or….. 'I'm a little bit concerned about your mark-up,' which was code for 'I think you're on the fiddle.'

Another phrase was 'there's an appeals procedure you can use,' which was our code to cover ourselves when we'd found a possible under-declaration of VAT which was speculative and what we really meant was 'my assessment will be based on hypothetical figures, but I'm behind with my targets so I'm desperate.'

Another was 'I'm really sorry to trouble you, but there's a bit of a problem,' which was our way of saying 'you owe us a lot of money,' ...and so on. We were learning the art of public relations I guess, who knows.

During training, I once did a VAT visit to a sort of pyramid business that involved party plan sellers for perfume and cosmetics and it was registered from a home address not far from Spaghetti Junction.

It was mid-September and the schools were back, and term-time traffic increased my journey by 40 minutes. I'd only got lost once, and nearly collided with a lorry when I emerged from an underpass at Smallbrook Queensway, but apart from that, the journey was straightforward. There was even a parking space outside the house, and after several embarrassing attempts trying to reverse into the slot, I managed to get my car tucked in between a dilapidated van and a rusty old Land Rover. I was sweating profusely with the exertion of my poor parking skills, and I desperately hoped that my wheel hubs would be intact when I returned at the end of the visit.

Mrs Primrose Wells was the sole proprietor of her business trading from a small terraced property. The tiny garden was overgrown with weeds and Russian Vine which covered most of the front window. I rang the bell and a lady in an unflattering tracksuit answered the door,

'I'm Miss Smith from Customs and Excise, I've got an appointment with a Mrs Wells?'

'That's me luvvie, come on in.'

Now I confess that the name 'Primrose' had conjured up in my mind someone who might have walked off the set of *Dallas*, but in reality, Mrs Wells was quite the opposite of that image. The incongruity lingered as she showed me into the front room, which was full of untidy plants, some half dead. And cats. Lots of cats. There were cats on the sofa, cats on the bookcase, cats on the windowsill, cats on the armchair, and a cat on the table where the accounts were.

The room was dark and dank - the Russian Vine outside had blocked out most of the natural light. Even though it was a bright sunny day Mrs Wells had to put the light on. The dull 40-watt bulb gave the room an eerie greenish glow. It was grim.

'Let me make a cuppa and I'll come back and show you the books luvvie, tea or coffee?'

'Tea please, milk no sugar, thank you very much.'

I was not gifted in the area of logic, and to this end, I struggled with the concept of a pyramid business and was immediately out of my depth with the inspection. I extracted all the information I could out of Mrs Wells during my 'interview' and settled down to inspect the accounts, not really knowing exactly what areas of risk I should be looking for.

Mrs Wells disappeared out the back, where the sound of a TV in another room dulled as she closed the door.

As I was jotting down some notes, a cat plonked itself on my notebook (as they do). We stared at each other for a few moments. I tugged at my notebook to shoo it off. A bad idea, as the cat thought I was playing games and its claws fanned out in a flash hooking my right thumb, drawing blood. It then departed by turning its back on me - arse about face - with a flick of its tail, victorious, and leaving the telltale signs of fleas on the pages of my notebook: tiny black specks - flea droppings. I began to itch. All over.

To distract myself from the itching, I tried to get to grips with the concept of the business and how it operated. I'd established during my interview that Mrs Wells, as the 'representative', earned commission and margin from sales, and also from recruiting other agents. I got bogged down trying to identify the contractual relationships but decided that Mrs Wells seemed to be on the ball and knew what she was doing. She told me that she didn't give any parties herself (just as well I thought, as it wasn't the most welcoming of places for a party) but she did attend the parties of her 'hostesses' as an 'organiser'. She blinded me with numerical science about how she calculated the VAT on goods at reduced prices for the hostesses and talked about cash commissions. I was completely bamboozled by it all. I have to confess it was one of those visits I hadn't got the mental energy or technical ability to go into much detail, and in the end, I trusted my instinct that the trader knew what they were doing.

I was glad when the visit was over, and I winged it in my report. Lord knows if I missed anything big, but at least my wheel hubs were still in place.

△△△

Visits to farmers were always a bit of a treat involving a pleasurable drive into the country, conducted in homely farm kitchens usually accompanied by home-baked cakes. All except one that is, when I visited an arable farm perched in a far-flung corner of our LVO.

I'd taken joy in motoring along country lanes once I'd passed suburbia; this was the kind of driving I loved best - windows down, drinking in the outstanding natural beauty, whiffing the cow dung being carried on the warm, southerly October breeze, listening to Bach Brandenburg Concertos on my cassette player in the car.

The previous visiting officer had left a useful note in the trader's file: 'Turn right at the Pig and Whistle pub, carry on for about a mile, the farm is at bottom of lane'. I duly followed the directions and sure enough, there was a sign 'Greendale Farm'. I drove into a large yard and parked. It was full of tractors and other farming machinery - massive motors with enormous engines. Some of them were old and derelict, and some were new and shiny and it was for this reason that Greendale Farm had flagged up for a VAT inspection because the farmer had reclaimed huge amounts of VAT on the purchase of a combine harvester and several other new tractors and machinery. It was down to me to verify that the claims were all bona fide and legitimate.

I looked for the farmhouse, but couldn't see one, and wondered if I'd missed it along the way. Then a man in dungarees and wellingtons jumped down from a tractor and came over to me. It was Mr Webster, the farmer himself. He'd been expecting me he said, and after I'd inspected the impressive array of agricultural apparatus, Mr Webster informed me that the accounts were in a caravan about half a mile away. We walked over to a small tractor where he instructed me to 'hop up, we'll be there in a jiffy.' After a bumpy journey over a farm track caked with stones and dried mud, we arrived at the caravan in the middle of nowhere. *Is this another ploy to get rid of me quickly? Another crafty ruse to freeze me out?*

There wasn't a lot to check. I'd finished the visit within an hour and a half and scrutinised all the purchase invoices for the new machinery, including the combine harvester where the farmer had claimed £9000 on that item alone. Everything had ticked all the Customs & Excise boxes and it was time to leave, but a couple of mugs of tea that the considerate farmer had poured out of a flask had run their course, and I needed the loo. The tiny, ageing caravan was basic and didn't have any toilet facilities. Mr Webster said the only place I could go was in the barn across the field as there was no loo back at the yard either. I needed to go, so had little choice but to head for the 'barn' which in reality was derelict and draughty, and more like a giant gazebo.

As I squatted to relieve myself behind a small pile of hay, I just hoped he didn't have a pair of binoculars.

△△△

On the subject of toilets, visits to small industrial units were often a hit and miss affair regarding lavatories, usually because of the lack of a regular cleaning routine. Engine oil and paraffin odours accompanied the loud mechanical hubbub, hissings and rowdy radios.

Finding somewhere clean for me to inspect the records and accounts could be a challenge for the trader, who often stuffed me up in a corner, or a greasy, untidy office. I once did a visit standing up for three hours checking the accounts on top of an oily machine. My toes were squished like sardines in my stiletto shoes as I hobbled to the loo.

Toilets at these places were always cold and draughty, even in summer, but invariably they had the joy of a cistern with a chain to pull. And one toilet even had moss growing in the bowl. I stared at it in wonder: myriads of minute, furry green shoots climbing up the sides of the pan, thriving on a diet of urine and other things.

So along with Mr Satchwell's toilet plumbed up on a podium, visits to the powder room could be a curious affair.

△△△

Performance Appraisal

My stint in Training District was coming to a close and soon I was to move on to a 'proper' District, but not before I had my first 'Performance Appraisal' with Kay. I was keen to read her report. *Just give it to me with both barrels, I can take it.*

The period of the report was from 1 January 1989 to 31 December 1989. My job title was 'Executive Officer, VAT Control' and my job purpose 'To protect the revenue'. Kay made it clear I was 'still on a learning curve' and so, on a scale of 1 to 5, my performance as a VAT Control Officer was judged:

1. Outstanding - None

2. Performance significantly above requirements - None

3. Performance fully meets normal requirements of the grade - I got nine ticks at this grade '3' for the planning of work, effective use of resources, well presented written work, numerical ability, relations with staff and traders, adaptability, plus ability to produce constructive ideas.

4. Performance not fully up to requirements, some improvement necessary - *I also got nine ticks at grade '4'. Needless to say, it included 'Oral communication' with the comment 'quiet personality - has found it difficult to interview traders'.*

Other misdemeanours were also noted by Kay:

- Makes careless errors on work returns.
- Has not always completed casework promptly.
- Needs to show that duties can be carried out without as much supervision.
- Must keep on top of casework at all times. (Oooops)

5. Unacceptable - *Fortunately, none of my work reflected this mark.*

It was noted about my performance generally that 'some good quality assessments had been issued' but that an area of weakness was my inability to bring casework to a close within a period of six weeks. My 'Forward Job Plan' made it clear that I had to complete my casework more quickly.

My 'Overall Performance' mark was a '4' with the comment *'The box 4 markings are due to her inexperience in both the grade and the job'* which was in truth a fair and accurate remark which I accepted.

The Surveyor had to countersign Kay's comments and it was good timing that Mr Pins-and-Wool-Travel-Expense-Jobsworth had by this time left to 'hang his hat on a pension', and for the past several months a new and vibrant Surveyor - Fiona - had replaced him. Fiona took a genuine interest in all the trainees. She brought something of a breath of fresh air to the Training District with a lively, effervescent personality, being a good role model, and she empowered her trainees by taking us out on the occasional VAT visit. On my staff appraisal, her evaluation of me read,

'With increased experience, Dawn's skills will develop and I have no doubt that she will become a most capable officer.'

It was a small but encouraging remark and this positive comment kept me going during the times I felt like packing it all in.

At the end of February 1990 I moved on to a 'proper' District within the same building, and a new trainee took my place as a rookie. …..pity my Performance Appraisal report had ended in December 1989. I never did get the credit for the two frauds I discovered with GlamourPuss and J&J Builders.

22. TIPPEX AND TANTRUMS

Not long after my staff appraisal report, I did a joint visit with Kay to a big civil engineering firm to reinforce my understanding of accounts at larger businesses. After we'd finished what turned out to be a very mundane visit where we didn't find a penny in under-declared tax, she invited me back to her house in Walmley for some refreshments before I headed home.

Although I never got the credit in my staff report for finding the false invoices at GlamourPuss and J&J Builders, over a cuppa and some of Kay's homemade fruit cake I got a verbal 'well done' for my powers of observation.

She then went on to tell me she also once discovered a trader forging purchase invoices in order to reclaim large amounts of VAT. He'd done it over a four year period to the tune of nearly £100,000 and Kay told me he'd used quite a different method of forgery which wasn't anywhere near as sophisticated as GlamourPuss or J&J Builders.

Kay said the methods he used were so crude that even a five-year-old would have probably spotted it and she was amazed that the trader had even attempted it. He'd simply used Tippex and a photocopier to inflate the amounts of VAT he'd claimed on the invoices.

'What happened to him?'

'I can't remember his fate apart from one of the fraud guys telling me several months later that the trader threw a tantrum in court and accused Customs and Excise of heavy-handed tactics to trap him. But it didn't do him any good, and confiscation proceedings went ahead to recover the stolen money, along with a prison sentence.'

Me: made a mental note to check more carefully for use of Tippex and photocopied invoices.

'Have you been involved in any really big fraud cases?'

Kay confirmed that in reality most officers rarely uncover any real wrongdoing, but that her husband Rob, who was also a VAT inspector, had once stumbled across a trader who'd set up a succession of fake businesses in order to reclaim large amounts of VAT using bogus invoices.

'How did he discover that?'

'I can't remember the exact details, but it was partly bad luck for the trader because Rob was sent out to visit two of the businesses within several months of each other.'

Kay went on to explain what had happened. The trader had formed a whole series of counterfeit identities for himself as the owner of more than ten different businesses - all of which he had registered for VAT. These businesses claimed to sell various goods and services ranging from gifts, make-up, jeans and T-shirts to working as designers and management consultants.

None of these businesses ever actually traded, yet they submitted VAT returns every three months deceitfully claiming back VAT allegedly paid on business expenses for the firms.

'But it was Rob's memory of the trader's hair which had a distinctive white patch in his fringe. Rob realised it was the same man but with a different name and identity.'

It turned out, Kay said, that he'd been doing this for over four years and had swindled nearly half a million pounds in false VAT claims. He was jailed and then taken back to court by Customs to confiscate his assets to recover the VAT he'd stolen.

Me: made a mental note to be more observant of identifying features when meeting traders.

23. NEW DISTRICT

As we strolled hand in hand through the field, we basked in the sensual warmth of the sun. Shimmering heat mirrored the grass caressed by a gentle breeze. We stopped in the shade of a tree and turned to face each other. Pulling me close, he leaned in to kiss me, unzipping the dress....

My alarm went off and with it the realisation that the dream showed me only one thing: I really, *really* did fancy Phil Birdwhistle.

I'd been in my new District for about six weeks and Phil was one of the senior officers. We sat opposite each other and I saw him every Friday on office days, but we rarely spoke apart from a cursory nod and a 'hello'.

He was married and we'd all been made aware that his wife wasn't well, and here I was dreaming of a romantic moment with him. How embarrassing. We both had quiet personalities, and any interaction between us was always within the group dynamics of our colleagues. I wasn't even aware I'd fancied him at all. Why was I dreaming about him? Although I enjoyed being single, my personal life had been colourless lately. Was it a Freudian hiccup? ....or maybe learning to play Chopin's tender Nocturne in C sharp minor had sparked an amorous yearning?

When I was six I'd married Dick van Dyke after seeing him in the 1965 film 'Mary Poppins'. I'd dressed up in my mother's clothes, high heels, jewellery, lipstick and all, and there, at the altar of her dressing table, me and Dick had tied the knot. My mother remembered it well - she came into the room just as we were saying our vows. Phil Birdwhistle was something of Dick van Dyke lookalike so maybe he'd triggered those childish longings, igniting the flame of desire which had oxygenated repressed lust. It was all promptly snuffed out by my embarrassment, and I hoped I'd never have a dream like that again. ….Mind you, I didn't fancy being called 'Mrs Birdwhistle' anyway.

Pushing the fantasy away, I got up, made a cup of tea and got ready for work. I was visiting a pub called The Shamrock. In my new District, I had more complex businesses to inspect, with larger turnovers.

The bitter March morning smattered the Midlands with a mantle of thin white frost. I arrived at the premises in Newtown near the city centre, but at 9.30 in the morning public houses are all double bolted and locked. It took me fifteen frosty minutes wandering around the premises knocking on every door, to get a response.

On my third attempt, a cheerful Irish man opened the bar door, and after introducing myself, he took me through to the main lounge where the miasma of stale beer and nicotine ascended from the carpet, a mass of stagnant stickiness. Mr O'Reilly, the proprietor, was a friendly Irishman and throughout the visit, I wasn't quite sure whether he was deliberately winding me up with his Irish wit.

When I asked him when his 'Financial Year End' was he replied in a lilting Irish accent, 'I'm not sure. I tink it's de tirty first of February,' completely deadpan as if he meant it. And then when I enquired about cashing up the takings he said, 'Takings? What's dem tings? I don't take nothing.'

And so it was that my interview with him wasn't very productive due to my inability to navigate his masterly responses. Not being skilled in the art of banter, I moved swiftly on to inspecting the premises - the part of the visit I liked best. VAT visits often involved looking around the 'Principal Place of Business' (PPOB for short) - unless it was a home address where there were no business premises as such.

Inspecting the premises at a pub was essential and I was on the lookout for condom machines, tampon machines, gaming machines, cigarette machines, sweet machines, jukeboxes and any other sorts of machines - all sources of VAT.

I discreetly scanned the bottles of liquor behind the bar playing a game of 'spot the difference' with my eye searching for any 'duty-free' labels which would need investigating - though in truth the only brand I could remember from training was Gordon's gin. I recalled Rhys telling me there'd been several pubs in the city caught using duty-free liquor. But I was out of luck, and the Gordon's gin bottle was all green and white like a bunch of fresh snowdrops.

Mr O'Reilly had recently taken over the pub as a 'Transfer of a Going Concern' (TOGC for short - another 'can of worms'), and this aspect only added to my inadequacy. It was an angle that would require some additional probing, though I was quite clueless about what sorts of probes I should employ and had no idea about verifying a TOGC from a VAT perspective. I'd just have to wing it.

I struggled through all the relevant checks and was at a loss how to ensure the VAT which had been paid was accurate. I needed the support of a senior officer, but there was no way I could call for assistance, I just had to battle on. There weren't even any annual accounts yet - if only an accountant had had a stab first I might have made a better job of it, and also made more sense of the TOGC.

The overall mark-up and VAT declared appeared to reflect the level of takings in such an establishment, so after 5 hours of checking as much as I could, I decided to call it a day, head for a bite to eat and kill some time in the warm city library, before attending my choir practice nearby.

I was a member of one of the prestigious city choirs where I sang 2nd soprano. We were rehearsing Beethoven's 9th - a rousing masterpiece that would clear my head and melt away the stress of my VAT incompetence.

For several weeks the choir been practising under the Chorus Master and we were all excited about performing the work with our world-famous conductor and symphony orchestra. The time had come for the renowned Maestro himself to put us through our paces before the final orchestral rehearsal, and he bounced up onto the podium, energetic with his baton in hand, conducting us with flourishes of arm and bouncy wild hair, pulling thespian faces in an attempt to milk us for musicality. It was a blast, and after belting out top A's at full volume, I was light-headed with oxygen. I could have floated up to the ceiling.

All was going well until we hit the *'Ihr Sturtz Nieder'* section and our Maestro wasn't happy,

'No, no, no, no, no,' he intoned descending in pitch, 'that's just *so* bland ladies and gentlemen. You must sing it with much more......with more......' we watched him enthralled and mesmerised waiting for him to deliver his poetic image which would elevate and transform our singing to new heights, '........to sing it like.......' his eyes hit the ceiling as he searched for the right scene, then exhaled '......like panting dogs, copulating.' *Panting dogs? Copulating?* (I kid you not!) ......*great, just what I needed to top off my inadequate VAT visit to an Irish pub.*

ΔΔΔ

For several weeks after my embarrassing dream, I found it difficult to get Phil Birdwhistle out of my mind as he randomly popped up at intermittent intervals. So I had to admit I was attracted to him. Thankfully there was nothing to suggest he was attracted to me, and even if he was, there's no way either of us would have embarked on a path to make our personal lives chaotic. A romantic dalliance with him was impossible. So I channelled my energies more and more into my artistic interests.

My personal observation and experience of relationships between the opposite sex in the Civil Service were about as interesting and exciting as the two volumes of VAT Law I carried around in my briefcase - everything was squeaky clean and all above board. The British Civil Service was one of the unsexiest places to work in the world. But I liked it that way. The focus was always on the work to be done, and for me, I always found it a safe environment.

In my new District, I had a different Line Manager to lick me into shape called Rob. By a quirk of fate, he was Kay's husband, and he was responsible for overseeing the continuation of my learning. I'd just about got used to leading visits under Kay's watchful eye, but now I had to lead a visit in front of Rob too so that he could assess my performance and progress. He was an affable personality with a lively sense of humour, yet his easy-going persona did not help my nerves on our first visit together. I hoped he wouldn't notice my anxiety and hesitancy during the interview. But he did notice, 'Dawn very nervous', he wrote in his feedback.

Mind you his driving didn't help to calm my nerves. He liked his snazzy new car, showing off the key fob which remotely locked and unlocked the doors - a newfangled thing that I coveted. On our way to the visit, we pulled up at some traffic lights passing a driver who'd got out of his car to get something from the back seat, and Rob managed to brush the man's backside with his passenger wing mirror.

'You've just clipped my arse with your wing mirror!' the man shouted, banging on Rob's window. Fortunately, the lights changed and with a 'Sorry mate!' Rob was off, tyres screeching….

After a couple of months, Rob rarely accompanied me on visits and I began to feel I wasn't completely incapable. But change was in the air and a staff reshuffle within the LVO mixed us all up: I was moved to District 18, Rob defected to 'the other side' by landing a highly paid job at GKN Ltd as their 'VAT Advisor', and the rest dispersed to pastures new. Phil Birdwhistle faded into a distant memory.

24. WHEN IS A BISCUIT NOT A BISCUIT?

My new Line Manager in District 18 was Gina. Softly spoken yet bubbly and vivacious, she drove her car in bare feet - a habit I adopted myself, for how can one drive in stilettos without ruining the heels with scuff marks? Gina also only worked part-time and I liked that idea. She worked just three days a week to ease the burden of her child-care fees. If I could get a promotion to Higher Executive Officer maybe I could work part-time and do other stuff - stuff that I enjoyed. Such as music. A good plan. An incentive to keep on keeping on.

Gina was responsible for visiting some of the biggest 'large traders' in the LVO. They were known as '999' traders and were a world away from the paltry '301' traders I'd visited in Training District such as milkmen and butchers. The numbers '999' indicated that the trader was big: a national or multi-national company. Quite what the reasoning behind allocating the number 999 was, I had no idea. This numbering system was just another quirk of Customs & Excise. Maybe it was intended to put the officer on high alert? Was there a psychological angle to it? ......999 being the number for the emergency services?

Under Gina's wing, I continued to build my expertise and at the end of my second year in September 1990 my 'Performance Appraisal' marks had improved a tad. My overall mark went up a notch to grade '3', and I'd even managed to achieve one mark at level '2' (performance significantly above requirements) for 'ability to produce constructive ideas'. I was full of ideas, making frequent submissions to the 'Staff Suggestion Scheme' and even though my ideas were usually rejected, my innovative mind was always thinking of ways to help VAT inspectors be more organised in their work.

I'd made no progress with my interviewing technique, however. *'Can be hesitant when interviewing'* wrote Gina. *Drat.* By now I'd developed some kind of blockage in that area.

Gina's overall assessment of me was *'a competent and hard-working officer whose skills as a VAT Control Officer have developed as the year has progressed.....Miss Smith has shown that she is keen to extend and develop her skills and has demonstrated particular aptitude to the systematic approach necessary at the larger traders.'*

.......Perhaps I might get that promotion after all.

△△△

During 1990 the wind of change blew through the Department. There were buzzwords such as 'performance-related pay' swanning around the office, so it was no surprise to us when 'performance indicators' became a reality under the Thatcher regime. Officers were now required to keep individual records detailing the size of their assessments in addition to their Work Returns - in other words, we had to sing for our supper and show our worth. A dull joke began to circulate in VAT Offices: 'What's the difference between a VAT Inspector and Robin Hood? A VAT Inspector has more targets to aim for.'

It's possibly true that some of the more mature officers weren't putting in that much effort - they were just 'grazing' (to use an in-house term bandied about at that time) until they retired. So there was some merit in making us sit up and keep tabs on whether we were worth our salaries. But there was a problem: we were employed to ensure that traders were compliant and conversant with VAT and VAT law. If we did that job well, then it should mean that we rarely found any under-declared tax. But with the introduction of 'performance indicators,' it was now in our interest to allow traders to make big mistakes, which would then mean we could find large assessments to look good on our performance sheets. Of course, we never did that but 'protecting the revenue' was as much about educating traders and encouraging them to be compliant as it was about finding under-declarations.

Gina had a nose for sniffing out under-declared tax like a Custom's dog sniffing out drugs. She could put many of her colleagues in the shade with the size of her assessments and was one of the top scorers. I learnt a lot about work at '999' traders and 'credibility checks' under her supervision. One of her 999 traders was a well known high street bakery chain at the time (now long since gone), with stores throughout the UK. Their HQ was registered in our District and I accompanied Gina to a routine inspection there.

Visits to 999 traders involved many more complex accounting checks and an officer could spend a whole week in the Accounts Department at a large trader, rummaging through their records which involved scrutinising the audit system, investigating 'transaction and exception reports', sniffing out subsidiary records and devising 'Internal Control Questionnaires' (ICQs for short). I came in very handy for Gina on these 999 visits because she gave me the extremely laborious - yet very necessary - routine checks to undertake, and I spent many hours searching through reams of paper to identify certain figures, or verifying the validity of large purchase invoices. This sounds easy enough until you discover that the one you want is one of 5000 on microfiche. Microfiche was a sheet of transparent photographic film which contained small-scale images of invoices and other printed matter. These miniaturised images were typically reduced to 4% of their original size and they were too small to read with the naked eye. They had to be viewed through a special machine that magnified the images on a dull display screen. Microfiche was a very popular method used by many large traders to store hundreds of thousands of documents. But it was like trying to find a needle in a haystack, and the repetitive monotony of searching the images made me go funny in my tummy. At the end of a two-hour stint on a microfiche machine checking dozens of purchase invoices, I was left with a mild headache from eye strain and a sharp pain between the shoulders from being hunched over it. I'd quit my clerical job to get rid of boring chores and here I was doing boring chores. But it was necessary to learn how large traders operated if I wanted to become a senior officer myself, so I had to just get on with it and 'quit bellyaching' (as my father would have said).

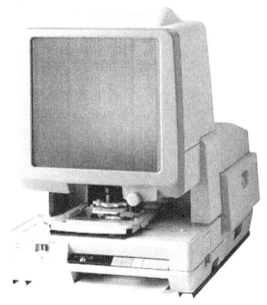

Microfiche machine, circa 1990

Gina had a tax-searching mind, and after spending two days in the Accounts Department where not a penny in under-declared VAT had been found, she decided we'd go out on the road and inspect some of the local bakery shops. It was important to observe how the tills were operated she said. And besides, Birmingham was in the grip of a glorious heatwave, why spend it cooped up in an office? So we zipped around several bakeries, Gina driving barefoot, car windows down with our hair blowing feral in the steamy August heat, nattering, chattering, singing along lustily to Bombalurina's *Itsy Bitsy Teeny Weeny Yellow Polka Dot Bikini* on the car radio. We were like two mischievous cats revelling in an orgy of freedom.

The bakery shops varied in size ranging from well-appointed stores in middle-class suburbs to small takeaway kiosks dotted around the city centre. We visited several shops scrutinising how the tills worked, and Gina also had a thing about biscuits and their VAT 'liability'. Biscuits were 'zero-rated' which meant the customer didn't have to pay any VAT on them, but when was a biscuit not a biscuit? That was the question. Who would ever have thought that the humble biscuit would be liable to anything? But it could be liable. Very liable. Especially if the biscuit had morphed into 'confectionery' because then it became liable for VAT, and the customer has to pay extra for the pleasure of whatever it is that makes the biscuit a piece of confectionery. Gina wanted to make sure all the biscuits were ordinary biscuits, and woe betides any biscuit found masquerading as 'confectionery'.

Quite what the criteria we were to use to differentiate between a good biscuit and a naughty one was unclear, but we decided chocolate would be a major culprit. And Smarties. But how many Smarties would alter the status of a biscuit to confectionery? If a biscuit was peppered with Smarties, it might hold up well in a VAT tribunal as a biscuit liable for VAT. If we found such sugary delights being put through the till as 'zero-rated' when they should be 'standard-rated' then a nice big fat assessment could land in Gina's lap.

So the plan was that while she was scrutinising how the tills were operated, I'd be scanning the bakery displays for misbehaving biscuits and any other camouflaged confectionary delights.

Gina's keen nose for tax was convinced if any money was to be found, it would be on how the staff operated the tills which had two buttons. There was a button for food with VAT on it, such as delicious hot pasties, sausage rolls, bacon and cheese turnovers, and then there was another button for food with no VAT on it, such as crusty loaves of bread, cobs, biscuits and cakes. I kept an eye open for any biscuits masquerading as confectionery, while Gina chatted to the staff about how they operated the tills.

By the end of the day, we were feeling deflated. Nothing. Not a thing out of place - and all the biscuits were behaving themselves. On a whim, Gina decided to do one more inspection and visit one of the tiny Kiosks in the city centre before we trundled home. We got there just in time as the young sales girl was closing up and printing the 'Z' reading from the till which Gina examined, and suddenly she went into 'gotcha' mode,

'Why aren't there any totals for standard-rated food?' asked Gina, 'you've put all the hot food through the zero-rated button.' The poor sales assistant was floored.

'Eh? I dunno what you're talking about?' she queried in a cowed voice, 'no-one's never told me nothin' about no zero buttons.'

We interpreted her quadruple negatives to mean that she had not been trained about the VAT liability of the food she sold and it was clear she'd just bunged the lot through the 'zero-rated' button. Gina told the girl not to worry and she'd take it up with Head Office.

As we left, huge cumulus clouds tinged with pink stretched high into the sky like giant candy-floss above the city buildings, and as we drove to Gina's house where I'd left my car, my frequent wont for day-dreaming became urgent. The clouds looked good enough to eat and my mind slipped back to my childhood days being taken to the fairground at Cannon Hill Park, where giant pink and white candy floss would sit top-heavy on a weedy stick.....I could even taste the sugary mass and hear the fairground hubbub, a mishmash of shoutings, laughings, music, popgun shots.....it would be a nice tasty hotdog to eat next with soggy onions and tomato ketchup.... I could smell it.....

'Are you OK?' Gina's question bounced me out of my reverie and my eyes left the fairground scene to see the houses speeding by along the A5127 as we travelled towards Wylde Green where she lived,

'Yes, I'm fine thank you.'

'Only you've gone quiet.'

'Oh, sorry, yeah I was just reminiscing, the clouds reminded me of candy floss.'

'Candy floss? They look more like my dirty puffs of cotton wool after I've taken my mascara off!' she said, glancing up through the windscreen.

As we got out of the car and I went in for a cuppa before I headed home, the turgid heat surrendered its grip as giant drops of rain began to fall......

Gina worked hard on her bakery case and established that the company had not given adequate training to the sales girl in the city kiosk about VAT liability or how to operate the till correctly. This led Gina to issue one of the biggest assessments of her career and it came to over half a million pounds. She based her assessment on the number of kiosks all around the UK making a similar error. It was later reduced on appeal because not only was the assessment 'speculative', but the size of it almost indicated fraud which the trader vehemently denied. But it was still a whopper of an assessment for Gina, and it looked very good indeed on her 'Performance Indicator' chart. *If only we could earn a 10% commission on our assessments.*

△△△

A year later, we heard that a different bakery company had won a VAT tribunal case with the issue of Jaffa Cakes. When was a cake not a cake? The judges had agreed with the trader that Jaffa Cakes were indeed cakes and as such were zero-rated, despite being covered in chocolate. Customs & Excise ended up with egg on their face. Well, you can't win 'em all as the saying goes.

I mused on the minefield of VAT liability and the delicate status of cakes and biscuits. *Good job I turned a blind eye to the Snowballs*.*

*Snowballs were chocolate-covered marshmallow cakes, sprinkled with flecks of desiccated coconut.

25. LIFE AT THE SHARP END

'As Prime Minister, Mrs Thatcher spent much energy denigrating and disparaging the civil service.'

(Michael Coolican, *No Tradesmen and No Women: The Origins of the British Civil Service*)

M ore buzzwords buzzed around the office - words such as 'Keith III' and 'Serious Misdeclaration Penalty' and 'default interest'. These words came from the buzz of bees in Whitehall bonnets, but they were the wrong sorts of bees and made traders, accountants and VAT officers edgy. Keith I and Keith II had already happened before I'd arrived on the VAT scene, though no one had ever mentioned Keith* to me. I'd never heard of the bloke. *Who is Keith, and what is he? Why is he cropping up now, threatening to make life on VAT Control more difficult?*

Under Margaret Thatcher, VAT Control was perched on the cusp of change, morphing into a mildly neurotic department, bringing fresh challenges to officers working at the coal face of VAT. She brought in a range of different 'Surcharges' and 'Penalties' on under-declarations - a type of interest on the underpayment, which ranged in severity depending on the type of assessment it was. The 'Serious' Misdeclaration Penalty (SMP for short) was what it said on the tin: it was 'Serious' implying dishonesty by the trader, to evade tax. At a whopping 30% on top of the assessment, it was a completely different level of penalty and it was much more than mere commercial restitution.

It didn't make our job any easier and flew in the face of

promoting good public relations with the trading community. But in Birmingham Collection there was something of a silent rebellion egged on by the tacit encouragement of our Surveyors and - like a game of pass it on - it was spread abroad in muted tones on office days that we would apologise to traders for the penalties, and advise them to lobby their MP about the draconian legislation, 'it's the only way that change will come and there will have to be a review,' we advised them, spurring them on in their whinnyings about the unjust penalties. I complied willingly with this unofficial mutiny.

I genuinely felt sorry for many traders. We all knew there were dishonest ones - crooks who would try and milk the system and get away with it - but overall our experience was mainly of hard-working honest business people. My job exposed me to the business bank accounts of traders and I witnessed the extortionate bank charges and saw from their Annual Accounts the pitiful drawings they took out of the business for themselves. It seemed they were working very hard for very little. I was pleased I had a regular job with a regular monthly salary.

The threat of VAT penalties also overshadowed the tone of VAT inspections and a drizzly cloud seemed to hover above many visits, particularly when errors were found. I felt the distaste and once saw the bitter fruit of its sting on a visit I did to a delivery business in Perry Barr. It was a limited company where the husband and wife, a Mr and Mrs Maddex, were the company directors. The business was registered from their home address, and as I was shown into the spacious lounge it was like walking into a building site with steel poles holding up the ceiling, and the floors were bare and cold with most of the furniture covered in dust sheets. I could only think they had some kind of serious structural issue with their property.

During the inspection, I discovered the company had reclaimed VAT on a monthly rental fee for a small warehouse they used for storage not far away. I had to disallow it because rent is exempt from VAT, but the continual monthly error over the previous four years had mounted up to a significant sum, and they would have to pay it all back to Customs & Excise, plus a surcharge. It was a careless error.

At the end of the visit in the mopping up session, I broke the bad news to the couple explaining why they had to pay it back and that unfortunately there would be a surcharge and possibly a penalty on top. I handed the VAT Notice on penalties and surcharges to Mrs Maddex, and she just stared at it wide-eyed in horror, choked speechless. Then she broke and was gone in a flash, with the thump thump thump of her feet on the staircase, stifling sobs. I was left holding the VAT Notice in my hand and felt the complete VAT villain. Mr Maddex remained calm and explained how his wife had struggled with things lately. On top of all the problems with their crumbling home, her mother had died the week before.

VAT inspectors never knew what personal problems their traders were going through, and it was outside of our remit to make any allowances, but it was something we were mindful of. The last thing some people want at a difficult point in their life is a VAT inspection.

△△△

Three Jobs

One sodden November day I had a VAT visit to a Catholic school in Tamworth in Staffordshire. It had rained hard and I'd had the joy of driving through several large roadside puddles, sending spray high up into the air. It had been a long but straightforward inspection working through my lunch hour so that I could pop off at 3.30 pm sharp, but it had been a singularly peculiar visit in that me and the school Secretary (who kept the accounts) had clicked on several deep and profound levels, bonding us in a fleeting 'womance', and concluding in a sisterly hug before I dashed home. Normally a hug with a trader would be completely unthinkable, but in this case, a sisterly hug with a Catholic school secretary seemed perfectly natural.

I had an hour's drive home before my first piano pupil arrived at 4.30 pm. I was starving and yaffled a packet of stale crisps which I found in my glove box, and hoped that there'd be no traffic jams on the M42. I made it with just five minutes to spare - enough time to go to the loo, make a cuppa and stuff a banana down before little Gemma arrived for her weekly half-hour lesson. Then after Gemma there was Jason, and after Jason, there was my adult pupil Wendy, then after Wendy, I had half an hour to wolf down a microwave meal, then set off on a 20-minute drive to Stock & Bradley Parish Council where I'd be taking the minutes of their bi-monthly Parish Council meeting. I didn't particularly enjoy taking minutes but I was the Parish Clerk and paid to do it. *How much longer will I have to keep this lark up?*

I got home at 10 pm, and after a cup of cocoa I went to bed, but I couldn't sleep even though I was whacked. I got out of bed, made more cocoa, and decided I'd type up the minutes of the meeting while they were fresh in my mind. It would save time in the end, knowing that trying to decipher my rusty shorthand strokes would take much longer if I left it until the weekend. I finally collapsed back into bed at 1 am.

The alarm roused me at 7.00 am. I had a VAT visit booked at a haulier in Lichfield two counties away at 9.30 am, and I was determined to eat some breakfast before I left. I was fed up feeling hungry all the time on VAT visits.

This work frenzy was all Margaret Thatcher's fault. Not only had she made life difficult for VAT officers and businesses alike with her lust for whatever it was she was lusting after, but she was making life difficult for everyone by losing control of the chaotic economy. It was the crippling mortgage rate of 14%, fuelled by a crazy gazumping hysteria in the property market, which pressed my financial button; I'd had to find other sources of income to supplement my salary to avoid getting into arrears with my mortgage, and I was well pigged off that I had no disposable income to enjoy life a bit more. I'd planned to go abroad, but a holiday was impossible with my dwindling finances.

My full-time job wasn't covering my basic cost of living, so I had to resurrect my old skills of teaching music, and at the same time took the opportunity to update my old friend Barbara about this turnaround in my career, letting her know I was now utilising my music degree that she'd helped to pay for. I hoped it would appease her taxpayer's outrage at my 'superfluity of naughtiness' when I'd shelved my music ambitions a decade previously, but she'd obviously forgotten the incident.

I needed special permission from the Assistant Collector to be a music teacher as it was considered an 'involvement in an outside occupation.' I was duly informed -

"...approval is given for you to carry on in business as a music teacher provided that this activity does not conflict with your official duties. If there is any change in circumstances you should notify me immediately.

Yours sincerely......"

And so after spending a whole Saturday morning writing out adverts and putting them in newsagents, I'd set myself up as a piano teacher. But it wasn't that easy to find pupils, and I still needed more regular income, so I'd responded to an advert in the local paper - Stock and Bradley Parish Council needed a Parish Clerk, and the job paid a small honorarium. It seemed to be a good little number with just six meetings a year to attend, taking the minutes and typing them up, and a little bit of filing. Little did I realise the job involved many more hours with miscellaneous duties, along with a trolley load of files, filing cabinets, and computer equipment that filled my spare bedroom.

These two part-time jobs however saved me from getting into debt, plus I'd been an unsuspecting punter when I'd taken out a small loan to purchase my second-hand Maestro, totally unaware that inflation and interest rates would rocket. I got caught out; I had no savings, no contingency plans, and no way of funding this debt. It was an additional financial burden I couldn't afford, so I asked my Surveyor if I could work two weeks of my annual leave. It would mean I'd get paid an extra two weeks' salary which would help pay off the loan. My request was granted and it kept me afloat. After all, what were just two weeks' leave? I couldn't afford to go on holiday anyway and I'd just be moping around at home. *I might be able to do this every year - quids in.* But it proved an unwise decision, and the relentless routine of work, with no break, was surprisingly physically and mentally draining.

Cash Jobs

Early in December 1990, I woke up one Saturday morning to a dead silence. I could hear the heavy snow outside. While I'd slept, blizzards had blanketed the Midlands. Pulling back the curtains the little grove where I lived was transformed as if someone had smothered it in thick, smooth icing. A murmuration of fine sherbet snow was swirling, and it all looked good enough to eat. My car was silhouetted in a seven-foot drift, with the ground pasted in virgin snow, inviting the first tread.

I put on my fleecy dressing gown, turned up the central heating, put bread in the toaster, and switched the kettle on - its gentle steamy hiss soothing the raw chill. As I turned to get some butter out of the fridge a dark shadow above caught my eye. The weight of the snow on my roof had caused water to ingress into the ceiling in my kitchen diner - the last thing I needed on top of all my debts. My father came to the rescue and offered to pay, 'Well that's what Dads are for,' he said, 'get three quotes, and choose the one in the middle.'

So I did as I was told and the one whose quote was in the middle informed me that he could 'do-it-a-bit-less-for-cash' - which was code for 'I won't charge you any VAT'. So I booked him up to do the job, and mused on my dilemma: what was I to do? If anything? We'd been given instructions about this scenario where VAT officers were offered 'cash jobs' as private individuals

-

1) always insist on paying by cheque (to cover yourself), and

2) send a note to the LVO where the dishonest trader was registered alerting the next visiting officer, and include details of the transaction with a copy of any documentation.

He arrived early one Saturday morning and had completed the job by early afternoon. I paid by cheque to make sure I covered myself. But I couldn't bring myself to snitch on him. Life was hard for everyone during those latter Thatcher years and beyond. But I was itching to tell him, 'I'm a VAT inspector you know!' .....though I didn't let on.

The moral of the tale is this: if you're a VAT registered business, bear in mind that you never know who you might be talking to. VAT inspectors don't go around with 'I am a VAT inspector' stamped on their foreheads.

Soon Thatcher's Ministers would oust her from her position. They couldn't allow the insanity of high inflation and soaring interest rates to continue.......as for Keith III and the Serious Misdeclaration Penalty, it proved to be a perfect example of ministerial misjudgement and it backfired. What was intended to bully traders into being more compliant morphed into a backlash from traders and their squealing accountants. There had to be a 'Review'. The stark language was of Freudian proportions - 'Serious' (we're on to you); 'Misdeclaration' (you're at it mate); and 'Penalty' (we're punishing you for your dishonesty) - were band-aided over with gentler terms such as 'period of grace' and it was all downgraded. In the 'Review of Serious Misdeclaration Penalty and Default Interest Keith III' reference was made several times to the Keith 'regime' and how this 'regime' was originally intended to 'improve compliance' which dissolved into an admission that it 'wasn't working as hoped', concluding that it didn't distinguish between fraudulent misdeclarations and negligent or careless errors: a more discretionary 'regime' was needed. The lobbying of MPs by the trading community had had an effect.

But the cogs of VAT Control worked in mysterious ways and I

profited from Keith III with yet another of my Good Ideas and a letter landed in my pigeon hole informing me -

"Dear Miss Smith

STAFF SUGGESTION SCHEME

Thank you for your suggestion concerning the provision to Control Officers at Pre Keith III Trader Reports. I have been asked by the Staff Suggestions Committee to inform you that the suggestion has been accepted in a modified form and an award of £50 has been recommended......

   Yours sincerely,

      A.T.H.........
      Suggestions Liaison Officer
      Birmingham Collection"

......Thank you Keith*, whomever you are.

Lord Keith of Kinkel.

26. CITIZENS CHARTER

'John Major, as he lost his grip on power, referred to Cabinet colleagues as bastards.'

(Michael Coolican, No Tradesmen and No Women: The Origins of the British Civil Service)

D isclosing the antics of naughty traders is only a part of my confessional in a job where I was struggling to get into the VAT groove, but a chapter revealing the internal modification of the Civil Service during the government of the day is not without place and is of some historical interest.

In September 1990 Brian Unwin, Chairman of the Board of HM Customs and Excise, sent round a 'People' booklet to all staff that set out several 'ideals' the Board wanted to achieve making it plain that -

"...we all need to work together to make the ideals a reality."

These were words of commitment. Underscore noted. It gave the feeling we were being buttered up for something, but we weren't quite sure what - it was somewhat vague as to what the 'ideals' were, so we were clueless about how to make them a reality.

By November 1990 Thatcher had gone. John Major had replaced her, and everyone wondered what changes might be ahead. In December Brian Unwin wrote another letter to all officers regarding the 'Customs & Excise People' initiative. It was difficult to discern what the real agenda was behind it, but we all felt a slight sense of foreboding. Here is a taster of it:

"Dear Colleague,

CUSTOMS AND EXCISE PEOPLE

I hope that you will all have had a chance to read, and discuss with your line manager, the "People" booklet......

2.   In visits to Collections and in Headquarters since the launch I have been greatly encouraged by the impact the initiative has made and the interest you have shown in it. But I am very conscious - and this goes for all my Board colleagues too - that words alone will not make it a reality......

3.   I want, therefore in this letter - as a starter - to let you know of some of the positive and new actions we have already taken or are planning in the spirit of the People initiative ......

4. You will already be aware of our move to fully open reporting and the use of a relocation company for Crown transfer moves of home.........

5.   Personnel Directorate will also be developing new strategies on accommodation - a subject which I know is of very great importance to you - and communications......

6. Communications are also central to the People initiative. We have therefore brought in a firm of professional communications consultants, People in Business, to review Departmental communications......

7. I set these initial measures out for you to show that the People initiative is not just about words but about practical action also......

8. With my very best wishes to all of you for a Happy Christmas and prosperous New Year.

*   Yours Sincerely,*

> *Brian Unwin*"

It all seemed a bit nebulous and no one was quite sure what it all meant (except his final point wishing us all a happy Christmas).

In the Budget of April 1991, Chancellor Norman Lamont increased the rate of VAT from 15% to 17.5%. For us as VAT inspectors it meant that the VAT fraction (which was needed to work out the VAT on VAT inclusive prices) changed from $^3/_{23}$ to $^7/_{47}$ - so we had to press different buttons on our calculators. There were rumours that the rise in VAT was to pay for people who didn't cough up their Poll Tax.

Then in July 1991, another government publication landed in our pigeonholes - a White Paper about the 'Citizen's Charter'. Brian Unwin wrote a third letter to all the staff:

Sir Brian Unwin KCB
Chairman

Board Room
H M Customs and Excise
New King's Beam House
22 Upper Ground
London SE1 9PJ
Direct Dial 071-865 5501
Telephone 071-620 1313 Ext 5501
GTN Number 3913 5501

23 July 1991

Dear Colleague,

CITIZEN'S CHARTER

The Government have just published a White Paper about the Citizen's Charter. Its main purpose is to set out what the public are entitled to expect from public services. It also deals with such themes as greater responsiveness to consumer needs amongst staff dealing with the public, publicly declared standards of service, and stronger complaints and redress procedures when services fall below acceptable standards. This is an important development for Customs and Excise, and I thought I should explain personally to you how we shall be tackling it.

2.   We already have a tradition of trying - within our overall objectives - to serve the public and reduce the burden on businesses. Indeed, in some ways - for example, through the Taxpayer's Charter and existing grievance procedures - we have already anticipated the Citizen's Charter. This has been recognised by Ministers who have paid tribute to our performance.

3.   But we cannot rest on our laurels, and we have been considering what more we can contribute to the new Citizen's Charter. The Taxpayer's Charter is now five years old and ripe for review. As a first step we have agreed with the Inland Revenue to issue a newly designed general document covering both Departments. But we shall then go on to support it with our own mini-Charters reflecting good practice in specific areas of our work - for example, a new Traveller's Charter. In keeping with our People initiative we shall, of course, consult with staff on the content and implementation of the Charters and supporting measures; and we shall assess how we measure up to them through service and performance indicators.

4.   All this will reinforce our continuing commitment to public service and underscore a reputation of which we can be proud. We already receive remarkably few complaints relative to the extent of our contacts with businesses and the travelling public, and we must aim to reduce these still further. I am sure that, with the professionalism and dedication that you already apply to your duties, you will succeed in doing this, and I am very grateful to you all for your hard work and the service you are giving to the Department and to the public.

Yours sincerely

BRIAN UNWIN

This time however he enclosed a copy of a letter from the Prime Minister himself, Mr John Major, who was also very fond of underscoring:

"By now you will have seen that I have published the Government's Citizen's Charter programme. No Government anywhere has ever set out such a thorough programme for improving the quality of public service.

The individual users and the taxpayers who pay for them deserve high quality services. <u>And I know you want to supply them.</u> Those who provide public services therefore have a special duty to respond to the needs of their customers and clients.

Delivering this higher quality depends first on the front line staff. Many of our public services are outstandingly good. But I think we all know that some other services leave much to be desired. I know that throughout the public service there are <u>many people</u> with energy, enthusiasm, initiative and ideas, working often in difficult circumstances. I want all <u>staff, both front line and those who back them up,</u> to have the scope and incentive to use all those qualities to serve the public. The Citizen's Charter puts people first. And it depends on you to make it a reality. The citizen will know, by the treatment he or she receives at the place where services are actually delivered, whether the Citizen's Charter principles mean something in practice. It is up to each of us to make sure that they do.

> *John Major,*
> *22 July 1991"*

I couldn't help thinking that he was playing a bit of a subtle guilt card, but we all just carried on as normal and nothing much changed in reality. No one was sure exactly how this might impact our jobs.

It was around this time, rather mysteriously, a gift in the form of a Customs & Excise headscarf was issued to female staff (and I believe male staff received a tie). How much that cost the department will never be known, but it must have been a fair bit, even though they were only made of polyester. Mind you, they were made in England, so it was good that the government was supporting British business. I never did wear it on VAT visits, but it was a nice thought. I still have it to this day as a memento.

Due to a staff reshuffle, I had a new Line Manager. Marie was my fourth senior officer in just over two years. She was a little younger than me and had risen the ladder from within the Department, beginning her Civil Service career as an Executive Officer in Registration District. She made light of doing the job properly without being a jobsworth and had a quiet personality like myself. We got on well together.

By July 1991 it was time for my third annual staff appraisal. What would Marie think of my performance for the past year?

There was a slight improvement in my marks and I achieved five ticks at grade '2' with my overall mark coming in at another grade '3', but this time I got a tick next to the box for 'likely to become fitted for promotion within 2 years.' *Part-time work here I come!*

Regarding my interview technique, however, it seemed I'd developed a different problem -

"Miss Smith has a confident approach and good preparation enables her to ask relevant and direct questions. She must on occasions remember to listen and evaluate traders' replies."

.....Ooops.....

27. THERE'S ALWAYS ONE....

I once shared a car journey with Marie to a VAT visit in Lichfield. After driving to her house in Boldmere we made our way up the A5127 in her car to a large rubber components company on the outskirts of the city, nattering about her forthcoming wedding, the latest Cher 'Shoop Shoop Song' number one in the charts, and whether we liked the chocolate version of HobNob biscuits or the original. Marie had clocked up seven years of experience in VAT Control and I asked which one of her visits was the most memorable.

She told me how several years back she'd accompanied a senior officer to a steelworks company where they'd uncovered a multi-layered web of deceit by a Mr Foley, the sole proprietor, who'd wangled the VAT in several devious ways to line his own pockets with public money over a period of three years.

It all started with spotting errors reclaimed by the business as input tax (that is the VAT claimed on expenses), and to this end, the trader had made nearly every input tax blunder in the book. He'd reclaimed VAT on all kinds of things which were not allowed such as private items (including a new set of golf clubs), business entertaining and personal clothing and footwear.

In addition to all of that, the trader had reclaimed VAT of 15% on invoices that had no VAT on them at all - from ridiculously small amounts claimed on milk, newspapers, TV Licence Fee, bank charges and even parking tickets, to the great where he'd claimed large amounts of VAT on horse racing betting slips, utilities, and insurances. The input tax crimes were unrelenting, Marie said, where the trader had also claimed VAT back on several purchase invoices which had gone 'missing' due to a 'flood' in the office. He'd also claimed VAT twice on the same goods - once on the original invoices, and again on proforma invoices.

'As for the sales side,' said Marie as we both popped some chewing gum in our mouths while stopped at some traffic lights, 'the business records were sloppy and incomplete. We found dozens of sales invoices missing which, when located, the VAT owed totalled over £54,000. He'd stolen nearly £85,000 including all his input tax cheats.'

'I wonder why he did it and how he thought he'd never get caught?'

'Just pure greed I think. The cheeky blighter denied he'd done anything wrong, and appealed and it went to tribunal. Then at the tribunal, he tried to wriggle out of his guilt by saying he was suffering from depression due to financial problems, which was ridiculous considering the amounts he'd spent on betting and other luxuries.'

Marie explained that her senior officer had to be a witness at the tribunal and although Customs won the case, the judge had been lenient believing the trader's sob story, to which end he got away with a lighter sentence.

'The judge told him not to rely on VAT due or falsely claimed as an interest-free loan to ease his financial problems. He got off lightly, but he'll probably try it on again.'

'Maybe there is some merit in these new Keith III penalties,' I mused.

'Possibly, yes, a bit of a deterrent to the Mr Foley's of this world, but they're a rare beast thankfully.'

△△△

When I was in Training District I did a joint visit with an experienced officer called Amir who was one of the few inspectors in the LVO who didn't own a car and was happy doing visits on public transport. On this occasion, he travelled with me in my old banger (just a few weeks before I learnt the engine was 'hanging by a thread' and could have killed us both if it had dropped off on the motorway).

We were on our way to a firm of solicitors and Amir would be making sure I got to grips with things like disbursements, recharges, place of supply and other boring VAT bits and bobs peculiar to solicitors. As we sped along the M6 northbound to Tamworth, I made the remark that I imagined traders like solicitors and accountants would surely be honest, and Amir related to me a few stories where this was not always the case, though he agreed his experience was rare.

He explained that it was back in the early 80s when he and his senior officer had visited a solicitor where they uncovered an attempt to hoodwink £125,000 from Customs and Excise involving sophisticated and elaborate methods by laundering dirty money.

'What's dirty money?' (I'd never heard of the term).

'It's illegal money.'

'Illegal money?' I queried, still none the wiser.

'Yeah, money obtained dishonestly.'

He explained that his senior officer had homed in on a large amount of money in a client's account and had noticed that the client lived in Spain - this being the red flag that prompted a deeper investigation by Customs & Excise resulting in the trader being struck off as a Solicitor after he'd been jailed for his part in a money laundering gang.

'So you never can tell. I guess the thing is to be aware of anything that sticks out like a sore thumb,' was Amir's advice.

He then went on to tell me how he once did a visit with his Surveyor in the late 70s to an accountant who'd siphoned off over £60,000 VAT by forging a company's cheques.

'How did you pick that up?' I probed, hoping to learn a new trick.

'Well I can't remember exactly, but the tell-tale sign was that we picked up the request for the customer to pay another entity which is not the company itself, again it stuck out like a sore thumb.'

'I see,' I lied, not having the foggiest idea what he was talking about, 'well I'm glad you're with me to spot any sore thumbs!' We laughed at the imagery.

As it turned out, there were no sore thumbs on our visit, and we didn't detect any irregularities on our inspection, but the conversation with Amir was a heads up that there's always one.

28. TRICKS OF THE TRADE

Marie moved to another District and I had a new senior officer, my fifth Line Manager in three years. Nigel wasn't far off retirement, and he took a keen interest in my progress, empowering me to achieve becoming a senior officer myself. We got on well together, and he was a sort of VAT Control fatherly figure, easy to talk to, good sense of humour, and I was comfortable under his supervision. I continued to expand my experience and also put into practice what I'd learnt from Gina and Marie.

Gina had taught me a really good trick where Annual Accounts were concerned and it was astonishingly simple: all I had to do was instruct the trader to contact their accountant and ask for the VAT balance under 'Liabilities' on the 'Balance Sheet'. It was an effective check, and why Kay or any other senior officer hadn't told me about it I'll never know. I can only guess they weren't aware of it. We weren't even taught about it on the six-week training course. It's quite possible that other LVOs used this check, but I only learnt about it from Gina. How Gina came to know about this hidden gem I never found out - maybe it was because her partner was a VAT registered trader himself, and he'd let her in on its bounteous secret.

I never did completely comprehend Annual Accounts on a technical level, and to help my inadequacies I used imagery to understand this complex document. I saw it as being like a pair of un-identical twins: the first twin is the 'Profit and Loss' account, and the second twin is the 'Balance Sheet'. Taking the imagery further, I saw the Balance Sheet as a pair of scales; assets are on one side of the scale and liabilities are on the other, and the scales have to balance evenly like a Libra birth sign. In Training District it was the Profit & Loss account we'd usually homed in on, with a cursory glance at the Balance Sheet for any 'Closing Stock' figures if we needed that information. But we'd been generally clueless as to what lay behind the blind window of the Balance Sheet where VAT was concerned. Or so it seemed to me.

The secret that Gina revealed to me was this: the exact amount of VAT that the trader owed to Custom & Excise at the Financial Year End was tucked away right there in the Balance Sheet. Of course, it had to be in there somewhere if one thought it through because VAT was a liability. It was an amount of money the trader owed (unless it was a repayment trader and then it was all 'arse about face' and the VAT was shown as an asset - but we won't go there). Once Gina had told me about it, the blind window of the Balance Sheet magically transformed into crystal clear glass revealing potential nuggets of underpaid VAT.

More imagery helped me to understand that the VAT Balance in the Balance sheet was a bit like a marriage. It had to be a perfect match where there's a glorious consummation of two figures: the VAT figure on the quarterly VAT Return should perfectly match the VAT balance in the Balance Sheet. But if the two figures were adrift, then the disharmony meant only one thing: that the accountant had found VAT errors.

I uncovered many under-declarations using this effortless check which didn't involve me doing any work whatsoever. The discrepancies disclosed during this check usually revealed the sale of an asset that hadn't been declared, or occasionally it was bookkeeping errors, or incorrectly claimed input tax. In other words, the accountant had done all the hard work for me during their detailed audit, and all I did was reap the fruit of their findings. Bingo! No matter how amazing a VAT inspector was, it was impossible to replicate the very detailed audits which were done by accountants. Some of the underpayments I found were historical errors going back many years which had lain undetected by previous officers and the accountant had just carried them forward year on year.

It stood to reason that any historical VAT errors found by the accountant were a liability, and they had to plonk it somewhere in the accounts. After all, they have their professional standards. But for me, it was a glorious fast track to finding hidden VAT owed to Customs & Excise. Simples. If only I'd known about this check earlier in my training. How much underpaid VAT had I missed in the past? Visions of traders and accountants laughing their socks off at me behind my back - the clueless VAT inspector who didn't have the first idea about the Balance Sheet and the hidden VAT underpayments lurking within....

Well, this check proved to be something of a trump card for me once when I visited one particular trader who had a reputation for asking to see an officer's Commission. It was unheard of for any trader to ask a VAT inspector to see their Commission - it was something they just did not do. Except for this one. And he did it in order to judge the length of service (and thus the experience) of the VAT inspector. So it was no surprise to me before I'd barely stepped over the threshold of his business premises, that he asked to see my Commission which I fished out of my briefcase.

I presented it to him observing a faint smirk as he clocked my short three years of service. At the end of the interview about his business records and accounts, I asked him to contact his accountant for the VAT balance on the Balance Sheet in the Annual Accounts. *And I won't even have to make any adjustment because his financial year-end ties in exactly with his quarterly VAT return. Good-oh.*

He did it right there and then picking up the phone, narrowing his eyes at me,

'I have a Miss Smith here from Customs and Ex-ercise, sitting before me wearing her red lipstick, wanting to know what the VAT balance is in the Balance Sheet.'

I was unsure why he'd deliberately mispronounced 'Excise' -

a common error with traders as they often mispronounced it as 'Exercise' - but surely not this one? .....or was he nervous about something? And I couldn't make out what the reference to my red lipstick meant if anything, but I detected it was a pathetic tactic to humiliate and intimidate me in some way. He wrote down the figure on a compliment slip and handed it to me in silence.

It turned out that the VAT balance in his Balance Sheet did not match the VAT paid for that quarter because the accountant had uncovered the sale of two large assets three years previously and no VAT had been paid over to Customs & Excise. The transactions had been neatly concealed in the bankings, with only two proforma invoices as evidence. I would never have found the error but for this simple check, and I issued an assessment for over £15,000 - a good notch on my 'performance indicator' chart. Thank you, Gina.

29. SPYCOP

O ne dim and dismal autumn day I did a visit to a Chinese takeaway. It had cropped up for an inspection because Customs & Excise had picked up a significant drop in sales for the past two quarters, so I was sent to do a routine visit and investigate the reason for the change in pattern. The takeaway was nestled between an Off-Licence and a Newsagent in a long row of shops on a busy main road in Washwood Heath and I parked on a side road in front of a block of flats. I'd arrived a little early, cocooned in my warm car, being ravished by the flawless tones of Emma Kirkby singing 'Nulla in Mundo' on Classic FM. I closed my eyes for a few moments before starting the day, luxuriating in the brief solace.

I got out of the car to the smell of wet dogs and traffic fumes and made my way to the main road, nearly slipping on a dog turd hidden under some mouldy leaves.

The takeaway was a limited company with several family members being directors and a Mr Ling - one of the directors - let me in. He had a bright permanent smile and pointed to a pile of papers on the counter.

'I just need to ask a few questions before I look at the accounts. Is the business still a limited company?'

'Yes still same'

'Is this the Principal Place of Business?'

'Yes, this is business place.'

'And is your Financial Year End still the 31st of March?' There was silence, and momentarily Mr Ling's smile was replaced by a slight frown.

'Ahhhhh!' he said raising a finger, the smile reappearing,

'come, please!' he said, motioning me to follow him. Perplexed, I followed him out the back where he showed me a machine that made potatoes into chips, '*Mach*ine, very good,' he said in broken English with a beaming smile. *Is he winding me up?* I smiled and nodded back at him, and decided to give him the benefit of the doubt believing his English was genuinely not good. So I stopped faffing around,

'The money in the till has gone low?'

'Till good, always press buttons.'

I tried a different tack, 'not many customers?'

'Yes, yes, we have many, many customer, we very, very busy, very busy.'

So it was a bit of a mystery. I tried weighing him up: he didn't seem like a crook or a fraud at all. He was very open and honest - face glowing, eyes twinkling - there was nothing shifty or evasive about him whatsoever. I went back to the accounts and he left me to do the inspection, which I had to do standing up with all the business records spread on top of the serving counter. I noticed the purchases of food for the previous eight months had risen significantly, even though the takings had drastically gone down. So something was definitely 'arse about face' (as Alf would have said).

The records were very well kept and I noticed that the business used a local bookkeeper. I'd spotted her quarterly invoice in the purchase records - *Mrs Dodwell, Bookkeeper & Cleaner.* Maybe they got two for the price of one? She hadn't queried the ratio of purchases to sales at all; she'd just totted up all the figures and filled in the VAT returns, without thinking through the discrepancy.

All the 'Z' totals on the till receipts matched the bankings, and all the purchases were in order. I was unable to establish why the takings had dramatically dropped. After two hours of checking as much as I could, I thanked Mr Ling for his help and informed him that I couldn't determine the exact reason for the drop in sales and that another visit would be necessary in a few months in order to monitor the difference in takings. He smiled and nodded, clearly not understanding a word I'd said, shook my hand firmly and said 'thank you, thank you,' and I took my leave.

After the visit I decided I had to get creative with a 'credibility check' and I came up with a plan. I'd worked out that the average cost of a meal from the takeaway was around £5 or £6 per person (a main, a few spring rolls, some fried rice and a bag of prawn crackers, and maybe a banana fritter). If the takings declared in the past six months were correct it meant they didn't have many customers at all. So I decided that one evening after work I'd park my car near the takeaway and sit and count how many customers went in from opening time until the time it closed.

I also planned to go in and buy a meal myself to determine the average cost of a takeaway and get a receipt. But this presented a problem in that I could be recognised by Mr Ling - unless I went in disguise, incognito. But the idea of donning some dark glasses and a wig didn't appeal to me, even though it would have been a new experience, to say the least.

I decided that ideally, I should have a witness with me when I executed this plan: what if I uncovered some kind of fraud and it ended up as a VAT tribunal case? I discussed it with Nigel and he agreed to come with me on this venture.

So one evening we met outside the takeaway and sat together in his car from 6 pm when it opened counting the punters who turned up in droves. There was a queue forming outside waiting for it to open when we got there. A steady stream of customers arrived as time went on, and it was clear there was no way that the takings recorded had been correct. We sat there for an hour, with me making a note of the number of customers.

'I wonder if they're involved with the Triads,' Nigel mused, 'it might be a Triad ring.'

'Triads? What are they?'

'Have you never heard of the Triads?!'

'No, what are they?'

'They're an organised crime group, the Chinese equivalent of the Mafia,' said Nigel, telling me all he knew about them from his vast general knowledge.

Our bellies began to rumble, so Nigel went in and bought a takeaway for us to eat in the car. It was rare to have such a feast as an officer of Customs & Excise. What a treat! I had the works; spring rolls for starters, then chicken chow mein with egg fried rice, prawn crackers and a pineapple fritter to round it all off.

The act of buying a meal from the takeaway and keeping the receipt would assist our 'test eat' invigilation, and give us some hard evidence along with an idea of how much an average meal cost if it was ever needed in court. I was seeing a nice big fat assessment arise which would look good on my performance record.

When Nigel came back with the food he looked mildly dazed. I asked him if he was all right.

'You'll never guess!' he shook his head '...... never guess in a million years what's going on in there!'

'What is it?' *Maybe it is something to do with the Triads after all.*

'The person serving is only charging £1.02p for every meal no matter how big it is!'

'What?!! How come?'

'Well, we'll to have to find out I guess, but I didn't want to make a scene in the shop.'

No wonder the takeaway was busy. The word had got around that they were only charging £1.02p for every meal, no matter how large.

We'd become chilled to the bone sitting in Nigel's car for an hour and were stubborn with cold. The hot meal thawed our shivering bodies, as well as misted up the windows. Goodness knows what the passers-by made of the steamy car, but it was perfectly innocent!

There was no point in monitoring customer numbers any longer, so we made for home after our feast, and I rounded off the evening by watching an episode of my favourite TV series *'Cagney and Lacey'* about two female cops on the streets in New York. I chided myself as a glimmer of identification with them surfaced. *Oh for crying out loud Smithy, a VAT Control Officer in Birmingham is a world away from being a cop in New York City!*

△△△

To cut a very long story short, we had to come clean with the trader about our spy mission and when we returned to sort it all out, a younger family member helped to interpret for us, so that we could find out what was going on. It transpired that the main 'director' - who was the owner and also a Mr Ling - had decided to spend a year in China with his family visiting relatives.

To keep the takeaway going while he was abroad, he'd roped in his cousin who was a director in name but who'd never worked front-of-shop before. Cousin Ling had only previously worked out the back operating the chip machine and preparing food. When Owner Ling was showing Cousin Ling how to take orders front-of-shop and operate the till, he'd given specific instructions in Chinese:

'So if you get an order for a bag of prawn crackers costing 50p and a banana fritter for 52p, it will come to one pound, two pence. In English, you say to the customer 'that will be one pound two P please' and you press this button and that button on the till.' But Cousin Ling had misinterpreted the instruction and he just charged £1.02p for every meal.

So that was it. My big assessment evaporated. There was nothing we could do. The takings were what they were - very, very low, and Owner Ling was in for a big shock on his return from China when he would find his profit margins in the negative. His accountant would have a jolly old time with that. All goes to show that sometimes things aren't always what they seem.

30. PROTECTING
THE REVENUE

T he unrhythmical thud of train doors slamming trailed off to a hush. Then the shrill whistle of the railway guard pierced the air. Another fleeting silence heralded the single thud of the guard's door that slammed just milliseconds before the train shunted out of New Street Station like a slug creeping out of a hole.

The familiar fug of stale money, stale newspapers, worn-out clothing and greasy railway uniforms sealed the train's aura. I was travelling to Swindon to do an 'AAT' Course (Advanced Accounts Training), an unexpected but welcome break from the routine of VAT visits. I settled back in my seat, shored up and hemmed in by my bags, books, magazines, Walkman and a watery take-away coffee in a polystyrene cup. Then, hit by a wall of weariness after an early morning start, I drowsed as the somnolent rocking of the carriage accompanied by soothing railway rhythms rocked me into a stupor.

An hour later, brutally woken up by the ticket collector, but still sluggish, I gazed out of the window where the landscape was now rural, speckled with trees like broccoli florets, green and burnished in the early autumn ambience. My coffee had gone cold, and the batteries in my Walkman were dead. Too weary to read, I dozed intermittently in between discreetly observing my fellow passengers, wallowing in the wealth of time and ordinary-ness: the man munching an apple after wiping it in his groin (was he a cricketer?); the yawn of a pensioner with ill-fitting dentures; the youth plugged into his

Walkman earphones and pump-pump-pumping his heel with knee bob-bob-bobbing. And then the smart - and very attractive - middle-aged gent in a suit reading a manual, manically writing notes, constantly pushing up his designer reading glasses.......all of us cocooned in our separate microscopic galaxies.

The journey passed in a blur of scenery, and on arrival, there was no time to explore Swindon. The taxi dropped me outside the hotel where the course was taking place. It was posh. I'd never stayed in such a prestigious hotel in all my born days. It had a palatial Reception area, contemporary decor and smart furnishings everywhere, a large double room - all to myself - complete with an ensuite bathroom, a bowl of fruit and bottled water. *Well, this is a nice surprise. Roll on dinner.*

The week's course started that afternoon with about 20 VAT Control officers all seated around a triclinium table. Every session was dry and tedious, and I was like a meerkat on watch duty trying to stay awake. I stifled many yawns, and when I was awake I had to resist my urges to indulge in my frequent daydreaming. I had a new fantasy which was flying an imaginary plane nurturing my love affair with Velocity. I was a brave pilot flying a small Hawk jet, 'looping the loop and defying the ground,' hurtling down to the earth at terrific speed, the G-force disfiguring my face........the officer next to me passed the water carafe and my daydream evaporated.

I wondered how much it had cost Customs & Excise to send us to this plush hotel but I learnt very little from the course. On the journey home I mused as to whether I'd been sent because I was crap at accounts or because I was a promising candidate for promotion. And to this day I have no idea if the course helped me in any way to 'protect the revenue'.

However, I can definitely boast that I saved the taxpayer over £330,000 in revenue that year, and over £150,000 of it was from a single assessment I found on a VAT visit I did to a clothing manufacturer. I discovered the under-declaration through a credibility check, however, not because of any new accounting skills I'd learnt on the AAT Course. The amount of under-declared VAT which I found begged the question: when is a fraud not a fraud? Answer: when it's a liability issue. Although it was technically a fraud, it wasn't a case the fraud squad were particularly interested in, despite the large amount of VAT I'd uncovered.

The visit had begun ordinarily enough, and everything was going well. The trader was very polite and obliging with all my requests and questions, and near the end of the visit, I decided I ought to do some kind of credibility check and that's where the issue flagged up. The problem was with his trousers (so to speak). I noticed the trader had purchased huge amounts of adult trouser belts which I expected to see mirrored in his sales of adult trousers. But the mirror of sales to purchases presented a poor reflection; he'd sold very few adult trousers.

I examined his stock of adult trouser belts *(maybe he was stockpiling them somewhere?)* but the stock levels were low: so where were all the tens of thousands of adult trouser belts he'd bought? Then it clicked. His records showed he also sold children's clothing, and children's clothing has no VAT on it (it is 'zero-rated'). The mirror became clear: he was passing off sales of adult trousers as children's trousers on his invoices, thus under-declaring VAT. This was also advantageous to him because it meant that he could sell his garments cheaper than his competitors And this was one trader who hadn't had the presence of mind to suppress his purchases to match his suppressed sales. If he'd not been so greedy and claimed back the VAT on all the adult belts then I might never have found the under-declaration. It was one of the biggest assessments of my career, boosting my performance chart for that year. *If only I could have 10% commission on it.*

I was expecting the trader to appeal against my assessment (could this be my very first tribunal case? ....would I be stepping up into the dock in a courtroom?), but the trader paid up no problem and my assessment wasn't even questioned. It was then that the thought crossed my mind: what did I miss? ....

maybe I should have checked the adult zips against the sales of adult anoraks. *Drat. My assessment might have been doubled!*

Nigel did my fourth annual 'performance appraisal'. Whether he was just being kind to me I'll never know, but his report showed significant improvement all around. Regarding my interviewing technique, he wrote,

"*Interviews trader efficiently from well-prepared notes.'*"

I deduced he was indeed being kind to me because in reality, I was still using my shopping list of trigger notes to prompt the relevant questions, but he seemed to think it was OK, and the rest of my performance panned out real good. For the first time ever I got two ticks at grade '1' ('performance significantly above requirements'). One was for 'Ability to produce constructive ideas' where Nigel noted -

"*Full of ideas. Has designed and introduced several useful aids and checklists for control.*"

My flair for coming up with new ideas was irrepressible. And I also had a grade '1' for 'Drive and determination' -

"*Her drive and enthusiasm have never wavered, producing a consistently high standard of assessments.*"

I'd never considered myself to have much drive and determination at all, particularly in this job which I struggled with on many levels. But someone else's perspective can inspire self-belief, and my overall performance mark went up a notch to grade '2' and I was marked 'Fitted for promotion', rounding off with -

"*Miss Smith has consistently performed throughout the year to a high standard in all aspects of work undertaken.*"

It had been a good year and buoyed up with confidence, a tendril of optimism curled around my trepidations of doing this strange job. But then new self-doubt unfurled - what if I was becoming hardened to the job? How could I judge whether the VAT pheromones which pervaded the department were changing my behaviour? Changing me? I was beginning to feel part of the VAT Control species after all. In truth, I was still feeling doubled-minded about the job because I wanted a job where I was popular. But I wasn't paid to be popular. I was paid to be efficient.

It was true that I fell into line with the culture of discipline in the department, along with my colleagues like sailors detailed off and piped to drill on the ship's deck, and we carried out every new directive to the letter. But this rigorous ethos was underpinned by a genuinely empowering element which was evidenced when a letter landed in my pigeon hole in February 1992:

"Dear Miss Smith

I am pleased to inform you that you have been awarded a special bonus of £200 under terms of G3-1 TA 5/89.

Your managers are impressed by your initiative, creative ability and organisational skills in the VAT control field. The overall application and dedication is a credit to you. Congratulations on your award which will be paid with your monthly salary.

Yours sincerely......"

Crikey. What a surprise to see the word 'creative'. How to find creativity in VAT Control? Maybe once an artiste always an artiste - even as a VAT inspector. *Perhaps the job wasn't so bad after all.*

PART THREE – THE REDUNDANT VAT INSPECTOR

**'Sit on your arse for fifty years and
hang your hat on a pension.'**

(Louis MacNeice, *Bagpipe Music*)

31. PASTURES NEW

A vacancy for a VAT Control Officer cropped up in Droitwich and I was at last able to apply for my long-awaited transfer. I was successful and it was the first time I'd felt mildly excited about doing VAT Control work. It meant I'd be covering postcodes in Worcestershire, the County where I lived. I did a further six months at Birmingham North LVO until all the paperwork was sorted. Nigel remained my Senior Officer during this time and in his final 'performance appraisal' he was even more glowing than before, giving me five marks at grade '1' and rounding off the detailed report with,

"She continues to be a strong candidate for promotion and has already risen to the challenge of work at a higher grade."

Thank you, Nigel. So in March 1993, I bade farewell to my colleagues in Birmingham North LVO. My leaving card was quirky and written in curvy comical font and a comical message bearing the words -

"The Works Escape Committee wishes to congratulate its most successful member!! .....Congratulations on your escape and all the very best for the future....from the rest of the inmates."

In reality, I was only escaping from Birmingham North LVO, not from Customs & Excise, but perhaps whoever chose the card had either a secret yearning to escape Customs & Excise themselves, or had read me well enough to know that I felt polarised about the job. But I was a 'civil servant' and as such, it had been made clear to us in our 'Terms of Employment' that:

"The first duty of civil servants is to give their undivided allegiance to the State at all times and on all occasions when the State has a claim on their services."

…..well, I might not like the job that much, but at least I'd tried to fulfil those Terms of Employment with everything I had. A simple dictionary check of the words 'civil' and 'servant' makes it plain that the person holding the post is not doing the job for themselves, but serving others, 'nolens volens'.

Droitwich LVO was situated in an attractive, sleepy rural Spa town, housed in a squat, one-storey building that had once been an army barracks during World War 2 - very quirky premises for a government department. Almost hidden from view with large shrubs and trees, it nestled peacefully in a quiet road. Inside, the spacious open plan office had neat regimental rows of desks, paired facing each other, resembling an army dormitory, with private quarters for the Surveyors - their higher grade gifting them each a separate office. What stories could those walls tell if they could speak?

As I sipped my ever-stale tea, my frequent daydreaming spells would rewind the reel of time fifty years to 1943 and I could see soldiers and officers moving around the place, larking, laughing, smoking, farting, swearing, fighting, sweating, eating, drinking, all in a jumble of earthy smells.

But now - silence. All I could hear was the random shuffle of papers, a lone desk drawer being stretched open, intermittent hushed voices, or the muted ring of a telephone resonating from a Surveyor's office, all swathed in the faint scent of paper and office chairs.

I loved working at Droitwich LVO; there was something quite dreamy about it. Its somnolence soothed many 'what ifs' and it was a beautiful drive through country lanes, and with just five or ten minutes travel when I had the occasional visit in Redditch where I lived, I could enjoy a lie-in for an hour, completing the languid routine.

At Droitwich, I was a 'Practical VAT Trainer' and regularly took new recruits with me on VAT visits. One trainee, Tamsin, accompanied me on a visit to a wholesaler of household goods. We arrived at the small warehouse in Worcester where one of the directors - a Mrs Jenkins - greeted us and made us welcome.

I did the usual routine with the interview and asked Mrs Jenkins to contact her accountant for the VAT balance in the Balance Sheet which she duly did without delay. We then inspected the premises and stock before settling down to wade through the business records and accounts.

I used the visit to teach Tamsin about wholesalers, double-entry bookkeeping and invoice traders. Mrs Jenkins made us tea, and we'd finished the visit in just over four hours. The VAT balance in the Balance Sheet was a perfect match to the quarterly VAT return so that drew a blank, but it was useful to disclose this gem to Tamsin who thought it was a brilliant VAT control check.

I discovered only two things wrong during the inspection - three purchase invoices were missing and I needed to see them to verify a significant amount of VAT that had been reclaimed, and Mrs Jenkins found them easily enough. The other thing that I'd noticed was input tax reclaimed on some new flooring at a private home address, so I had to disallow it. I informed Mrs Jenkins calmly in my usual professional manner that this expense was not allowable, and that it would have to be repaid. I thanked her for her help and hospitality, and we left, returning to the office where Tamsin had left her car.

I'd barely got my notebook out to write up the report when my Surveyor, Tony, called me into his 'quarters',

'I've just had a 'phone call from Mrs Jenkins about you.'

'Really?'

'Yes, she's complained about you…..'

'Complained?!'

'…. but don't worry,' he said waving his hand dismissively, 'I don't believe a word she's said. I've come across this tactic a lot lately from neurotic traders.'

'What's going on then?'

'Well, there's a thing going around the trading community at the moment where, after they've had a VAT inspection, they ring up and complain about the visiting officer.'

'Why?'

'I really don't know. It never achieves anything. It's been going on for several months now. You're not the first and you won't be the last.' I was speechless for a moment before adding, 'well I'm glad Tamsin was with me as a witness.'

Tony told me that Mrs Jenkins had accused me of being 'heavy handed' and that I'd 'demanded' to inspect the premises and stock. She said I'd 'accused' her of fiddling by claiming VAT on flooring at a home address and to top it all off, she said I'd been rude by falsely accusing her of hiding away some purchase invoices. She wanted me 'reprimanded'.

Tamsin was as surprised as I was when I told her, but we both saw the funny side. Tony told me not to worry about it assuring me he'd back me up. He knew the trader was fabricating the whole thing. I never heard any more about it. But it goes to show - there's always one.

32. SHROUDS AND SHRIVES

J ust before I left Birmingham North LVO I did a VAT visit to a funeral director called Morton & Sons (a rather appropriate name for an undertaker I thought) though in reality there were no sons - only Mr Morton (a widower) and his three daughters who ran the family business which had been handed down from his grandfather.

I was armed with my VAT Notice 701 detailing all the intricacies of VAT concerning burial, cremation and commemoration of the dead. I'd also done some homework before the visit familiarising myself with the areas I needed to home in on. Generally, services supplied by funeral directors were exempt from VAT, unless it was the burial or cremation of an animal, but some things were liable for VAT such as coffins, urns and shrouds (unless they were part of a funeral 'package'), flowers, commemorative items, newspaper announcements and any catering supplied for wakes - such things were taxable.

The idea that there would ever be a dishonest funeral director seemed almost obscene, but nevertheless, I had to wade through the necessary areas to make sure the VAT returns were accurate. Plus I'd learnt from Amir that there's always one.

As it turned out it was a textbook visit with not a thing out of place. Mr Morton was very thorough in every detail and aspect of his business, including the accounts by ensuring there was an immaculate audit trail that verified and substantiated every transaction made. One of his daughters, Rachel, was the bookkeeper and it was apparent it was a job she enjoyed and took pride in, with everything neatly recorded and expertly filed and documented.

The visit sticks out in my mind however for a different reason in that Mr Morton - an immaculately dressed gentleman - was slightly eccentric in some of his views and topics of conversation which he was not shy in speaking out about, much to the embarrassment of his daughter.

'You do know what Mark Twain said about death don't you?' he asked as I was ploughing my way through a pile of invoices checking the VAT claimed on shrouds,

'I'm afraid I don't.'

'It's a very famous quote of his, very famous, everyone should know it. He said he didn't fear death because he'd been dead for billions and billions of years before he was born, and had not suffered the slightest inconvenience from it.'

'Well now, that's most interesting. I really like that because strangely I've had that very thought myself a couple of times and thought I was going barmy!'

'Well, you're in good company. My late wife had it read out at her funeral.'

Me: thinks that's going a bit too far.

The other odd thing about Mr Morton was he had a thing about tax - not just Value Added Tax, but any tax, and in particular income tax. Concerning VAT, he was not a happy bunny about being an 'unpaid tax collector for Customs & Excise' and he was a very very unhappy bunny about paying the Inland Revenue income tax.

'Taxes just do not work you know,' he said as Rachel bought us all a mug of fresh tea, 'they don't make a country richer.' He unceremoniously dunked a Rich Tea biscuit which seemed quite incongruous with his proper mannerisms, 'Churchill got it right when he said for a nation to tax itself into prosperity is like a man standing in a bucket and trying to lift himself up by the handle. Don't you agree?'

'Dad!' interjected his daughter as she turned to look at me, 'you'll have to excuse him, income tax is one of his bees in his bonnet.'

'Well I've never really thought about it to be honest, but

surely taxes help pay for things like education,' I ventured, remembering my friend Barbara driving it home that her taxes had helped to fund my music degree.

It was rare - in fact unheard of - for a VAT inspector to get into a debate with a trader over anything, let alone taxes, but Mr Morton was genuinely passionate about the subject and he'd whetted my appetite.

'Yes but it depends on the type of tax,' he continued unabated, 'they're a necessary evil I agree.'

'What did Churchill propose instead then?' I probed, now genuinely inquisitive.

'He wanted to shift taxation from labour to land. Very sensible idea. He wanted to tax wealth, not wages. Much better to tax land, don't you agree?'

'Well yes sounds good, though I'd be out of a job if VAT was abolished,' I ventured a weak laugh.

'Taxes are a governmental intrusion that's what - a threat to our personal freedom.'

'Dad!'

....now I was beginning to think he was off on a tangent. *Governmental intrusion? Threat to our personal freedom?*

'Well I don't like having to pay over a third of my wages in taxes, but I can't see any other way of doing it now,' I confessed.

'The public lost the battle back in the 1700s over it. There never used to be income tax in Britain before then, did you know that?'

'No, I didn't, I thought there'd always been taxes. Is that a fact?'

'It sure is. Income tax was brought in by William Pitt the Younger in 1799 to pay for weapons for war with France. They should never have allowed income tax to happen because once you give up the right to freedom you never get it back. There should have been a revolution.'

'Dad!'

Revolution? Over income tax? The idea seemed preposterous.

'They should have kept the Window Tax that's what,'

continued Mr Morton.

'Window tax? A tax on windows?! You're joking!' I nearly spurted out a mouthful of tea.

'I'm deadly serious - go to the library and read about the history of taxes. Taxing windows was a much better idea.'

A spontaneous laugh escaped from myself and Rachel. Mr Morton certainly was entertaining even though he was serious.

'Well, I'd be quids in if my windows were taxed. I've only got six!'

'Exactly.'

'Well I must say it's been an education, I'll certainly look at my payslip in a new light from now on.'

'Yes, and your job would be a lot easier if you were a Window Tax Inspector. All you'd have to do is go to the property, count the windows and Bob's your uncle. No hassle. No fraud. People can't do fraud with windows.'

Well, he had a point there. Window Tax Inspector. Yes, that certainly would make a tax inspector's job a lot easier.

The visit concluded with an inspection of the premises. I'd never seen a dead body before and hoped there wasn't one lying on display as we entered the Chapel of Rest - thankfully it was vacant. I followed Mr Morton around the spacious building as he proudly showed me some of his most expensive oak coffins lined with real silk, and also his fleet of hearses parked out the back. He certainly loved his job.

33. A JOB FOR LIFE

'While politicians often criticise the civil service for being too big, and Chancellors of the Exchequer relish announcing job cuts, the fact remains that it is politicians who create the jobs in the first place and who pay insufficient attention to cutting out unnecessary tasks.'

(Michael Coolican, *No Tradesmen and No Women: The Origins of the British Civil Service*)

In May 1993 the 'Review for Promotion' panels in Birmingham Collection was in full swing and I was selected for an interview. If I was to realise my dream of working part-time, it was now or never, so I accepted the invitation.

I received a copy of *'Notes for Candidates appearing before Promotion Boards'* which disclosed *'The Criteria'* for promotion along with advice such as *'Try to Relax'* and the assurance that the interview panel *'will not be trying to catch you out'*. But nerves were never an issue when I was being interviewed - I only got nervous when I was interviewing traders.

'The Criteria' for promotion to Higher Executive Officer were laid bare in plain English:

Judgement - do you show perception, flexibility and open-mindedness? Can you draw balanced conclusions and take a wide view of issues?

Analysis - can you identify the implications surrounding issues and understand the relationship between them?

Communication - are you logical, lucid and concise? Can you listen carefully as well as speak? Are you convincing?

Leadership and Motivation - do you have the ability to get things done through people? Can you give positive guidance to get the best from your staff? *(Thank goodness being a VAT inspector doesn't involve staff management!)*

So I bluffed my way through the interview and was successful. In the ever quaint but mercantile language peculiar only to Customs & Excise I was informed -

"your name has been placed on the Birmingham vetted list from which promotions will be made."

Having therefore been "vetted", in August 1993 I took up the post of Higher Executive Officer and was appointed to work for Central England Regional Large Trader Control Unit in Coventry. My time in Droitwich LVO came to an abrupt end after just five short months, during which time I'd become strangely attached to the place. It had been a pleasant place to work - an oasis - where VAT visits were less stressful too (well, apart from neurotic traders who made complaints about me, that is).

By now Customs & Excise had caught up a little with technology and a rather thick, weighty laptop the size of a small paving slab was available to officers who wanted one to type up reports and then print them out at the office. I was first in the queue for this trendy device, finding a childish pleasure and a yuppy-ish glee at having a laptop in my briefcase. Rhianna, one of my colleagues, even bought herself a mobile phone. It was the size of a brick, but she loved it, 'you'll all be using one of these in a few years' she prophesied. How we all laughed at her. *No way!*

In At The Deep End

At Coventry LVO I was responsible for ensuring VAT compliance at several large traders, including Warwick County Council and a

Very Large German Retailer (which I shall call GR Ltd for short) - a 'no frills' supermarket that prided itself on excellent quality at low prices.

Early in September 1993, I did my very first VAT visit to GR Ltd. The Headquarters were situated in a small, rural market town giving me the gift of a 45-minute pleasurable country drive across three counties.

As I pulled up into the extensive car park my gaze siphoned towards the building of GR's Headquarters - a custom-built roofless monolithic rectangle. It was like an elongated triple-decker train, with red-brown bricks layered between shiny grey paned glass which mirrored the sky. *Very smart.*

At either end of the building, an illustrious glazed portal invited the visitor through the palatial entrance. The structure was no architectural masterpiece, but the song of its symmetry and minimalism charmed me, and I stood momentarily hypnotised by its stark beauty. Even their lorries were minimalist - unbranded pure white juggernauts - which were lined up at slight angles like identical dinky toys in neat rows in the spacious car park.

A jaunty sun was playing peek-a-boo behind transient clouds as I walked towards the glassy entrance. Inside the Reception area, e-v-e-r-y-t-h-i-n-g was immaculate, and after checking in, I was taken to meet the Accounts Manager. His office was sparse and impeccable; his desk was bare except for a phone and a Filofax. *Clean desk policy - nice!*

'Good morning, I'm Dawn Smith from Customs and Excise, I've taken over from Dermot Palethorpe.' We shook hands.

'Good morning, do take a seat.' I plonked my heavy briefcase and handbag at my feet and I sat facing Mr Accounts Manager, ready to begin my 'interview' as his clean desk lay between us like a subliminal message. I'd decided to attempt the interview (which I'd rehearsed) without reference to my notebook. Just to look a bit more professional, like.

I took a discreet deep breath and went for it. But soon I was slipping and I slid on the icy plane of inexperience. Although

I'd visited large '999' traders before with Gina, as I sat before the competent Accounts Manager my self-belief deserted me; I was now a learner driver responsible for driving this VAT juggernaut of a trader.

Overcome by my inadequacy, my confidence deconstructed and goodness knows what Mr Accounts Manager made of that first interview. I felt as if he could see right through me, and that he'd politely summed me up as being a useless officer and crap at my job. I just hoped that when I asked him for the VAT balance in the Balance Sheet I'd at least shown some degree of accounting knowledge and redeemed myself somewhat.

I moved on to inspecting the premises as I always did when I was blundering my way through a shoddy interview. Mr Accounts Manager took me into the huge open plan office where all the product lines were displayed on several large tables, laid out all neat and tidy in rows as if they were items on show at a raffle. There were more 'clean desks' with people working at them, and along the walls, there were rows and rows of smart built-in filing cabinets. It was all very white, clinical, and shiny and it could have been an operating theatre. Random shards of dark green fronds from handsome tropical palms stole into the whiteness. Green and white - a calming combination. After spending five years inspecting British businesses in their untidy, cramped offices, this was definitely different.

Mr Accounts Manager introduced me to some of the staff just as the window blinds leisurely descended, cooling the office to an ambient temperature.

'They're automatically triggered by the solar gain,' explained Mr Accounts Manager with his permanent polite smile as I stood and watched the magic show for a few moments.

He ordered me a coffee and then left me to mooch among the items, giving me permission to 'ask for anything' I needed. I spent a happy hour inspecting the different lines sold - packets of biscuits, tinned foods, toiletry items, household items - they all looked so different from the brands I was familiar with in Tesco. I'd never seen anything like them before. I made notes of the cost and selling price of each item to get an idea of mark-ups, while the window blinds moved silently up and down in response to the antics of the cheeky sun waxing and waning behind the playful clouds.

I'd done some pre-visit homework on GR Ltd by reading Dermot's reports where he'd flagged up some interesting stuff. GR Ltd sold up to a hundred lines, none of which had any prices stamped on them. Stamping items with a price was an unnecessary job in their eyes (the prices were displayed for the customer to see above each line in the shop). A red light flashed in the recesses of my faint accounting mind.

Dermot had also detailed the unique method used at the cash tills: GR Ltd trained all their check-out staff to memorise the price of every item sold. It was a scientific fact - Dermot annotated - people can be trained to memorise the prices of up to a hundred lines. But any more than a hundred, then errors would creep in. GR Ltd also only ever accepted cash and no cheques or credit cards were allowed. More red lights flashed as I picked up the drift of Dermot's 'risk areas'. *Crikey, even a small error at the tills could mean tens of thousands of pounds in under-declared VAT.*

So it was agreed with Mr Accounts Manager that I should visit one of their supermarkets, fill a trolley with goods, and put it through a till to test out their system and he accompanied me to oversee this venture. It was unlike any other supermarket I'd been in before. It was more like a warehouse - very basic yet fat with stock.

I filled my trolley with about two dozen items - some goods were vatable, some were 'zero-rated' and I made a note of the selling prices. Then, sidling my way up to the tills for my mock checkout, I unloaded my trolley and watched the checkout girl perform her stunt - a magnificent display of masterful till operation as her left hand picked up my items, and her right hand punched in the price and correct VAT button like a one-handed typist typing at 100wpm. She never even had to look at the till, her eyes were firmly on the goods.

She presented me with my receipt and a smile after which Mr Accounts Manager moved in to tell her it was a dummy run. We examined the receipt and it was 100% correct. I tried the same with two other checkout staff, one of whom was a young lad, *he's bound to get it wrong.* But both were tiptop and had no mistakes.

So I decided I wouldn't waste any more time with that little exercise. We left and I had a stab at devising an updated 'Internal Control Questionnaire' instead. But there was never anything out of place at GR Ltd. I never found any under-declared tax. Ever. Everything was 'all fair and above board'. German precision at its best. It was a short straw for me for my performance targets. *Bugger.*

△△△

At the end of my first year as a senior officer, my performance indicator chart was rubbish. I'd found bigger assessments when I was an EO visiting smaller traders and I discovered that it was much harder to find under-declared tax on '999' visits. Big businesses had better accounting systems in place and were more VAT compliant. They had professional accounts managers and often employed ex-VAT inspectors to ensure 100% accurate VAT returns - especially since the draconian 'Keith III' legislation had kicked in. How was I to rake in big assessments with these squeaky clean large traders who had immaculate accounting systems? How was I able to pitch my brains against experienced ex-VAT Control officers who'd defected to the other side, making it impossible for me to find mistakes? Should I join the defectors? Maybe I could get a job like that? They were much better paid. Top salaries. Company car. Mobile phone. Bigger and better.

Thankfully Greg, my new Surveyor, was supportive and he knew I couldn't get blood out of a stone. He was a jolly Geordie with a keen sense of humour, very helpful and a bit of a fatherly figure, taking a genuine interest in the welfare of all his staff.

He slipped me a few 'high risk' traders to visit. At least it gave me a chance of finding some under-declared VAT so that my performance indicators wouldn't show a grand total of Nil.

All Change

On 13 July 1994, another 'White Paper' was published called *'THE CIVIL SERVICE - Continuity and Change - A Guide for Staff.'* I rarely read these missives which arrived in my pigeon-hole from the government. But a cursory glance at the booklet made one word jump out: **'redundancies'**. *I thought this was a job for life? Am I going to be made redundant because the total sum of my annual assessments is zero?*

It was true that I'd had unsettling doubts about spending the next 30 years in VAT Control, but to be made redundant? I wasn't sure I fancied that either, especially if it meant going out like a soggy air biscuit because my 'performance indicators' were below par. It wasn't my fault that all my large traders were 100% VAT compliant.

Crikey. I didn't see any of this coming. It was all rather unsettling.

The White Paper was a megaphone message to all civil servants announcing in no uncertain terms: 'WE ARE GOING TO MAKE STAFF CUTS.'

The fiscal famine was now a reality. A huge cull in manpower was imminent. On the first page of the White Paper were two personal messages: one from the Prime Minister (again) - Mr John Major himself, and the other from the Head of the Home Civil Service, Sir Robin Butler.

Their messages were capped by their photographs: John Major looking friendly, calm and distinguished with a hint of a smile. Then Sir Robin, again with a hint of a smile but looking decidedly worried, his eyes overshadowed by a slight frown, betraying concern. The document began with John Major buttering us all up with praise before delivering the punchline:

"Britain is fortunate in having a Civil Service of the highest

quality. I, and all my Cabinet colleagues, recognise the continuing need for a first-class Civil Service, able to serve successive governments with the integrity, dedication and impartiality for which the British Civil Service is renowned........But the Civil Service cannot be immune to change......"

.....followed by Sir Robin continuing the theme:

"The Civil Service is going through a period of change which has caused understandable uncertainties. This White Paper does not promise an end to change. Nor should we expect it to.......I hope that we will all respond constructively."

Constructively? What is that supposed to mean?

**MESSAGE FROM
THE PRIME MINISTER**

Britain is fortunate in having a Civil Service of the highest quality. I, and all my Cabinet colleagues, recognise the continuing need for a first class Civil Service, able to serve successive governments with the integrity, dedication and impartiality for which the British Civil Service is renowned.

In this White Paper you will find our commitment to upholding these qualities spelled out very clearly. But the Civil Service cannot be immune to change. It has already made enormous strides in recent years in improving standards of service and efficiency. And I believe it can achieve still more in the future. To do this, the path ahead needs to be clearly mapped out, so that all civil servants can see what is expected of them, and what the opportunities are. That is what the White Paper sets out to do. It is a challenging programme. But it is one that with your help I believe can raise standards still further.

**MESSAGE FROM
SIR ROBIN BUTLER**

I welcome the Government's decision to publish this White Paper as I hope you will. It contains important messages for everyone in the Civil Service.

Not least of these is that it confirms the Government's commitment to a key role for the Civil Service in supporting Ministers in policy work and in managing and delivering public services. It stresses the continuing importance of the values on which the Civil Service has been built.

The Civil Service is going through a period of change which has caused understandable uncertainties. This White Paper does not promise an end to change. Nor should we expect it to. But it sets out clearly what the Government wants from us and puts forward ideas - on which it invites comment - on how the management of the Senior Civil Service should develop.

I hope that we will all respond constructively.

On the next page headed **SOME KEY QUESTIONS**, my eyes went straight to the redundancy question:

Q. Will there be compulsory redundancies?
A. Wherever possible the Government will deal with reductions in the size of the Civil Service by not replacing staff who leave. If redundancies are required in some areas, staff will be treated fairly. A number of flexibilities are already available to help - and further flexibilities, within current exit terms, are being considered.

Flexibilities. I liked that spin on it. 'Flexibilities' didn't sound too bad. If I was booted out, at least it might be with flexibility and some dignity.

34. SO LONG, FAREWELL...

Hot on the heels of the White Paper spilling the beans that the Civil Service was to be drastically downsized, another fanfare sounded in our pigeonholes from Valerie Strachan, Chair of HM Customs & Excise. She'd taken over from Brian Unwin, and like him began her epistles with a handwritten opening - she wrote:

*"**Dear colleague,** (note the small "c")*

Today all Civil Servants are being sent a summary of the Government's White Paper on the Civil Service. I wanted to let you know my own reactions to it, and to help put it in context with some of the changes that you know are already happening.........
The reference to Civil Service numbers, which are expected to fall significantly below 500,000, is likely to attract attention. Although this will affect all departments, it will not, in our case, be on top of any staff reduction resulting from the Fundamental Expenditure Review.......Finally, you will see that the Government intends where possible to deal with reduction in Civil Service numbers by voluntary means. This will certainly be our own approach......our aim will be to ensure that any rundown is, as far as possible, done on a voluntary basis; and above all, that those who do leave do so with support and a feeling that they have been treated properly and fairly.
As promised earlier, I will do my best to ensure that you are kept informed whenever there are developments to report.

Yours sincerely,
Valerie Strachan"

This was a reassuring letter and as compassionate as any Government Department could navigate drastic staff reductions. It was all down to the 'Fundamental Expenditure Review' by HM Treasury - they were meaningless words to me, but I got the drift: the government needed money and was desperate to save money. Cutting back on Civil Servants, and in particular VAT Control officers, made sense: why pay our salaries to ferret out unpaid VAT at traders who were either 100% compliant, or whose turnovers were so trifling it wasn't worth the effort? No point in spitting in the wind.

NEWS UPDATE

Keeping you in touch with developments in Customs and Excise

13 July 1994 — Issue 49

This special issue of News Update is being distributed to all staff, together with a summary of the Government's White Paper on the Civil Service, which is published today. The Chairman, Valerie Strachan, gives her own reactions to the White Paper.

Dear colleague,

Today all Civil Servants are being sent a summary of the Government's White Paper on the Civil Service. I wanted to let you know my own reactions to it, and to help put it in context with some of the changes that you know are already happening.

First, you will see that, although change will continue to be a way of life for the Civil Service, Ministers have chosen to start by reaffirming traditional values such as honesty, fairness and objectivity which we in Customs and Excise have long upheld.

Some of the policies announced are ones on which we have already embarked. Pay and grading is to be delegated to all departments and agencies: but we already have our own pay agreement and a strategy for reforming our grading structure. Staff development is to be given higher priority: we already invest substantially in people although we have more to do. These and other steps are, I believe, welcome.

The reference to Civil Service numbers, which are expected to fall to significantly below 500,000, is likely to attract attention. Although this will affect all departments, it will not, in our case, be on top of any staff reductions resulting from the Fundamental Expenditure Review. In effect, the FER will be the means of deciding our contribution.

Finally, you will see that the Government intends wherever possible to deal with reductions in Civil Service numbers by voluntary means. This will certainly be our own approach. Much will depend on the outcome of the FER, but our aim will be to ensure that any rundown is, as far as possible, done on a voluntary basis; and above all, that those who do leave do so with support and a feeling that they have been treated properly and fairly.

As promised earlier, I will do my best to ensure that you are kept informed whenever there are developments to report.

Yours sincerely

Valerie Strachan

The letter was a glimmer of hope, however, and at least I'd be politely offered the opportunity to leave of my own accord if things got really bad. It would be voluntary. As I stared at Valerie's words *"those who do leave do so with support and a feeling that they have been treated properly and fairly"* I thought back to my training days when we had all believed that our jobs were safe forever. Who'd have thought it was all so transient? So ephemeral? So much for 'a job for life' being 'safe and secure'. *Wherever did we get that idea from?*

Seismic decisions from Whitehall instigated a tsunami headed for HM Customs & Excise to swallow the department up. The picture became more clear: the government had taken a magnifying glass to the whole approach to VAT Control for several years, and the VAT Registration threshold had doubled to £45,000 by 1 December 1993 triggering a torrent of small businesses de-registering from VAT, alongside many new small businesses which didn't even need to register for VAT at all. Who needed all those VAT inspectors?

By the end of 1994, we all learnt what the word 'flexibilities' actually meant: we were being paid to leave under a 'Flexible Early Severance Scheme' for those wishing to appropriate it. *Very tempting.* Was it to be fight or flight?

Marriage, Moving and Motherhood
During 1992, a holiday romance led to marriage in March 1994. And now I was pregnant and would be moving to the South West where my husband lived. Devon was a place with large pockets of stunning scenery spread around its suburbs, flanked by a coastline full of stories, pirates, paths, coves, and palms. I didn't need much persuading to move south. But I did need a transfer to Exeter LVO and who knows, maybe the VAT officers there might all be nearing retirement and I could be in with a chance? I was even willing to drop a grade to Executive Officer (at least I'd find more under-declared VAT at that grade). So I wrote to Personnel Department and had a reply from Joan who'd been one

of my senior officers in the Training District. She'd moved over to work in Personnel as a Staff Assistance Officer - a good move, I reflected, recalling her warm, and caring personality. She wrote,

"Our LVO at Exeter is to become a 2 District VSO (VAT sub-office)...they are being forced to reduce numbers and any members leaving through natural causes are not being replaced. It is unfortunate that the time you need to move to the South West is at a time when the Civil Service is contracting......If I hear of any news at all I will contact you."

So that was the end of that. Giving up work was alluring and I was becoming reconciled to it - but I'd miss the money. I was earning just over £16000 as an HEO, rising incrementally each year until I reached the top of the scale. Still, I decided I'd tell Greg, my Surveyor, that I'd opt-in for the Flexible Early Severance Scheme. So one Friday I knocked on his ever-open door to surrender and wave my white flag, but ever-resourceful and on the lookout for his staff Greg had spotted some HEO vacancies at the Crown Prosecution Service: what did I think about transferring to another department? He'd give me a glowing reference, he said. Without hesitating, I thanked him for thinking of me, and I applied for the job. I'd worked hard for both of my promotions, and I still fancied working part-time which would be ideal as a new mother. But despite Greg's flattering reference, a fully-fledged VAT inspector was completely useless to the Crown Prosecution Service, and I didn't even get an interview. So in January 1995, I 'swallowed the anchor' (as they say in the Navy), handed back my Commission and received £12,108.67 as a lump sum payment. A new life awaited me in the South West as a wife and mother, and at least I had a bit of a handout.

𝕿𝖔 𝖆𝖑𝖑 𝖙𝖔 𝖜𝖍𝖔𝖒 *these Presents shall come* Greeting.

𝖂𝖊 the Commissioners of Her Majesty's Customs and Excise *pursuant to the powers in that behalf vested in us* 𝕯𝖔 𝕳𝖊𝖗𝖊𝖇𝖞 *appoint*

Several months later, having settled in Devon, I was chopping carrots and trying to feed my baby son at the same time. The BBC news cackled on our portable TV in the kitchen as I decanted a jar of chocolate pudding and my ears snatched up the words '...... ***the state pension age for women will increase to 65 ......***' I tuned in my attention to the report - yes, it was true: the government had raised the State Pension Age for women from 60 to 65 under the Pensions Act 1995. Just like that.

'What! They cannot be serious!!' I said to my husband who was peeling potatoes, scratching my head as I did some sums reckoning up the loss which the announcement had caused me, 'they've given me money in one hand and they've just taken it all back with the other!'

'Well, that's equality for you.'

'I get that, but it's just cost me thousands of pounds.'

'I guess it had to come at some point.'

'Well, you'll lose out too - if we both live that long.'

And so it was that in one fell swoop the government not only repossessed by stealth the £12,108.67p they paid me to leave Customs and Excise, but they also gained at least a further £50,000 by raising my State Pension Age to 65 (and later they raised it again to 66). Plus I'd have to pay National Insurance Contributions for an extra five years to boot. But like many people in their thirties, I wasn't overly concerned. The age of 65 seemed a very long way off. Becoming a 'pensioner' was almost incomprehensible and I carried on chopping the carrots. Mind you, the Department for Work and Pensions never did write and let me know how much money I'd be losing, or give me any advice on how I might make any contingency plans. Besides, by raiding our pensions in the name of 'equality', the government had appropriated a good source of money for HM Treasury which was used to reduce the national debt.

Ten years later on the 1st April 2005, HM Customs and Excise was dissolved. Typical of the government to abolish it on April Fool's Day. *Was there a subliminal message in there somewhere?*

Value Added Tax was hoovered up by the Inland Revenue under the new umbrella department of HMRC - Her Majesty's Revenue and Customs. It had always been a bone of contention as to why Customs & Excise were allocated the responsibility of collecting VAT rather than the Inland Revenue - now finally they had the pleasure of collecting and controlling it.

I wonder what happened to all those green folders?

35. LES DAWSON AT THE MIDNIGHT MASS

Don't shoot the pianist (she's doing the best she can)
(Attributed to Oscar Wilde)

'Are you the artiste?' asked a very smartly dressed man smoking a cigarette as I walked through the hotel doors.

'I am, I'll be playing the piano during dinner,' I cooed as I clumsily dragged my heavy briefcase-on-wheels full of sheet music up the step while trying not to trip over my long evening dress in a pair of high heels. Some things never change.

How that word 'artiste' sounded so good! That's what I'd always wanted to be, some kind of 'artiste'. After mothballing my musical ambitions for over thirty years, I was finally living my dream as a professional pianist. It wasn't quite what I'd originally planned, but I found merry-making during hotel dinners surprisingly fulfilling.

Then one year I was approached by the Rector of a local Anglican Church.

'We have a bit of a problem,' he murmured down the telephone, 'our organist is stepping down, are you able to play for our services please?'

'I can't play the pedals,' I confessed, half hoping that this would disqualify me from a job that I wasn't sure I could do.

'That doesn't matter, we just need someone to play the tune.'

So that was it. Church organist I was.

However, it wasn't always plain sailing. One Christmas Eve, after playing for nearly three hours at a country restaurant during dinner, I dashed the 20 miles from the hotel to the church so that I could rehearse the choir before Midnight Mass began. At 11.30 pm the church was full of Yuletide worshippers - most of whom had piled in from the pub next door. They'd all come to see the baby Jesus doll being placed in the manger by the Vicar, as well as enjoy singing some traditional Christmas carols.

Midnight Mass was a sung Eucharist, and I'd played it many times during Sunday morning services, but as midnight approached the only place I wanted to be was fast asleep tucked up in a warm cosy bed. My penchant for nodding off very nearly happened during the Sanctus and I ended up playing a fistful of wrong notes. The strange harmonies woke me up and I swiftly recovered and picked up the right tune. Thankfully most of the congregation was completely unaware of my mistake - *good job it didn't happen during a well-known carol.* But it completely threw the choir,

'You really kept us on our toes there,' they quipped without malice, 'nice little variation that,' they teased in good humour.

I could only apologise, 'yes sorry about that, nothing like a bit of Les Dawson in the Midnight Mass, eh?' was all I could say, making light of my blunder. The following year I made sure I had an afternoon nap on Christmas Eve before repeating the routine.

I'd kept in touch with my old friend Barbara who reached a good age well into her eighties and I was able to tell her that I'd made it as a professional musician after all. She'd long forgotten her outrage at funding my musical education as a taxpayer. And it's true - nothing we do in life is ever wasted.

Being a musician is much more my kind of work except in respect of one thing: as a self-employed person, I found it much harder to keep records and accounts than I ever did to check them! ....thank goodness for accountants.....

EPILOGUE

Despite my initial difficulties and misgivings about VAT Control work, Customs & Excise had been extremely kind to me on many levels. I was grateful for the opportunity the Department had given me for two promotions, and for the challenges that VAT Control work forced me to respond to. In return I'd tried to summon up as much enthusiasm, dedication and loyalty as I could in my role as a 'civil servant', doing my best in a job I didn't choose or want.

I can't deny that I was glad to leave the world of VAT behind, but in the words of Gill Powell in her writings *Careering: 40 Jobs in 40 Years* - "I've learnt lots along the way; the most important lesson was WHO you work with is often more important than the work itself." And that was certainly true in my Civil Service career - the people I'd had the privilege of working with had made all the difference, and I was richer for their input.

I would love to read stories of former VAT inspectors and am hoping that this book will inspire them to share their very personal journeys and confessions.

ACKNOWLEDGEMENT

I began writing some of the stories in this book over 25 years ago, inspired by James Herriott's book *It Shouldn't Happen To A Vet,* but it has only been during the Lockdowns that the currency of time has gifted me the many hours necessary to complete it.

First, I would like to thank my husband Don for being a writer's widower for many days and evenings.

I would also like to thank Cathy Rentzenbrink for an excellent memoir writing course on Curtis Brown Creative, along with Shannon Leone Fowler, my tutor and professional reader on the writing course, without whose advice, writing tips, suggestions and above all belief in my book as a "unique and entertaining work", I would have given up.

I'd like to thank Cheryl Zimmerman who proofread my very messy first draft, made suggestions and encouraged me on my writing journey.

Finally I'd like to thank all my HM Customs & Excise Surveyors, Senior Officers and Colleagues from all those years ago who truly made the Department a safe, happy and empowering place to work.

PERMISSIONS & CREDITS

Every effort has been made to obtain the necessary permissions with reference to copyright material, both illustrative and quoted. I apologise for any omissions in this respect and will be pleased to make the appropriate acknowledgements in any future edition.

Contains public sector information licensed under the Open Government Licence v2.0

TEXT PERMISSIONS & CREDITS:

- Part One Epigraph from Poirot, quoted courtesy of ITV archive.

- Chapter Epigraphs by Michael Coolican taken from *No Tradesmen and No Women: The Origins of the British Civil Service* © Michael Coolican, 2018, reprinted by permission of Biteback Publishing.

- Part Three Epigraph from 'Bagpipe Music' from *Collected Poems* by Louis MacNiece (Faber & Faber) reproduced by kind permission by David Higham Associates.

IMAGE PERMISSIONS & CREDITS:

Chapter 8 - Cartoon of duty-free gin bottle by Lee Shetliffe. Used with Permission.

- Image of Commission used with kind permission of Paul Walsh, retired Officer of HM Customs & Excise.

Chapter 19 *Raising the Marriage Bar* Cartoon by Alan Bennett, originally from the Home Office Red Tape magazine, August 1946. Image from www.civilservant.org.uk. With thanks to Alan Bennett. Used with permission.

Chapter 24 - Minolta RP600Z Microfiche machine. Image used with permission of microfilmworld.com

Chapter 34 - Cancelled Commission. Thanks to Keith Anderson, a retired officer for this image, used with permission.

ABOUT THE AUTHOR

Dawn Fallon

Dawn Fallon was born in Birmingham in 1959 to working-class parents. After studying music she graduated in 1980 but laid aside her musical ambitions when she entered the Civil Service. She really was a VAT inspector after obtaining a promotion. She currently lives in Devon with her husband and works as a hotel pianist.

GLOSSARY

D1507 - A printout showing quarterly VAT return figures of a business due for a VAT inspection.

Daily Gross Takings (DGT) - all payments received for goods or services supplied for each day.

Drawings - Sums of money that a sole trader or partner takes out of their business bank account.

Input tax - VAT reclaimed on purchases and expenses by a business

Internal Control Questionnaires (ICQs) - questions that auditors can use to evaluate a company's internal controls.

LVO - Local VAT Office

Output tax - VAT charged to customers by a business on sales

Principal Place of Business (PPOB) - the primarily location of where a company's business is performed

Purchase Day Book - A list of purchase invoices

Sales Day Book - A list of sales invoices

Tax Point The date which VAT is due - usually invoice date, or date cash is received - whichever happens first in most cases.

Trader - A generic term for any entity from a small business to a large multinational.

999 - large trader.

301 - small trader (with a 300 being a medium sized trader!)

Transfer of a Going Concern (TOGC) - transfer of a running business which is capable or being carried on by the purchaser as an independent business.

WE LOVE MEMOIRS

Printed in Great Britain
by Amazon